Willing Migrants

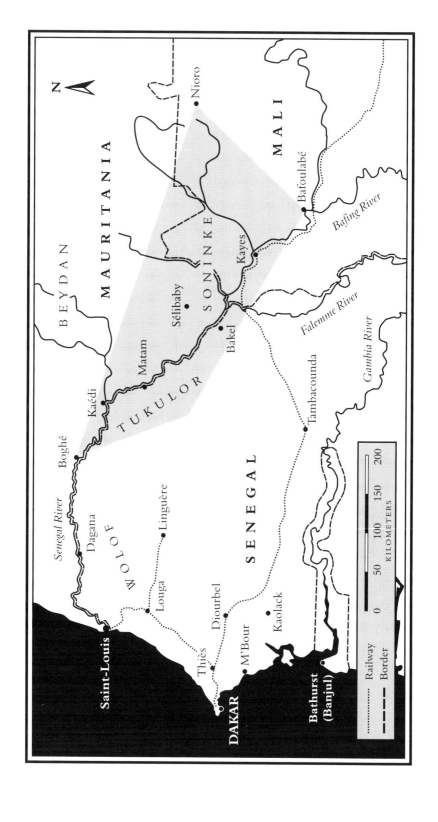

Willing Migrants

SONINKE LABOR DIASPORAS, 1848-1960

François Manchuelle

OHIO UNIVERSITY PRESS

ATHENS

JAMES CURREY PUBLISHERS

LONDON

Ohio University Press, Athens, Ohio 45701
© 1997 by Ohio University Press

James Currey Ltd
73 Botley Road
Oxford
OX2 0BS

01 00 99 98 97   5 4 3 2 1

Book design by Chiquita Babb

Library of Congress Cataloging-in-Publication Data

Manchuelle, François, 1953–1996
     Willing migrants : Soninke labor diasporas, 1848–1960 / François
Manchuelle.
          p.   cm.
     Includes bibliographical references and index.
     ISBN 0-8214-1201-9 (cloth : alk. paper). — ISBN 0-8214-1202-7
(paper : alk. paper)
     1. Soninke (African people)—Employment—Foreign countries.
2. Soninke (African people)—Migrations. I. Title.
DT549.45.S66M35   1997
331.6'2367044—dc21
                                                    97-27492
                                                    CIP

British Library Cataloging in Publication Data available

Manchuelle, François
     Willing migrants : Soninke labor diasporas, 1848–1960
     1. Soninke (African people)—Employment—Foreign countries
     2. Soninke (African people)—Migrations.
     I. Title.
     331.6'2367'044
     ISBN 0-85255-755-8 (cl)
     ISBN 0-85255-756-6 (pbk)

Frontispiece: Regions of Origin of Black African
Migrants in France in the Early 1960s.
From Diarra, Travailleurs Africains noirs en France, *p. 904.*

To Minimax

Contents

Tables

Foreword

In the spring of 1985, I received a letter from a graduate student at the University of California in Santa Barbara asking if I would read two chapters from his thesis. I agreed to do so, not only because I enjoy reading the work of young scholars, but because he was working on questions that had a bearing on the book I was writing on slavery and French colonial rule.[1] The Soninke were important to my study as slave traders and as the architects of a very harsh slave system. They also produced a large grain surplus in the early twentieth century in spite of what looked to me like a hostile environment. I was struggling with several questions. I was trying to understand the complex and very dynamic Senegal river trade system of the nineteenth century and why so many slaves stayed with their masters in the early nineteenth century during a period of a massive slave emigration in French West Africa, when perhaps a million returned to earlier homes.

The chapters Manchuelle sent me made an original argument on Soninke labor migration. The role of the Soninke in the river trade, as sailors in the French fleet, and as the first African migrants to France was well known, but, like many, I had assumed that the first to migrate were the poor, perhaps runaway slaves. In fact, Manchuelle argued that it was the nobles who migrated, and that they did so not because they wanted to leave, but because they wanted to reinforce their position within traditional society. Furthermore, his documentation was solid. The most original part of Manchuelle's argument was why they did it. I was so fascinated that I asked to read the whole thesis and invited him to give a paper at a conference in Canada.

The Soninke are a particularly interesting people. They founded the first of the great empires of West Africa, Ghana. After the fall of Ghana in the thirteenth century, there were no large Soninke states, but a Soninke diaspora spread trading communities across much of West Africa. Known as

---

1. Forthcoming from Cambridge University Press under the title *Slavery and Colonial Rule in French West Africa*.

Marka or Juula, these communities often assimilated local languages, but because of their involvement in commerce, maintained their distinctiveness and their pride in Soninke origins. Manchuelle argues perceptively that the Soninke entrepreneurial tradition developed because of their role as commercial arbiters between the desert and the savanna. The desert-side area was commercially one of the most important areas in Africa. The Soninke were in many ways the product of this interaction, and certainly the people best equipped to exploit it. Nomads needed grain and cloth and could offer livestock and salt. Those with entrepreneurial skills could use those goods to trade further south for slaves, gold, kola nuts, and other commodities.

In recent years, the Soninke have been noted for another kind of migration. Although they are not very numerous, in the 1950s and 1960s the Soninke made up the vast majority of an increasing African migration to France. Their origins, their collaboration, and their dormitory-style living arrangements were frequently discussed in the French press during the 1960s and attracted a great deal of scholarly interest. They lived frugally, shared meals, helped each other find jobs, and faced common problems of illness and death. Few writers, however, traced the history of this migration or saw that there was a link between the entrepreneurial skills of the sharpest traders in West Africa and the appearance of Soninke sanitation workers doing the humblest kinds of work in late-twentieth-century France. Labor migration was rooted in commercial migration and often contributed to new forms of commercial activity. The humble Soninke who sweeps the streets of Paris may have two taxis on the streets of Bamako, often driven by brothers or cousins, and when he retires, will probably farm with hired labor. He may also have a cousin driving a truck in the Ivory Coast or trading precious stones in Zaire.

Manchuelle's study makes several important arguments about migration. For one, migrants do not always come from poor areas, nor is it always the poorest who migrate. This is also clear for long-distance migration elsewhere. Those who came to North America by steerage a century ago had to be able to pay for their passage, and the same is true for those seeking a better life today in North America and Europe. Manchuelle also argues that migration was not rooted in the impoverishment of the Soninke homeland and did not contribute to its impoverishment. The strength of Manchuelle's argument is that he seats it in an understanding of Soninke society and history.

The small, weak Soninke polities were marked by intense competition, which provided an incentive for people to seek resources from outside. Thus, seasonal migration for trade, the accumulation of slaves, and an eagerness for wage labor on the river and the high seas were all linked. Manchuelle also moves clearly from one form of migration to others. He not only links the labor migrations in the Senegal River valley to earlier commercial migrations, but also describes new migrations in the early colonial period, especially seasonal migration to the peanut fields and long-term migration to the two Congos. He describes how maraboutic networks competed with the nobles and how former slaves moved into those networks.

Manchuelle also answers the question I first asked. Why did so many slaves remain within an exploitative social structure, and when they migrated, why did so many return? The slaves who left were primarily those who remembered an earlier home. Those who remained were not necessarily passive. They were rooted in Soninke society and chose to struggle, sometimes ineffectively, within Soninke society. As in many parts of West Africa, there was a struggle for the control of the labor of those who remained, essentially a process of renegotiating social and work relationships. Masters were most effective in maintaining control of persons where they controlled the land. The Soninke areas were relatively dry regions with small areas of rich floodplain controlled by established families. Slaves won a certain degree of autonomy, but could not shake the domination of the noble class. When the master could not provide land, a former slave could often get it from another master, but he could not change his status. Many remained not only because they could get land within the system, but, as Manchuelle explains, because they had access to migratory networks.

I learned a lot from François and always enjoyed our exchanges. He did not bend easily to the ideas of others, but he was always gracious in debate, often gentle, and always eager to refine his argument and get the response of others. He was also very well informed. He wrote on a wide variety of subjects and read widely. He assumed that there were regularities in the way human societies operate, and sought for parallels in literature on other parts of the world. The ability to see migration in comparative context is one of the strengths of this manuscript. Perhaps the most important thing Manchuelle has done in this book is to prove how relevant history is to understanding a contemporary situation. By looking at how and why different sectors of

Soninke society have migrated over time, he contributes to our understanding of the Soninke. By constantly setting the Soninke in comparative context, he contributes to our understanding of migration. He has written a book that is original, that challenges accepted ideas, and that will be much debated. We can only regret that he will not be here to take part in the debate.

Martin A. Klein
University of Toronto

Editor's Preface

In Remembrance of François Manchuelle (1953–1996)

François Manchuelle died tragically on 17 July 1996 in the explosion of TWA Flight 800 off the coast of Long Island. This disaster cut short a vital scholarly career. In addition to a stream of academic articles on the intellectual roots of nineteenth-century French colonization policy, the cultural dynamics of precolonial West African labor migrations, the political emergence of Africans in Senegal, and the origins of cultural nationalism in French Africa, François had just recently finished *Willing Migrants*, was deeply engaged in a large study of the intellectual origins of African cultural nationalism that traced the linkages between intellectuals in the Caribbean, Europe, and West Africa, and was in the process of editing a special issue of the *Cahiers d'Etudes Africaines*, on whose editorial board he served. François died in the midst of making major contributions to the history of Africa and of Africans in diaspora.

François's other métier was as an academic administrator. After completing his doctoral degree at the University of California at Santa Barbara in 1987, François accepted a teaching post in the Department of History at Georgia Southern University, and while there found time to secure a major institutional grant, ensuring the future of the Black Studies program. Later, after a teaching stint at Bowdoin College, François accepted a position as associate director of Africana Studies and the Institute for Afro-American Affairs at New York University. At NYU François devoted his time to strengthening the university institutions devoted to the study of Africa and of Africans in diaspora, taught seminars in African history, and brought forth as executive editor the first issue of *Black Renaissance/Renaissance Noire*.

With his death, François Manchuelle's far-flung network of intellectual and collegial relationships, maintained through careful correspondence and an ever-willingness to pick up the telephone, was ruptured. But at the age of forty-three, his lifespirit had such trajectory and quiet force that his intellectual legacy and his warm personal presence will continue to influence those of us who were fortunate to know him. Colleagues in Europe, North America, the Caribbean, and Africa all remember him with affection.

James L. A. Webb, Jr.
Colby College
February 1997

Select Bibliography of Works
by François Manchuelle

1996 "The 'Regeneration of Africa': An Important and Ambiguous Concept in 18th and 19th Century French Thinking about Africa," *Cahiers d'Etudes Africaines,* vol. 144, no. XXXVI-4, 559–588.

1995 "Assimilés ou patriotes africains? Naissance du nationalisme culturel en Afrique française," *Cahiers d'Etudes Africaines,* vols. 138–139, no. XXXV-2-3, 333–368.

1992 "Le rôle des Antillais dans l'apparition du nationalisme culturel en Afrique francophone," *Cahiers d'Etudes Africaines,* vol. 127, no. XXXII-3, 375–408.

1989 "Slavery, Emancipation, and Labor Migration in West Africa: The Case of the Soninke," *Journal of African History,* vol. 30, no. 1, 89–106.

1989 "The Patriarchal Ideal of Soninke Labor Migrants: From Slave Owners to Employers of Free Labor Migrants," *Canadian Journal of African Studies,* vol. 23, no. 1, 106–125.

1988 "Origines républicaines de la politique d'expansion coloniale de Jules Ferry, 1838–1865," *Revue française d'histoire d'outre-mer,* vol. 75, no. 279, 185–206.

1985 "Origines républicaines et philanthropiques de la politique d'expansion coloniale de Jules Ferry (1838–1865)" *Proceedings of the French Colonial Historical Society,* 1985, 193–205.

1984 "Métis et colons: La famille Devès et l'émergence politique des Africains au Sénégal, 1881–1897," *Cahiers d'Etudes Africaines,* vol. 96, no. XXIV-4, 477–504.

Willing Migrants

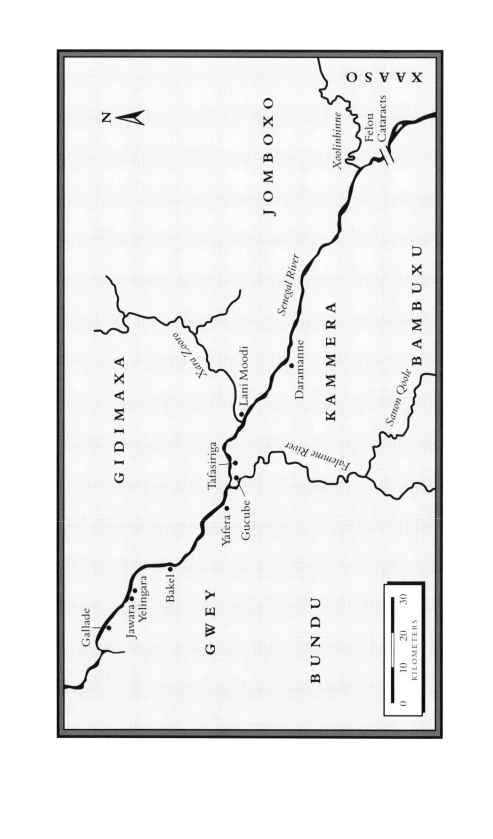

Introduction

WHEN I BEGAN this study, I was strongly influenced by the radical politics of the late 1960s and early 1970s. I chose to focus my doctoral research on labor migration from Africa to France because I wished to document an aspect of the theory of "neocolonial dependency," that is, I wished to show that the migration of workers from Africa to Europe was one symptom of the exploitation of the impoverished Third World by the capitalist West. The results of my investigation proved to be quite different from what I had expected.

There has been for half a century in France a large community of Third World migrants, the "Arab" (in fact, Arabo-Berber) North Africans, who are among the most oppressed people in the country. The question of their integration into society has been a burning issue in French politics in the last four decades. At the time when I began this study, however, this proletariat had its own underworld: the Black Africans, who lived in the shabbiest housing in the neighborhoods inhabited by North Africans and who took the jobs rejected by them. Any visitor to Paris in the 1960s and 1970s would have noticed that most of the menial jobs in the French capital, in particular in sanitation, were carried out by Black Africans, often (incorrectly) called "Senegalese." Black Africans also worked (in fact, in greater numbers than in sanitation) as unskilled workers in automobile plants in the Parisian suburbs, such as Renault-Billancourt, Citroën-Aulnay, of Talbot-Poissy.

The Black African community in France in the 1960s and 1970s was small in comparison with the North African community. Its concentration in the French capital, however, gave it a certain visibility. Moreover, it was growing extremely rapidly. In 1953, the official figure for African workers in France was 2,000. Ten years later, the official figure stood at 20,000, while unofficial estimates ranged between 30,000 and 60,000. Since this time, the Black African community in France may have grown to 660,000, its size increasing by a factor of ten during the last twenty years. This raises the remote but not unrealistic possibility that it may one day become as large as the North African community itself. Judging from the severe problems posed today by xenophobic feelings in French society, the integration of large numbers of Black Africans may prove a formidable problem in the decades to come.

When it began, roughly around 1960, Black African migration in France presented all the characteristics of a *labor migration*. This term must be defined: *labor migration* designates an economically motivated, *temporary* form of migration. Labor migrants are generally young men from rural areas, often unmarried. They have no plans to settle abroad but shuttle between their villages and places of employment (cities and more developed agricultural areas), a movement often described as "return" or "circular" migration. Labor migrants are an important proportion of the world's labor force, especially in developing areas, and more especially in sub-Saharan Africa: in 1965, the economist Elliot J. Berg estimated the number of migrant laborers in West Africa to be about one million, or *half* of its labor force.[1] In fact, all of the main export producing regions of Africa—the "peanut basin" of Senegal; the "cocoa belt" of Ghana, the Ivory Coast, and Nigeria; the "copper belt" of Zambia; and the mining regions of South Africa and Zaire—owe their economic success to the in-migration of temporary laborers. Black African migration to France was thus connected to a wider phenomenon of labor migration in Africa.

In 1968, Souleymane Diarra published the first scholarly study of Black African labor migration to France.[2] Its startling revelation was that 85 percent of the migrants came from a single region of West Africa, a triangle of 520 x 480 x 210 kilometers between the Mauritanian town of Boghé and the Malian towns of Nioro and Bafoulabé, covering roughly equal amounts of Senegalese, Mauritanian, and Malian soil (see map). Moreover, within this territory, 85 percent of the migrants were members of a single ethnic group, called in Senegal the Sarakole, but who call themselves the Soninke, a branch of the large Mande-speaking group, which also comprises the Bambara and Malinke peoples.

What made this information so interesting was the fact that the Soninke have long history of migration in Africa. In the nineteenth century, they were among the first *navétanes* (agricultural labor migrants to the peanut fields that are the mainstay of Senegal's economy). During the colonial period, the Soninke also migrated to the Ivory Coast, Cameroon, and the Congo-Zaire basin. They had a tradition of employment in the French merchant marine, which eventually led some to settle in French harbor cities—the origin of their present migration to France. In Soninke villages, one can meet former sailors who have been to the United States, Mexico, India, Japan, and so on. Today the Soninke live not only in France, but also in Sierra Leone, the Ivory Coast, Zaire, Congo, the Central African Republic, Zambia, Tanzania, Libya, Spain, Belgium, even Sweden, and there even appears to be a tiny Soninke community in New York City, probably established prior to the Second World War.

The "tradition" of migration among the Soninke actually goes back to the precolonial period. The Soninke probably were the first *jula*, or itinerant traders of West Africa. Their Mande-speaking descendants, the Marka, are found in most commercial centers of the Western Sudan. Today an important proportion of the Soninke continue to be merchants. Soninke merchants fly to Hong Kong to buy the Japanese watches and pocket calculators that flood the marketplace of Bamako, Mali. Many have made fortunes without having a formal education. In one interview, a Soninke merchant in Bamako said: "I cannot read, but I can count."[3] And Soninke merchants indeed can count, as shown by the success of such businessmen as Adan Kébé, rumored to have bought two beachfront hotels in Dakar "for cash" and to have been the private banker of the former President Mobutu of Zaire.

From the beginning, therefore, my research had to resolve an interesting contradiction. I wished to show that the migration of poor Black African workers to France was the result of Africa's exploitation by France, thus, in keeping with Marxist theory, that it was the result of *economic* factors. However, historical evidence pointed to the fact that Soninke migration predated the domination of Western capitalism and may have been related to *cultural* factors. But was premodern migration connected to present migration? I felt it was necessary to address the history of Soninke migrations in order to answer this question.

Theories of African Labor Migration

Early colonial explanations of labor migration in Africa often emphasized the role of ethnicity. Ethnic groups that migrated more than others were deemed to have a cultural "propensity to migrate." Such a "propensity" was never theorized, but rather was part of a set of Western prejudices about the supposedly odd or backwards economic behavior of Africans. The colonial "bright lights theory" held that Africans, particularly the young, migrated because they were attracted by the often fallacious promises of city life. The "target worker" theory asserted that Africans sought paid employment solely in order to reach specific economic "targets"—buying a bicycle, a sewing machine, and so on. Once the "targets" were reached, it was said, the migrants went home, with the paradoxical result that higher wages resulted in a higher turnover and eventually a lower supply of labor. What these "theories" had in common, therefore, was the suggestion that Africans were not, unlike modern Europeans, rational economical beings.

Modern sociological and economic studies have proven these conceptions wrong. Although African migrants value the excitement of city life, they are, in fact, looking for cash. Elliot J. Berg showed that in Africa, as in the rest of the world, higher wages result in a larger labor supply. Berg attributed the high turnover rates noticed by employers in the early days of colonization not to high but to low wages.[4] As economic and sociological studies have progressed, scholars have increasingly emphasized the rational economic motivations of African labor migration. J. Clyde Mitchell pointed out that most migrants gave an economic reason (often the need to pay taxes) for migrating and that even when a noneconomic cause was invoked, the real cause was almost always economic. For example, migrants may declare that they migrated because of disagreements with relatives, but in the majority of cases, these disagreements have an economic basis.[5] J. Van Velsen noted that in the matter of periodic returns to their home villages, "school" ("westernized") migrants of East London, South Africa, behaved no differently than "Red" ("tribal") migrants even though their attitudes toward the modern world sharply differed. The purpose of periodic returns home was to maintain a stake in family lands in the migrants' villages. Village lands are the migrants' "pension funds," and migrants must make certain that they are still considered part of their original communities in order to retain access to these lands, which are communally owned or controlled.[6]

Sociological and economic literature has made great progress in understanding African labor migration but, at the same time, it has brought new questions: assuming that economic causes are determinant, what type of economic causes provoke migration? Essentially, there are two answers to this question. For some scholars—we may call them the "neoclassical" school, whose best-known representative is Elliot J. Berg—each migrant makes a personal choice, after balancing the advantages and disadvantages (economic and noneconomic) of staying at home or migrating.[7] The neoclassical school emphasizes job opportunities in the region at the receiving end of the migration, that is, the "pull" factor of economic growth. The opposing "school" (which is by far the most popular today) believes that migrants were "pushed" away from their home region by adverse economic conditions and/or various forms of coercion. According to a growing body of literature, colonial taxes were the "trigger" to African labor migration, in particular because they were imposed in money currency, which was available only in the coastal areas dominated by the colonial economy.[8]

From what precedes, it is clear that the debate has become increasingly historical in nature. In fact, history would appear as essential in the study of migrations, which are processes of social change that necessarily develop over a long period of time. Yet even though a growing number of studies use historical material and methods, African labor migration has been investigated almost exclusively by sociologists and economists, and there is almost no major study of African labor migration by a trained historian.

The theory that African labor migration is the result of economic deprivation and colonial violence is, as I mentioned, by far the most prevalent today. However, there are very important differences between the migratory behaviors of various African ethnic groups that economic factors do not seem to explain. Among migrants to France, for example, although local Pulaar-speakers from the Upper Senegal River Valley in the region of Matam (called "Tukulor" by colonial scholars)[9] do not exceed 14 percent of the adult male population,[10] the Soninke comprise around 36 percent. These differential rates of migration to France are not the result of differences in the economic conditions of the two ethnic groups, which are roughly similar. Particularly interesting in this respect is the fact that Soninke village enclaves in the mainly Pulaar-speaking districts of Kanel and Ourossogui have migration rates as high (36 percent) as the predominantly Soninke-speaking Bakel region upstream, *in spite of the fact that these villages are situated in the midst of Pulaar-speaking villages,* which have at least a *four times* lower rate of migration to France.[11]

Explanations of labor migration as the result of economic deprivation and violence, although very popular among Africanist scholars, have been criticized by recent Europeanist and Americanist labor migration historians. A book as popular in its time as Oscar Handlin's *The Uprooted, The Epic Story of the Great Migrations That Made the American People* today evokes more criticism than praise.[12] Although the image of uprooted migrants continues to be popular with the general public, contemporary Europeanist and Americanist scholarship emphasizes such factors as income differentials and *kinship networks* as determining factors of modern labor migrations. Kinship networks were crucial in making rural populations aware of better income opportunities and in facilitating their migration and eventual settlement abroad. Finally, and this is very important for the subject at hand, this scholarship has also shown that there is a direct link between modern migrations and older, preindustrial migrations—the periodic migrations of traders, craftsmen, and laborers for which many regions of Europe were traditionally famous. Contrary to what is generally assumed, European premodern populations were not isolated, self-sufficient communities.[13]

Considering this, one may wonder why the theory of "uprooting" is so popular in the study of African labor migration, while the bulk of African migration scholarship today emphasizes similarities between African and European economic behavior. Oddly enough, the literature on African labor migration often gives the impression that modern migrations in Africa could not have occurred if Africans had not been *forced* to migrate. Specialists would perhaps connect this view with the "substantivist" anthropological theory, which had a profound impact on African studies—in particular Marxist African studies. The "substantivists" believed that early ("primitive") economies were "redistributive" economies not organized around the market principle. To put it simply: wealth is accumulated in such societies by chiefs or powerful individuals through nonmarket means, such as communal labor, rents, or tributes, and redistributed to the people in the form of gifts, giving birth to networks of clientage and allegiance. Early substantivists maintained that there was a fundamental difference between market and nonmarket economies and that in "primitive" societies neither land nor labor could be bought or sold. This, of course, implied that labor migration did not exist in precolonial African economies.[14]

Most anthropologists, however, today would argue that although precolonial African economies indeed contained strong "redistributive" sectors, there was no fundamental incompatibility between market and nonmarket systems. All precolonial societies, to one degree or another, had market institutions, susceptible of growing into "capitalism" whenever external contacts made this possible and desirable. A logical consequence of this reasoning is that there is no longer any need to think that "tribal" economies *had* to be disrupted in order for labor migration to take place.

But the idea of African labor migration as the necessary result of economic disruption is, in fact, present in all shades of African scholarship—whatever their relation to substantivist theories. As a brief illustration I will quote from Elliot J. Berg, who used to be ritually vilified by Marxists as one of the chief exponents of the "neoclassical" school,[15] something which would have placed him among the "formalists," or opponents of the substantivist theory:

> Put in its simplest terms, the [labor] recruitment problem in Africa arose from the tenacity of social systems. Well-knit, integrated social systems yield stubbornly to change, and this is particularly true of tradition-oriented preindustrial societies facing the onslaught of economic change. It is universally observable that people in pre-industrial agricultural societies do not ordinarily relinquish, even temporarily, the security and certainty of their traditional way of life unless certain changes occur within their societies. In most cases people in these societies *have to be pushed from the land; rural life must be made untenable for them*. . . . In Africa it was particularly difficult because of abundant land and *limited needs* in the villages.[16]

The idea that precolonial African societies were self-contained and resistant to change is one of the most deeply ingrained in Western thought, despite the warnings of the leading specialists. Philip Curtin writes:

> Perhaps the most durable of all myths about precolonial Africa is the belief that it contained myriad, isolated economic units—"subsistence economies," where the village group if not each individual family actually produced all it consumed. . . . In point of fact, it is doubtful that *any* African economy of recent centuries was absolutely self-contained, without trade of any kind, even the most isolated parts of the continent.[17]

The concept of African traditional economies as isolated, self-sufficient "subsistence economies" was characteristic of colonial thinking. It was the reason why so many colonial officials believed in the value of forced labor: if Africans had "limited needs" and were content with their lot, how could Africa develop economically? Many colonial officials thus believed that

Africans *had* to be coerced in order for the continent to progress. To say this, however, is not to say that coercion had the desired impact on migration. The evidence available on some of the most famous taxation policies introduced to create labor migration is that they failed.[18] It was, in fact, easy for colonial administrators to exaggerate their power over their subjects. Governor Angoulvant of the Ivory Coast believed in 1908 that he could force Africans to become wage laborers and export-crop farmers with a personal tax of 0.50 to 4.50 francs *a year*, while Baule peasants easily earned 0.30 to 1.00 franc *a day* in local agriculture and craft production.[19] Blunt coercion, moreover, could act as a *deterrent* to labor migration; such was apparently the case in the Ivory Coast, toward which converged thousands of migrants from Burkina Faso and Niger after the abolition of forced labor after the Second World War—migrants who had previously gone to Ghana, where forced labor was unknown after the First World War.[20]

In this study, I strongly stress the internal dynamics of the labor migration process. African societies were not passive recipients or victims of external changes, but societies that faced specific historical choices, which they made according to their own historical, cultural, social, and political backgrounds. I also argue against explanations of labor migration based on taxation and coercion. My contention, of course, is mainly based on the study of the Soninke, but it would be useful if such evidence contributed to a reexamination of the issue by historians. Few of the scholars who cite taxation and coercion as a cause in labor migration have made a critical assessment of the question on the basis of available documents, in particular quantitative commercial and taxation records.

ONE

Soninke Society and Migration

Nineteenth Century[1]

PHILIP CURTIN has questioned the widespread notion that precolonial Africa was the land of autarchic "subsistence" economies.[2] It is interesting to note that the book containing this comment is largely devoted to the economic history of a Soninke region (the precolonial kingdom of Gajaaga in the Upper Senegal River Valley). Indeed, the Soninke had one of the longest histories of involvement in trade and commercial agriculture in West Africa. This history is tightly bound to the issue of migration. In this chapter, I will give a description of precolonial Soninke society and economy: unless indicated otherwise, this description is based on documents relative to the nineteenth century (French travelers or administrators' reports, as well as Soninke oral tradition).

Geographical and Historical Outline of the Soninke

The Soninke are the northern branch of the large Mande-speaking group. Because censuses are difficult to interpret (for a variety of reasons), it is difficult to assess their number today. In the 1970s, they were perhaps 200,000 to 300,000, mostly in the Republic of Mali (districts of Kayes, Yélimané,

Nioro, and Goumbou-Nara), with smaller communities in Senegal (districts of Bakel and Matam) and Mauritania (district of Sélibaby).[3]

The region inhabited by the Soninke is a narrow belt stretching about 800 kilometers along the southern edge of the Sahara between Matam in the Upper Senegal River Valley and Sokolo in the Republic of Mali, not far from the Niger River. This is an intermediary sector between the Sudanese and the Sahelian vegetation zones, which has been severely affected by the drought of the last two decades. Desertification is not new to this area: in past centuries, the Soninke homeland extended far to the north in the Tagant and the Adrar, which today are desertic. Because of this, it is often believed that the precolonial Soninke migrations were a response to the ecological fragility of the region.[4] It is worth noting, however, that the climatic conditions of the Soninke homeland are not very different from those of the most populated areas of Senegal. Roughly speaking, Bakel is on the same latitudinal parallel as Thiès or Dakar, Nioro is on the same parallel as Mekhé north of Thiès, and Kayes is on a parallel slightly north of Kaolack. Because of this location, the environment of the Soninke is quite certainly preferable to that of northernmost Wolof regions such as Jolof.[5] Rainfalls recorded between the 1930s and 1960s in Bakel, Yélimané, Nioro, and Sélibaby averaged between 500 and 600 millimeters annually. These were ordinary figures for the area between the 14th and 16th parallels in Senegal, Mauritania, and Mali, and they were more than sufficient for agriculture.[6]

The Soninke homeland can be divided into two geographical regions. The "western region" encompasses the hydrographic system of the Upper Senegal River. Hayre-Damga, once a province of Gajaaga, was the most westerly precolonial Soninke polity *(jamaane)*—in the nineteenth century, it was part of Fuuta Tooro. Upstream, the kingdom of Gajaaga was situated along the southern bank of the Senegal River, while the region of Gidimaxa covered the northern bank and extended along a number of tributaries to the north—the most important being the Xaara Xooro. Above Xaaso, an area of the Upper Senegal River Valley lost by Gajaaga to Fuulbe migrants in the seventeenth and eighteenth centuries, the valley of the Xoolinbinne, a major tributary of the Senegal and of its own tributary the Terekolle, was the location of a string of Soninke polities (Jafunu, Tiringa, Soroma, Gidyume, and Kenyareme). The "eastern region" is a wide plateau once well-watered by temporary streams (polities of Kingi and Baaxunu), ending in vast oasislike sandy depressions set in semidesertic areas containing the polities of Wagadu

(Gumbu) and Soxolo (Sokolo). The eastern part of the Soninke homeland is more ethnically diverse than the western part: indigenous nomadic Fuulbe and descendents of Fuutanke invaders who came with the religious conqueror Al-Haj Umar Tal in the mid nineteenth century live in the region of Kingi, while in the easternmost regions of Baaxunu, Gumbu, and Soxolo, the Soninke are often intermixed with other groups, especially the Bambara.

Soninke farmers have been particularly skillful at using the variety of agricultural milieux dispensed by their environment. Today, they especially practice rainfall agriculture on riverbanks *(falo)* and clayey depressions, which retain humidity better than the lands in the interior *(jeri)* and are therefore less prone to drought. But in the past, a large proportion of their rainfall crops also came from rainfall agriculture on the more sandy soils in the jeri.[7] In the western region, Soninke farmers also practice dry-season agriculture on the fertile floodlands *(waalo)* of the Senegal, Xara Xooro, and Xoolinbinne river valleys. Waalo floodlands in the Upper Senegal region are small, especially when compared with those in the Middle Senegal River Valley, but they once provided an important complement to local agricultural production. The Soninke in the western region thus practiced three types of agriculture during the year: rainy-season agriculture on the jeri, rainy-season agriculture on riverbanks, and floodland agriculture during the dry season. It is true that the labor requirements of these various types of agriculture often conflict during the course of their respective agricultural cycles (to take the most important example, the harvest of jeri lands and the sowing of waalo lands must be done concurrently),[8] but larger households with many dependents and slaves could exploit the various environments to the fullest. We shall see that slavery provided farm units with a large additional labor force in the precolonial period (and even in the colonial period).

Agricultural conditions have dramatically altered with the chronic drought of the last two decades.[9] This has meant unpredictable harvests and lower yields in the jeri. More prolific long-cycle varieties of sorghum are being replaced by short-cycle varieties such as *nabane*, which need less rainfall.[10] In the 1800s, and probably up to the 1960s, long-cycle sorghums dominated—such as the famed *gajaba*, which has the best yield (and whose stalks have a high sugar content and thus make an excellent fodder). Gajaba made up more than half of the sorghum consumed in Gajaaga in the nineteenth century, the remainder being made up mostly of shorter-cycle *nyeniko*.[11] According to informants in Jafunu, gajaba was once the only variety cultivated in this region (probably until the early to mid twentieth century).[12] Gajaba was often cultivated on riverbank lands together with maize (sometimes in alternating rows on the same field).[13] There are no colonial data on the proportion of maize in Soninke agriculture, but a comparison of sources leaves the impression that its cultivation (which requires more water than sorghum or millet) has also receded. Smaller yields are the result of both the retreat of superior varieties of grain and of the drought itself. While the probable average yield today in *riverbank* agriculture is no more than one ton per hectare, yields vastly superior, going up to amazing maximums of two tons and a half per hectare, are recorded for the colonial period.[14]

It would thus be a mistake to assume that the currently depressed condition of Soninke agriculture also prevailed in the precolonial and colonial periods. In these periods, occasional crises and even famines did certainly occur, but overall, a wetter climate and the additional labor provided by slaves made it possible to grow higher-yield varieties of grain in a wider variety of environments than today. For these reasons, Soninke agriculture was able to produce surpluses, and even to export sizeable quantities of grain (especially to desert areas to the north).

In precolonial times, this ability to produce a grain surplus was the foundation of a particularly dynamic commercial system. The Soninke homeland's configuration as a long belt of territory bordering the Sahara Desert made the region a center of very active commercial exchange between sedentary and desert nomad populations—the so-called "desert-side" trade. In the dry season, nomads descended from the desert to pasture their herds on Soninke lands. They bought cereals produced by Soninke farmers, in exchange for livestock, and especially for rock salt produced in mines in the desert in Ijil and Tishit, north of the Soninke homeland. The Soninke then formed trading expeditions to reexport this livestock and salt farther south. They also exported cotton cloth, which was woven by their slaves, and cattle and horses raised in the Soninke homeland. They came back from these periodic migrations with slaves, whom they mostly used to further develop their own agriculture.

"Desert-side" trade, and the periodic migrations that it generated, were not the exclusive preserve of the Soninke: both were practiced by all of the peoples of the West African Sahel from Waalo on the estuary of the Senegal River to Kanem along Lake Chad. But the geographical location of the Soninke was better than that of most of their Sahelian neighbors. Situated in a reasonably fertile area, they were close, toward the south and southeast, to the well-populated Middle Niger River Valley, which was an important market for their goods and an avenue of penetration toward markets farther south. They were close, toward the southwest, to the Gambia River Valley, less populated than the Niger Valley to be sure but another potential market for their goods. Finally, they were close to the gold-producing regions of Bambuxu between the Falemme River and the Upper Senegal River and Bure on the Upper Niger. The Soninke took salt, livestock, and slaves to these regions, from which they bought gold that they eventually reexported into the trans-Saharan trade.

The outlines of the Soninke desert-side trade no doubt changed in history. Salt, in particular, may have been more of a rarity in medieval times.[15] Nevertheless, one is struck by the similarities between nineteenth-century accounts of trade in Soninke regions and much earlier accounts. Thus the medieval Arab traveler Al-Bakri noted that the king of Ghana (a Soninke kingdom, as we shall see) taxed *salt* entering the kingdom, and that the "best *gold*" of Ghana came from the town of Ghiyaru, that is, Gunjuru, an important Soninke town in the Upper Senegal River Valley located not far from the Bambuxu goldfields. Speaking of the trade of the town of Sila in the Upper Senegal region, Al-Bakri notes: "For money the inhabitants of Sila use *sorghum*, *salt*, copper rings and *lengths of fine cotton*. . . . They own many *cows* but no sheep or goats [my emphasis]." Finally, Al-Idrisi noted that the inhabitants of Barisa (Yaresna, another early Soninke town in the Upper Senegal River Valley) "are *itinerant merchants* . . . , who pay allegiance to the Takruri."[16] These authors gave descriptions very similar to the nineteenth-century patterns that I am going to describe in detail in this chapter.

All this explains how the Soninke came to play such an important role in the trade and history of the Western Sudan.[17] In medieval times, they were the first in the Western Sudan to establish commercial relations with Arabo-Berber traders from North Africa, and they were among the first to become *jula* (itinerant traders) in West Africa—as we shall see. The first of the great medieval kingdoms of the Western Sudan known to historians was a Soninke kingdom, called *Ghana* by Arab travelers and *Wagadu* by the Soninke. Today, all important Soninke families claim descent from Wagadu aristocrats. However, even at the time of its greatness, Wagadu was not the only existing Soninke polity. Al-Bakri and Al-Idrisi thus mention the kingdom of Jafunu and a "kingdom of Sila," which was the historical ancestor of Gajaaga.

Wagadu declined after the twelfth century, when it was overshadowed by Soninke "successor states" such as Jafunu, Mema, Jara (Kingi), and Soso

(Xanyaga), and then by the Malinke state of Mali, rising under Sunjata Keita in the thirteenth century. With Mali, the focus of economic activity in the Western Sudan began to shift toward the Niger Valley, but the Soninke homeland remained important in the economy of the region. When Mali declined, the Soninke states regained their independence. Among them, the most important was the kingdom of Jara, centered in Kingi and ruled by the Jawara dynasty. In the western Soninke region, the kingdom of Gajaaga, conquered at an unknown date by a branch of the Sempera family—who claim to descend from the governors of the province of Soxolo (Sokolo) in medieval Ghana—had a period of greatness, dominating most of the Upper Senegal region (including Gidimaxa, Jafunu, and Xaaso). Internal divisions, Fuulbe invasions, and especially the rise of the Bambara states, however, eventually sapped the power of Soninke polities. In the eighteenth century, the Soninke lived in small polities dominated by their more powerful Bambara and Beydan (Arabo-Berber) neighbors. But the wealth of the Soninke remained and was noted by all observers in the nineteenth century.

The preceding outline shows that the Soninke had a comparatively prosperous economy in precolonial times, and that this prosperity rested largely on their participation in seasonal itinerant trading expeditions, that is, in *periodic return migration*.

The Politics of Clientage

The basic social organization of the precolonial Soninke was similar to that of their Mande-speaking neighbors and ethnic relatives, the Malinke and the Bambara.[18] The first in social status among Soninke aristocrats were the *tunka lemmu*, or members of the royal families.[19] Below them came aristocrats of nonclerical status, the *mangu*, who were either descendents of the military retinue of the *tunka* (the chief) or members of important indigenous clans who retained some importance after a conquest. Free men who are not casted artisans are generally called "nobles" in the specialized literature, but many were, in fact, commoner peasants *(jambuuruni)*, subject to various taxes and *corvées*. The poor *(miskino,* or "small" people) are described by villagers as immigrants—in other words, they were people who had not lived long enough in a village to be granted a voice in its affairs and consequently had no firm right to land (land was allocated either by the families of the first settlers of an area or by the political authorities). Islamic clerics *(moodi)*, called *marabouts* by the French, were the descendents of the first families to convert to Islam. As among all Mande-speaking peoples, they were denied the rank of "warrior" and could not fight. As a result, they could not become chiefs and were generally the clients of aristocratic and notable families. However, they regarded themselves as superior to the "pagan" warriors, and they were influential and often wealthy because of their religious and trading activities. Below warriors and clerics came the artisans *(nyaxamalo)* who, as elsewhere in West Africa, belonged to endogamous castes. They were subject to various forms of social indignity, but their skills and the patronage of important families made them quite secure financially. Finally, at the bottom of the social scale were the slaves, who were extremely numerous in Soninke precolonial society (between one-third and one-half of the population). Not all slaves were chattel slaves, however. Particular categories of crown slaves,[20] called "great slaves" *(komo xaaso)* by the Soninke, participated as members of the aristocratic class, although their slave status continued to affect them in various ways (they could not marry people of free status or become chiefs). Their function in society was either military or administrative (tax and toll collectors).

The case of the "great slaves" shows that in Soninke precolonial society, status and "class" did not always coincide. A closer examination of Soninke society and politics reveals another kind of hierarchy, in which slave and casted clients of the tunka lemmu (royals) stood in reality far above the commoner jambuuruni peasants, who were in theory their superiors. This hierarchy will become clearer after an examination of the Soninke political system.

Soninke "Segmentary States"

The distinction between "state" and "stateless" societies is conventional in African studies; however, many precolonial African systems were neither "state" nor "stateless" but something in between. In a recent contribution (inspired by E. R. Leach's *Political Systems of Highland Burma*), Jean-Loup Amselle has argued that many Sudanese societies actually experienced *both* "state" and "stateless" modes, but at different times in their history; that is, they went through a continuous cycle of death and rebirth.[21] When these societies were in their "state" mode, their state institutions remained elementary: they had no standing army or bureaucracy, state powers were in the hands of a royal clan and its clients, and the state limited its intervention to foreign affairs and arbitration between family groups.[22] As the royal clan increased in size, however, its constituent lineages grew more and more distant, until the point when their rivalries split the state apart. Society then entered its "stateless" mode, but this situation was also temporary because all clans competed to gain followers and build up influence; eventually one clan imposed its authority through peaceful or violent means, and the state was re-created and the cycle began again.

This model seems to apply quite well to the Soninke. In the nineteenth century, the Soninke lived either in "segmentary states" such as Gajaaga or Jafunu or in "independent villages" such as in Gidimaxa, Gidyume, or Kingi Jawara. At this time, however, the "states" of Gajaaga and Jafunu were at a rather advanced level of decay. Jafunu, although still considered one jamaane (country) by its inhabitants, had split (perhaps as early as the Middle Ages) into two diminutive polities ruled by branches of the Dukure clan based in the towns of Gori and Tambakara.[23] Gajaaga divided in the mid nineteenth century into the polities of Gwey and Kammera, dominated by rival factions of the numerous Bacili clan.[24] Similarly, "stateless" Gidimaxa had been a kingdom in the past, while the "republican" Jawara clan of Kingi had once ruled the powerful kingdom of Jara. Some polities probably had gone through similar phases of decay in the past: Gajaaga was ruled originally by the Siima, who were replaced by the Bacili; Kingi (Jara) by the Niaxaate, who were replaced by the Jawara; and Gidimaxa was ruled successively by the Sumaare and the Kamara before it finally reached its "stateless" phase.[25] What we know of the evolution of the rules of kingship illustrates the inevitable fragmentation process at work in Soninke polities. In Jafunu, and probably in Gajaaga as well, it appears that the king was originally the oldest man in the *eldest branch* of the royal clan.[26] As the royal clan became larger and larger (a process encouraged by polygyny), ties between its component lineages became more and more distant and the risk of rebellion increased among the junior branches that were ineligible for kingship. For this reason, all distinctions between the various lineages in the royal clan were abolished, and it was decided that the king would be the *oldest man among all royals*.[27] The rule preserved (for a time) unity among royals, but it also weakened kingship since the kings were always very old men, who were often impotent or senile.

In such a society, clientage was an essential basis of power. As is well known, clientage is found in all societies where state organization is either weak or absent. As a social form, clientage is elusive and often difficult to de-scribe. Its origin lies in what sociologists call "generalized exchange": the ways in which individuals and social groups maintain good relations with each other, for example, courtesy, intermarriage, and the exchange of gifts. These forms of exchange imply a reciprocity, but they can be transformed into sources of power whenever one of the parties can give others important favors in exchange for their support. Clientage over time tends to take an in-stitutionalized form, but informal relations always play an essential role in its operation.[28]

In Soninke polities, royal families ruled through two institutions of for-malized clientship: the *laada* and the *jonghu*. The laada (Arabic *al-ada*: custom) generally involved the performing by clients of rituals at family ceremonies of their patrons (baptisms, circumcisions, marriages, funerals, etc.) in exchange for well-defined favors, such as gifts or tax exemptions. For example, the Darame and Jaaxo maraboutic families officiated at funerals of the Bacili in Gajaaga. The jonghu was an inviolable oath between families, involving mutual protection, the avoidance of shedding each other's blood, and joking relationships. The jonghu was in principle an alliance between equals (there were jonghu between noble families and even collective jonghu between inhabitants of different jamaane), but in practice royal families used the institution to establish patron-client relationships.[29]

Both laada and jonghu made clients symbolically a part of their patrons' family, creating a formal setting for clientship. The material rewards of clientship, however, were mostly contingent on the will of the patrons. Royal families rewarded their clients well, with land grants, tax exemptions, and gifts. In Gajaaga, according to the the the words of the Gajaaga epic song dedicated to the Bacili royal family known by its refrain *"Kenyu do Gande,"* "All those who have anything in their possession in this country; They owe it to the Bacili."[30] According to Abdoulaye Bathily, the mangu of Gajaaga lived partly by the gifts made by the Bacili tunkalemme;[31] and the same was true also of those maraboutic (such as the Jaaxo and Darame) and casted families who were the clients of the Bacili. Royal families were not the only ones to have clients: all noble families had maraboutic (clerical) and casted families attached to them, who officiated at family ceremonies *(griots* [praise-singers] at baptisms and marriages, blacksmiths at circumcisions, marabouts at funerals).[32]

For the Soninke, the hierarchies implied in such relationships are in theory immutable. But history and Soninke oral tradition itself contradict that. As already mentioned, different royal clans ruled in succession in Gajaaga, Gidimaxa, and Kingi. Other changes of fortune are documented at lower levels. In Gajaaga, the most important mangu family, the Gunjamu (members of the prestigious Jaguraga clan), lost its preeminence among mangu clients of the Bacili royals to the benefit of newcomers (the Jallo, Tuure, and Timmera) in the eighteenth century. Likewise, still in Gajaaga, the Darame supplanted the Jaaxo as marabouts of the Bacili royal clan at an unknown date.[33] Clans and families were thus in a perpetual state of tension and competition. Within the royal clan, lineages and individuals competed for kingship[34] or to become influential advisers of the king. Outside of the royal clan, aristocratic families competed to gain influence and build their own power bases.

Ostentatious gifts to clients (in particular to griots) demonstrated the wealth and generosity of the donors, thereby establishing their status as powerful patrons.[35] The oral literature of the Soninke is filled with references to such generosity and to the wealth that made it possible. The praise-song of Jaabe Siise, the first *manga* (emperor) of Wagadu, also called Manga Kuya ("The Generous Manga"), says:

He is rich in gold, Jaabe Siise

He is rich in silver, Jaabe Siise

The prosperous son of Dinga, Jaabe Siise
The lucky son of Dinga, Jaabe Siise
The Manga who offers a hundred of each, Jaabe Siise
The Manga Kuya Manga, Jaabe Siise[36]

The "hundred of each" in this song is a form of gift often mentioned in Western Sudanese and Senegambian epics, in which the "each" represents a valuable item. For example, in the Soninke "Legend of the Dispersion of the Kusa," the Dukure (who are the ruling clan in Gumbu and in Jafunu) give to their 101 praise singers, the *Kusa tange:* 101 red horses, 101 horses "of the twelve races," then 101 pots of gold, 101 pots of silver, 101 gold blankets, 101 silver blankets, 101 uncircumcised slaves, 101 pubescent girls, and so forth.[37] The praise-songs of nonruling clans also emphasized their wealth and generosity. Here is an example of one for the large and prestigious Jaguraga clan:

Jammera, son of Birama, son of the genie and the demon, the beautiful tunka, the upright tunka, the popular tunka, the generous tunka, the dauntless tunka, Jaguraga![38]

Competition in the kingdoms among aristocratic groups, therefore, was keen. It was a competition for power—a power that was obtained in building a clientele through generosity and prestige. The same kind of competition was visible at the village level.

Soninke Village Society

Given the periodic breakdowns of central authority in the Soninke jamaane, villages were important social units. The central authority in villages, as in the kingdoms, was often weak since the chief was always the oldest man in the family of the village founders. The elders of all village families, however, acted as a relatively efficient informal village council assisting the village chief. Soninke villages, moreover, often had a certain social homogeneity, that is, each tended to be dominated, numerically and politically, by a certain social group. (It is important to remember that although such a dominance was easily discernible, no village was inhabited exclusively by one social group.) Some were royal villages; with polygyny, royal families were very large, and several royal villages vied for power in a kingdom such as Gajaaga. Maraboutic villages were wealthy and well-populated for reasons that we shall explore below; because marabouts could not be chiefs, however, these villages were headed by a "warrior" (nonmaraboutic) family. Some villages were dominated by mangu families (nonclerical aristocrats). Finally, there were occasionally artisan or even slave villages (the latter were rare among the Soninke).

Villages were important units of everyday life; for example, as elsewhere in Africa—and still today—children of similar age are organized into age groups. Male and female village youth associations have a "chief," who is the oldest member belonging to the chiefly family of the village. The "chief" is assisted by other members of the chiefly family and by another youth belonging to a client family of the chiefly family who acts as treasurer or town crier for the association. At the association's feasts, cooking is done by a youth of slave status. The youth association has a building of its own and a budget, whose funds come from members' regular contributions and from fines levied for various offenses. They organize dances and entertainment for the young people of the villages and occasionally take on tasks of public utility. Ties forged in age associations continue into adulthood and, indeed, into old age, giving greater coherence to the village community.[39]

Intravillage solidarity was therefore real,[40] but deep conflicts of interest nevertheless divided villagers, in particular concerning the ownership of land.[41] In villages, as in kingdoms, families competed for leadership, wealth, and clients. The founding families of the villages, which owned or administered the land on behalf of the state, dominated "stranger" families (many of whom had lived in the village for generations), who depended on them to receive land. The fortunes of village notables, however, fluctuated with time. Indications about such changes of power are more difficult to obtain for villages than for kingdoms, but some are available. For example, the French colonial administrator J.-M. Colombani noted around 1925 that in the large Gidimaxa village of Jagili, the Yatera, who were originally Malinke from Bambuxu (and who for this reason must have been considered as "strangers" of inferior status), contended for leadership with the Jabira, who were the founding and chiefly family of the village.[42]

In their competition for power, families emphasized their prestige and their wealth in praise-songs similar to those of aristocratic families. Here is, for example, the praise-song of the Saaxo-Wakkane, chiefly family of the large maraboutic village of Jawara (Gajaaga), who claim to descend from Wakkane Saaxo, one of the four *fado* (kings or governors) of ancient Wagadu:

> Wakkane the rich, Wakkane of Jajiga, Wakkane the son of the one who refuses humiliation, Wakkane Saaxo.[43]

Clientage and Honor

All societies in which clientage plays an important role have a strict conception of honor. Honor in modern Western societies either refers to notions of personal morality or courage or to a now old-fashioned sexual morality based on the "purity" of women. In societies where the concept of honor is important, however (such as Mediterranean societies or European societies before the French Revolution), honor appears primarily tied to the realities of influence and wealth. Honor in these societies results either from a connection with the powerful (which brings prestige) or more simply from the ability to provide for one's family (which guarantees one's independence).[44]

In such societies, the "people without honor" are the poor, who have no connection with power and who also must beg from or work for others in order to survive. Because they depend on others for their living, the poor are incapable of preserving the integrity of their kind. (This is where questions of courage and sexual morality come into play; because of their poverty and helplessness, poor men are probably less likely to fight back during confrontations with their superiors, and "their" women are deemed more prone to accept money in exchange for sexual favors.) Thus defined, clientship contains a contradiction: on the one hand, it is prestigious to be a client of the powerful, in a sense, to be dependent; on the other hand, it is dishonorable to be too dependent on others.

Such contradiction is apparent in the Soninke concept of honor. Tradition maintains, for example, that some royal slaves were originally free men who had been driven by circumstances to throw themselves on the generosity of the royal clan, thus becoming the "things" of the royals.[45] The story may or may not be true, but it certainly expresses social disapproval of too complete a dependence on patrons, even prestigious patrons. It is significant that marabouts and casted artisans, who were the most visible clients of noble families, were to varying degrees considered as not entirely honorable, even though they were free; marabouts were considered "women" who could not fight, and casted artisans married only their own kind and were subject to rules of physical avoidance.[46] Thus families struggled, not only in a positive sense to increase their wealth and to gain followers, but also in a negative sense not to "fall behind" and become too dependent—a kind of social "fear of falling."

In order to be considered wealthy, and thus "honorable," one had to own slaves, cattle, one or two horses, filled granaries, and secondarily, jewelry and money.[47] All stages in life, moreover, were occasions for a necessary ostentation of wealth. Marriage was probably the most expensive stage in the life of a Soninke man. As recently as in the 1960s in Jafunu, courting involved two major visits by an intermediary (usually a slave or a casted client) to the family of the fiancée. During each of these visits, gifts were made to future in-laws of a value of about one month's earnings in local wage labor. In addition, the suitor had to make many regular visits to the fiancée's household, which were also followed with gifts. The dowry itself usually cost between one-and-a-half and three months of local wage earnings, but richer families paid far more.[48] In Gidimaxa in precolonial times, the prestigious Sumaare family paid dowries equivalent to the value of fifteen cows.[49]

Among the Jawara of Kingi, the dowry was made up of several payments, one of which amounted on average to six cows: four were given to the father of the bride, one was given to the griots, and one was slaughtered for the wedding meal.[50] And at the wedding (in Gidimaxa in the 1920s):

> [The bride] is brought by her friends to her husband's house amidst singing, with a band escorting her; together with the bride, her luggage is brought: *pagnes*, clothes, etc. crammed into baskets or enormous calabashes carried on the heads [of her escort]; the more baskets a woman has, the more she will be considered.[51]

Women's apparel continued to advertise the family's wealth after her marriage. In Gidimaxa in the 1920s, according to Saint-Père, rich women wore gold rings from top to bottom of their ears, gold ear pendants, gold necklace ornaments, bracelets, an amber pearl bracelet on the right arm, silver bead anklets, and heavy silver ring anklets that could weigh up to 2.5 kilograms![52]

Conversely, poverty was castigated. Ritualized insults in joking relationships today refer to the alleged poverty of the relative or mate, a reference that would be supremely offensive in normal circumstances.[53] The idea of poverty and that of slavery (understood as a metaphor of abject dependence) were associated in the minds of the Soninke. Slaves were recognized by their "shabby appearance"; they sat in the "poor man's sitting position" (*misikina taxe*, with legs tucked under their body as a sign of humility), and slave women "had songs expressing the poverty of the slaves and the gratitude that they were supposed to feel for their masters." Slaves and freedmen were not expected to have any dignity: they begged, they had "uncouth manners," men and women slaves performed obscene dances.[54] In precolonial times, therefore, poverty and slavery provided a negative image of honor. In Soninke society, it was (and remains) very important to hold one's rank, and rank and honor were understood (not only but primarily) in terms of wealth.

Soninke Traditional Economy

The Acquisition of Wealth: Military Power, Land, and Slaves

Wealth was obtained in a variety of ways in the precolonial period. Tunka lemmu and mangu obtained wealth in war, either from booty or plunder. Indeed young tunka lemmu aristocrats, easily recognized by their yellow

clothes and braided hair, were above the law and often behaved as mere bandits, plundering peasants and travelers at will.[55] (Mungo Park was stripped
in this fashion of all his valuables by young tunka lemmu as he went through
Gajaaga in 1795).[56] Soninke polities were small, however, and their military
forces were small. Moreover, apart from royals and mangu, the Soninke
were considered a peaceful people, far more interested in raising their
income through agriculture and trade than in waging war. Unlike many
Sudanic peoples, Soninke peasants did not engage in periodic raiding expeditions against their neighbors.[57]

All dominant families (tunka lemmu and their mangu and maraboutic
clients in particular) derived income from their connection with the state or,
in its absence, with power and influence at the local level. As in ancien régime
France until the seventeenth century, the only direct taxes levied by states
were exceptional war contributions, which were especially unpopular.[58] In
the absence of regular taxation, land rents from free tenants were an important source of revenue for the state, and in the absence of a state, for the
powerful. Land ownership customs varied, but in general royal, aristocratic
and chiefly families owned the best lands in each polity. The details of the
precolonial situation are difficult to reconstruct because certain customs (in
particular, those related to ownership of jeri lands) appear to have fallen into
disuse.

In Jafunu, all lands (including jeri lands) were apparently owned by the
families of the "masters of the land," either descendents of the first inhabitants of the polity, segments of the ruling family of the Dukure, or aristocratic families granted land by the Dukure.[59] In Gajaaga, all lands were in
theory owned by the ruling Bacili, who by right of conquest had deprived
the lineages of original "masters of the land" of their property. As villages
were established, the Bacili granted some of the riverbank lands to client lineages at the same time they allowed them to found a village. These lineages
later granted part of this land to other lineages, who were either their own
clients or clients of the Bacili. The Bacili also granted riverbank lands to
client lineages of mangu or marabouts, and they retained an important part
of these lands for themselves as a kind of *ager publicus* providing revenue for
the state.[60] Jeri lands in Gajaaga were also owned by the Bacili, and some
portions by the founding families of villages as well, but there is little data on
the latter.[61] In Gidimaxa, riverbank lands were owned by the founding lineages of villages, who later granted some to other lineages. The ownership
of jeri lands in Gidimaxa, however, is not clear; it is probable that they were

owned by the founding families of villages.[62] There is only fragmentary information on landownership custom in the eastern Soninke region.[63]

As this account indicates, there was apparently a difference in the ownership of jeri lands and riverbank lands. Jeri lands today are not subject to the payment of land rents: they are considered *jamankafo-nyinyo* ("collective land") for the village. As we have just seen, this was probably not the case in the past, when jeri lands were owned by royal families or lineages of prominent "masters of the land." As today, however, access to jeri lands was open; except for a few more fertile lands, any family could farm any unoccupied spot on the jeri. The richer riverbanks and floodlands, on the contrary, were owned by a number of lineages, who either farmed these lands themselves or rented them to landless peasants. This difference is probably the result of differing types of cultivation. On jeri lands, a kind of shifting agriculture is practiced. These lands are situated far from the village, often ten kilometers or more. Very long periods of fallow (sometimes up to twenty or thirty years) alternate with short periods of cultivation of three to five years.[64] Families thus continually move on the jeri, and with the exception of some more fertile spots, they never stay long enough in one area to begin to claim ownership. As a result, landownership in precolonial times remained in the hands a small number of royal families, original settlers, and founding families of villages, who collected land rents but allowed open access to the land. Riverbank lands, on the contrary, were close to the village, and needed less fallow (and thus were cultivated more continuously); they were more productive and in shorter supply than jeri lands. For these reasons, property and usership rights in riverbank lands were more sharply defined than in the jeri and have survived to the present day.

The ownership of land was a source of political power as well as of wealth for aristocrats and village notables. With very rare exceptions, slaves and nyaxamalo (casted artisans) were excluded from the ownership of land. Landowning families allowed free men of "stranger" status who owned no riverbank lands to farm on their surplus of such land in exchange for the payment of a rent, which amounted in theory to one-tenth of the crop (rents of one-third of the crop are reported on some lands, presumably the most productive riverbank lands, in Gajaaga and Gidimaxa).[65] Such payments, however, could be reduced to a symbolic amount if the owner so chose. It was important, therefore, for "stranger" lineages to build a good relationship with village notables. In time, "stranger" tenants could probably obtain riverbank lands in full with the support of a notable of royal lineage or a founding family of a village, which alone could grant them land. The ownership of land, therefore, was a critical element in the building of clienteles.

However, in order to be fully productive, land had to be cultivated by a sufficient labor force. Slaves provided such a labor force in precolonial times. Not surprisingly, wealthiest in slaves were the royal families and their clients, who had direct access to revenue from war and land rents. These families left farming entirely to their slaves in precolonial times.[66] But the largest number of slaves in precolonial times was probably obtained through revenues gained from trade.

The Acquisition of Wealth: Traditional Trade Migration

As mentioned, the great majority of the Soninke live in an area of contact between the desert and the Sahel. Sahelian territories to the north of this belt are not properly speaking desertic, but they are mostly fit for pastoralism. Further north in the desert are oases in the massifs of the Assaba, the Tagant, and the Adrar, and several salt mines (the most famous was in Ijil, north of the Adrar, followed in importance by Tishit, north of the eastern Soninke region, which produces *amersal* salt for livestock consumption). During the year, Arabo-Berber pastoralists (whom the French called "Moors" and who call themselves "Beydan," i.e., "whites") migrated, descending south toward the cultivated areas during the dry season, and ascending north toward the desert in the rainy season. In the dry season, the Beydan usually arrived on the lands of the agriculturalists in January, shortly after the main harvest of rainfall agriculture was completed.[67]

Beydan families customarily had Soninke families as their hosts. Their herds pastured on their hosts' freshly harvested fields, fertilizing them with manure. In return, they received "gifts" in cereals, which had just been harvested in November and December. And there were additional transactions which allowed the Beydan to have access to much-needed grain. The Beydan traded highly-valued bar salt from the desert for millet and sorghum. They exchanged some of their sheep and cattle for cereals. And the pastoralists transported loads of grain on the backs of animals for their hosts, and for these services they were likewise remunerated in millet and sorghum.[68] These transactions were generally arranged through Soninke hosts, the *jatigi*, who acted as middlemen.[69]

The Soninke "desert-side" trade thus produced two commodities that were in great demand further south: livestock and desert salt. Salt, of course, was a very important item of precolonial trade. Salt intakes are important in hot climates because of the major salt losses that take place in perspiration, which the body must replace in order to maintain a proper chemical balance.[70] Salt is nowhere to be found in sub-Saharan West Africa, except for lesser-quality maritime salt on the coast, which is friable and therefore less easy to transport. Salt was especially in demand in the great Mande center of population in the Niger Valley, which is situated inland and far from the desert.[71] In the late nineteenth century, out of a total of 3,000 metric tons (official French figures) imported from the desert into what is now the Republic of Mali, some 1,700 metric tons (57 percent) came through the Soninke regions, the rest presumably through the Niger Bend markets such as Banamba and Timbuktu.[72] As for livestock, it had also a great importance in West African precolonial north-south exchanges, although the details of this trade are less known. Almost all of the West African livestock (including horses, donkeys, sheep, and goats) is found between the 12th and the 18th parallels north. Above the 18th parallel, the climate is too dry, and below the 12th parallel, the tse-tse fly makes cattle raising practically impossible, hence the necessity for the well-peopled areas to the south to import most of their livestock.[73] The Soninke homeland was precisely in the middle of this livestock-raising zone. In addition to the animals obtained from the Beydan, the Soninke had large holdings of cattle, which were entrusted to Fuulbe herdsmen, and raised horses, which were in great demand farther south for their use in the military or simply for purposes of ostentation.

The Soninke, or rather their slaves, also produced cotton cloth, which was in great demand in the Sudan and Senegambia. Philip Curtin noted that the sale of cotton cloth was so lucrative in the seventeenth and eighteenth centuries that European merchants became involved in its trade, making profits as high as 100 percent by carrying indigenous cloth from the Upper Senegal and Gambia Rivers to the Senegambian coast. The Soninke regions were among the main producers of indigenous cloth in the region. This cloth was produced exclusively by Soninke slaves (the Soninke, like many Senegambian peoples, but unlike their neighbors the Fuutanke, have no artisanal weaver caste).[73] Finally, the Soninke also produced numerous household crafts, such as hides and crafted leather, mats, pottery, and calabashes.

In the dry season, the Soninke formed trading expeditions to carry salt, cattle, cloth, and household crafts farther south. Goods were usually carried on donkeys, but sometimes headloaded, in small, heavily armed caravans of twenty to fifty people. Caravans traveled before the return of the rains, which called everybody back to the farms. As trade was essentially a seasonal operation, there were geographical limits to the range of Soninke migrations. Migrants in general could not wander farther than 1,000 to 1,500 kilometers and be back in time for the rains and tillage. The extreme point reached by Soninke migrations, therefore, was the area corresponding roughly to the Kankan region in the Republic of Guinea and the northwest region of the Ivory Coast. This is another ecological contact zone, somewhat like the Soninke homeland, between the forest and savanna zones of West Africa, and it was the area where kola nuts, another extremely valuable item of West African trade, could be obtained.

Most travelers probably did not go that far, but exchanged their goods to secondary markets on the Niger Bend. The Soninke from western Gajaaga and Gidimaxa were relatively far from this zone and may not have gone any farther than the cities of the Niger Bend, for example, Nyamina, Segu, or Banamba in the nineteenth centuries.[75] They compensated for this by a secondary western trade network, which took them to the goldfields of Bambuxu and also to the Gambia, where they could obtain maritime salt. In the eighteenth and nineteenth centuries, European trade grafted itself onto the Gajaaga Gambian network, which now served to exchange slaves from the interior of Africa for European manufactured products.[76]

The trade migrations of the Soninke may already have existed in the Middle Ages, as we have seen. During this era, Soninke migrations left trading colonies throughout West Africa. Most commercial families *(jula)* in the Western Sudan today claim a Soninke origin, a claim that appears substantiated by the large number of Soninke *jamu* (clan names) among the jula.[77] Among groups claiming a Soninke origin, one of the most important is the Marka (this is the name given by the Mande to the Soninke) who settled in the Middle Niger River Valley, probably at the time of the kingdom of Ghana.[78] The Marka were the quasi-official traders in the Bambara kingdom of Segu in the eighteenth century and its nineteenth-century successor, the Umarian state.[79] Farther east, the Yarse (the name derives from the town of Yaresna, in the Upper Senegal region), who formed merchant communities among the Mossi, also have a Soninke origin, probably by way of the Middle Niger. The Soninke also had a strong influence on the Songhay. Soninke traders were the financiers and brokers of the Songhay empire, and it is also worth mentioning that Askia Mohammed, the founder of the great Askia dynasty of the Songhay empire, was of Soninke origin.[80] In the southern Mande area, the important trading city of Kankan was founded by families claiming a Soninke origin.[81] All the groups mentioned, however, no longer speak Soninke, but the language of the peoples among whom they settled (mostly Mande).

In its occupational meaning, the term *jula* refers to a full-time trader. Most Soninke were *occasional* traders, but as mentioned, there were full-time Soninke traders as well. Soninke jula, as is the case throughout the Western Sudan, were members of maraboutic (clerical) families. There were several reasons for the dominance of clerics among traders. First, of course, Islam created ties of brotherhood among traders in the Sudan and between traders in the Sudan and in North Africa. Second, Islamic clerics were excluded from political power, and as a result, they often redirected their ambitions into trade. Finally, maraboutic families accumulated large numbers of slaves because students in Islamic (Koranic) schools, the *talibe*, were requested by custom to give their teacher a gift of a value not inferior to one slave at the end of their studies; moreover, talibe worked on their teachers' farm during their studies. Freed from farm labor by their talibe and their slaves, members of maraboutic families could thus engage in trade as a full-time activity.[82] This reason also explains why clerics were especially involved in the slave trade in the precolonial period. Because of all these factors, Islamic clerics came closely behind royal families and their clients as large slave owners.

In Soninke society (as elsewhere in the Western Sudan until the Islamic revolutions of the nineteenth century), custom prevented clerics from holding political office. However, clerics were wealthy, and as we have seen above, wealth was the source of power in Soninke society. This created a kind of hidden tension between the clerics and "warrior" aristocrats. Oral tradition highlights the differences in lifestyles and ethics between clerics and "warriors." Clerical proverbs collected by Abdoulaye Bathily praise hard work in a fashion reminiscent of Max Weber's "Protestant ethic,"[83] while on the contrary, tunka lemmu and aristocrats emphasized military values, even brute force.[84] Tradition has also kept alive the memory of armed conflicts between royals and clerics.[85]

Tradition, however, gives a conventional and stereotypical view of royals and clerics, which overemphasizes the opposition between them. Ties of clientage linked warrior aristocracies and clerics. In Gajaaga, for example, the Darame and Jaaxo were very close clients of the Bacili, who performed at the funerals of the tunka. Clerics, in fact, needed such patronage in order to devote their life to the proper clerical pursuit—which was not trade, but religious study.[86] Clerics of the Darame family, one of the two most prestigious clerical families in Gajaaga, even considered trade an improper activity, outwardly preferring to live from the gifts bestowed by the Bacili.[87] Other prestigious clerical families probably felt the same way, although lesser clerical families emphasize that the Prophet Muhammad had been a trader, as if to legitimate their participation in this occupation. Conversely, "warrior" aristocrats did participate in trade (which they affected to despise)—indirectly or even directly. Hence, aristocrats financed jula trading expeditions, later sharing part of the proceeds. Better still, they were careful to participate in annual trade expeditions through the intermediary of their slaves, their clients, and even their young unmarried sons.[88] In Soninke precolonial society, trade (and trade migration) was an important way to accumulate wealth and through this wealth to obtain or to maintain power and influence. This observation was valid for all classes of society.

Soninke Slavery and Farm Production

The Soninke invariably came back from their trading expeditions with slaves. Few of these slaves were resold to the Beydan; the majority were kept by the Soninke and put to work on their fields in order to produce more millet to be sold to desert nomads. This form of reinvestment of trading gains was extremely profitable: at the end of the nineteenth century, for example, it took only three years for the marketable production (cereals or cotton cloth) of a single slave to become equal to the value of another slave.[89] Over time, Soninke society thus evolved into a slave-owning society. Slaves at the end of the nineteenth century never comprised less than one-third of the population, and in some regions they made up well over one-half.[90] Such figures were quite common in the Western Sudan and Senegambia, especially in those areas touched by the desert-side trade, but they certainly were not general: by comparison, in the Sereer part of the Senegalese kingdom of Bawol, a relatively self-sufficient and prosperous peasant society, only one-sixteenth, or 6.25 percent, of the population were slaves.[91]

The Soninke's need to maintain control over such large numbers of slaves related directly to their brutal treatment of slaves. Nineteenth-century observers were unanimous in reporting the harsh treatment of slaves in Soninke society, and these reports are confirmed by interviews made in the 1960s and 1970s of former slaves. These reports give lie to the idea, once current in Africanist literature, that African slavery was milder than American plantation slavery. Whippings, beatings, and infants half-buried in the sand in the shade of a tree to keep them quiet while their mothers worked in the fields were commonplace.[92] In the years when crops proved insufficient, masters supplemented their food reserves by taking away from the slaves' rations.[93] Slaves had no rights and no dignity. In many villages, they were segregated in a special quarter, an arrangement that has persisted until today.[94] In spite of its brutality, however, Soninke slavery was relatively stable because slaves tended to be progressively integrated into the system of clientage.

FARMING SYSTEMS

In order to understand how slaves were used in the Soninke homeland, one must first understand the labor arrangements of family units. Contrary to their ethnic relatives, the Marka of the Middle Niger River Valley (the Marka are Bambara-speakers of Soninke origin), the Soninke did not cluster their slaves into "slave villages," set apart from their town.[95] Most slave owners among the Soninke owned only two to four slaves.[96] This does not mean necessarily that most Soninke slaves were owned by such small holders, but we have no numerical information on the proportions of slaves owned by small and large holders respectively. According to Eric Pollet and Grace Winter, about half of all slave owners in Jafunu worked in the fields alongside their slaves.[97] As already seen, aristocrats, especially members of royal families, left farming entirely to their slaves.[98] In Gajaaga, aristocratic slave holdings of fifty to a hundred slaves were not rare.[99] The numerous slaves of aristocratic and maraboutic families were placed under the authority of a head slave,[100] and they were sometimes regrouped in separate cultivation villages (farming camps) on the jeri during the rainy season.[101] There are no reports, however, that the labor arrangements on aristocratic estates were different from those of commoner households. In all cases, therefore, slaves were integrated into labor arrangements that were patterned after those of the extended family.

Soninke families, still today, are production units based on the labor of younger dependents organized in a hierarchy of labor duties. Each family head, the *ka gumme*, controls the family lands (which are either obtained from the lineage head if the family is part of a lineage of "masters of the land" or otherwise rented from a family of such lineage). There is a variety of possible situations, but a commonplace arrangement is as follows. In the morning, each ka gumme farms the *te-xoore*, the "great field" or family field,[102] with the help of his sons. ("Morning" is defined as the portion of the day between sunrise and about two o'clock, the time of the midday meal, which is provided by the family head.) In the afternoon and evening, the family head farms alone on the "great field," while each of his sons farms on his individual plot *(saluma;* pl.: *salumo)*. If the father is no longer alive, he is replaced in his duties as ka gumme by the eldest son. In this case, the eldest brother leads his younger brothers on the "great field" in the morning. In the first part of the afternoon (between two and four), the eldest brother farms alone on the "great field," while the next oldest brother works on his own saluma aided by all younger brothers. These in turn have the rest of their afternoon and evening free to work on their own salumo. These kinds of arrangement usually prevail during four or five days of the week. During the two or three remaining days of the week, the sons work on their salumo, or if the family head is the eldest brother, the second oldest brother farms his saluma in the morning helped by his younger brothers (the second brother must then provide the midday meal), who farm in the afternoon on their own plots.[103]

Soninke women also have fields, whose status bears some similarity with that of the salumo of dependent men. Like the salumo, these fields are allocated by the family head—thus in strictly legal terms, there is no female property, or even tenancy, of land.[104] As with the salumo, the product of women's plots is the property of the women who grow it, with the caveat that wives must provide the ingredients of the sauce that accompanies the main courses of cereals (for this reason, peanuts are the most common women's crop). The difference with the salumo is that women do not owe a portion of their time to the family head in exchange for their plot, although their participation is required in certain tasks on the "great field," such as sowing, protecting crops from animal predators, and harvesting. Working arrangements on the women's fields vary; each woman may work alone on her plot, or work may be organized as on the men's fields, with daughters working for their mother in the morning and for each other in the order of their filiation in the remaining time.[105] As elsewhere in Africa, there is a gender division of labor in agriculture. While men farm cereals and cotton, women farm peanuts, rice, and indigo. But this gender division should not be taken as absolute. Today, due to the migration of men, it is not infrequent to see women grow sorghum, while there are past and present examples of men growing peanuts.[106] Finally, in contrast with many regions of Africa, women's agriculture is less important than that of men. Although it is impossible to evaluate the production of women in the precolonial period, a relatively recent estimate in the Upper Senegal River region indicates that slightly less than one-third of agricultural production comes from women's plots.[107] The figure may be biased because about one-third to one-half of adult men in this region are today away as migrants.

THE USE OF SLAVES

The name "slave," if we except the peculiar case of the "great slaves," designated three different conditions among the Soninke, as among most Senegambian and Western Sudanic peoples. These conditions should be distinguished from the classic colonial designations of *captifs de traite* (first-generation trade slaves) and *captifs de case* (second-generation slaves born in the household). Second-generation slaves were indeed treated better than trade slaves, but the colonial designations, as well as the Western Sudanic terminology in which they originated, are confusing. Far more useful, at least for the description of the *economic* situation of slaves (the legal situation is another matter), is the distinction that James Searing has drawn between "actual slaves" and "serfs," and his comparison of the condition of "serfs" with that of Russian serfs in the preemancipation era.[108]

"Actual slaves" lived within the household of their owner and were fed and clothed by him. They were in general first-generation trade slaves, but they also comprised second-generation slaves born in their master's household who were not yet married. In Gajaaga and Gidimaxa, "actual slaves" worked in principle six "mornings" a week for their masters, and they had six afternoons and the whole day of Friday to work on a plot alloted to them by their masters.[109] In Jafunu, the "best custom" was to make these slaves work until two in the afternoon for the family head, from two to four for the head slave (if there was one), and from four to six for the second brother or eldest son of the family head or on a plot allocated by the family head.[110] In Gumbu, such slaves also worked on the plots of brothers and sons of the family head, in addition to the "great field" of the family head, and remained on call for whatever tasks had to be done the rest of the time.[111] In all regions, the family head was obligated to feed the slaves while they worked for him, and he also had to clothe them. Most of these descriptions, however, portray a theoretical arrangement. In practice, the treatment of "actual slaves" depended on the arbitrary will of their master, who could requisition their work at will, and who often did not fulfill his obligation to feed and clothe them (the slaves had to feed themselves from the product of their plots).[112]

Slaves who were married and who lived in their own household, independently from their master's household, had a condition more akin to that of a "serf" than a slave.[113] Such slaves were called *saarido* (born in the house) in Soninke.[114] As their name indicates, the saarido were second-generation slaves. However, first-generation slaves who were allowed to marry and to form independent households had a condition similar to that of the saarido.[115] Contrary to the once popular descriptions of African slavery, second-generation slaves could be sold, but such an action was considered shameful since it demonstrated the ruin of the family, and it seems to have happened only in exceptional cases, such as the liquidation of the inheritance of an insolvent family head.[116]

As in the Wolof system of slavery described by James Searing, there were two systems of "serfdom" among the Soninke. The first was probably the most common. Similar to the Russian *barschina* system of serfdom, it was based on the provision of a rent in labor by the serf to the slave owner. Slaves under this kind of arrangement were called in Jafunu *woroso* (Bambara for "born in the house"), and *komo woroso* in Gumbu.[117] In the *cercle* (administrative division) of Bakel (i.e., in Gwey, western part of Gajaaga), they worked four to five mornings a week on their master's fields.[118] In the cercle of Kayes (Kammera, eastern part of Gajaaga), they worked five mornings a week.[119] In Gumbu, they worked six mornings a week for their master. In Gumbu, therefore, there was less difference between such "serfs" and "actual slaves" than in other Soninke regions—perhaps an influence of the harsh "plantation" system in neighboring Beledugu, which spread to Gumbu at the end of the nineteenth century.[120] An early colonial report for the cercle of Nioro mentions that Soninke slaves there worked six mornings a week for their masters, without indicating what kind of slave status was described, which may suggest that the difference between a "serf" and an "actual slave" was less marked there, too.[121] In all regions, serfs owing a rent in labor worked in their free time on personal plots provided by their owner. They were fed by their master only when they worked for him. During the dry season, they (and "actual slaves") made cotton cloth; females made cotton thread and males wove cloth. They paid half of the gains from this activity to their owners.[122]

A second kind of "serfdom," similar to the Russian *obrok* system, was based on the provision of a rent in kind to the slave owner. In Gumbu, such "serfs," called woroso, owed their owner a yearly rent of 150 *mudd* of grain grown on their plots (a mudd is a measure of capacity roughly equivalent to about 2.25 kilograms of sorghum).[123] In Kammera (presumably in Gwey as well) and Gidimaxa, slaves had likewise the possibility to "get themselves out of the hands [of their master]" for a yearly payment of two *pièces de guinée* (cloth used as currency in the Upper Senegal in the nineteenth century), which Charles Monteil tells us had been once equivalent to 100 mudds of grain (it certainly was worth far less at the time); 100 to 150 mudds correspond roughly speaking to the average grain surplus of an adult producer.[124] Monteil further indicates that "it was always possible" for a second-generation slave to gain this status; for a married male, it was when one of his sons was circumcised and could replace him on the master's fields, and for a married female, when one of her daughters married (and thus would beget slave children for the master).[125] Monteil's rather imprecise sentence suggests that the decision was contingent on the will of the master. In Gumbu, access to this condition was indeed dependent on the will of the master, who would organize a formal ceremony to mark the change in status of the slave.[126] In Gumbu and probably elsewhere, the condition of "serf" owing a rent in kind was not reserved for second-generation slaves; first-generation slaves also had access to it if their owner so chose.

"Serfs" were allowed to participate in activities other than agriculture or weaving. With their master's permission, they could engage in trade. Male "serfs" could work on trading caravans, or they could in the nineteenth century become labor migrants in the Gambia or in French colonial centers for periods of two to three years or become sailors on French boats.[127] That slaves were allowed to migrate of course appears surprising, but since these slaves were married, they left behind their wives and children as hostages— the slave master had the right to sell the children of a serf if he did not pay his rent in kind.[128] There is some imprecision in the sources as to what category of "serfs" was allowed to migrate, but the second category (owing a rent in kind) is more probable.[129] Claude Meillassoux mentions that certain subordinate occupations in trade, such as the brokering of slaves or retailing in markets, were especially reserved for such slaves.[130]

As was generally the case in the Western Sudan, most Soninke slaves were women. According to 1894 French reports, among slaves in the cercle of Nioro 25 percent were men, 40 percent women, and 35 percent children (this figure included Soninke slaves as well as slaves of other ethnic groups). In Kayes, among Soninke slaves, 24 percent were men, 50 percent were women, and 26 percent were children.[131] Oral testimonies as well as contemporary eyewitness reports indicate that first-generation female slaves ("actual slaves") generally worked on the "great fields" of (male) family heads alongside male trade slaves.[132] This was, of course, in contradiction to the traditional gender division of labor in African societies, but well in keeping with the dehumanized status of first-generation slaves. Maraboutic and pious families, however, spared their male and female slaves the humiliation of working together on the same field; female slaves in these families worked on women's plots only.[133] In addition to their work in the fields, women slaves relieved free women of the hardest and most labor-intensive household duties, such as pounding grain or fetching water. During the dry season, they spun thread and dyed cloth woven by male slaves.[134] Spinning was an important activity of female slaves since it took eight hours of spinning to provide enough thread for one hour of weaving.[135]

Women slaves generally fetched a slightly higher price than men.[136] This was in part because they were easier to control and in part because they bore children, which added to their master's wealth (children were the property of the mother's owner). But as Martin Klein noted in his contribution to *Women and Slavery in Africa*, this was also because women could be used to integrate male slaves.[137] Slave owners provided their male slaves with their first wife. It was at that time, as we have seen, that slaves left the category of "actual slaves" to become "serfs" owing a rent in labor. Later, when children of the slave ménage had grown into adulthood and could replace their father on the master's fields, their parents could become "serfs" owing a rent in kind, thus progressing toward a greater autonomy. One should not see in this a kind of ineluctable "process model"—there were second-generation married slaves who remained on their master's compound, and access to the condition of a "serf" owing a rent in kind, as we have seen, was apparently contingent on the master's will.

Access to the condition of a "serf," or woroso, provided greater autonomy, but it did not provide security for one's old age. Children of the half-emancipated slave ménage were the property of their mother's owner. Although small children apparently remained with their parents, once they were circumcised (and thus became legally adult), they worked for their master.[138] This could become a serious problem when a "serf" became old and was no longer able to support himself. But there were solutions: a "serf" could buy a slave, who worked for him only;[139] better still, a male "serf" could buy a woman slave and make her his wife or buy back his own wife.[140] In this case, the children of this union would work only for him. Buying a slave, of course, presupposed that the "serf" had been able to accumulate substantial savings. Hard work was clearly important, but so was the good will of the owner of the "serf." The slave owner would or would not decide to allocate the "serf" a reasonably productive field, he would or would not make a male slave an overseer (and therefore a beneficiary of labor obligations, or prestations, in the beginning of the afternoon), and he would or would not allow a male slave to trade or to hire himself abroad.

Slaves could also buy back their freedom.[141] This was extremely expensive since it cost the value of two slaves, which was paid to the owner of the slave.[142] There was little advantage for a slave in buying his freedom and not the freedom of his spouse and children as well, but the cost of buying back a whole family must have been prohibitive. A slave owner, however, could decide to lower the amount of the redeeming payment, or even waive it altogether. Finally, a slave could buy himself or herself back only if the master agreed to it. For these reasons, there were very few *dubangandi komo* (redeemed slaves) in Soninke society.[143] Not surprisingly, redeemed slaves remained the clients of their former masters, a dependence expressed in the symbolic participation of such slaves in family ceremonies. Redeemed slaves could not marry free Soninke, but they married into the class of the "great slaves" and were customarily considered part of that category. "Great slaves" did not work or make payments to anyone, they married under the same custom as free Soninke, and they had access to village lands (presumably lands in the jeri and, through renting, to riverbank lands).[144] Although the number of redeemed slaves was very small, the possibility of reaching a status almost similar to that of the free must have given hope to many Soninke slaves. Indeed, Claude Meillassoux's informants in Gumbu indicated that "serfs" of the second category (owing a rent in kind) only married their daughters to, and celebrated festivals in the company of, slaves of their own category and "great slaves."[145]

To sum up, Soninke slaves over time could acquire greater and greater autonomy and could even hope for a condition akin to freedom, but this progression was mostly dependent on the will of their owner. It was the slave owner who arranged the marriage that was the first step in the progression of the slave toward autonomy. Later, it was largely the slave owner who made it possible (or not) for a "serf" to buy a slave or a wife and thereby ensure support in his old age. And finally, it was with the authorization of the slave master, and often thanks to his generosity regarding the amount of the redeeming payment, that a few privileged slaves could regain their freedom (but only a portion of their honor). In other words, in order to better their condition and inch their way back toward freedom, Soninke slaves had to become the clients of their masters.

Soninke slavery was harsh and exploitive. If we did not have the testimonies on the bad treatment of slaves that I summarized above, we would know this from colonial statistics on the demography of Soninke slaves. As we have seen, the proportion of children among Soninke slaves was very low (around 25 percent)—quite a remarkable fact considering that most first-generation slaves were either children or women of childbearing age. Soninke slaves did not reproduce themselves at a net positive rate of population growth.[146] But at the same time, the structure of clientage in which Soninke slaves were integrated, the tight interpersonal relations between slaves and their owners, and the hope that the slaves had of bettering their condition over time gave great stability to the system—a stability demonstrated when slavery came to an end in the Western Sudan.[147]

Conclusion

The precolonial economic system of the Soninke was remarkable in that it resulted, through the practice of trade migration, in a form of productive investment, slaves—an investment that is repugnant to us today, but one that was nevertheless morally acceptable then, and also extremely profitable. The Soninke were not, as was asserted by a number of colonial writers, a "people of traders" in the sense of a people specializing in trade as a permanent activity, but rather agriculturalists producing for a market, who migrated periodically to sell the products obtained in exchange for their commercial agricultural production and who used the product of these transactions to reinvest in their production system in the form of slaves.

Soninke precolonial migrations contradict the view of African societies (and, indeed, of peasant societies in general) as sedentary and resistant to change. In fact, such migrations were rather common in precolonial Africa. As noted, all West African "desert-side" populations practiced periodic trade migrations in the precolonial period: the Fuutanke, the Mossi, and especially the Hausa.[148] The Fuutanke and the Mossi, however, were less well-placed geographically than the Soninke: Fuuta Tooro is bordered to the south by the Ferlo semidesert, while the Mossi are separated from the desert to the north by the Niger Bend.[149] By contrast the Hausa, who are in contact with the desert edge to the north and with well-populated regions to the south, had a geographical situation as favorable as that of the Soninke. This no doubt explains why the Hausa played such an important role as traders in the Central Sudan and neighboring regions. If we turn our attention toward continents other than Africa, temporary migrations were also quite common. European mountaineers in particular, for example, in Auvergne or Savoie, took advantage of long winters to trade livestock or products of their environment, such as cheeses and woodcrafts, to the surrounding countryside.[150] Such migration often led a favored minority of migrants to become full-time traders, as with the case of the Auvergnat trading "diaspora" in Spain in the seventeenth and eighteenth centuries.[151]

Environmental factors thus played an important role in the emergence of premodern temporary migrations. Migration was a way to maximize productive time in farming societies that would otherwise have remained largely idle during seasonal periods of agricultural inactivity (dry season in Africa, winter in Europe). Environmental factors, however, were not the only causes of migration. For example, in Africa, forest populations such as the Dida of the Ivory Coast, who live in an area where there is little seasonal agricultural inactivity, also mounted periodic trading expeditions.[152] Two additional factors played a role in this case. The first was commercial opportunity: forest populations in the Ivory Coast and Ghana could trade with both Sudanic regions to the north and with Europeans on the coast to the south; they also had valuable items to trade (kola nuts, gold, and slaves). The second was the decentralized or fragmented character of their political and social organization: in societies where the state is weak, there are few or no restrictions to movements of population. There is also a great amount of pressure to accumulate wealth and, through wealth, to accumulate clients and, therefore, power (the other side of the coin being that if one does not accumulate enough wealth, one will lose independence and, therefore, lose honor). In premodern times, trade migration was one of the ways in decentralized societies to attain wealth and power.[153]

The reverse case, which is offered as a plausible hypothesis to be tested rather than as a certainty, further illustrates the point: in premodern times, it appears that state societies tended to regulate trade in order to prevent the emergence of wealthy individuals or families who could interfere with the influence of the state. In Asante, for example, long-distance traders had to enlist as "chief's men" in officially approved caravans, and traders who were too successful were often stripped of their wealth by the state.[154] In China, temporary traders came from the mountain regions of Szechwan, Yunnan, and Kueichou, which had a long period of winter inactivity but which also were beyond the pale of imperial authority. Conversely, Han (mainstream Chinese) populations in the Chinese plains, who were well controlled by the state, were legally tied to the land.[155] The European situation historically mirrors that of the Chinese.

Thus if one looks for a common denominator for peoples involved in premodern trade migrations, one such denominator may be statelessness or the weakness of the state. This is also valid for European premodern migrations: a simple look at the map of traditional temporary migrant groups in Europe reveals that these came from regions with strong extended family structures, strong village allegiances, and little or no clear allegiance to central power, for example, the highland societies of the Auvergnat, the Scots, the Welsh, or the Savoyard.[156] What has obscured the connection between "statelessness" and migration in the European case is that European mountain societies were usually very poor and that this poverty seemed to explain both their migrations and their social "backwardness" (i.e., their extended family structures and lack of allegiance to the state). In the African case, however, examples abound of groups that were at the same time "stateless societies" and heavily involved in return migration while by all accounts they were comparatively rich. The Baule are a good example.[157]

To conclude, the Soninke homeland in precolonial times was at the same time a comparatively wealthy region of commercial agriculture and a region "exporting" temporary migrants. There was no contradiction between the two activities. In fact, the more the Soninke participated in commercial agriculture and the more they were involved in temporary migration, the wealthier they became. This observation clashes with the dominant view of African modern migrations as the result of deprivation and colonial violence. That the Soninke were heavily involved in temporary migration in the precolonial period suggests it is continuity, not disruption, that lies at the center of explanations for their modern migration.

T W O

From Traditional to Modern Migration

1822-1855

THE DOMINANT VIEW among Africanists today is that labor migration emerged as a result of colonial taxation and coercion and the impoverishment of rural areas during colonization (see Introduction). Yet as we have just seen, the Soninke had a long history of migration in precolonial times. We shall now see that when their modern (labor) migrations began, their economy was comparatively prosperous as a result of the desert-side trade and French commerce. As for colonial control, it was not established in the Upper Senegal region before the middle of the nineteenth century.

The Upper Senegal River Valley in the Eighteenth Century

The French began to trade in the Upper Senegal region in the eighteenth century.[1] This period is marginally important for our topic, but a brief outline will help to put into perspective the regional pattern of trade in the following century.[2] A newcomer, French trade became integrated in an already established pattern. The region's commercial foundation was the "desert-side" trade—the exchange of grain for salt and livestock brought by the Beydan. The Soninke reexported this salt and livestock to the neighboring gold-producing region of Bambuxu (Bambuck). But gold production in

Bambuxu depended upon the labor of slaves and migrant laborers,[3] all of whom this region apparently could not feed; so, answering the demand for food, Soninke in Gajaaga and especially in the Falemme River Valley also exported grain. With gold obtained in Bambuxu, the Soninke went to the Middle Valley of the Niger (and earlier in the seventeenth century to the Jawara kingdom of Jara), where they obtained slaves. The Soninke then either kept these slaves to produce more grain in Gajaaga for the Beydan or in the valley of the Falemme River for Bambuxu or sold them in Bambuxu, where they were used as gold miners. The Soninke of the Upper Senegal region, therefore, handled an important trade in slaves. This explains why they became the privileged partners of the French slave trade in Senegal. Gajaaga, in fact, became Senegal's most important supplier in the Atlantic slave trade of the eighteenth century.[4] The French slave trade itself caused a new expansion in grain production in the Upper Senegal region. With salt from salt pans near the estuary of the Senegal River, the French bought grain to feed the slaves kept in French forts while they awaited shipping. In time, the French also bought grain for the consumption of their colonial outpost of Saint-Louis, which was situated in the comparatively infertile region of Waalo.[5]

The point to remember in this quick overview is the importance of grain in the pattern of exchanges in the Upper Senegal region. Grain was important primarily in the desert-side trade with the Beydan (which indirectly fed all the other types of trade), but it was also an important item in the gold trade to Bambuxu and in the French slave trade.

The French in the Upper Senegal Region

In the eighteenth century, French trade in the Senegal River Valley had rested especially on the export of slaves, although gum arabic became increasingly more important in the last decades of the period. During the French revolutionary wars, however, the colony of Senegal (then little larger than the trading towns of Saint-Louis and Gorée) fell to the British, and contacts with the upper river region ceased completely. When Senegal was returned to French control in 1817, its economy was in shambles. The slave trade had been abolished by the British in 1807, a prohibition that was confirmed by an Anglo-French agreement in 1814. Meanwhile, the French had lost their most important colonial possession, the Caribbean sugar-producing island of Saint-Domingue. The recovery plan of the new French governor of Senegal, Julien Schmalz, combined the philanthropic aspirations of the times and the desire to recoup the losses in the Caribbean. Since slave labor could no longer be transported across the Atlantic, Schmalz's plan proposed creating plantations where the manpower was, that is, in Africa. The plantations were to be managed by Africans as independent producers. A limited number of European colonists were to be settled, but they were to serve as living examples of the European values of thrift and hard work rather than as planters and overseers. The area to be colonized was the valley of the Senegal River, which had been the natural route of French penetration since the seventeenth century. Three colonization bases were to be established in the lower, middle, and upper valley. The Upper Senegal, where former commercial contacts could be reestablished (many former trading partners of the French were presumably still alive), understandably was to come first. Such were the reasons behind the establishment of the fort at Bakel in lower Gajaaga, or Gwey (called Goye by the French), in 1818.[6]

Plans for agricultural colonization in the Upper Senegal region, however, quickly receded into the background. The region, situated some 800 kilometers from the coast, could be supplied only during the five or six months of the year (between July and December or January) when the river was navigable. Instead, the French soon embarked, under Governor Jacques-François Roger, on an ill-fated colonization scheme in Waalo in the lower valley of the Senegal River.[7] Yet the idea of creating a hub of agricultural development in the Upper Senegal region never completely died out, as we shall see.

The French "official mind" had initially little interest in products other than agricultural ones, but from the start, Beydan from the desert had brought gum arabic to Bakel and demanded a greater involvement in the gum trade by the French monopolistic charter company, the Compagnie de Galam. Gum arabic was fast becoming the main item of trade in Senegal due to rising demand in the European textile industry (where gum was used in the dyeing process). Gum arabic is a secretion of several species of acacia tree. Most of the gum-producing trees are found south of the Sahara, in a belt extending from southern Mauritania to Somalia. Until the end of the nineteenth century, when the Anglo-Egyptian Sudan became dominant in the trade, the Senegal River Valley was the principal place in the world where gum arabic could be obtained. Most of the Senegambian acacia trees are situated to the north of the Senegal River Valley and were controlled in the nineteenth century by Beydan, usually from *ẓawaya* (or maraboutic) tribes. They traded their gum on the Senegal River to Afro-French middlemen, the *traitants*, who were métis (Creole) or Black Saint-Louisiens.[8]

The Upper Senegal region participated in the general expansion of the gum trade after 1818, although on a lesser scale than the lower valley, which was accessible by river boat all year. This expansion was especially apparent after 1830, when steps were taken toward the establishment of free trade in Senegal. In 1831, the French government decided to allow Senegal to export gum directly to countries other than France,[9] which led to the years of "gum fever." The agricultural colonization scheme in Waalo was abandoned, to the great relief of Senegalese merchants who had more or less been coerced into investing in it.

In 1832, the Compagnie de Galam was freed from the obligation of maintaining an agricultural settlement in Bakel.[10] Administrative records, however, show that the French colonial administration had by no means renounced the idea of agricultural colonization in the Upper Senegal River Valley. A document from Bakel in 1847 spoke about creating a "second Waalo" in the Upper Senegal region.[11] All such reports characteristically envisioned agricultural development as planned from the top, disregarding the importance of the commercial market: for French administrators, "civilization was the source of commerce" and if the Upper Senegal had not developed into an agricultural export area, it was because the administration was too lenient with traders and no longer requested that they develop agricultural plantations.[12]

French administrators were not entirely blind, however, to the relationship between commerce and agriculture. One report stated:

> If the Saracolets [the Soninke] . . . today only seek in their crops what is necessary for them to live, it is that, located far from the great centers of consumption, they do not find advantageous outlets for their crops, [but] let them be encouraged by [good] examples, let them be certain that they will derive ample profit from their land and they will soon engage . . . in cultivation. Already we have a striking example of this under our eyes: *as the price of grain* ["*mil*," in this region, sorghum] *has risen because of the purchases made by the Moors, the amount of land under cultivation has become twice as large as in the past.*[13]

While this report was intended as a criticism of the Saint-Louis traders, it was the first direct record of the expansion that was taking place in the agricultural economy of the Senegal River Valley as a result of the gum trade.

Indirect Effects of the Gum Trade on Agriculture in the Upper Senegal Region

The rising importance of the gum trade in Senegal had a critical impact on Beydan society in the nineteenth century. In 1848, writing about the entire Senegal River Valley, Captain Bouët-Willaumez noted that "for a number of years, grain (*mil*, i.e., sorghum or millet) has become part of the diet of the Beydan, and is especially used for the consumption of the numerous captives [slaves] employed in gathering gum in the mimosa [acacia] forests."[14] Nineteenth-century French sources on the gum trade concur that the Beydan involved in this trade bought more grain in the Senegal River Valley, but Bouët-Willaumez's account is implausible for two reasons. The first is, of course, that grain had become part of the Beydan diet long before the nineteenth century. The second is that the number of slaves employed in gathering gum by the Beydan must have been very small. The Upper Senegal region exported a yearly average of 300,000 kilograms of gum at the beginning of the nineteenth century. According to James Webb, during the gum-producing season a slave collected on average about four kilograms of gum per day.[15] This can be translated into 75,000 days of work. Since the main gum harvest lasted about three months, the gum-export figure for the entire Upper Senegal region corresponded to a workforce of about 830 slaves only! Given a generous estimate of one kilogram of grain per day to feed an adult male slave, the Beydan would have had to buy from the Soninke no more than seventy-five metric tons of grain. This hardly would have caused a revolution in food production in the Upper Senegal River Valley.

That said, however, it is clear that desert nomads did buy more and more grain in the Senegal River Valley and in general in the whole sub-Saharan belt in the nineteenth century.[16] The reason was climatic change in the Saharan area. The western "Sahelian" zone experienced a trend toward increasing aridity beginning in the late sixteenth or early seventeenth century. The desiccation initially caused famines, but by the middle of the eighteenth century, farmers in the Senegal River Valley had begun to adapt to the drier environment. They abandoned maize as a dominant crop in favor of a mixed agriculture based on maize and sorghum—the latter becoming increasingly more important.[17] Meanwhile, nomads increased both their raiding of sedentaries and their commercial exchanges with them. The salt trade became more important, providing the Beydan with the resources needed to buy grain. The gum trade filled a similar role after the beginning of the nineteenth century.[18]

The desert populations were thus thrust into a cycle of commercial expansion that had repercussions to the south among agriculturalists. The demand in cereals grew and the Soninke (and other Senegal River Valley populations, such as the Fuutanke) responded to the demand by increasing production—resulting in the increase in cultivated land noted in the 1847 report quoted above.

The Senegalese River gum trade in the nineteenth century was a kind of "triangular trade": French traders or mulatto middlemen, settled in Saint-Louis in the estuary of the Senegal River, imported from French India pièces de guinée or bafts, the indigo-dyed cloths that had become for all practical purposes the currency of the Senegambia. Officially registered middlemen, the traitants, carried these guinées upstream during the season when the Senegal River was navigable, between July and January. The traitants were the only traders allowed to buy gum on the river, in a limited number of official gum-trading posts, the *escales*. In January, the Beydan began to arrive in the Soninke homeland, where they pastured their herds and bought recently harvested cereals. The Beydan did not have gum to sell at that time of the year, since the main gum season was between February and July, so the traitants lent their guinée cloths to the Beydan in exchange for the promise of a certain quantity of gum. The Beydan then traded some of their guinées to Soninke farmers in exchange for cereals.[19] The Beydan tended to buy grain close to the desert edge[20] in order to cut down on transportation costs, to take advantage of lower prices for cereals at the beginning of the dry season, and also probably to keep their herds away from the less salubrious river areas. This gave an advantage to Soninke regions situated to the north. The French, with their equation of trade and civilization with centralized societies, were puzzled by the evidence of a far greater agricultural activity in the "anarchistic" region of Gidimaxa on the northern bank of the Senegal River (where the highest authorities were the village chiefs) than in the kingdom of Gwey on the southern bank.[21]

It is worth examining for a moment these Beydan who brought gum to the French and who purchased grain from the Soninke. There were two gum escales in the Upper Senegal region before 1848. In Bakel, by far the most important trading post, gum was sold by the Idaw Aish. Further upstream, a lesser Beydan group, composed of the Awlad Koisi and Asker, acted as a middleman for the Awlad Mbarek (of which the Awlad Koisi and Asker were themselves a subgroup) at a *comptoir flottant* (a floating trading post) anchored near Maxanna in Kammera.[22] Together with the Awlad Koisi and the Asker, the Awlad Naser are also mentioned in 1848 as participants in the trade of a comptoir flottant near Kenyu (near the present town of Kayes).[23]

The names Idaw Aish, Awlad Mbarek, and so forth, refer to "nations"— that is, hierarchized "confederations" composed of warriors, clerics, and tributaries—which are known by the name of the dominant warrior group. But dominant warrior groups did not trade; they lived from the taxation and exploitation of traders, who were members of the maraboutic groups (zawaya). There are only scattered references to the maraboutic groups that traded gum in Bakel. The clearest reference dates to 1842 and specifies that the Laghlal traded "[t]wo hundred thousand [metric pounds] of gum,"[24] that is, a hundred tons. This corresponded roughly to *one-third* of the gum traded in the Upper Senegal region at the time.[25] Another report of 1850 mentions an attempt made by a French trader to buy gum in the village of Jagili (Gidimaxa) from "the caravan of H. T. [Hamet Taleb]." This can only have been Ahmed Taleb, son of Mohamed Mahmud Wuld Abdallah, who was at the time chief of the Ahl Sidi Mahmud. The Ahl Sidi Mahmud, a branch of the Idaw Al-Haj, were a maraboutic group but behaved as warriors, and established hegemony over various tributary and maraboutic subjects of the Idaw Aish in the mid nineteenth century.[26]

Additional information can be obtained by confronting secondary literature with primary documents. The main maraboutic subjects of the Idaw Aish, the Ahl Sidi Mahmud, and the Awlad Mbarek were the Laghlal and the Tajakant, who are presented in the colonial literature as important traders of gum.[27] As for the Awlad Naser (mentioned as trading near Kenyu in 1848— see above), according to Georges Poulet they acted as intermediaries for the trade of the Kunta.[28] At the time when Poulet wrote (1904), the Kunta sold gum, livestock, and salt (from Tishit as well as Ijil) in the cercle of Nioro. The Kunta are briefly mentioned as trading in Bakel in 1884, but this was an exceptional occurrence due to a temporary alliance of the Kunta and the Idaw Aish against the Ahl Sidi Mahmud. In normal times, the Kunta were the enemies of both the Idaw Aish and the Ahl Sidi Mahmud, and they were not welcome in Bakel, although they must have traded in Médine after its foundation, as they probably did at the comptoir flottant near Kenyu mentioned by Bouët-Willaumez in 1848.[29] Among other exceptional mentions, the Meshduf, a group that emerged in the Hodh in the middle of the nineteenth century, are also noted as trading in Bakel in 1885. Their coming was due to floods that prevented them from selling their gum in Médine, as they did usually.[30] Again, the name Meshduf refers to the dominant group in a "nation" rather than the maraboutic group that actually traded the gum, which was apparently either Laghlal or Tajakant.[31]

The various mentions of the Laghlal (especially the 1842 mention specifying that they brought one-third of the gum traded in Bakel) are interesting because this group acknowledges a *Soninke* ancestor, Mohammed Roll, whom tradition also presents as the ancestor of the Masna, a group of traders of Soninke origin living in the oasis of Tishit.[32] (The Masna are apparently a remnant of the Soninke populations that inhabited southeastern Mauritania in the Middle Ages, prior to the desertification of the region.) These blood ties of the Laghlal, real or not, are an indication of old commercial ties with the Soninke homeland. They are also an indication of a historical link between the gum trade and the salt trade since an important part of the salt trade in the Soninke homeland came from Tishit. It is also worth noting that the three maraboutic groups especially mentioned above—Laghlal, Tajakant, and Kunta—were the most important participants in the salt trade in the region.[33] In general, this information strongly suggests that the gum trade grew on the basis of the commercial network earlier created by the salt trade.

The Beydan were not the only ones to buy Soninke-grown grain in the nineteenth century. Grain from the Upper Senegal was also carried away by a fleet of small boats owned by small Saint-Louisian traders, the *marigotiers*, named after the seasonal tributaries of the Senegal River (*marigots*, or creeks) on which these traders traveled to get to the smaller settlements. Some of the grain bought by the marigotiers in the Upper Senegal region may have served the trade with Saint-Louis, but in fact, most was destined to be sold in the Lower Senegal River Valley to the Trarza and Brakna Beydan, who gathered the most important portion of the gum exported from Senegal. These grain imports were necessary because the lower valley of the Senegal is generally an area of poor agriculture, owing to saline infiltrations from the Atlantic Ocean into the estuary of the Senegal River. Much of the grain eaten by the Trarza and Brakna during the summer months had to be imported from upstream, primarily from Fuutanke villages in the middle valley or Damga, to be sure, but from Soninke areas as well.[34]

It is possible to give a rough estimate of volume of the grain trade of the marigotiers. Bouët-Willaumez estimated the number of marigotiers who traveled each year to the Upper Senegal "delta" (i.e., Gajaaga, Gidimaxa, and probably Jafunu and Xaaso) at between 100 and 240 boats of two to twelve nautical tons burden (cargo weight).[35] A nautical ton is equivalent to 2.83 cubic meters of burden. We know from nineteenth-century documents that a *barrique* of sorghum contained 225 liters, or again, 0.225 cubic meters of grain weighing 216 kilograms.[36] From this, we may estimate that a boat of two nautical tons burden carried at least four metric tons of grain.[37] Even if we consider that the majority of the boats used by the marigotiers were of the smallest size of two nautical tons burden, some 400 to 1,000 metric tons of grain were carried away each year from the Upper Senegal region. This minimum figure should be appreciated in comparison with the population of the Upper Senegal region at the time. Pollet and Winter evaluate the surplus grain production of a Soninke farmer (after deduction of his personal consumption and that of his dependents, the constitution of a security reserve, and minor expenses) at between 200 and 233 kilograms a year.[38] Hence, the minimum figure of 400 to 1,000 tons of grain represented the commercial production of between 2,000 and 5,000 individuals. These individuals were essentially adult males (since females in general did not grow sorghum). Including the families of these producers, we obtain a minimum figure of 8,000 to 20,000 persons who were directly affected by the marigotier trade. As the combined populations of Damga, Gajaaga, Jafunu, and Xaaso (representing the entire Upper Senegal population) amounted to about 80,000, a minimum of 10 to 25 percent of the mainly Soninke population of the Upper Senegal was directly affected by the marigotier trade.[39] These figures could be biased by a number of factors,[40] but they provide an indication of the importance of the trade of the marigotiers.

The suppression of the monopolistic Compagnie de Galam, and of many concomitant restrictions on riverine trade that followed the French Revolution of 1848, resulted in expanding exports for the Upper Senegal region. It brought about a flourishing of French trading posts *(comptoirs)* in river villages, staffed by Saint-Louisien traitants or *sous-traitants*. The creation of such trading posts is thus documented for the villages of Kungani (Gwey);

Jagili (Gidimaxa, opposite Kungani on the other side of the river), where the buying of grain by the French is documented as early as 1837; Jogunturo; and Sollu (Gidimaxa). The purpose of the comptoirs was to buy grain in exchange for salt and small manufactured objects on behalf of a Saint-Louis *négociant* since the gum trade was forbidden outside of Bakel and Maxanna even after 1848. These village trading posts were to multiply in the years to come.[41]

Further upstream still, Beydan (such as those under the domination of the Awlad Mbarek) who had been until then prevented from trading with the French commercial network by the monopolistic practices of the Compagnie de Galam, began to bring their gum after 1848, especially after the foundation of the fort at Médine in 1855.[42] A further expansion of trade followed in this region. In 1854, the traitants of Bakel complained in a letter to the governor that a local war above Médine stopped all communications with the marigot of Logo, which was the destination point of caravans from Kaarta and Bambuxu and where the peanut crop was "particularly abundant."[43] The mention of a peanut trade in Logo at the very extreme point of navigation on the Upper Senegal River (most of Logo is, in fact, above the Félou cataracts, generally considered as the extreme point of navigation on the Senegal River!) underscores that by the middle of the nineteenth century, few regions were unaffected by the growing French trade in the Upper Senegal.[44]

General Prosperity of the Upper Senegal Region before 1855

The French, in the midst of this commercial expansion, had by no means renounced their ideal of agricultural colonization in the Upper Senegal region and continued to wish for enterprising colonists. In 1851, noting with satisfaction the changes brought by freedom of trade, the commandant of Bakel observed that "Saint-Louis is poor, it has a great surplus of inactive laborers. Its inhabitants have little inclination to go seek their fortune [outside of the river valley] but they like Galam [the Upper Senegal region] a lot and would like to settle there" and that he thought that they should be encouraged in doing so. There were at the time perhaps as many as 500 Saint-Louisiens residing in Bakel. The wealthiest among them, the Black traitant Macodé Sal, owned a house valued at 12,000 francs. In 1851, a shipment made in his name to the lower Senegal and Saint-Louis amounted to a staggering 200,000 francs. In an obviously buoyant mood, the French commandant noted that

Bakel would one day become "a city [and] a great center for populations who are far more intelligent than those living around Saint-Louis." Yet, remarking on the presence of Bambara laborers in Senudebu (Sénoudébou), a short-lived French trading outpost in Bundu, another commandant noted in 1853:

> As regards immigrants, we need farmers, [they are] the most difficult to obtain among the people of Senegal [i.e., the people of Saint-Louis]. These [Saint-Louisiens] abound in Bakel but they are nothing but parasites who hate farming and come to Bakel only because life is easier and there is the least amount of work.[45]

Despite the irate comment, however, the French colonial administration could not help but note that agricultural development was taking place in the Upper Senegal, even if it was not in the way that it had devised. Administrative dreams of planned agricultural development were now revived as a result of this spontaneous expansion. In 1855, Fréderic Carrère and Paul Holle (later of colonial fame for his defense of the French fort at Médine against Al-Haj Umar Tal in 1857) outlined in *De la Sénégambie française* a grandiose dream of commercial development based on peanut production in the Upper Senegal. Carrère and Holle envisioned a fleet of barges towed by powerful tugboats making as many as six trips a year between Podor, in the lower valley, and Bakel and Médine. Peanuts brought to Podor would then be transhipped by thousands of laborers onto boats headed for Saint-Louis and Europe. Carrère and Holle believed that through such an improvement of river transportation, the volume of trade in the Upper Senegal, then equal to 4 or 5 million francs, could be trebled. A similar proposal had been made in 1851 in the petition by the French merchant Marc Maurel, which inspired Governor Faidherbe after 1854.[46]

The time for commercial peanut production in the Upper Senegal was yet to come (although a considerable 1,007 tons of peanuts were apparently exported from the region in 1853).[47] Economic expansion in the region, however, was beginning to create problems for its inhabitants and for the French. A long and fruitless civil war broke out in 1833 between rival segments of the royal clan of Gajaaga, the Bacili, over the "customs," or tribute, paid by the French to local rulers.[48] Gajaaga eventually had to be partitioned under French guidance into two separate states, Gwey, near Bakel, centered on the royal village of Tiyaabu, and Kammera, above the Falemme River confluence.

An ominous element of this conflict was the tendency of opposing parties to appeal to powerful neighbors. The Upper Senegal region increasingly came to be at the center of a formidable conflict between the "pagan" Bambara of Kaarta and the Islamic militant Fuutanke, which exploded in 1855 with the religious wars of Al-Haj Umar Tal.[49]

The French tried to make the best of the situation. In the 1850s, the Beydan so pressured the richer province of Gidimaxa on the Senegal's north bank that villagers asked the Almamy of Bundu (south of Gajaaga) for permission to emigrate to his lands. The French, who believed that the agricultural success of Gidimaxa was due to the more hard-working character of its inhabitants, tried to divert the would-be emigrants toward Gwey near Bakel in order to foster agricultural development there, too.[50]

In spite of the turmoil, the prosperity of the Upper Senegal trade in the early 1850s was impressive. In 1853, a letter from the Senegalese traitants to Hilaire Maurel, the most prominent French merchant in Saint-Louis, noted that since the introduction of free trade, annual gum exports from the Upper Senegal region had trebled.[51] A year earlier, Governor Protet had written to the Ministry of Marine and Colonies:

> . . . for two years, the gum trade in Galam [the Upper Senegal] has equaled that of the lower river *escales*, and the value of the trade in gold, peanuts, and other products must be at least as important as that of gum. It cannot be said, therefore, that free trade in Galam did not have a positive result and that the upper Senegal does not appear as a most promising place in this colony.[52]

It is true that disturbances in the Lower Senegal region in the early 1850s redirected part of the gum trade from this area to the Upper Senegal region and generally made trade in the Upper Senegal appear more important in relative terms than it would have been in normal years.[53] Nevertheless, the quote by Protet shows that nongum exports from the Upper Senegal were becoming very important.

The year 1854 saw the first direct trip by an oceangoing steamship from Bordeaux to Bakel. Leaving Saint-Louis on 19 September 1854, Captain Jean-Baptiste Pontac, commanding *L'Aquitaine*—drawing 0.42 meters, with a carrying capacity of 600 nautical tons—arrived in Bakel on 30 September and was back in Saint-Louis on 17 October.[54] Such trips became commonplace in the following years, until the beginning of the twentieth century.[55]

It is clear from this account that the French were not trying to foster emigration in the Upper Senegal. Indeed, it was an influx of people in the region which they sought. They tried to encourage Frenchmen, Saint-Louisien Africans, Bambara, and finally Soninke from Gidimaxa to settle near their fort in Bakel. All along, the aim of the French administration was to further agricultural development in the region. Although administrative efforts were rather misguided, French trade in gum all along the Senegal River Valley stimulated cereal production in Gajaaga, Gidimaxa, Xaaso, probably Jafunu, and even beyond. In addition, there was a beginning of a promising peanut-export production. On the eve of the wars with Al-Haj Umar Tal, the French were preparing to create with the help of modern transportation an even greater agricultural development in the Upper Senegal region.

Migration at a Time of Prosperity

The Navetanes

The word "*navétane*" is derived from the Wolof language. It is a recent creation, appearing around the 1920s, nearly seventy years after the first report of migrant laborers in the Gambia. *Nawet* is the rainy season, which is also the cultivation season in Senegal. The word can also be used as a verb, meaning "to spend the rainy season." The *nawetaan* is thus the rainy season laborer (his counterpart is the *nooraan*, "he who spends the dry season"). Until the 1960s and 1970s, the navetanes came as seasonal laborers during the rainy season to work on the peanut fields of central and coastal Senegambia. This migration, known by its French derivative, "*navétanat*," was one of the most important seasonal migrations in the modern history of West Africa.[56]

Although the practice of navetanat later spread to the whole of Senegal's central plain, it began in the Gambia River Valley, a traditional destination of Soninke precolonial migrations. The Gambia, which is only two weeks away on foot from the Upper Senegal region, was part of the traditional trade network of Soninke from the Upper Senegal region (Gajaaga and Gidimaxa especially). Traditional migrants to the Gambia were attracted by the prospect of trading in sea salt, which is found in both natural and man-made deposits along the Gambia River Valley. The Soninke carried large amounts of this salt to the region of Bambuxu, where they exchanged it for locally produced gold.[57] Trade networks based on the salt trade, and probably on some slave trade as well, were thus in place when British traders first came to the Gambia in the seventeenth century. Through their commercial networks in the Gambia, Soninke traders supplied the British in slaves throughout the seventeenth and eighteenth centuries.

Philip Curtin has described how slave merchants in eighteenth-century Gambia, in order to offset the "storage cost" of slaves, that is, the cost of feeding slaves while they awaited shipment, rented plots of land locally where slaves were put to work. The land rented by the jula was planted in grain, which served to feed the slaves awaiting shipment, but also to provision the ships of the slave trade and probably to feed the European settlements on the Senegambian coast as well.[58] But slaves were not the only laborers involved in the commercial grain production in the Gambia. According to Curtin, by the 1780s and probably earlier, young men came from inland regions such as Bundu to grow grain near the salt pans. Their aim was to earn enough to buy trade goods (presumably salt and European manufactured goods), which they sold inland at several times their initial cost.[59] Although Curtin makes no mention of other regions than Bundu, it seems obvious that the young migrants must have come also from neighboring Gajaaga and Gidimaxa. For these migrants, spending an agricultural season in the Gambia was an easy way to obtain the trading capital necessary for trading in Bambuxu and elsewhere.

Along with a demand for grain, the slave trade also created a commercial network for buying grain along the Gambia River. This network was still in place in the nineteenth century. In 1831, for example, the trading post of Albréda, a French enclave in the Gambia (where a semiclandestine Atlantic slave trade continued well into the 1840s) was reported as exporting most of the rice consumed in Bathurst, Gorée, and even Saint-Louis. Similar commercial exports of cereals (rice and millet or sorghum) to the growing European coastal cities took place at other sites along the Gambia at this time.[60] This development facilitated the transition to an agricultural export economy that followed the adoption of the "legitimate trade" policy by the British and the French at the beginning of the nineteenth century.

After experimental shipments were made to London in the 1830s, peanuts became the main export in the Gambia, later spreading to Senegal.[61] Soninke migrants who had been involved at an early date in sales of grain to Europeans for the provision of the slave trade were among the first to convert to peanut production. In 1848, Governor MacDonnell of the Gambia wrote:

> The Sera Woolies [Sarakole, or Soninke] and Tilli-bunkas ["man of the east" in Mandinka, i.e., probably Malinke or Bambara][62] often visit the countries near the Gambia, frequently coming not less than 500 or 600 miles from the interior. . . . The greater portion of the groundnuts exported is raised in this manner by parties who have no permanent connection with the soil they cultivate.[63]

These were the first navetanes. By 1849, navetanes grew more than half of the peanuts sold in the Gambia.[64] As the reference to "Tilli-bunkas" indicates, the Soninke were not the only ethnic group represented in the migration, but they may have been the majority among early navetanes. In 1860, Governor D'Arcy referred to the Soninke as the main peanut cultivators in the Gambia.[65] References to Soninke migrants, at any rate, are numerous for this period and this area. A few refer specifically to Soninke from Gwey (lower Gajaaga) and the Bakel area.[66]

The earliest detailed description of the navetane labor system was provided by E. Bertrand-Bocandé in a report published in 1856 about the Séd-hiou region of Casamance, which is geographically and culturally close to the Gambia:

> These bands of agricultural migrants come and settle during the rainy season around the European trading posts; there, they grow peanuts on unoccupied lands. When they have sold their crop, they bring back their profit to their homeland and they come back the next year. During their stay, these laborers spend little; they are housed by local people whom they pay back in helping them till their fields; in this fashion, work and production expand.[67]

This account may be compared to the following description of mid twentieth century navetanat by Philippe David:[68] Senegambian farmers, called *jatigi*, fed the navetanes during the duration of their stay in the peanut-producing areas. In addition, they provided them with individual plots, on which the navetanes grew peanuts, which they sold for profit. In exchange for the board and lodging and the plots, the navetanes worked four or five days on their jatigi's farm. In some cases, the navetanes gave a portion of their crop to the jatigi, and worked fewer days on the jatigi's farm. It is easy to see that such an arrangement is virtually the same as the one described by

Bocandé. The similarity between it and the organization of slave and family labor in the Senegambia and Western Sudan (see Chapter One) is also obvious and has been pointed out by Ken Swindell, who was the first to call attention to the early history of navetanat.[69]

Why, given the wide availability of slaves in the Western Sudan at the time, did Gambian agricultural development take place with the help of free labor migrants?[70]

A first answer to this question is that navetane arrangements were advantageous from the point of view of employer and laborer alike. Navetanes could reap the full profit of cash-crop agriculture by obtaining the use of a plot on which to grow their own crops instead of being paid a flat daily sum as wage laborers. As for employers, the system allowed them to obtain laborers without having to disburse anything, as they would have if they had bought slaves or hired wage laborers. Employers simply had to provide land, and all sources concur that there was generally an overabundance of land in nineteenth-century Gambia.

Another possible answer is that slaves were needed as year-round laborers, while navetanes were needed as seasonal laborers. As is well known, most agricultural work in the Senegambia is concentrated during the very short rainy season. Some tasks connected with farmwork, however, are done year round, such as woodcutting, drawing water, and feeding animals. In addition, adobe and mud houses must be repaired in the dry season. All these tasks are quite labor intensive. In the Senegambian peanut basin today, they are done by family members and year-round migrants known as *surga*.[71] It can be presumed that in precolonial times, the work of the surga was done by slaves. It is thus possible that Gambian farmers at the same time bought slaves to use in year-round tasks and hired navetanes for the seasonal occupation of peanut growing. However, Gambian farmers could use also slaves who were not needed for dry-season tasks as weavers. Hence, it may still have been advantageous for farmers who had sufficient financial resources to buy slaves rather than hire navetanes.

One way to solve the apparent puzzle is to turn our attention toward Soninke traders rather than Gambian farmers. All sources concur that it was the Soninke rather than Gambian farmers who first grew peanuts for export. The end of the Atlantic slave trade must have posed a problem for Soninke slave traders in the Gambia. While their Gambian brokers (the jatigi) could reconvert to slave-based peanut production, choosing such an option was not really open to slave traders. Because of the day-to-day problems inherent in managing a slave farm, a jula would have had to abandon itinerant trade and settle permanently in the Gambia. Some traders may have done so, but the majority probably adopted another solution. This solution is described as follows by E. Bertrand-Bocandé, again referring to the region of Sédhiou in 1858:

> Peanuts are grown not only by the inhabitants of this country; caravans of laborers come from the tribes of the interior of Africa, who are more commercially minded and more hardworking than the tribes who live on the coast. . . . Formerly, when these oleaginous seeds were not in such demand, caravans from the interior brought only products having a certain value: beeswax, and ivory, which were loaded onto slaves, whom they sold upon departing. [But] the peanut trade has had this influence in the interior of Africa, that chiefs or merchants form a kind of association with *either free workers or with their slaves* [my emphasis]; they evidently do not consider their slaves as one form of merchandise that transports another.[72]

The text by Bocandé thus suggests that Soninke jula reconverted into peanut production by hiring free clients or slaves on a seasonal basis—something that allowed them to replace incomes made in the Atlantic slave trade without having to abandon the practice of itinerant trading. The "slaves" hired by these Soninke jula can only have been members of the favored category of "serfs" owing a rent in kind (see Chapter One). This would appear validated by the 1894 "Inquiry on Slavery" in the cercle of Bakel, in which Administrator Desmarets remarked that trusted *second-generation* slaves were allowed by their masters to go to work "in Saint-Louis, *the Gambia,* Kayes, etc." [My emphasis.] When they returned, they shared their earnings with their master and often used their share to purchase their freedom.[73] Abdoulaye Bathily has collected similar oral material on Soninke slaves being allowed to migrate to cultivate peanuts or to work on the docks of Saint-Louis, in exchange for a share in the profits.[74] As to the *free* migrants hired by the jula, many were probably miskino (poor) farmers who were the clients of the jula, and perhaps also present or former talibe (religious students) of Soninke clerics.[75]

Bocandé mentioned that migrants went not only to Casamance and the Gambia, but also to the Rio Grande region of Guinea.[76] The nineteenth-century French traveler Eugène Mage likewise met a Soninke migrant who had gone to grow peanuts on the coast of Sierra Leone.[77] These data once again reinforce the suspicion that there was a connection between the slave trade and navetanat, since the Upper Guinea coast was an important region of clandestine slave exports as well as peanut production in the nineteenth century.[78]

It may appear puzzling that free laborers were ready to do what had been traditionally "slave work" in the Gambia. But, in fact, the rewards were substantial enough to make the migration profitable. The price of 100 kilograms of peanuts in Rufisque in Senegal was 20 francs in 1846 and 26 francs in 1857.[79] In the Soninke region of Jafunu today, according to Pollet and Winter, the average area cultivated per agricultural worker is slightly more than one hectare, and the average yield per hectare is 600 to 700 kilograms for grain, 500 kilograms for peanuts.[80] These figures are low (David's book suggests an average production of one metric ton on navetanes' plots), but they can be used as a basis for comparison. The average size of a navetane's individual plot was about one hectare. Adopting Pollet and Winter's figures, each navetane produced on his personal plot a harvest valued at 100 to 130 francs a year. Since a navetane was fed and lodged by his Gambian landlords, his only expenses were a customary right of 10 percent in kind paid to his Gambian landlord and a tax of 12 shillings, or about 15 francs, paid to the Gambian village chief.[81] The profit of a stay in the Gambia in the late 1840s would, therefore, have been about 75 to 102 francs. Meanwhile a farmer who stayed at home in Gajaaga would have saved about one-third of his cereal production for trading—about 200 to 233 kilograms. With an estimated price for grain of 0.10 franc a kilogram,[82] the grain farmer around Bakel, once he deducted his family's consumption and various local expenses, could sell between 20 and 23.3 francs worth of grain a year per one hectare of land. The returns of a navetane were thus *five* times higher than those of a farmer in the Upper Senegal region.

Of course, my calculation does not take into consideration the production of family dependents and slaves (there is no practical way to estimate the composition of an "average" Soninke family in the nineteenth century). But it is clear that there was an economic advantage for families, in particular the poorer ones with no slaves, to send away at least one of their younger male dependents for a season in the Gambia. Furthermore, trips to the Gambia allowed migrants to resell cattle obtained from the Beydan,[83] and especially cotton cloth woven by Soninke slaves. On the return trip, European manufactured goods (which were much cheaper in the Gambia, owing to the lack of trade import barriers and the greater industrial advance of the British) could be brought back.[84] For family heads in the Upper Senegal, therefore, the temporary departure of one or more of their dependents was amply compensated by the returns of the migration—which according to Soninke custom must be remitted in full to the family head.[85]

The Laptots: Royal Migrants

Another indication that Soninke labor migration in the early nineteenth century was not due to a rather implausible impoverishment of the Soninke homeland is to be found in another contemporary Soninke migration—that of the *laptots*, or indigenous sailors.

As early as 1791, the French traveler Saugnier noted that the father of the chief of Maxanna—who was in effect the tunka (king) of Kammera (Maxanna was then the dominant royal village in Kammera in the Upper Senegal region)—had been a laptot "in Senegal," that is, in Saint-Louis, in his youth. Saugnier added that the chief of Maxanna "gives his best welcome to the laptots of Senegal, and each time [the French go up to Gajaaga] he persuades one [laptot] to stay [in Maxanna] by his gifts, especially those of the Saracolet [Soninke] nation. . . ."[86]

This quotation is the first of many referring to tunka lemmu (royals) having worked as laptots. Given what we know of the Soninke concept of honor (see Chapter One), it appears curious that royals not only worked as laptots, but accepted the son of a laptot as their chief. With regard to this question, the French traveler Paul Soleillet (who traveled in the Upper Senegal region around 1868) made a fascinating remark, unfortunately unique in our records for this period. Noting that there were numerous Bacili (members of the royal family of Gajaaga in Upper Senegal) employed by French commerce, Soleillet added that

> . . . in the Senegambia, the trades of mason, carpenter and joiner, commercial employee, *capitaine de rivière* (river pilot), laptot, are reputed for noble. Free men, even princes, do not see themselves as dishonored by the use of the trowel, or by the handling of the meter-rule, any more than the Breton gentleman by the driving of his plow. The occupations which are considered as vile in the Senegambia, are those of stokers on board of ships, of metal workers, and infantry soldiers. House servants and cooks are regarded as members of the family they serve.[87]

Many of these references are easily understandable in the idiom of traditional Senegambian culture. Metalwork must have been regarded as "vile" because it was a smith's work, hence work stemming from a caste. Likewise, infantry soldiers must have been regarded as slaves because this is what they often were in West African armies. The characterization of the laptot occupation as "noble," however, is at first sight problematic because many laptots were slaves until the mid nineteenth century.[88]

That many laptots were slaves, however, does not mean that the occupation was a "slave occupation." The first laptots in the seventeenth century were, in fact, free men (they were Wolof fishermen from the Saint-Louis area). Even in the late eighteenth century, when the employment of slave laptots was at its peak, free laptots still dominated. This was because sailing upriver was a seasonal occupation: given the high cost of food in Saint-Louis (Saint-Louis imported all its cereal from the river valley), it made little economic sense to own only slave laptots, who worked only during the five months of the annual trade expedition upriver.[89] In the late eighteenth century, out of about eight hundred laptots going to "Galam" (Gajaaga), four to five hundred were free laptots employed on a seasonal basis.[90] It is probable that the first Soninke laptots in the eighteenth century were hired in the Upper Senegal region, in temporary replacement of Wolof laptots who had died or fallen sick during the upriver travel. This led to their regular employment as seasonal workers later.

It is also worth noting that, for reasons that need not be discussed here, Saint-Louisien slave laptots had a privileged condition: most were owned by *métis habitants* of Saint-Louis who hired them out to French merchants and officials in exchange for half of their wages, but the other half was paid to the slaves themselves. The laptot occupation, therefore, was not a "slave occupation" that was also carried out by some free men, but rather a wage-labor occupation that was also carried out by slave workers whose treatment and pay were identical to those of free men.

The laptot occupation was considered "noble" in the eighteenth and nineteenth centuries because it was a prestigious military occupation. Until the middle of the nineteenth century, laptots were the primary French fighting force in Senegal. They defended convoys of river transports, which came under almost constant attacks (especially in Fuuta Tooro), and they participated in military expeditions along the river. Most laptots actually fought not for French authorities, but for Saint-Louis traders who maintained private armies of laptots. James Searing and Malcolm Thompson have both compared laptots to the Wolof *ceddo,* who were originally slave soldiers, but who over time became a military aristocracy.[91] A good illustration of this comparison is given by James Searing in his discussion of the career of a freed slave named Charles Scipio. After gaining his freedom, Scipio became a ship captain. He was the de facto leader of the river convoy in which Saugnier traveled to Gajaaga. Scipio's skills as a sailor and a warrior saved the convoy from destruction as it was attacked in Fuuta Tooro. Later, during negotiations with the tunka of Tiyaabu (Gwey), Scipio described himself as "the monarch of the river" and pretended to treat the Soninke king as an equal.[92] I doubt that Soninke laptots took Scipio's pretensions seriously; most probably looked down on Wolof slave laptots. Such contempt, however, obviously did not extend to the laptot occupation itself, which held all the attractions of the traditional military lifestyle of Soninke aristocrats.[93] Soninke aristocrats, at any rate, were used to hiring themselves out as mercenaries. Many Soninke thus fought as mercenaries in the Gambia around 1850, in the conflicts that preceded the civil wars of the 1860s.[94] This practice was apparently quite old: according to oral tradition, when the Bacili conquered Gajaaga in medieval times, they were themselves "knights errant" looking for booty and fortune in the Western Sudan.[95] Soninke kings valued the laptots' military skill, which explains in part why the chief of Maxanna referred to in Saugnier's text was so anxious to obtain the services of former laptots. For the same reason, the rival Bacili factions that fought each other during the civil wars that tore Gajaaga apart after 1833 competed for the loyalty of former laptots.[96]

For the laptots, one of the main attractions of the occupation was the lure of booty (including slaves, whom the French allowed their African troops to capture until the end of the nineteenth century), but laptot wages were also very attractive. In the middle of the eighteenth century, laptots were paid three "bars" (a currency of account in use in the Senegambia) or nine livres a month—thus fifteen bars or forty-five livres for a five-month trading campaign. In addition, the laptots who went to Galam, received a "gift" of one mudd of salt (of about three to five livres in value, which could be sold for much more in the Upper Senegal). To give an idea of the real value of such wages, it was possible in the early eighteenth century to purchase 1,600 pounds of grain with one bar.[97] According to Philip Curtin, a laptot's pay for the five-month voyage in the late eighteenth century "came to more than

half the cost of a slave bought in Gajaaga."[98] Curtin noted that this remuneration was close to that of an ordinary European seaman in the British
slave trade.[99] For the Soninke of Gajaaga, such wages were a very large
amount of money if we compare them with the farm incomes given above in
my discussion of the Soninke economy. Curtin also estimates the wages of a
laptot, specifically for Gajaaga in 1826 and 1829, which are shown in the table
below:

Table 2.1 [100]

Laptot Wages in Gajaaga, 1826–1829

Year	Annual Wages	Monthly Average
1826	121.76 francs	10 francs
1829	479.59 francs	40 francs

Such high incomes enabled laptots after their return home to make gifts to
powerful individuals in order to build clienteles and, thus, to compete for political power. I shall return to this topic in following chapters. Moreover, the
occupation of laptot in the eighteenth and early nineteenth centuries was
probably the first step in becoming a traitant, that is, an agent of the Saint-
Louis commercial houses.[101] The father of the chief mentioned by Saugnier
thus rose from laptot to broker *(courtier)* for the French chartered company
holding the monopoly of the Upper Senegal trade. He then became collector of the "customs," or taxes, paid by the French to the tunka of Tiyaabu,
who then ruled Gajaaga. He sent his son to be educated in Saint-Louis, who,
in turn, became so powerful that he eventually became independent from the
tunka of Tiyaabu.[102] In this case, becoming a laptot had enabled a young
tunka lemme (member of a royal family) to rise to a strategic position of
broker between French commerce and the Soninke political system, which
eventually led him to power. This politically sensitive character of trading
relations encouraged the tunka lemmu to monopolize such occupations for
their class. As late as 1851, the Upper Senegal traitants complained in these
terms of the pretensions of the Bacili (royal family of Gajaaga) of Maxanna
(Kammera, upstream from Bakel):

> [The Bacili] are very interested in the *escale* [trading post], one could say
> that they control it; they are brokers, *maîtres de langue* [interpreters], couri-
> ers. They would not suffer that other princes in the land be involved in [Eu-
> ropean] trade, nor that a *traitant* choose a *maître de langue* who would not be
> a member of the family.[103]

In the first half of the nineteenth century, the French traveler Soleillet collected information on the careers of two Bacili agents of French commerce. Samba Njaay Bacili (Samba N'Diaye Bathily) was a hostage of the French in Saint-Louis from age eight or ten to age twenty. He returned to Tiyaabu, his hometown (the royal capital of Gwey) under "Governor Grammont" (Bourdon-Grammont) in 1846, and established a *comptoir de traitant* (a full-fledged trading post). Tambo Bacili, born in Laani, another Bacili village, was a sous-traitant in Gajaaga on behalf of the agent of a Saint-Louis commercial house in Bakel. Both Tambo and Samba Njaay Bacili joined Al-Haj Umar Tal in 1857 and became leading counselors of his son Amadu Sheku, playing an important role in Franco-Umarian diplomatic relations.[104] These examples are somewhat puzzling in regard to the traditional dislike of Senegambian aristocracies for commerce. French commerce, however, with its "customs" payments, was too sensitive a political issue to be left in the hands of nonroyals.

Conclusion

The beginnings of the modern migrations of the Soninke were linked to European commercial penetration in Africa in the nineteenth century. It was the expansion of export trade in the era of "legitimate trade" that created for the Soninke in the Upper Senegal region opportunities for both commercial agriculture at home and labor migration abroad. But the Soninke were made aware of the latter through their traditional trade migrant networks, which had been in contact with Europeans in the Senegal and Gambia River valleys since the eighteenth century.

This account runs counter to the widespread characterization of precolonial African economies as autarchic and indifferent to profit. Reflecting on Karl Polanyi's distinction between "primitive" and "archaic" and "modern" economies (see Introduction), Philip Curtin noted that traditional Senegambian societies in the eighteenth century had all the potential features of a capitalist economy, and that the impetus of an African or European demand for African products was all that was needed for currency to circulate, land to be rented, capital to be accumulated, and, finally, labor to be hired.[105] Curtin's remark appears especially relevant to the case of the Soninke, who were involved so early in commerce and commercial agriculture. That there was no fundamental opposition between "archaic" and "modern" economies is, in fact, illustrated by the migration of Soninke aristocrats as laptots: it is true that the Soninke political system functioned on a "noncapitalist" redistributive basis, but the customary obligation of making gifts did not lessen aristocratic interest in making a profit. On the contrary, it increased it; in order to build a clientele, contenders for political power needed cash, preferably generated from outside—this gave them greater independence. Again, I shall discuss this topic at greater length in following chapters.

This being the case, it should no longer appear surprising that the Soninke moved so easily from traditional forms of migration into modern labor migration. There was, indeed, no fundamental difference in the search for profit in traditional migrations and in modern migrations—except for the fact that earnings were higher in labor migration. Such a smooth transition from "traditional" to "modern" migrations was rather common in world history. European economies during the Industrial Revolution were largely dependent on flows of temporary migrants who themselves were the heirs of centuries-old traditional migration currents. As mentioned, traditional migrants in Europe were often mountaineers who used the long winter periods of seasonal inactivity to sell products of their environment. Transhumance, the selling of cheese and wooden carved objects in the French plains, was the first historical form of migration by such well-known migrant peoples as the Auvergnat of the Savoyard.[106] Eventually, they became the first labor migrants in France. The Auvergnats became hay harvesters, grape pickers, sawyers, hemp combers, navvys, and river sailing hands in the French plains of Aquitaine or the Rhône valley and later made their way to employment in French cities.[107]

The main historical difference between European and African migration was, of course, that in the Senegambia, labor migration was the historical successor of the slave trade. Indeed, the slave trade in Africa could be considered an early form of labor migration; Stefano Fenaltoa has argued recently that the slave trade and contemporary labor migration were caused by the same economic forces.[108] According to his demonstration, whenever the cost of transportation makes it too expensive to export products from a given area, the people who would otherwise cultivate these exports may either be themselves exported or migrate to places where such products can be exported at a reasonable cost. Bertrand-Bocandé spontaneously made the same judgment with reference to the migration of navetanes in the mid nineteenth century when he wrote:

The peanut load of a man coming from a distant country would not be worth the strain of the journey . . . ; hence the caravan head brings the production site closer to the selling site, and instead of selling his [the merchant's] slaves, when he returns to his homeland, . . . seeks to increase their number and to bring new caravans back himself.[109]

It is true that the Upper Senegal region did export agricultural products, to both the Beydan and the French, but the returns of such exports were lower than those of cash-crop agriculture in the Gambia.

When the slave trade disappeared, free labor migrants began to take the place of slaves. This will appear puzzling only if we assume that "slave jobs" were undesirable and unproductive, but cash-crop cultivation in the Gambia actually brought very substantial returns. This was not the only instance of "slave jobs" attracting free laborers; the plantations of Brazil, for example, attracted scores of European migrants after slavery was abolished at the end of the nineteenth century.[110]

The transition from slave trade to labor migration was made easier by the fact that among the Soninke, the slave trade, the professional trade of the jula, and seasonal migration of farmers as petty traders were linked and followed the same age-old routes. When the slave trade ended, young Soninke, and young men from other ethnic groups that had provided seasonal trade migrants (such as the Mande), were ready to enter the emerging free labor market. At the same time, professional traders, who were involved in the slave trade and in slave-based commercial agriculture, were ready to channel them into the new forms of employment. These observations are probably valid for other regions of Africa than the Senegambia. The Asante-Akan region of Ghana and the Ivory Coast, for example, was in precolonial times one of the most important destinations of the slave trade in West Africa, as well as (especially in the nineteenth century) an important "consumer" of slaves for kola nut production and trade. Later, this region became the leading world exporter of cocoa. This success was achieved with the help of seasonal agricultural migrants from Sahelian regions such as the Mossi or the Zabrama (Songhai). These ethnic groups were involved in both slave-trading and seasonal trade migrations to the Asante-Akan region in the precolonial period. This suggests that there was more continuity than is usually assumed between the periods of slave and free labor in Africa.[111]

THREE

Taxation and the Soninke Economy

1855–1885

FOR THE GREAT MAJORITY of colonial and contemporary authors, colonial taxes were the "trigger" of labor migration. In addition, many contemporary scholars believe that colonial taxes were deliberately manipulated in order to force African villagers to migrate, and to seek in cities and coastal areas the cash resources that were not available in their homelands. Yet, in the case of Senegal, the archival record shows that colonial taxation was not created with a view to cause migration. Furthermore, its value in the Soninke homeland during the period considered in this chapter was initially very low and affected only a minute portion of the population. Finally, French control over the Upper Senegal region was scant and precarious until at least the late 1870s. Meanwhile, trade in the Upper Senegal region continued to expand after a difficult period in the mid 1850s, and the 1860s and the 1870s were years of exceptional prosperity. But labor migration continued to grow, and it probably became a major feature of Soninke society during these two decades.

Institution of the Personal Tax in Senegal

If we did not have sufficient evidence of the economic importance of the Upper Senegal region in the nineteenth century, we would find additional confirmation in the events surrounding the *jihad* of Al-Haj Umar Tal in the Upper Senegal. In February 1855, in answer to the French decision to place an embargo on arms sales to his forces, Umar sent his lieutenant Alfa Umar Balla to confiscate all merchandise in the French trading posts of Gajaaga and Xaaso, that is, the Upper Senegal River Valley. Although Bakel was well protected by its fort and was not attacked by Umar's troops, French merchants experienced losses due to raids on the smaller village trading posts, which they later estimated at between 100,000 and 150,000 francs, or the equivalent of 10 percent of the annual budget of the colony of Senegal.[1]

Following these events, Umar turned his attention toward the conquest of the Bambara empire of Kaarta. The French took advantage of this temporary respite to build their fort at Médine in Xaaso on the Upper Senegal. In 1857, Umar returned to the region and met a momentous defeat under the walls of the fort of Médine commanded by the famous métis Colonel Paul Holle. Umar's failure at Médine ended his attempt to establish an Islamic state in the Senegambia, but it did not put an end to hostilities with the French. In April 1858, Umar built his own fort at Gemu in Gidimaxa on a major caravan route of the gum trade to Bakel and brought to a halt the trade campaign of 1858 to 1859.[2]

The Gemu fort was destroyed by French troops in the fall of 1859. The temporary shutdown of Bakel's lifeline had been brutal, for the colony was experiencing its worst economic depression since the beginning of the nineteenth century. The prosperity of Senegal depended on gum arabic: in the 1830s the price of a kilogram of gum in Senegal had been two francs;[3] in 1858 to 1859, it plunged to an all-time low of 0.60 francs.[4] The Gemu blockade, moreover, revived worries that had troubled the French for some time about progress in the fabrication of dextrin, an industrial ersatz of gum arabic.[5] These considerations were on the minds of the officials and merchants' representatives who gathered at the meeting of the advisory Conseil d'Administration of Senegal on 11 October 1859, shortly after the destruction of the Gemu fort. The object was to debate a proposal by Governor Faidherbe to reform the tax system of the colony.[6]

In his opening address, Faidherbe reminded the council of the recent fall in the price of gum on French markets, then proceeded to enumerate the taxes that weighed on the gum trade. These were a 4 percent tax paid by merchants upon leaving the river lands where gum was obtained to pay "customs" (tribute) to Beydan and African chiefs, which could be neither reduced nor suppressed given the current military situation; a 2 percent tax in kind collected upon entry to the port of Saint-Louis, originally created to aid the traitants' guild but now collected by the Senegalese treasury since the guild no longer existed; and a 13.5 percent tax collected at the port of entry in France. Of the latter three, only the 2 percent tax in kind collected at Saint-Louis could be suppressed immediately, costing the colony an annual revenue of 30,000 to 40,000 francs. To replace this income, Faidherbe proposed to establish a new tax on property and a personal tax in Senegal. The governor asserted that the head tax was already paid in all the other French colonies. The head tax would first be established in the outskirts of Saint-Louis and the adjacent province of Waalo and, later, cautiously extended to the conquered peoples on the river.

The head tax, in Faidherbe's mind, had more than a financial purpose. It was also to be a "visible sign of the allegiance of [Senegalese] populations to France." The tax was to support the creation of a Direction de l'Intérieur, that is, of a real internal administration in Senegal. The French during the first half of the nineteenth century had maintained control only of Saint-Louis and Gorée, plus a number of forts in the interior such as Bakel. Outside these points, they had a fluctuating and ill-defined influence over the small Senegalese polities, depending on the state of commercial relations and French interests. Relations with client states were handled since 1844 by the Direction des Affaires Extérieures.[7] Faidherbe's proposed Direction de l'Intérieur was to oversee the formal French territories of Saint-Louis, Gorée, the Cap Vert peninsula, and Waalo. Bakel was to remain under the Affaires Indigènes, but the Direction de l'Intérieur would have a say on all matters concerning trade. (This arrangement shows that Faidherbe's designs for territorial expansion did not yet apply to the Upper Senegal region.)

In the discussion that followed among members of the Conseil d'Administration, the French wholesale merchant Albert Teisseire (settled in Saint-Louis) observed that the high taxes on gum had been acceptable as long as the price of that commodity had remained high, but that the new commercial situation might force producers to devote their energies to other products. Two government officials, the contrôleur colonial and the head of the judiciary, noted that although the revenues of the colony were insufficient, the treasury of Senegal was fed only by export duties while the majority of the Senegalese paid no taxes. Acquiescing to the arguments put forward by the governor and the various speakers, the Conseil d'Administration agreed to the introduction of personal taxation in the colony.

It is difficult to find in the above any evidence supporting the contention that personal taxation was introduced in order to force Africans to emigrate. *All the data presented here strongly suggest that the head tax in Senegal was introduced for reasons that had nothing to do with labor migration.* The use of taxation as a means to provide labor was, in fact, unknown to the French until the turn of the nineteenth century. For example, in the fifth edition of his *De la colonisation chez les peuples modernes*, written in 1891, the famous colonial propagandist Paul Leroy-Beaulieu devoted his chapter on "labor in the colonies" entirely to a discussion of foreign immigration (European and "coolie" immigration). It was only in the sixth edition, of 1908, that Leroy-Beaulieu added a section devoted to the "treatment and recruitment of black labor."[8]

The motives behind the creation of the personal tax in Senegal were economic, budgetary, and political. Faced with declining world prices for its main commodity, Senegal sought to lighten the burden weighing on the gum trade and to create sources of revenue other than export duties.[9] The switch to direct taxes, incidentally, was in keeping with contemporary liberal European opinion. It was the time when direct income tax was slowly introduced in England, while indirect taxes were considered socially unjust and economically unsound.[10] Finally, Governor Faidherbe, in keeping with the report of the interministerial commission of 1850, which had recommended a more assertive French presence in Senegal,[11] seized the opportunity to create an embryonic administration in Senegal, copied from other French colonial territories. The new direct administration was quite modest in size: apart from the director of the interior himself, it was composed of one delegate in Gorée, two senior clerks, and two junior clerks, at an annual cost of 20,000 francs. Modest also was the amount of the contribution requested from the taxpayers when personal taxation was established in 1861: 3 francs a year in Saint-Louis and 1.5 francs outside of the Senegalese capital, calculated on the basis of the value of three workdays of an ordinary laborer in Senegal.[12]

Institution of the Personal Tax in Bakel

The situation in Bakel in the aftermath of the wars with Al-Haj Umar Tal was not a bright one. In May 1859, N'Diaye Sow, the chief of the Bakel traitants, wrote to the Director of the Affaires Extérieures of Senegal: "Famine reigns in Galam, we have never had before anything like it. We are dying of hunger."[13] In Bakel in December 1859, at a time when the famine was apparently over for the local population, two thousand refugees still left the village every morning to gather wild fruit for their subsistence.[14] The war had affected the entire Upper Senegal region: David Robinson has shown how wartime destruction and the migration of 40,000 people from Fuuta Tooro, who followed Umar, resulted in one of the most tragic famines ever experienced in the history of Senegambia and the Western Sudan.[15] Not surprisingly, trade was slow to recover, even after the capture of Gemu.[16] These were inauspicious conditions for the introduction of direct taxation in the region. Yet the local administration was soon to face the prospect of collecting direct taxes in five left-bank Soninke villages between Bakel and the Falemme River.

The annexation to France of these villages in 1858 was a kind of historical footnote: its purpose was to secure a corridor between Bakel and the Falemme River leading toward the gold fields of Bambuxu, which were the cause of a gold mirage among French colonial officialdom at the time.[17] The small kingdom of Gwey was thus divided into a *Goye Annexé*, upstream from Bakel to the Falemme River, and a *Goye Indépendant*, downstream from Bakel to the Middle Valley region of Damga. The Goye Annexé (Kungani, Golmi, Yaafera, Arundu, and the village of Baalu on the banks of the Falemme River) was subject to the personal tax as a French territory. The French began to take measures for its collection only in 1862, after the famine had subsided.

Abdoulaye Bathily has argued that

> The institution of [personal] taxation, decided by Faidherbe and carried out by his successor Jauréguiberry met rapidly with violent opposition on the part of the populations. It created a movement of emigration towards the Niger and the Gambia [River valleys] and led several village chiefs to disobedience. In May 1862, the chiefs of Kungani (Kunghel) and Yafera were put under arrest following the refusal of the inhabitants [of Goye Annexé] to pay their taxes. Disturbances occurred in 1863, 1864, 1865 around the same problem.[18]

It is impossible, however, to follow Bathily in his conclusions here when referring to the original source, the correspondence of the Bakel administrator, Commandant de Pineau, with the governor of Senegal, Jauréguiberry.

The emigration to the Gambia is mentioned in a letter of May 1862, *that is, before tax was actually collected.*[19] The first record of tax collection for Goye Annexé is for December 1863.[20] Moreover, the French administration was rather lenient. To be sure, two chiefs were arrested, but arguing that the region had just begun to recover from the years of war and famine, Commandant de Pineau urged against collecting head tax in 1862.[21] Head tax, in fact, was not collected that year. It is not known how long the arrested headmen were kept in detention, but in August, they and the other village chiefs of Goye Annexé participated in a meeting in Bakel where the principle of taxation was agreed on. The French seem to have represented that as a French territory Goye Annexé would be entitled to protection from Beydan raids.[22] During the following months the French even briefly considered naming the chief of Yaafera, who had apparently led the resistance to personal taxation, the chief of Goye Annexé, on account of his influence and the support that he eventually gave to the taxation project.[23] Finally, the 1863 tax was not collected, apparently on account of the bad crops that year.[24] It is clear that there was no such brutal confrontation as implied by Bathily in the paragraph quoted. There was rather a process of pressure and negotiation with some amount of give and take on both sides.[25]

In fact, Bathily's mistaken appraisal of the role of the Bakel commandant in 1862 had its origin in a controversy that was only indirectly connected with the question of taxation. The period of the administration of Commandant de Pineau in Bakel coincides with the governorship of Jauréguiberry. Sandwiched between two gubernatorial terms of the illustrious Faidherbe, the period of Jauréguiberry's administration in Senegal has been neglected by scholars. From what we know, it was marked by an aggressive and somewhat unsuccessful policy of military expansion and, quite in contrast with Faidherbe's administration, by recurring squabbles with the Saint-Louis merchant community. We know also that Jauréguiberry received instructions from the Ministry of Colonies in Paris to encourage the production of cotton in Senegal.[26]

Commandant de Pineau followed instructions to encourage cotton (and also peanut) production in Bakel by paying frequent visits to the villages in the company of a military escort. Governor Jauréguiberry asked him to stop doing so in March 1862. Following this, Commandant de Pineau ran into open conflict with the French merchants.[27] Saint-Louis and Bordeaux merchants feared a repetition of the fiasco of the 1820s, when the administration had forcibly drafted them into investing and managing unprofitable plantations in Waalo.[28] Commandant de Pineau apparently confirmed such fears when he spoke of introducing a system of premiums to farmers and of fixed prices for cotton and peanuts[29] (such as had been in use in the Waalo scheme).

The effectiveness of Pineau's coercive methods was very limited: return cargoes from the Upper Senegal for 1862 and 1863 do not show *any* cotton export, while there was a marked increase in peanuts traded in Bakel from 292,593 kilograms to 853,153 kilograms in 1863. In other words, the Soninke of Gwey yielded to pressure for peanuts, something that was in their interest, since peanuts fetched their highest price in this period (reaching an all-time high of 25 francs for 100 kilograms during 1860 to 1867). But they stubbornly refused to produce any cotton.[30] It was probably in anticipation of such resistance that when the personal tax was introduced in 1862, it was made payable in cotton, which probably renewed fears in the merchant community that it too was going to be coerced into the administration's development scheme.[31] This explains why attacks on Commandant de Pineau focused on taxation. On 23 January 1863, the *Journal de Bordeaux*, an organ of French colonial merchants, attacked the institution of direct taxation in Senegal, writing that it was not worth the money it cost and that "[r]eigning with gunshots in order to colonize is a thing of the past."[32] The denunciation of colonial exactions, in particular in Algeria, was a popular theme in liberal circles, and in the Algerian case, protest against restrictions to economic freedom went hand-in-hand with opposition to military rule.[33]

The press campaign about personal tax soon affected Governor Jauréguiberry himself, who had to face the general opposition of the merchants of the colony, and was finally recalled in May 1863.[34] The same month Commandant de Pineau asked to be recalled "for health reasons." He departed from Bakel about the same time that Governor Faidherbe arrived in Senegal for a second term.[35] This seems to have been the end of forced cultivation in the Bakel area.

Direct taxation, however, was not immediately abandoned (even though payment in cotton was quickly dropped). Did it have an effect on migration? We should remember that the French tax applied only to five villages in Gwey plus Bakel itself. What stands out is the small number of people required to pay the tax and the small sum required from the "annexed" Soninke: the first census, made by village chiefs, produced 125 taxpayers for

Goye Annexé, which had a population of 1,200 to 1,500. These 125 taxpayers paid in December 1863 an absurdly low 12 pièces de guinée, that is, 192 francs.[36] The French colonial law on direct taxation in Senegal set the level of personal tax to the equivalent of three days of labor or 1.50 francs (outside of Saint-Louis).[37] All individuals from age eighteen to sixty were to pay it, except for married women, invalids, and indigent people.[38] We see that with 125 taxpayers among a population of 1,200 to 1,500 persons, there was quite a bit of flexibility in the practical definition of indigents: certainly no less than one-fourth of the population (300 to 375 persons) must have been composed of adult males, and of these, two-thirds were declared unable to pay tax by the chiefs! It was only in 1877 that a new census was conducted, and this time through agents of the commandant: 239 able persons were found, a less implausible number.[39]

If we consider that 1863 was an exceptional year in economic terms, let us consider the credulity of the new commandant. Indeed, he recalled that he had believed at first that the chiefs had wanted to cheat him, but that he had changed his mind after visiting some desperately poor villages in Bundu.[40] But there was no comparison between the situation in Bundu—inland, devastated, and almost completely depopulated by Al-Haj Umar Tal—and the situation in Gwey.[41] Actually, 1863 had been an exceptional year for agriculture. According to the *Feuille officielle* of Senegal, exports of cereals and peanuts alone from Bakel in September 1863 (at the height of the trading season) amounted to 350,000 francs.[42] Of course, not only Gwey traded in Bakel. Villages on the right bank did as well. Caravans of camels or donkeys brought produce to French posts.[43] A fair estimate of Bakel's commercial range, as far as agricultural products are concerned, must have been around 200 villages.[44] It is plain that the five villages of the Goye Annexé, with an estimated income of 1,750 francs *per village* from peanuts and cereals, could very well pay a total tax for *all* villages of 192 francs. And I have not taken into account the indirect income of the gum trade.

What probably motivated the new commandant's timidity was, of course, the memory of Pineau's downfall and the conciliatory attitude toward traders of the new Faidherbe administration. Successors of Faidherbe proved even more lenient. After 1865, under Governor Pinet-Laprade and then Governor Valière, the personal tax was simply allowed to fade away.

The period after 1865, following the disasters of the French expedition to

Mexico and the Franco-Prussian War, was one of colonial retreat. In Senegal, the French colony was reduced to Saint-Louis, Gorée, and the line of French posts along the river, and the coast south of Dakar.[45] The effects of retrenchment are visible in the Bakel periodic reports. In February 1866, the Bakel commandant asked if he should tax the villages since they had suffered from grasshoppers and a cattle disease that year. An exemption was granted the following month.[46] The Soninke were quick to seize the opportunity by turning it into a precedent for not paying the tax. They were encouraged in this by the attitude of the administration; in April of the same year, the Bakel commandant reported that he was following the governor's orders not to intervene in local affairs unless commercial freedom was violated—without, however, formally renouncing the existing treaties with local populations.[47] In fact, the policy of abstention, the practical renunciation of taxation, was equivalent to an abdication of French authority. In November 1866, the chief of the "annexed" village of Yaafera made the French commandant wait eight hours until he finally appeared precisely at the time fixed for the commandant's departure.[48] The chiefs of Goye Annexé made no mystery of their desire to live independently, under the authority of their tunka.[49]

It would be unnecessarily fastidious to recall year-by-year the events related to taxation in Goye Annexé. By 1867, the French recognized privately what was already in evidence: they no longer exercised any power over the Soninke outside Bakel. They continued to send letters to the village chiefs asking to discuss with them the issue of taxation, only to meet various kinds of humiliating rebukes.[50] In fact, the French were even unable to insure the safety of their traders. In 1868, the chief of the annexed village of Baalu drove away a French traitant who had brought him a letter from the commandant, telling the traitant that he would have him "shot like a dog" if he did this again and that he wanted "neither order nor request" from the whites.[51]

The waning of French authority in this region that experienced an unprecedented period of agricultural prosperity had important consequences.

Agricultural Prosperity of the 1860s and 1870s

I have already noted the Bakel peanut trade figures for 1863, which was the year when Bakel began to file monthly commercial and agricultural reports containing numerical information. These were sent regularly until the end of the nineteenth century.[52] Peanut production reached what was perhaps an all-time high in 1865 with 3,500 metric tons and generally maintained itself in the 1,000 to 2,000 metric tons range into the early 1870s.[53]

These figures were exceptionally high for the time. Granted, today 3,500 tons is minuscule compared to the contemporary peanut export of Senegal. But placed in the proper context, this was impressive. In 1867, for example, the 5,600 tons of peanuts exported from Rufisque, soon to become Senegal's main peanut-exporting harbor, were sufficient, according to Roger Pasquier, to provoke a "veritable euphoria."[54]

What had made this prosperity possible was the transportation revolution envisioned by Carrère and Holle in *De la Sénégambie française* in 1855. The local archives repeatedly refer to fleets of *chalands*, or barges, towed by tugs, coming to Bakel and the Upper Senegal.[55] In 1886, Commandant Frey described the traffic of riverboats bringing supplies to Kayes in preparation for the military conquest of the Sudanic interior:

> On the Senegal [River] then, for several months we see nothing but armed sloops [*avisos*] flanked by one or more barges [*chalands*], sometimes as large as the boats themselves; [and] powerful tugs, having to their sides, or towing behind them, fifteen, twenty barges, sometimes more. They are slowly, laboriously, moving upstream, followed by a minuscule forest of little masts. The journey from St. Louis to Kayes takes eight to ten days. The return, made easier by a violent current, is done in three times less. After a period of rest in St. Louis, during which most of the crew gets acquainted with the Navy hospital, the little fleet goes back on with a new cargo, and up again for the same journey as long as the waters remain high.[56]

A visible sign of the rising fortunes of the Upper Senegal was the multiplication of secondary trading posts in Soninke villages: Ganyi, Ambidedi, Somankidi (Gidimaxa), Baalu (Goye Annexé) are thus variously recorded,[57] while the Bakel commandant reported that "our trade has a host of settlements [trading posts] in Gidimaxa villages."[58] In 1873, the commandant was suspicious that some traitants created trading posts in order to conceal part of their trade and to avoid paying tax. Indeed, it appears that a significant proportion of the trade of the comptoirs went unreported.[59] Meanwhile, the trade of the marigotiers continued to flourish, and peanuts were brought to the river on pack animals from inland villages. Gajaaga and Gidimaxa villages sold predominantly peanuts, while Soninke villages in Damga traded mostly cereals, but Gajaaga and Gidimaxa also exported cereals.[60]

The year 1873 was an exceptional one for peanuts in Bakel. Unfortunately, no figures are available for this year, but according to the Bakel traitants, this had been the most exceptional harvest ever. It came after a series of good years: 1865, discussed above, and 1867 whose figures were granted the honor of print in the official *Moniteur du Sénégal*. In 1868, "every man, woman or child wanted to have their field planted in cotton, *mil* [sorghum or millet] or peanuts"; although results in this year proved disappointing, 1869 saw a "very abundant" crop.[61] In 1872, the stores of a single trading agent burned in the village of Ganyi in Gidimaxa: the damage was estimated at 10,930 francs[62]—that is, more than fifty times the entire tax of Goye Annexé in 1863 and half the budget of the Direction de l'Intérieur at its creation by Governor Faidherbe in 1859. In 1865, the commandant in Bakel estimated that French traders owned in Gidimaxa "products or merchandise for more than 600,000 francs."[63]

After 1873, with the overall fall in prices due to the opening of the Suez Canal and competition from British India,[64] peanut exports plummeted although some improvements came in the last years of the decade. The decline of peanut exports, though, were offset for the whole region by the expansion of the gum trade in the post of Médine, upstream from Bakel, as shown in the following figures:

Table 3.1[65]
Upper Senegal Exports, 1860s–1870s
(Figures in brackets are incomplete)

	1860s			
Product	Bakel Volume (in Metric Tons)	Bakel Value (in Francs)	Médine Volume (in Metric Tons)	Médine Value (in Francs)
Gum	558.95	558,953.8	[112.9–225.15]	[112,907–225,159]
Peanuts	1,587	296,774	[280.7]	[40,960]
Cereals	830	[65,320]	[?]	[?]
Total		[921,047.8]		[153,867–266,119]

Total 1860s for Médine and Bakel: [1,074,914.8–1,187,166.8]

Product	Bakel Volume (in Metric Tons)	Bakel Value (in Francs)	Médine Volume (in Metric Tons)	Médine Value (in Francs)
Gum	458.18	502,668.4	[306.303]	[306,303]
Peanuts	750	[75,890]	[222.900]	[20,565]
Cereals	[278.5]	[31,793]	[?]	[?]
Total		[610,361]		[326,868]

Total 1870s for Médine and Bakel: [941,354]

These incomplete figures seem to indicate a relative economic decline for Bakel as compared to Médine due to the fall in peanut prices in the 1870s. Yet there is no evidence that this decline had any impact on migration: mentions of origin for laptots, which are the only ones available for the 1870s, indicate that they came in equal numbers from the Bakel region up to the Falemme River (the kingdom of Gwey) and the region above the Falemme (the kingdom of Kammera), which was within Médine's commercial range.

The Soninke as Laptots and in Saint-Louis

As we have seen in the first chapter, the Soninke had been laptots since the eighteenth century. At the time, they were still a minority among them. But the number of Soninke laptots increased dramatically in the nineteenth century. In 1855, Carrère and Holle noted that although the occupation of laptot was highly regarded in the past, it was now considered by inhabitants of Saint-Louis as "vile" and that "the government's ships are obliged to recruit their personnel among foreigners or people newly settled [in Saint-Louis] (Bambaras, Saracolets [Soninke])."[66] Carrère and Holle noted that the main ambition of Saint-Louisiens was to become involved in commerce, in other words to become traitants. Indeed, according to some reports, already before the general emancipation in Saint-Louis (a result of the French Revolution of 1848), slaves refused to be anything but commercial employees.[67] By instituting free trade on the Senegal River, the Revolution of 1848 created new opportunities for the Wolof of Saint-Louis, including freedmen.[68] As trade on the Senegal River expanded, most became traders or commercial agents, leaving the less profitable occupations to the Soninke. This is the first instance in this study of what I believe to be a basic cause of labor migration: economic expansion enables its beneficiaries to graduate to better occupations, leaving a vacuum at the bottom of the social ladder, which is filled by migrants.[69]

It is difficult to obtain information on the laptots employed by the Saint-Louisien traders, who apparently left very few archives.[70] But we are remarkably well informed on the Senegal River service of the Senegalese *station locale* of the French Navy. By 1872, all Wolof laptots had left the French Navy river service. Captain Rebel, who wrote a report on the matter, blamed it on a reform that at some point had suppressed the class of indigenous quartermasters or *gourmets* in the station locale. The reform also specified that *capitaines de rivière*, or indigenous pilots, whose knowledge of the treacherous course of the Senegal River was indispensable in journeys to the Upper Senegal, would no longer be recruited among the gourmets but among a specially trained class of pilot cadets. In other words, advancement from the ranks had become impossible, and the Wolof, who according to Captain Rebel could find better paying jobs as laptots or laborers with the Saint-Louis trading houses, left the French Navy en masse. They were replaced by laptots from the Senegal River Valley, who were mostly Soninke from Gajaaga and Gidimaxa, and also some Fuutanke.[71]

At least by the 1870s, the Soninke dominated employment on commercial river transports as well: the first mention dates from 1877, but the information has secondhand value because it comes from a Navy report —the Soninke were probably the majority earlier.[72] Commercial transports paid better wages, which explains why the Wolof remained there longer than on the state vessels. The Wolof, in fact, never completely left commercial sailing but moved into skilled jobs and in time became a sort of aristocracy among Senegalese sailors.

Around the time the Soninke came to dominate the laptot occupation in Senegal, they also were seen more and more often seeking work as simple laborers in Saint-Louis, often shifting from one occupation to another as suited their convenience. A letter from a local French Navy official in 1877 asserted: "The laptot of today will introduce himself tomorrow to serve as an animal drover with the Army or a male nurse at the military hospital."[73] A similar report in 1880 mentioned that among the laptots, many had been "successively in occupations apparently as incompatible as gardener, horseman, Public Works laborer, etc."[74] Such versatility was not surprising since the first laptots in the Upper Senegal were jacks-of-all-trades who performed a variety of tasks. But the rapid job turnover of the Soninke also had other causes, as we shall see below.

Where did these migrants come from in the Soninke homeland? The available information for this period reinforces the view that Soninke labor migration was not the result of poverty and economic disruption. The villages of origin of laptots were all situated along the river in the Upper Senegal region.[75] While it stands to reason that laptots would be recruited from river villages, these were also the very villages that were enriched by European trade. This implies that laptot wages were high enough to compete with incomes from a prosperous local farming economy. This logical deduction is confirmed by numerical data: laptot wages were completely out of proportion with agricultural incomes in the Upper Senegal region.

Laptot Wages

One of my biggest surprises in conducting this research was to discover how high were the wages offered to Africans in the French colonial cities at the end of the nineteenth century, not only in comparison with African agricultural incomes but with French wages as well.

French expansion in Africa pushed wages very high in the 1880s. In 1881, for example, laptots in the local station of the French Navy (this included the Senegal River service) received 30 francs a month; those who worked for the river commercial fleet earned the much higher wages of 50 to 60 francs a month. The various French expeditions, it is said, created a kind of "economic revolution," and explorers paid up to 70 francs a month.[76] This competition created a problem for French naval officers, who began facing recruitment problems and even strikes.[77]

It is difficult to know exactly the rate of wages of unskilled workers in French outposts who were not employed as laptots. The standard wage of a common laborer in the communes of Senegal was probably not less than 1 franc a day (this was the estimate made at the time of the introduction of the personal tax in 1859), but here again considerable pay raises may have occurred in the late 1870s and in the 1880s. In 1880, with the construction of the telegraph line in the Upper Senegal and the construction of the military post of Bafoulabé, dockers in Saint-Louis made 3.50 to 4 francs a day, that is, 90 to 100 francs a month (provided one could find work every working day).[78]

Such wages compare with contemporary French wages, especially if we choose to look at wages outside of Paris and in the French countryside. In 1885, farmhands (who were fed and lodged) in the impoverished region of Brittany earned 60 to 100 francs *a year* and day laborers earned 1.25 francs a day without food. At the same time in High Normandy, a quite well-off region, day laborers earned 1.25 to 1.50 francs with food on the farm, thus about the same as the Senegalese Navy laptots. In provincial French towns, workers earned an average of 3.90 francs a day, comparable to the dockers' wages in Saint-Louis in 1880.[79] Compared with the agricultural incomes in the Upper Senegal region discussed in the last chapter, laptot and urban laborer incomes were enormous.[80]

Causes of High Turnover among the Soninke Laptots

A recurring complaint of French Navy officials about Soninke laptots was that they rarely respected their two-year clause of employment. In fact, many did not even honor their minimum mandatory one year of employment. The French Navy in Senegal was in the curious situation of having sailors who worked as day laborers. French officers complained bitterly about the situation, recalling favorably the earlier time when most laptots were Saint-Louisiens.[81]

The situation can be compared with that described by economist Walter Elkan in his book, *Migrants and Proletarians,* on urban labor in Uganda in the 1960s.[82] The Soninke, like the Nilotic migrants in Elkan's study, were "migrants": their "commitment" to their employment was low, their turnover rate was high, and consequently their level of skill and pay was at the bottom of the scale. The Wolof, like Elkan's Ganda, were "proletarians": they were committed to lifelong employment, they were concerned with promotion, and they were generally better skilled and better paid as a result. Elkan used the word "proletarian" to describe what is in the African context a "labor aristocracy" in order to draw attention to the fact that the Ganda (proletarians) owned only small plots of land insufficient to ensure fully their subsistence, while Nilotic migrants had access through their extended families or clans to plots of land that were their primary focus of interest. The Ganda were a stable workforce because they depended almost entirely on wage labor for their living, while the Nilotic migrants sought employment in order to make investments on their farms. This theory applies to a degree to the nineteenth-century Senegalese situation, but with a number of caveats and explanations.

The Wolof probably fit into Elkan's definition of the "proletarian," at least for the great number among them who were former slaves in an urban setting and who presumably did not own any land. As for Soninke laptots, they cannot be said to have completely lacked "commitment" to wage labor for, in fact, a number of arrangements allowed them to keep their jobs even when taking frequent and extended leaves of absence. Thus a French Navy report of 1877 stated that the seventy or so laptots of the Senegal River flotilla were recruited from a pool of 155 registered men "who come and go, embark or disembark as they please."[83] And in 1888, Colonel Frey, referring to a situation probably prior to 1885, observed that Soninke servants employed by the French generally kept their job for several years before selling their position to a successor, "whom they invariably introduce [to their employer] as their brother."[84] Elkan's remark as to migration enabling "migrants" to make investments at home, however, was perceptive: it was indeed the case with the Soninke, but the preferred form of Soninke migrant "investment" on their farms was slaves.

The Laptots as Slave Owners

Colonel Frey noted explicitly:

> As soon as [a Soninke] has built up a small savings, he buys goods that he sends back to his homeland. He entrusts a relative or a friend with acquiring in his absence, whenever a good opportunity arises, one or more slaves, depending on the sum he has available. In the month of July, 1886, the governor of Senegal, having at his table Colonel Frey, back from his military campaign [against the Soninke revolt of Mamadou Lamine], was very surprised to learn from him that the butler who was waiting on them was a full-blooded [Soninke], owner in Galam of seven slaves whom he had bought in this fashion.[85]

Frey was here corroborated by a French Navy report, undated but probably of around 1880:

> Among [the Soninke], almost all men go abroad for a shorter or longer period, they come to Saint-Louis in order to obtain *pièces de guinée* [bafts, the currency of the river valley] which on their return will allow them to settle after buying wives and slaves [*captifs*].[86]

Similar reports were collected by the French traveler Soleillet who visited the Upper Senegal region in 1879.[87] Such behavior was fully in line with the historical behavior of Soninke migrants: the Soninke migrated to the Niger River Valley in order to buy slaves, which helped them expand their commercial agriculture. But there was one important difference between traditional and modern (labor) migrations.

The authors of these nineteenth-century texts do not speak of migrants saving their earnings to hand them over to family heads, as Soninke custom in principle requires.[88] In fact, all witnesses spoke about migrants saving money in order to buy slaves for *themselves* (not the extended family unit). A young Soninke migrant from the village of Gumal (Hayre-Damga) thus confided to Soleillet in 1878 or 1879 that after earning enough for bridewealth during his first visit to Saint-Louis, he was planning to go back for a second visit in order to earn money for merchandise, which he hoped to exchange for three or four male slaves and one female slave.[89] The intent to create an independent household was here quite clear. Several years later, Colonel Frey observed: "Like the caravan trader, the Soninke employee, as soon as he feels he has become wealthy enough, returns home and settles on his own. He becomes another family head [*chef de case*].[90]

In the traditional social system, although Soninke family heads had ultimate control over their dependents' earnings, younger sons, women, and even children had sizeable personal possessions, which could include even slaves.[91] This opened the possibility for young men to set up separate households of their own provided they had access to independent sources of income. In traditional society such opportunities were limited: in trade migration in particular, migrants needed an initial capital of trade goods, which had to be provided by the family group. In labor migration, on the contrary, it was the migrants' labor alone that generated income.[92]

The Laptots: Royal Migrants

In precolonial Soninke society, however, migration represented more than a simple "declaration of independence" from the elders. The fortunes earned abroad enabled migrants to do much more than that. In Soninke society, as noted earlier, wealth and clientage were the basis of power. We should not be too surprised, therefore, by the numerous historical examples of Soninke chiefs who were former laptots. The first Soninke laptot mentioned in the literature—in 1791—was the chief of Maxanna, for all practical purposes the tunka (king) of Kammera.[93] Later, examples of former laptots who were chiefs or members of chiefly families are numerous. Thus the villages of Golmi and Yaafera (Gwey) were headed in 1881 by former Navy laptots.[94] The son of the chief of the village of Somankidi (Gidimaxa) in 1878 or 1879 was a laptot who had served for eighteen years in the French Navy and had even been to the French harbor of Lorient in Brittany.[95] The village of Muusala (Kammera), which according to Soleillet (one of our main sources on the matter) contained the largest number of laptots, was a Bacili (royal) village.[96] At the beginning of the twentieth century, tunkas Samba Suuley, Amadu Sumbulu, and Demba Jangu Bacili were former laptots. At that time, the *chambre* of Tiyaabu, which was the seat of the migrants' organization from the royal capital of Gwey, was the hotbed of political contest for the kingdom.[97]

In fact, laptot and urban incomes were so high in comparison with village incomes that royal families in the Upper Senegal apparently maintained a kind of monopoly on these occupations.[98] This monopoly was easy to maintain since employers in Senegal recruited their personnel through recommendation from their own employees or workers, who introduced relatives or people from the same village as candidates for new jobs. For example, French Navy reports in Senegal mentioned that recruitments were made on such a narrow basis that crews on the same ship were often from the same village or family.[99]

Evidence of aristocratic migration may appear very puzzling, but actually the Soninke were not unique in using migration returns to build up political power. In the twentieth century, for example, most of the chiefs of the Kru of Ivory Coast and Liberia, who also migrated as sailors on European ships, had spent a considerable time in employment abroad accumulating wealth.[100] Soninke royal families were very large because of polygyny; competition for power between young royals was very keen. Soninke laptots invested their incomes in slaves, who provided a steady revenue from cultivation in the Soninke homeland. This revenue, in turn, would be used to make generous gifts to powerful elders, to build an entourage of clients by generous gifts and displays of wealth—without forgetting gifts to the griots, the praise-singers, who were the "advertising agencies" of this patriarchal age—and thus to compete for political power.[101]

Thus, while migration encouraged the emancipation of junior dependents in extended families, migrants did not wish to destroy the Soninke traditional family but to settle down after a polygynous marriage as wealthy patriarchs surrounded by their slaves and dependents, participants in the local political game. No sooner was the old order questioned in practice than it was re-created by the migrants. The migrants were not protesting the traditional society; they hoped to achieve promotion within it.

Slaves as Navetanes: The Baalu Slave Migrant Affair (1879)

Laptots were not the only Soninke to make substantial earnings in migration. There is practically no information on navetanat in the Gambia for this period due to the so-called Marabout-Soninke (no relation to the ethnic Soninke)[102] civil wars. These cut off all communication between European trading posts and the interior. However, indications from the neighboring Upper Casamance region of Southern Senegal, where navetanat continued to expand in the years 1860 to 1868, are that migration toward the Gambia persisted despite the war.[103] We have little information on the origin of Soninke navetanes, but all the available evidence concerns migrants from the Bakel area. This is not surprising since, of all Soninke regions, Bakel (Gwey) was closest to the areas of Upper Gambia and Upper Casamance where navetanat apparently began. And it once more reinforces the view that labor migration among the Soninke was the result of the "pull" of higher incomes abroad for, as we have seen, the Bakel area was experiencing unprecedented prosperity during this period.

In 1879 a very interesting case arose in the village of Baalu (Goye Annexé)[104] in which two men came to see the commandant in Bakel

> to complain that the people of the village of Baalu absolutely want that they be slaves [I translate literally the equivocal wording of the text], as they possess numerous slaves, and a fine herd. They [the villagers] want to take everything away from them. One of these men [the two plaintiffs] has lived during fifteen years in the Gambia, and this is where he acquired his fortune.

There are unfortunately no further details about the particulars of the affair in the archives, but the French apparently believed the plaintiffs. Led by their marabout, the villagers resisted French pressure to give satisfaction to the two men. The French director of political affairs, Galliéni, came to Baalu with a gunboat, which landed a small military party of six laptots and two French officers. The marabout and the village chief were arrested (the latter was subsequently dismissed) and the village had to pay a fine of fifty guinées.

The ambiguity of the wording of the passage quoted above suggests that the two plaintiffs actually were, or had been, slaves. Two scenarios are plausible. A first is that the two plaintiffs were "serfs" owing a rent in kind. As we have seen, such "serfs" were among the first Soninke navetanes. According to custom, they were required to pay one-half of their gains to their owners. Captain Mazillier's 1894 report on slavery in the cercle of Kayes also mentions another type of arrangement, in which the slave had to pay a set price upon his departure but "extraordinary gains" had to be shared equally with the owner upon the slave's return.[105] The dispute in Baalu may have concerned the sharing of gains made abroad. Custom also specified that a "serf" owing a rent in kind who did not make the required payments to his master could be forced to work again for his master, that is, he could be made again into a "serf." One of the two men from Baalu had been away for fifteen years, apparently without returning to the village. As a result, the villagers may have considered that he had not made his customary payments during that period and that he ought accordingly to be retroceded to the condition of a "serf." Why then did the man return to the village? It is possible that he hoped to buy back his freedom from his master with a customary payment of the value of two slaves. Sources mention that some slave migrants did use their earnings in this fashion.

Another possibility is that the two "slaves" were, in fact, redeemed slaves *(dubagandi komo)*. This would be suggested by another Bakel case from a later date (1897). Fajele Sise (Cissé) from Gemu claimed that he had bought his freedom back from his master by giving him one slave and the value of another slave. Later he went to work in Saint-Louis and brought back with him fifty pièces de guinée. He deposited them with his former master, who then kept them for himself, claiming that "the work of his captive belonged to him."[106] In this case, the slave master clearly went against custom, but the fact that the former slave could not gain redress in the village (as evidenced by the fact that he took the case to the French commandant in Bakel) suggests that slave owners in Gemu generally felt threatened by the economic success of a slave.

It is also interesting to compare these cases with another, brought to the Bakel commandant in 1897. In the 1850s, a slave went to work in Saint-Louis during the dry season with his master's authorization. However, instead of coming back to his master, he came back to live in the royal village of

Tiyaabu, in the house of a certain Amadi Sili, probably a member of the Bacili family or of a client family.[107] In this case, the slave succeeded in escaping the wrath of his master (and perhaps also in keeping the gains of his migration) by attaching himself to a patron who was more powerful than his rightful owner.

All of these cases indicate that Soninke slaves were finding in migration an opportunity to better their condition and to move toward freedom. It also appears that migrant slaves were often willing to take their disputes with their owners to the French. In later years, migration and French authority were going to bring about profound changes to Soninke slavery.

French and Umarian Taxes in the 1870s

The policy followed by the French after 1865 in the Upper Senegal region created a power vacuum, which did not remain empty very long. In 1866, the French administrator in Bakel noted that Gidimaxa villages were paying tax to an agent of the Umarian state residing in the village of Jogunturo.[108] This constituted a definite encroachment on the French sphere of influence tacitly recognized in the Franco-Umarian treaty of 1860, a sphere of influence that included not only the southern bank of the Senegal River, but Gidimaxa as well.[109] In the following years, the Umarians became bolder, and their authority was felt even in the region around the French fort of Bakel and in the nominally French villages of Goye Annexé. In 1870, diplomatic negotiations took place between the traditional authorities of Gwey, Kammera, and Gidimaxa and the envoys of Ahmadu Seku, who had succeeded his father, Al-Haj Umar Tal.[110]

Intelligence reports summarized in the correspondence of the Bakel commandant give us a unique insight into the understudied matter of African taxation systems, for the negotiations were centered around how much was to be paid to the Umarian empire. There appear to have been two kinds of taxes: ordinary and extraordinary. The ordinary tax was the annual Islamic *zakkat* (locally called *jakka*), theoretically of one-tenth of the harvest but actually probably much smaller (in figures below I have made an arbitrary minimum estimate of one-twentieth).[111] The extraordinary tax, which was collected in 1872 apparently in Gidimaxa alone, was of eighty horses, eighty rifles, and eighty pièces de guinée. The way it was set up (eighty of "each") shows that it was a "gift," in fact, an exceptional war contribution. Similar to taxes in ancien régime France, it was negotiated at length between the Gidi-maxa villages and the Umarians.[112] I have attempted an estimate of the bur-den of both taxes on the Soninke villages.

For the zakkat, I have chosen the hypothesis of an average village of 400 inhabitants.[113] Of these 400 inhabitants, certainly no less than 100 (one-fourth) were able-bodied men. According to Pollet and Winter, the average sorghum production today in Jafunu is 600 kilograms per hectare, with an average of one hectare cultivated per man. Using this conservative estimate (past figures suggest one metric ton and higher), the village owed: 600 x 100 ÷ 20 = 3,000 kilograms.

Since the price of grain stayed during this time at around 0.10 francs a kilogram, our village owed the equivalent of 300 francs annually to Nioro.[114] It is interesting to note that the *zakkat* was apparently collected in guinées rather than in kind.[115]

As for the extraordinary contribution, it was equal to:[116]

Table 3.2
Umarian Extraordinary Tax Collected in Gidimaxa, 1872

80 horses:	80 x 400 francs = 32,000
80 rifles:	80 x 94 francs = 7,520
80 guinées:	80 x 12.5 francs = 1,000
Total:	40,520 francs

Since there were 100 villages in Gidimaxa, each of them paid 405 francs in 1872. Moreover, the Beydan also levied tribute in Gidimaxa. The Bakel archives contain no figures concerning the ordinary Beydan tribute for this period (other than the indication that the Beydan "pressured [Gidimaxa vil-lagers] in horrible fashion"), but they give some figures for a number of Damga villages immediately downstream. These villages paid in 1866 from 400 to 1,000 mudd of cereals a year to their Beydan overlords, that is, 900 to 2,250 kilograms, or 90 to 225 francs a year.[117] Finally, the Beydan imposed on Gidimaxa villages in 1872 an extraordinary tax of twenty horses and twenty guns—9,880 francs, 98.8 francs per village. Adding figures for ordinary and extraordinary Umarian and Beydan taxes, we come to a figure of 961 francs per village. This data, incidentally, is not the only evidence that we have for this period that indigenous taxes were far higher than the French taxes im-posed after 1858 and largely abandoned after 1867: in 1889, the Bakel com-mandant reported that two Bundu villages, Allelui and Ololdu, located about ten kilometers from Bakel, would have preferred to be recognized as part of French-controlled Gwey so they would not to have to pay "tithe" (zakkat) to the Almami (ruler) of Bundu.[118]

These figures, in fact, question whether it would be possible that migration was caused not by French taxation, but by indigenous (Umarian or Beydan) taxation. If this had been true, however, there would have been a larger number of migrants from Gidimaxa than from anywhere else. The evidence we have for laptots is that an equal number of migrants came from Gwey, Kammera, and Gidimaxa. As for navetanes, the only indications of origin that we have are for Gwey or for the "Bakel region," which does not exclude Gidimaxa but certainly does not mean they were essentially coming from this region. Finally, it is obvious that if Bakel generated more than 500,000 francs of exports a year after 1870 (of which the greater part must have gone to Gidimaxa, which did the most trade with the Beydan and the French), the villages could pay such taxes. In fact, it may have been the realization that Soninke villages withstood such outrageously high rates of taxation (as compared with French rates) that gave the future "*officiers soudanais*," the Desbordes and Archinard, the idea that their future conquests in the Western Sudan could become a self-supporting colony through personal taxation, eliminating the continuous squabbles marking their relations with the Senegal merchant community and the French Parliament.[119]

Reestablishment of French Authority in Gwey (1876)

The French followed the political situation in the Upper Senegal region closely. They were concerned lest an incident disturb agricultural activity in Gidimaxa, which was said to produce "far more" than all the areas on the southern bank between Matam and Médine, that is, Damga, Gwey, Kammera, and Xaaso.[120] The French were also concerned with the potential consequences of Umarian authority for French traders in the area. The Umarians collected a tax of one-tenth of the value of all caravans *(usuru)* crossing their territory.[121] In 1870, as I have related, there were negotiations between Umarian envoys and Gwey, Kammera, and Gidimaxa. In 1872, Kammera on the southern bank began paying direct taxes to the Umarians.[122] The following year, the French began to request the payment of a personal tax in Goye Annexé again.[123] At the end of 1874, the tunka placed a tax collector in Kungani, the village in Goye Annexé closest to Bakel. This official was to collect a one-tenth duty on the value of all French goods.[124] By this time, an even greater threat for the French had arisen near their fort at Bakel itself.[125]

The origin of French authority in the village of Bakel (as distinguished from the French fort) dated from 1821 when the inhabitants of Bakel, the Njaay (N'Diaye), had sided with the French against the tunka of Gwey.[126] During the wars with Al-Haj Umar Tal, however, a number of Bakel Soninke had turned against the French, and as a result, their lands were confiscated.[127] Another subject of grievances was that the French, in the name of free trade, had abolished the duties originally collected by the inhabitants of Bakel on caravans and traders who crossed their territory. In 1873, the Soninke chief of Bakel declared that he recognized the authority of the tunka, implying he rejected that of the French. At the end of 1874 and the beginning of 1875, the matter came to open conflict: petty harassment by the Bakel commandant led to insults and violence and, finally, open rebellion. The Soninke quarter of Bakel was burned, it seems after cannon shots were fired from the French fort (there apparently were no victims). Throughout the crisis, the tunka of Gwey had looked on with interest—and presumably the Umarians had as well. These events explain why the French decided in 1876 on a show of force in Gwey.

The new governor, Brière de l'Isle, needed no encouragement to take action. A stern Navy officer, Brière de l'Isle was a steadfast supporter of French expansion in the Sudan, which meant having available a strong base of operations in the Upper Senegal. The matter was quickly settled. In August 1876, the governor arrived in Bakel on a Navy sloop. A number of cannon shots were fired over the village of Yaafera.[128] At the end of the month, the tax census was completed and the tax collected.

In addition to the 1876 tax, which had been set at a higher rate than in 1863, the village of Yaafera had to pay four times this amount as a fine, and the brother of the chief of Yaafera had to pay an additional fine of ten guinées. The total seems to have been around 95 guinées for all five villages, 50 guinées for Yaafera (including the fine of the chief's brother), between 6 and 12 guinées for the other villages. This came to about 1,187 francs for all villages—625 francs for Yaafera and between 75 and 150 francs for the other villages.[129] Compared with the figures given above for Umarian taxation in Gidimaxa, the "punishment" was mild indeed. The following year tax was collected according to the new census. I reproduce this tax census below.

Table 3.3
French Personal Tax in the Cercle of Bakel, 1877[130]

Village	*Taxpayers: men*	*Taxpayers: women*	*Taxpayers: total*	*Total of Tax (in Francs)*
Yaafera	46	4	50	75
Golmi	63	1	64	96
Arundu	17	4	21	31.50
Baalu	17	7	24	36
Kungani	71	9	80	120
Total:			239	358.50

These figures speak for themselves. They are even lower than the esti-mate made (without formal census) by the Bakel commandant in 1876 (the difference is 101.50 francs, i.e., almost one-fourth).[131] Also remarkable is the low number of reported taxpayers. Every man and woman, slave or free, of age fifteen to sixty-five officially had to pay tax.[132] Clearly more than 239 persons in a population of 1,200 to 1,500 qualified under this definition. When the Bakel administrator complained in 1878 that tax collection in-curred a loss of 2.50 francs per ten taxpayers because taxes were paid in over-valued guinées, Brière de l'Isle noted in the margin of his letter: "Personal taxation has not been created in order to [bring revenue?—illegible word] but as a moral sign of domination."[133] In fact, it is probable that without the events of 1873 to 1876, personal tax would have been abolished in Bakel. The Conseil d'Administration of Senegal (where the major French and Creole [métis] trading houses were represented) had asked unanimously in 1871 to suppress the personal tax. The tax was provisionally suspended in 1872 but had to be reintroduced the same year for budgetary reasons. In 1874, the Ad-ministrative Council reiterated its demand, but it made an exception for the river outposts for "very special political reasons," a reference to the tense Bakel situation.[134]

Speaking of the Soninke around 1885, Colonel Frey wrote:

[T]hanks to the complete security which the Sarakole [the Soninke] derived from our protection, owing to the vicinity of our [military] posts, their commercial inclinations were able to develop freely. All the Sarakole vil-lages had become important centers of trade for peanuts, cereals, and cattle, in particular since several years ago, because of the considerable needs that were the consequence of our new undertaking [the French conquest of the Sudan]. This commercial expansion had brought to the whole region an extraordinary wealth for the Blacks, who ordinarily do not own very much, or cannot keep what they have acquired; some family heads [*chefs de case*] owned more than a hundred slaves, possessed horses, cattle in large numbers; granaries were bursting with grain; the *tatas* [adobe fortifications around the villages] were fully stocked with powder and bullets; all able-bodied men were equipped with rifles, some of which were true luxury weapons.[135]

Yet, in spite of its economic prosperity, this period saw the consolidation of labor migration among the Upper Senegal Soninke: in 1885, during the Soninke religious revolt of Mamadu Lamin Darame, the French estimated that 1,200 to 1,500 of the rebels were former laptots or people who had been employed by the French.[136] As the population of Gwey, Kammera, and Gidimaxa numbered at the time about 42,500 people (including Bakel), the former migrants who were employees of the French in the region numbered at least (for we can assume that some of them did not join the rebellion) 11 to 14 percent of the adult male population.[137] This, it should be stressed, was a considerable figure: in the 1960s, a migration rate of 25 percent among the Fuutanke, the immediate neighbors of the Soninke in the Senegal River Valley, was judged sufficiently alarming by the Mauritanian and Senegalese governments for them to commission a large-scale economic study of the Middle Valley of the Senegal River.[138] And it should be added that the 1885 Soninke figure does not include the presumably larger navetane migration.

Conclusion

Taxation did not create labor migration in the Soninke homeland nor was it intended for that purpose by the French administration. Far more significant in this period than taxation or other nonexistent coercion and economic disruption was the attraction of high wages and incomes in an expanding coastal Senegambian economy. Why were laptots' wages so high in this period? Perhaps economists will be able to answer this question.

Higher wages and incomes were the dominant motivation for Soninke labor migration at this time, not because the Soninke were given "new needs" (such as "needs" for European goods), but because such incomes provided them with a potential for social promotion within Soninke soci- ety.[139] The possibility of raising money for bridewealth, of buying slaves, of setting up an independent household, and, for aristocrats, of competing more efficiently for political power were not "new needs," but ambitions that had always existed within the traditional society, ambitions, moreover, that had often been fulfilled through migration. As we have seen, the basis of power in the "semistateless" Soninke society was wealth, giving rise to a sys- tem of clientage. The successful individual was the elder, heading a polygy- nous, slave-holding household, which contributed enough resources to enable a patron to provide for many clients. While younger men endured the authority of the elders impatiently and migrated abroad to gain greater per- sonal independence from them, they also hoped to amass enough resources to become one day successful elders themselves.

Again, comparisons with other parts of the world help to place these con- clusions in perspective. I have already referred to the case of former Kru sailors who became chiefs. In Europe, migrants often migrated in order to return as village notables.[140] In Corsica, aristocrats such as the d'Ornano or the Bonaparte migrated as mercenaries in Italian and French armies in order to build up personal and family wealth.[141] In Greece in the eighteenth and nineteenth centuries, migrants from the Mani region of Cape Tainaron in southern Peloponnesos used their accumulated savings to build castles and attract followers, eventually becoming warlords and territorial chiefs.[142] It is worth noting that both Corsica and the Peloponnesos had a decentralized so- ciety, which recalls stateless societies in Africa. Indeed, the description given by John N. Andromedas of the society of southern Peloponnesos, with its juxtaposition and alternation of village "republicanism" and regional war- lordism, is strongly reminiscent of precolonial Soninke society.[143]

FOUR

A Time of Troubles

1880–1894

UP TO THIS POINT, Soninke labor migration has appeared to have been caused by the "pull" factor of opportunities abroad rather than the "push" of an adverse economic situation at home. After 1880, following the creation of the Administration du Haut-Fleuve (which became the colony of French Soudan in 1892), the situation of the Soninke became more perplexing. The Upper Senegal region was effectively subjected to colonial rule, in its least desirable form as a military administration: the ambitious French officers who governed the region until 1895 (when Bakel and the western half of Gidimaxa were returned to Senegal) imposed high taxes and forced labor. The period also witnessed the Islamic revolt led by Mamadu Lamin Darame (Mamadou Lamine Dramé), followed by a period of repression. Lastly, in the 1890s the price of gum slumped dramatically on the world market. Yet these political and economic tribulations did not produce a process of generalized economic decline. And the data on migration for this period certainly do not substantiate the thesis of a colonial "trigger" to population movements.

Migration and Coercion

Although the Third Republic gave a mandate to the French military to conquer the interior of West Africa, the way in which they carried out this mandate was hardly disciplined or disinterested: the military's thirst for glory and professional advancement, their disregard of injunctions of restraint, and their cavalier and often brutal treatment of the conquered populations are now well-known. The Soninke homeland was the base of French operations in the Sudan. After 1880, it came under the jurisdiction of the newly created military administration of the commandant supérieur du Haut-Fleuve, then theoretically under the authority of the governor of Senegal, but soon to become the colony of French Soudan. The military requisitioned laborers to build their telegraph line and their new administrative capital of Kayes near Médine, to unload ships, and to pull their river transports when stranded in the shallow waters of the Senegal River. They requisitioned donkeys to transport their supplies, and occasionally cattle to feed their troops. Abdoulaye Bathily saw in these events a major cause of the revolt of Mamadu Lamin Darame in the Upper Senegal in 1886.[1]

A closer examination of the documents, however, shows that the impact of the French military in the region was relatively minor. The number of requisitioned workers before 1886 was small; even projected figures (as distinguished from the number of men actually recruited) never were greater than 200 or 300 men at one time, and the largest number of men actually recruited at one time was 115.[2] With one short-term exception (a period of three days), the French conscripted workers only after all agricultural work had been completed.[3] No recruits were made to work in locations more distant than Kayes, and even though the conscripted workers were paid irregularly, they were paid at a rate not inferior to that of the market.[4] Villagers helping stranded barges were apparently paid.[5] Donkeys and cows were actually bought.[6]

Why this moderation? The French needed to protect their supply line to the Sudan and their base of operations in the Upper Senegal.[7] They could hardly afford a revolt in this area, and they knew from their recent experience in 1873 to 1875 that this was a possibility. Soninke reactions to coercion reinforced this perception. In January 1881, the chiefs of Gwey, Kammera, Xaaso, and Bundu met in Daramanne (Kammera) and swore on the Koran that they would not provide a single laborer to the French. Not surprisingly, only a small number of men could be conscripted and desertions were frequent. Desertions eventually were so numerous that Chinese and Moroccan laborers had to be brought in.[8] The chief of the village of Golmi, a former laptot, hid donkeys lost by a returning French expedition and, when called into Bakel by the commandant, simply refused to go. The commandant wrote that he could not go to arrest him in his village: "It would be bad politics and would bring about a conflict."[9] In 1880, a particularly bad year for river navigation, Commandant-Supérieur Borgnis-Desbordes himself was reportedly insulted by the tunka of Kammera when he requested help for his stranded boat near the village of Tanbunkaani.[10] Bakel documents make no mention of recruitments after 1881, and there is reason to think that this was indeed the case until the revolt of Mamadu Lamin Darame.

The Revolt of Mamadu Lamin Darame [11]

Even though the hardship created by French military expansion was relatively limited, resentments arising from the growing French presence probably did play a role in the revolt led by the Soninke cleric Mamadu Lamin Darame among the Upper Senegal Soninke in 1886. Recent scholarship, however, has shown that the revolt had mostly religious motives. It began as a crusade against the pagan Malinke state of Gamon (in Bambuxu), and it was only after Bundu, a longtime French ally, had refused to authorize the crossing of its territory by Lamin's army and was subsequently attacked that the French intervened. Ensuing events made clear that Mamadu Lamin Darame's followers harbored deep resentments against the Umarian empire and its ruler, Al-Haj Umar Tal's son Amadu Sheku, whom they accused of betraying his father's Islamic ideals. The revolt, therefore, was the result of the progress of militant Islam among the Soninke.[12]

Soninke royals, the tunka lemmu, who traditionally looked upon clerics with contempt, had remained aloof from the growing religious fervor among their countrymen until relatively late in the movement's rise. In 1881, Soninke laptots of the Compagnie des Mécaniciens Indigènes (who were presumably tunka lemmu), caused a riot in Saint-Louis when they reportedly walked carrying their regulation Navy wine rations near a mosque at the time of prayer.[13] During the revolt of Mamadu Lamin Darame, however, some 1,200 to 1,500 former laptots or former employees of the French fought in Lamin's army. These appeared to be among the leaders of the revolt and the most courageous in battle. The French were shocked by this episode, which they saw as a mark of ingratitude on the part of their former employees.[14] In fact, the participation of laptots in the revolt showed that Soninke warrior aristocrats (tunka lemmu essentially) were now committed to the movement of religious reform. The circumstances of the 1881 riot notwithstanding, Soninke laptots and laborers must have been influenced by the religious atmosphere in Saint-Louis, then one of the most active Islamic centers in West Africa. As elsewhere in Senegambia, with the conversion of traditional aristocrats to reformed Islam, military ethics transmuted into religious zeal, giving birth to what David Robinson has called a "crusading ideal," a longing of young aristocrats to prove their worth by fighting the *jihad*.[15]

After the Revolt

The revolt of Mamadu Lamin Darame and the repression that followed were costly for the region. Yet the impact of the events of 1886 did not consume the region's wealth. Colonel Frey stated that the sale of war booty made during the revolt enabled the French administration to make a gift of 150 francs to each soldier who had fought in the war. There were 140 French soldiers and 380 Senegalese *tirailleurs* in Frey's column.[16] Many died in the campaign, mostly from heat and disease. Ignoring these deaths (which I cannot estimate), the reward would come to 78,000 francs. There were also 2,000 African auxiliaries, who most certainly received nothing from the French but took booty as well (taking booty must have been for many of them their main reason for participating in the repression of the revolt). Counting an equal figure for the auxiliaries' booty, we come to 156,000 francs. Bathily also mentions a "war contribution" (was that the same as the reward to soldiers mentioned above?) of 530,000 francs paid by the populations of the Upper Senegal.[17] Adding this, the total estimate comes to 686,000 francs. In 1893, a French census for the eastern Soninke provinces of Kingi, Kenyareme, and Gidyume recorded that they owned 2,100 horses, 3,000 cows or oxen, and 100,000 sheep; or the equivalent of between 1,916,000 and 3,150,000 francs.[18] Gwey, Gidimaxa, and Kammera, which were affected by the French repression, had a population of about half that of these three provinces, but they were also much richer, due to their location on the banks of the Senegal River.[19] In point of fact, a Bakel political report of 1889, three years after the revolt, spoke of the "great affluence" and of the "prosperous state" of Gwey, and in 1892 the region was said to be particularly rich in livestock.[20]

The Soninke, moreover, were able to recoup their losses in the war due to the buoyant state of the Upper Senegal economy in the second half of the 1880s. The revolt of the Mahdi in the Egyptian Sudan suppressed for a time a dangerous emerging rival of the Senegalese gum arabic.[21] From 1885 to 1888, gum exports from Bakel probably were at a level of 1 million francs a year, that is, at the level of the overconfident years following establishment of free trade after 1848.[22] Finally, exports other than gum continued to come from the region, especially grain, which was much in demand to feed the French army in the Soudan.[23]

After the repression of the revolt, the French evidently were in a better position to demand services from the Soninke, but they used this ability sparingly as far as labor recruitment was concerned.[24] The French probably feared a new outbreak of violence if they showed themselves too demanding. They were also concerned with maintaining their grain and livestock supplies from this region.[25] In addition, the policies of the officiers soudanais came under sharp scrutiny in the French Parliament after 1888, and orders were sent against the use of forced labor. The region from Bakel to Kayes, well-frequented by Saint-Louisien traders, could not hope to escape attention, as did the remote regions to the east that the French were then conquering.[26] Finally, forced labor recruitments were politically unwise given the role that the Soudanese officers had devised for Africans—providing wealth for the Soudanese treasury.

Following the revolt of Mamadu Lamin, the French annexed the former Goye Indépendant (now known as Goye Inférieur) and Kammera in 1888,[27] and later a number of Gidimaxa villages in 1891. An agreement with the rulers of Gwey specified that there would be no more conscription of laborers but that Gwey would now pay the personal tax.[28] As we have seen, the French were well aware of the very substantial taxes paid to the Umarians by the Soninke villages on the right bank of the Senegal River in the 1870s, which seemed to be easily collected. The French, however, tended to overestimate the amounts paid to the Umarians; in 1887, Colonel Frey believed that Gidimaxa paid an improbable 60,000 francs annually to Amadu Sheku.[29] There was an element of "wishful thinking" in these misconceptions, for the Soudanese officers were impatient to free themselves from the control of the Senegalese administration and the French Parliament, which both tried to restrain the pace of conquest in the Sudan. The military wanted to create an autonomous Soudan colony with its own budget and revenue. The problem was that French Soudan had no sea outlet and that Senegal obstinately refused to surrender part of its customs revenues, even though a sizeable proportion actually came from the export of Upper Senegal gum.[30] In an age when the income of most European colonies came from export taxes—that is, customs revenues—the projected Soudan colony would have to try to support itself on personal tax.[31]

Since the Soudan in 1888 was legally part of Senegal, it could not have a tax policy distinct from the mother colony. But Senegal raised its personal tax outside of Saint-Louis to 3 francs per person in 1888 in order to meet the growing expenses of the rapidly expanding colony.[32] (Even after this reform in 1889, only 315,000 francs, about 11 percent, of Senegalese revenues came from direct taxes, as against 2,439,500 francs in indirect taxes.)[33] Moreover, the number of taxpayers had been in the past so grossly underestimated in the Upper Senegal region that it was possible to obtain a considerable increase in tax revenues simply by applying the law.[34] The 1889 personal tax in Bakel yielded 6,500 francs. The following year, it yielded 22,000 francs.[35] Tax this year was collected for the first time in money rather than in cereals or in guinées. As there was an insufficient supply of currency in the region, French francs rose in real value (i.e., became overvalued in relation to the value of local exports) by about 25 percent, adding to the taxpayer's burden of an already vastly increased tax.[36] In 1893, with the incorporation of a number of Gidimaxa villages into the cercle of Bakel, the income from personal tax rose to 37,000 francs, 80 percent of which was paid in currency and 20 percent in guinées. Adding an estimated figure for Kammera (which was part of the cercle of Médine and on which I lack information) and 25 percent for the local inflation of currency, we come to a figure of about 60,000 francs for the Upper Senegal Soninke of Gwey, Kammera, and Gidimaxa.[37]

The Gum Crash

The increase in the tax burden came at the wrong time. The high price of gum in the years 1885 to 1888 was short-lived; as soon as the Mahdist revolt ended, the Anglo-Egyptian Sudan resumed its gum exports with a vengeance, driving down the price of Senegalese gum in devastating proportions, as the following figures for Bakel (no figures for Médine seem to be available) demonstrate:

Table 4.1[38]

Gum Exports From Bakel, 1888–1895

Year	Metric Tons	Price/Kilo (in Francs)	Value (in Francs)
1885–88	[ca.350]	[ca.3.0]	[ca.1,000,000]
1889	[350]	1.25	437,500
1890	225	0.83	186,750
1891	600	[1.2]	720,000
1892	157	1.0	157,000
1893	250	0.4–0.65	100,000–162,500
1894	122.5	0.43	60,224
1895	310	0.4	124,000
1896	329	0.6	197,400
1897	218	0.33	71,940

The fall in the price of gum was catastrophic for French trade in the Upper Senegal, and in Bakel particularly. Even counting other local exports, such as peanuts, the Bakel trade for 1894 came to an all-time low of 1.7 percent of all Senegalese exports, while in 1860 it stood at about 16 percent.[39] The fall in the price of gum, moreover, was lasting and definitive. The most immediate result of the gum crash was a vast deficit in the Bakel trade. The main problem for the region was not really taxation but that the revenue from exports no longer covered the cost of imports. In 1894 Bakel exports came only to 204,477.45 francs, while imports stood at 565,019.65 francs. These imports were composed mostly of cloth (63 percent) and African goods such as kola nuts and livestock (16 percent), with European manufactured goods other than cloth making up a mere 1.62 percent (this clearly goes against the stereotype of an African continent hungry for shoddy European goods). More than half of the value of imports was composed of guinées, which were given on credit by Saint-Louis traders to traitants upstream, who themselves sold the guinées on credit to Beydan in exchange for the promise of a supply of gum.[40] It was this reliance on credit in the gum trade that probably explains why the deficit was so large at the beginning of the crisis. Another reason was that the river was navigable only between July and January, while the main gum season lasted from February to July. Traders thus had to import their merchandise first during the second half of the year, taking a chance that they would be able to sell it to Beydan in the first half of the following year.[41]

Because of the importance of the desert-side trade, the gum crash was bound to have repercussions on the welfare of the Soninke. Their predicament was worsened by a series of adverse coincidences. A cattle epidemic destroyed most of the herds around Bakel in 1892, wiping out the farmers' "bank accounts."[42] There were also bad crops that year, and quarantine measures (apparently because of a cholera epidemic) made it impossible to import grain from Damga or Fuuta Tooro to relieve the food shortage.[43] In 1895, the cercle of Bakel was returned to the colony of Senegal. After Governor-General Chaudié, in a speech given in Bakel in November 1895, led the population to believe that the French no longer recognized slavery, slaves in Gwey and in Gidimaxa fled in large numbers. Although most subsequently were returned to their masters, at least two hundred managed to escape to Fuuta Tooro or the Gambia or to obtain freedom certificates from the French.[44] Moreover, under the administration of Senegal, taxes were no longer collected in December after crops had been harvested and sold, as had been the case while Bakel was part of the Soudan, but in the middle of the year, during the "hungry season," when farmers often had to borrow grain from traitants in Bakel. By a sad combination of circumstances, a severe drought hit the Bakel region in 1896. The archives for Bakel in 1897 give definite indications of serious economic distress. Villagers had to borrow grain brought from Damga and Soudan in order to survive during several months before harvest.[45] There was strong resistance to tax collection; village chiefs or notables from the villages of Kungani, Arundu, Yaafera, Allahima, Turime (Gwey), and Selibaby (Gidimaxa) were jailed, and the commandant threatened the tunka and the village chiefs of Gwey that he would station a platoon of *spahis* (Senegalese cavalry) on their territory, who would live off the land, until the tax was paid.[46] Some villages had to borrow guinées (which they used to pay the tax) from Bakel traitants, who loaned them at the usurious price of 10 francs (the current price was 7 francs), to be repaid in grain after harvest. Other villagers had to pawn their jewelry, their personal weapons, and even in some cases their clothes in order to pay the tax.[47] Crops were bad in 1897, too, and the following year was again very difficult for the population of the cercle.[48] The year 1900 was also bad because of drought, and some deaths by hunger were reported in Bundu, although not in Gajaaga.[49]

The decline of the Bakel region, which had once been so important in the economy of Senegal, was lasting. In 1908, former Bakel Commandant Frédéric Riembau described Bakel as "fallen to the rank of a very secondary market town," whereas twelve to fifteen years before, it had been a "very important trading post" where most of the larger trading houses were represented.[50] The decline of gum also brought about a gradual decline of the village trading posts. In Bakel itself, the newly installed French trading house of Marc Caland, which brought stiff competition to Saint-Louisien black traitants, preferred to exchange merchandise for currency instead of local products.[51]

This account from Bakel, however, somewhat overdramatizes the long-term impact of the gum crisis on the Upper Senegal Soninke. The Soninke continued to weave and export cotton cloth, which was in growing demand in urban and cash-crop producing rural areas. They continued to export livestock, and in this respect, they probably benefited in the short run from the crash since the necessity to repay debts must have encouraged the Beydan to sell part of their livestock at lower prices. Reports from Bakel for the beginning of the twentieth century mention dry-season migrations to sell cloth in Kayes, Rufisque, Bathurst, and generally all urban centers and trading posts along the Senegal River and railway, or again to sell livestock bought from Beydan in Nioro to buyers in Siin-Saluum and the Gambia.[52] The demand for cereals among the Beydan, moreover, was not likely to disappear because of the gum crash (although many Beydan, especially slaves and people of lower status, progressively turned to agriculture in the twentieth century). Finally the decline of French trade in the Upper Senegal region was never absolute. Gum, millet, and even peanuts continued to be bought in Kayes, Bakel, and the village trading posts.[53] Major Saint-Louisien trading houses did retreat from Bakel, but the old trade of the marigotiers quickly filled their place. In 1912, it was reported that villagers in Gwey found the price of 0.04 francs a kilogram offered for peanuts by traders in Bakel too low and that they preferred to sell them to Saint-Louisien and Waalo Beydan canoe owners, who offered twice as much.[54] The volume of such traffic should not be underestimated: between 1955 and 1963, canoe traffic on the Senegal River was estimated at 15,000 to 20,000 tons annually.[55] As evidence that the Soninke were able to recoup their losses in this period, the Bakel cercle was reported in 1904 (slightly more than a decade after the devastating cattle epidemic of 1892) as owning a herd of 8,500 cows, 8,200 sheep, and 8,700 goats.[56] This represented capital of about 930,000 francs, providing an annual increase in value of 60,000 francs, equivalent to my estimate for the taxes paid to the Soudanese administration in the *entire* Upper Senegal region in 1893 (see above).

Moreover, the decline of the Upper Senegal region was not general. While the Bakel region stagnated, the Médine-Kayes region continued to expand. In 1895, the quantity of gum exported from the French Soudan, that is from the Kayes-Nioro region, was already superior to the quantity exported from Bakel, about 500 metric tons. In 1898, it had reached 1,781 tons.[57] Furthermore, the region above Bakel benefited from the proximity of Kayes, which was the river port of entry into (and for a time the capital of) French Soudan. In 1900, the Soninke regions of Gidimaxa and Kammera were said to be the wealthiest in the cercle of Kayes. Peanuts were "in abundance" and taxes were collected "without pressure." That same year, it was reported that trading posts were opening in the cercle along the Senegal River, that is, in Kammera and the Soudanese part of Gidimaxa.[58] In 1910, some 8,000 tons of peanuts were exported from Kayes, most of them from the cercle, an impressive record if we consider that the much-famed contemporary 1913 "peanut boom" in Kano in northern Nigeria amounted to no more than the export of 6,000 tons of peanuts.[59] Yet Soninke districts in the cercle of Kayes were especially affected by labor migration.[60]

Immigration in a Land of Emigration

One of the striking illustrations of the fact that "push" explanations are insufficient to capture the complex reality of migration is the *in*-migration that took place at the time in the eastern part of Gidimaxa (located in the cercle of Kayes), which itself was also a region of *out*-migration. I quote the report for 1892 to 1893 from the French commandant in Kayes:

> The people of Jafunu, Kingi, and Kenyareme, although they inhabit a rich and fertile land, but one that is situated too far from trading centers, come to farm in Gidimaxa at the beginning of each cultivation season; [they] make one or two harvests, which they trade for guinée[s], and then return to their region of origin, bringing back with them the fruit of their labor.[61]

This was the first report of modern labor migration from the more easterly Soninke regions known to the French as the "Sahel"[62] and it becomes fascinating when one considers that these regions were indeed quite well-off (a 1893 French census of Kingi, Kenyareme, and the neighboring Soninke province of Gidyume found cattle holdings of a value superior to two million francs).[63] Again, this migration was motivated by differences of income between the migrants' regions of origin and destination. A kilogram of sorghum sold in normal years in the 1890s for 0.04 francs in Nioro and 0.15 francs in Bakel. Guinées cost 11 francs in Nioro and only 8 francs in Bakel.[64] With a yearly commercial surplus of 100 mudd, or 220 kilograms, a farmer around Nioro sold it for 0.88 guinées a year while a farmer in the Upper Senegal region sold it for 4.125 guinées.[65] Thus returns on commercial cereal production were *five* times higher in the Upper Senegal region than in the Sahel. Furthermore, as in the case of the navetanes, the migrants could buy a host of cheaper-priced European trade goods in Kayes, Médine, or Bakel and probably sell cattle or cloth there as well.

But why the employment of *free* laborers rather than *slaves* at this particular time? In 1894, slaves were still imported in the cercle of Bakel from the states of Tyeba and Samori. (They were, in fact, listed among other commodities in French commercial reports for Bakel!)[66] But the situation may have been different in Gidimaxa. The 1881 treaty of Nango between the French and the Umarian empire had given Gidimaxa to the Umarians, but the officiers soudanais, who probably remembered the political difficulties experienced in the Upper Senegal in the 1870s, never seem to have accepted this clause (the treaty itself was never ratified). In 1886, Colonel Frey took advantage of the revolt of Mamadu Lamin Darame to wage war on Gidimaxa, but he was disavowed by Paris. With the appointment of Louis Archinard as commandant-supérieur of the Soudan in April 1888, the military resumed its aggressive stance against the Umarian empire. Circumstances provided an opportunity to pressure Gidimaxa into asking "voluntarily" for its own annexation. Many Soninke families were then leaving the region to join the heartland of the Umarian empire. Their slaves often refused to follow them. They fled to Bakel to claim their freedom from the French. The French freed all the Gidimaxa slaves who asked for it, under the pretext of opposing emigration to the Umarian empire.[67] In 1889, Bakel's *village de liberté* was reported to be made up almost entirely of fugitives from Gidimaxa. In 1890, Gidimaxa villages gave in and the following year they were added to the French territory, at their own "request."[68] The most important point for us in this story is not the number of slaves liberated (the Bakel village de liberté never had more than 500 occupants), but that French policy made Gidimaxa for several years a hazardous place to buy or sell trade slaves (who were more likely to escape). This could explain why farmers, instead of importing slaves, had to depend on free migrants in order to meet the expanding labor needs of their commercial agriculture. It should be noted, however, that once Gidimaxa chiefs made their submission in 1890, the French returned escaped slaves to the villages—thus it was no longer risky to bring slaves into the area.[69] Perhaps the reason for using free migrants, then, was that they required a lower amount of investment capital than slaves (who had to be bought, in addition to being housed and fed).

There are other, later references to free *in*-migrants in the Upper Senegal region. Writing during 1898 and 1899, Charles Monteil mentioned migrant laborers called *nansoka* ("I work for you," i.e., hired laborers).[70] Some were *nansoka de mil* ("sorghum nansoka"), who worked in Gajaaga and Jomboxo (Xaaso)—that is, these were the migrants described in the 1892 to 1893 report quoted above—but others "came to cultivate peanuts." Monteil does not specify where these "peanut nansoka" were employed, although Gidimaxa, Kammera, and Xaaso villages along the Senegal River in the neighborhood of Kayes and Médine, close to the French trading houses, seem the most probable location. Monteil mentioned that migrant nansoka had to pay a certain quantity of their crop to their jatigi and to village chiefs. The mentions of jatigi and of the custom of making a payment to village chiefs strongly recall early navetanat.[71] Although Monteil does not describe the contracts between the migrants and their employer, Pollet and Winter have given a description of two contemporary nansoka arrangements in Jafunu. Under what seems to be the oldest type of arrangement,[72] the nansoka are housed and fed by their employer, and they receive their seed from him. In exchange, they work for their employer five mornings a week. The rest of their time they are free to work on their personal plot.[73] In other words, the arrangement is virtually the same as a navetane contract.

By the time Monteil wrote, the slave trade had lost its main provisioning source in the Western Sudan with the capture of Samori Ture by the French in 1898. By 1905 to 1910, slavery itself was to disappear, or rather, to transform in very significant ways (see Chapter Five). For these reasons, although we have no mention of nansoka in Kayes after the 1890s, it seems impossible that their migration did not continue in the area. In 1900, as I noted earlier, peanuts were mentioned as "abundant" in the cercle of Kayes, and by 1910, a considerable 8,000 tons of peanuts were exported from Kayes, most of them coming from the cercle. We shall see later that this expansion continued after the First World War—in the face of the end of slavery in 1905 to 1910 and 1918 to 1920 and of very high rates of emigration in the interwar period.[74] The migration of the nansoka must have helped maintain production during these years. There is mention of such migrants after the Second World War: the employment of migrants (who were in this case "most often haratin Moors") is mentioned by Boyer for Kingi Jawara in the late 1940s.[75]

The nansoka were thus the historical predecessors of the surga—the seasonal migrants who today work on Soninke farms while most of the Soninke are themselves away in migration abroad. In Gajaaga and Gidimaxa, the surga come from Soninke regions further east—as the nansoka did in the 1890s—but many are also Xaasonke and especially "Bambara," an imprecise term that probably includes Malinke as well as Bambara.[76] In Jafunu, according to Pollet and Winter, seasonal farm laborers are Beydan coming from regions to the north, as many were in Kingi Jawara in the late 1940s.[77] Most reports on the surga describe their employment as a recent development. But the evidence presented above, of course, contradicts this allegation. The Soninke, incidentally, were not the only ethnic group in the area to hire free labor migrants at the end of slavery; the Marka of Mali, who are ethnic relatives and geographical neighbors of the Soninke, succeeded in expanding their commercial production of cereals in the face of a general exodus of their slaves in 1905 to 1910, by replacing them with free migrant laborers.[78]

How did the migration of nansoka first develop from Jafunu, Kenyareme, and Kingi? The available documents give no indications, but we can make some plausible speculations. As is very often the case in West Africa, the same clans are represented across geographical boundaries. The Jawara, in particular, whose base is in Kingi Jawara, have a branch in the Gidimaxa of Kayes, where they form the nucleus of ten villages.[79] They are also represented in Jafunu.[80] There are also alliances, cemented by joking relationships, between clans and even between polities. Thus the people of Jafunu and Gidimaxa share a joking relationship and a particular form of intermarriage (with a faked abduction).[81] Looking into the details of clan and family history one realizes that the Soninke homeland is crisscrossed by clan ties and alliances, which are the result of past migration and history and which probably played a role in the emergence of modern migrations.[82]

Rare Detailed Data on the Migration: The Congo Migrant Sample

I have already discussed the numerical information on Soninke migration provided by Captain Brosselard that 1,500 to 2,000 former laptots or employees of the French participated in the revolt of Mamadu Lamin Darame in 1885 to 1886.[83] This seemingly modest figure actually suggests that labor migration was already well established among the Upper Senegal Soninke before the gum crash (since it represented *10 percent* or more of the adult male population of Gajaaga and Gidimaxa).[84] It, however, tells us little about the geographical or social origins of the migrants, although other sources give us some indications in this respect. The two documents analyzed below, by contrast, are invaluable detailed "samples" of the migration, at an early date and also at the crucial time of the gum crisis.[85]

In 1888, the Congo Free State began recruiting workers in Senegal for the building of what was to become the Matadi-Kinshasa railway, linking the Congo (Zaire) River basin to the Atlantic Ocean. Employers in Senegal's colonial towns, who feared a flight of their skilled labor force and a higher cost of labor, demanded and obtained from French authorities a complete ban on recruiting by foreign powers in the colony. During the following years, however, agents of the Congo Free State came to an agreement with Saint-Louis merchants, in particular with the powerful Creole (mulatto) Devès family. The Frenchman Albert Laplène, a relative by marriage of the Devès, began to recruit laborers in Gorée and Rufisque for the Congo Railway. Colonial authorities, however, continued to oppose the recruitment and prevented the departure of laborers from Senegalese harbors after 1894. During an enquiry in Gorée that year, the colonial police recorded the names, place of birth, occupation, and other details pertinent to the recruiting operations of 301 would-be migrants.[86]

The migrants were all recruited in colonial towns of Senegal and in Saint-Louis, but especially in Dakar and Rufisque. Most were temporary migrants who were looking for employment but without success since Senegal was going through a period of economic recession and urban unemployment at the time. The 1894 list, therefore, is a rare document on *temporary urban migration* in the Senegambia at the end of the nineteenth century.

I give below the information about the geographical origin of the migrants:

Table 4.2
Geographical Origins of the Congo Migrants, 1894

Locality	Emigrants	Percentage
Four communes		
St.-Louis & suburbs	8	
Dakar	4	
Rufisque	2	
Subtotal	14	4.7%
Other urban centers		
Thiès	1	
Tivaouane	1	
Subtotal	2	0.7%
Northern Wolof states		
Jambuur	4	
Jolof	3	
Kajoor	19	
Waalo	9	
Subtotal	35	11.6%
Southern Wolof and Sereer states		
Bawol	3	
Saluum	22	
Siin	1	
Nioro du Rip	5	
Rip	1	
Subtotal	32	10.6%
British Gambia	3	1 %
Fuuta Tooro		
Matam	3	
Podor	2	
Fuuta	63	
Tooro	13	
"Galam"	6	
Subtotal	87	29 %
Bundu	2	0.7%
Fuuta Jalon	2	0.7%
Casamance	1	0.3%

Table 4.2 (cont.)

Locality	Emigrants	Percentage
Soninke		
unknown	1	
"Goye Indépendant"	28	
"Goye Annexé"	2	
Bakel	8	
Damga	10	
Gidimaxa	7	
Kammera	15	
Jafunu	7	
Nioro	3	
Subtotal	82	27.2%
Soudan		
Urban centers	15	
Other	18	
Subtotal	33	11 %
Undetermined	8	4.2%
Total	301	100 %

First, we should note the distances traveled by some of the migrants; in 1894, as many as 11 percent of the labor migrants to Dakar came from the faraway French Soudan, a remarkable observation for such an early date. Second, the migrating regions were not necessarily the most densely populated; figures are almost negligible for the Sereer province of Siin and for Bawol, two of the most densely populated Senegalese regions today. Third, migrants often came from comparatively wealthy regions, such as Kajoor and Saalum, the main peanut-producing areas of Senegal at the time. Saalum, which was the region of origin of one-third of the migrants, like Gidimaxa, was both a region of in-migration (navetanes) and out-migration.[87] Finally, the main migrating regions were all situated along major communication routes, the Senegal River (Fuuta Tooro and Soninke homeland) and the Dakar-Saint-Louis railway (Kajoor)—this observation is also valid for Saalum, a river delta, well-frequented by coastal navigation at the time.

Let us now examine the Soninke in the "sample." Once again, we note the importance of the Senegal River: the great majority of the Soninke villages affected by the migration were situated along the river. Only eleven migrants out of eighty-two were not from riverine villages, and seven out of these eleven came from Jafunu, which was linked at the time to the Senegal River network by the Xoolinbinne River. The predominance of migrants from river villages suggests that migration from colonial towns among the Soninke was an outgrowth of earlier employment as laptots or as workers of the French commercial network along the Senegal River Valley.

The second observation about Soninke migrants is more puzzling. *Practically all* the migrants from Gajaaga came either from "maraboutic villages" (villages whose population belonged in majority to the clerical classes) or from royal villages.[88] Villages of casted artisans (Sebeku),[89] of Bacili excluded from royal succession (Gallade, Golmi, Arundu, Gunjamu, Segala), and villages of mangu (villages of nonroyal, nonclerical aristocracy: Gucube, Sengalu, Xaabu Kammera, Songone, Yaagine, Ambidedi) were not represented in the migration—with the lone exception of one migrant from the mangu village of Songone (Kammera).[90]

Table 4.3
Congo Migrants per Village (Gwey and Kammera), 1894

Village	Migrants	Maraboutic	Royal
Gwey			
Jawara	9	X	
Tiyaabu	10		X
Muderi	1	X	
Mannayel	5	[X]	
Yellingara	3	X	
Yaafera	1	[X]	
Kammera			
Tafasiriga	8	X	
Daramanne	1	X	
Laani	4	X	X
Gunjuru	1	X	
Songone	1		

* There are three Laani in Kammera: Laani Tunka is a royal village, Laani Moodi is a maraboutic village, and Laani Taxutala is a slave and state official (mangu?) village. They are situated side by side. Bathily, "Imperialism amd Colonial Expansion," p. 92.

Unfortunately, most of the 1894 emigrants did not give their family names (following in this the Senegambian custom of going by their first name followed by their mother's first name), but some did, providing an indication of their social origin (with an important reservation that I will discuss in greater detail below—clan names indicating a high social status are sometimes borne by persons of low status):

Table 4.4
1894 Congo Migrants: Gajaaga Names and Villages

GWEY:

Tiyaabu (royal village)		
Amat Bakili	Bacili	Royal family of Gwey
Silly N'Diaye	Njaay	
Amady Diawara	Jawara	
Jawara (maraboutic village)		
Samba Sakho	Saaxo	Village chief's family
Bakary Doucouré	Dukure	Maraboutic family
Samba Cissé	Sise	Family of notables
Mody Cissé	Sise	Family of notables
Séga Diahilé	Jaxite	Family of notables
Bouma Caita	Koyta	
Samba Kouloubali	Kulubali	
Maha Diop	Joop	
Muderi (maraboutic village)		
Deïa Diaye?	Njaay	Village chief's family
Mannayel (maraboutic village)		
Mamadou Caita	Koyta	Maraboutic family
Boubou N'Diaye	Njaay	
Yellingara (maraboutic village)		
Nalla Dialo	Jallo	
KAMMERA:		
Muusala (royal village)		
Mamadou Bathily	Bacili	Royal family of Kammera
Laani (royal village)		
Samba Tarawara	Tarawere	
Daramanne (maraboutic village)		
Mamadou Deramé	Darame	Very important maraboutic family
Tafasiriga (maraboutic village)		
Samba Soumaré	Suumare	Village chief's family
Mamadou Sow	So	
Ladi Tiam	Cam	
Tiéouliu Traovallé	Tarawere	
Bakary Fohana	Fofana	

Although some of the names hint at a low social status (such as Kulubali, a Bambara name indicating a probable slave origin), names usually borne by aristocratic and chiefly families, and client families, are in evidence. Going down the list in more detail, one notes:

1. IN GWEY:

In *Tiyaabu* (the royal village of Gwey), the Bacili are the royal clan of Gajaaga; and the Jawara are a lineage of casted clients of the Bacili.[91] In *Jawara* (a large maraboutic village), the Saaxo are the village chiefs, the Sise and Diaxite are notable families of the village;[92] and the Dukure are a maraboutic family. In *Muderi*, the Njaay are the village chiefly family. In *Mannayel*, the Koyta are a maraboutic family. It should be noted also that the village was founded by the Jallo, who are close clients of the Bacili.[93]

2. IN KAMMERA:

In *Muusala* (one of the royal villages that vied for power in Kammera), the Bacili are the royal clan of Gajaaga. I have no information about the Tarawere in *Laani*, but Laani Tunka is an important royal village and Laani Moodi an important maraboutic village. In *Daramane*, the Darame are the most important client lineage of the royal Bacili in Gajaaga. In *Tafasiriga* (an important maraboutic village, where the Darame have a strong presence), the Suumare are the village chief's family. In addition, it should be noted that the Suumare have a jonghu (blood brotherhood) with the Bacili.[94] I have no information about the Fofana of Tafasiriga, but the Fofana of Golmi (Gwey) were "great slaves" of the Bacili in Gajaaga.[95]

Finally, we have available another list of emigrants, drawn for intelligence purposes by the British administration in the Gambia in 1897 after French opposition to the emigration movement forced recruiters to move their headquarters out of Senegal.[96] Out of 156 migrants, 108 were Soninke and 120 came from the Bakel region.

The 1897 list must be treated with more caution since it gives no information on the villages of origin of the migrants. But some observations may be made. First, many of the names are the same as those in the 1894 list, leaving the impression that the migrants of 1897 were relatives of the migrants of 1894. Second, the 1897 list comprises several new names, some of which may have come from client families of the Bacili and maraboutic families. The

Table 4.5

1897 Congo Migrants: Names
(* indicates name present in 1894 list; see Table 4.4)

Name	Number	Village
Royal Family:		
*Bathily [Bacili]	3	Tiyaabu, Laani Tunka, Muusala
Camara [Kamara] (see below)		
Royal Clients:		
*Camara [Kamara]	6	
Timéra [Timmera]	(see below)	
Touré [Tuure]	(see below)	
*Diawara [Jawara]	1	
Sissoko [Sisoxo]	2	
Marabouts:		
*Dramé [Darame]	1	Bakel, Laani Moodi, Daramanne, Gunjuru
Diakho [Jaaxo =Tanjigora]	2	[Kungani, Jaxali]
Timéra [Timmera]	1	Yaafera
Touré [Tuure]	2	Muderi
*Soumaré [Suumare]	2	Laani Moodi, Tafasiriga
*Keita [Koyta]	4	Mannayel
Chiefs, village notables:		
*Sakho [Saaxo]	3	Jawara
*Cissé [Sise]	4	Jawara
*Diakhité [Jaxite]	1	Jawara
*N'Dié [Njaay]	1	Muderi, Bakel
Total	33	

Jaaxo (also called Tanjigora) are a close second behind the Darame in the order of maraboutic clients of the Bacili (according to tradition, they are even blood relatives of the Bacili). The Timmera and Tuure, together with the Jallo, were the main client "warrior" families of Gajaaga.[97] In addition, there are also clerical families of Timmera and Tuure in the villages of (respectively) Yaafera and Muderi. The Kamara are tunka lemmu in Gidimaxa, but the Kamara of Golmi (Gwey) are "great slaves" of the Bacili; nicknamed *kara-komo* ("death slaves"), they were a kind of elite fighting corps in Gajaaga.[98] Finally, the Sisoxo, originally griots of the Koyta, are clients of the Bacili, especially in Kammera.[99]

It is true that clan names are not an absolute indicator of social class. There are in the Upper Senegal region families of slave status, for example, who bear the royal name of Bacili (this occurs in particular with the practice of "adoption" of slaves by their masters' family, in fact, a form of clientage). However, the suggestion derived from clan names in the list is here reinforced by other evidence. First, as we have seen, only royal and maraboutic villagers migrated in 1894, not mangu villagers. Second, we have seen that there were many laptots who became chiefs or kings from the eighteenth century to the beginning of the twentieth century (see Chapters Two and Three), and one 1853 document even alleged that the Bacili royal family maintained a monopoly on employment in the French commercial sector in the Upper Senegal (see Chapter Two). Finally, we know that working for the French paid comparatively enormous wages, which were used by the migrants to buy slaves and probably to compete in local politics (see Chapters Two and Three). Taken together, the data suggest that many, perhaps most, of the Soninke who worked for the French came not from the lower classes of society, but from the upper classes.

Comparison with Fuutanke Migrants in the 1894 Sample

It is interesting to compare migrants from Gajaaga and Fuuta Tooro in the 1894 sample. I am most thankful to Jean Schmitz for helping me identify the villages of Fuutanke migrants on the yet unpublished ORSTOM anthropological map of the Senegal River Valley (unfortunately, this map does not include Gajaaga) and for providing me with data relative to the possible social origin of the migrants.[100]

The great majority of the sixty-eight Fuutanke migrants came from villages located on or in the vicinity of the Senegal River and its important branch, the Doué, which parallels a very large portion of its course. This was, of course, to be expected since Fuuta Tooro is a river valley. But the majority of the migrants (54 percent), also came from the region near the confluence of the Senegal and the Doué, situated between Kaskas and central Ngenaar, upstream from Kaedi.[101] This is the most populated region of Fuuta Tooro, but it is also an important node in the hydrographic system of the Senegal River. For French navigation, this was a dangerous zone: shoals in Kaskas, Salde (especially), and Oudourou (in Ngenaar, upstream from Kaedi) often forced boats to unload and reload, exposing them to pillage.[102]

It would have been logical for the French to hire additional boat hands in this region, thus initiating a movement of migration. These recruitments would have taken place mostly in fishermen villages, and in villages located near fords (which of course were shoals for French ships). This hypothesis appears confirmed by the relatively frequent presence of the Ceddo and Cuballo social groups in the sample.[103] The Cuballo are the Fuutanke caste of fishermen. The Ceddo, who appear to have been originally slave warriors owned by the state in Fuuta, had among their tasks that of guarding fords on the Senegal River and its affluents, and of collecting dues on river crossings.[104]

In contrast with the Soninke sample, there are not many chiefly names in the Fuutanke migrants' list.[105] There are two possible explanations for this. One is anthropological and was suggested to me by Jean Schmitz.[106] In Fuuta Tooro after the Islamic revolution of Abd-al-Qadir in the eighteenth century, chiefly functions were *elective*. Such a system required a constant presence at home of potential candidates to chiefly posts, thus preventing their migration. Among the Soninke, on the contrary, as among most Mande groups, society was *gerontocratic*. In such a society, where all authority and important functions were reserved to old men, it was logical for young men to migrate, both as a means to escape a stifling atmosphere at home and to build up capital (in particular, in slaves) that would enable them to become respected notables or chiefs upon their return home in their old age.[107] The other explanation is historical. Beginning in the mid nineteenth century, an important migration, which was at least in part motivated by considerations of religion, developed from Fuuta Tooro to the Umarian state in Kaarta (this migration was called the *Fergo Umar*). This migration continued in the late nineteenth century. It particularly affected the Fuutanke Toroodo aristocracy. "Not only were the Fuutanke pre-occupied with this movement, but those who remained behind were inundated with anti-French rhetoric from Umarian recruiters. Thus, many Fuutanke young men may have been deterred from entering the colonial service as laptots."[108]

Conclusion

Two features in the data for this period do not correspond to the usual view of labor migration as caused by deprivation and violence. First, beginning in the 1890s, the Soninke themselves had migrants working for them. Second, urban migration in the Senegambia in the 1890s affected not the poorest regions or social classes, but the more well-off.

The phenomenon of "immigration in a land of emigration," although curious, is, in fact, quite common. Thus in Europe in the 1970s (to take a number of examples among the countries traditionally renowned for their emigration) Spain had immigrants from Morocco and Algeria; Portugal, immigrants from the Cape Verde islands; Greece, immigrants from Egypt, Sudan, Ethiopia, and even Somalia; Yugoslavia, from Czechoslovakia and Poland.[109] Italy has had the fastest growing immigrant population in recent years; it approached a million in 1982, with very diverse origins. A large proportion of its migrant workers are employed in agriculture in the Mezzogiorno and Sicily—the epitome of regions of emigration in European consciousness.[110] In the nineteenth century, Corsican farmers, whose sons were away in mainland France accumulating money as migrants, employed Italian migrant workers on their farms.[111] Likewise, in West Africa, the Baule (who, like the Soninke, migrated in order to buy slaves in the precolonial period)[112] have migrated for the last four or five decades to the cities of the Ivory Coast, while the Mossi of Burkina Faso took their place on the farm.[113]

To be properly understood, this phenomenon of "immigration in a land of emigration" must be seen in a social rather than a geographical context. Out-migration often represents a possibility of social promotion. Young Soninke migrants, like the Baule in the Ivory Coast, migrated in order to accumulate resources (including slaves) to become family heads, in other words, because they did not want to remain powerless subordinates on their fathers' farms. Their place was taken by migrants, either brought by force (slaves) or who came on their own free will (labor migrants—nansoka, surga, etc.). In other words, as certain categories of a population are given a chance to take more desirable jobs and thus to move up in society, their departure from the lower echelons creates a demand that is filled by other groups at the periphery. This is, in fact, the reason behind Soninke migration to France since the jobs initially taken by the Soninke were those rejected by the French.

Regarding the second point, the Congo migrant "samples" show that migrants did not come from the poorest regions and social classes. Of course, they are not representative of Senegambian migration as a whole, although they give a good indication of urban migration: the economic plight of the

Upper Senegal in the late 1890s may have caused an increase in the navetane "commoner" migration to rural areas in the Gambia, Casamance, or Siin-Saluum (which cannot be ascertained at this point given the available data). But even admitting that navetane migration grew, it remains that the Congo migrant lists (whether one considers the Soninke or other ethnic groups), by showing that urban migrants often came from favored regions or social groups in the Senegambia, strongly suggest that poverty alone cannot be a satisfactory explanation of labor migration.

An increasing body of scholarly literature supports this assertion. Recent large-scale studies conducted in the Ivory Coast and Cameroon have shown that regions with a high level of migration to Ivoirien cities are often comparatively rich regions, while comparatively poor regions do not send migrants. In the Ivory Coast, the highest rates of urban migration today are not to be found in the poor and backward northeast (which has the lowest rates), but in the richer northwest and in the Baule homeland. Reflecting on this phenomenon, the author of the study, Yves Marguerat, suggested that migration is connected to historical factors.[114]

If this was the case for the Soninke, it also appears that an important factor behind labor migration was access to channels of information about job opportunities. The Senegambian transportation network—the Senegal and Gambia Rivers and the Dakar-Saint-Louis railway—apparently was a good channel for such information, as well as a good employer itself. A British historian, Arthur Redford, attempted during the 1920s to investigate the formation of the labor force of England during the Industrial Revolution by means of a compilation of regional studies. His conclusions, challenging Marx's theory on the impact of the "enclosures" movement, showed that most of England's urban migrants in the nineteenth century came from relatively well-off rather than impoverished regions. These regions were situated close to English towns, or to the railways that led to them.[115]

But the facts that the Soninke were so well represented in migrations to Senegal's cities and that expanding export crop regions and their royal and maraboutic groups were overrepresented in urban migration cannot be simply explained by the transportation network. Social factors also should be brought into consideration. The decentralized and gerontocratic nature of Soninke society encouraged young aristocrats to seek the most lucrative forms of migration as laptots and as workers for the French commercial sector in the hope of building capital that would later give them an important role in the community. But how did information about migration circulate among Soninke aristocrats? How did they support each other while away in migration? And why were there so many clerics among the migrants?

Recent studies of European migrations have emphasized the notion of "network" as one of the explanations of modern migrations. A network may be considered as the way a determined group in society monopolizes certain job opportunities, or at least certain information about job opportunities. [116] What exactly were these Soninke networks? We know already that family and clan ties and ties of clientage helped spread such migration, as well as monopolize it for aristocrats and their clients. But we will look at this question of networks in greater detail.

FIVE

Soninke Migrant Networks and Social Change

1895–1914

THE PERIOD BETWEEN 1895, date of the return of Bakel to the administration of Senegal, and the First World War is in some respects better documented than previous periods. French domination, which had been for so long a vague suzerainty at best, was finally taking shape. We begin to see, notably in the Bakel archives, more information about the local society. Also more available for this period is oral information—the turn of the century is for many older Soninke only a generation away. Conversely, however (and this is a reflection of the continuous economic decline of the Upper Senegal region), economic information in its quantitative form becomes scarcer and finally vanishes entirely from local documents after the turn of the century.

Oral information as well as archival documents confirm an earlier observation about Soninke migration regarding the importance of clerical and aristocratic families in migration. But by the beginning of the twentieth century, other classes in Soninke society were becoming involved in labor migration. Slave emancipation was an upheaval in Soninke society not because it provoked a general flight of the slaves away from their masters, but because former slaves gained access to opportunities for social promotion such as labor migration.

The Soninke Migrant Networks

Maraboutic Networks: Migration to the Congo in Oral Sources

Why were marabouts so prominent in the Congo migration "samples" of 1894 and 1897? In this section, I will discuss several accounts of the migration, especially from oral sources.

Among the persons suspected of recruiting for the Congo Free State, one Ibrahim Darame (Ibrahim Dramé), described as a notable of Dakar, attracted the attention of the French authorities in 1896. Two leading labor recruiters for the Free State (one was a Soninke) were living at his house at the time. Ibrahim Darame vouched for both in an attempt to have French authorities make an exception to the legal prohibition to emigration.[1] Darame is one of the two most prestigious maraboutic names in Gajaaga, and as we shall see (Chapter Seven), the Darame became quite prominent among the Congo migrants. It is very likely that Ibrahim Darame was acting as a host for Soninke migrants. This would explain in part the importance of maraboutic migrants in the 1894 and 1897 samples.

Villagers from the important maraboutic village of Kungani in Gwey tell an interesting story about the origin of the migration. According to them, the initiator of the migration was Ba Bintu Tanjigora, or Jaaxo (the two names can be used interchangeably), from Kungani, who first went to the Congo as a tirailleur (soldier). Ba Bintu Tanjigora came back from his journey with a large sum in gold. With such money in hand, he was greeted in Kungani with enthusiasm. In the words of one informant, "only six months [of work] were now sufficient to become rich." At the time, there was a famous religious teacher in the village whose school was attended by students coming from villages from the Gambia to what is today Mali. After seeing villagers who had come back from the Congo, and after being encouraged by the people of the village, the young talibe (advanced students in the school) decided to follow their example, with an eye toward earning enough for their customary graduation gift to their teacher, which had to be equal to the minimum value of one slave. Later, when the young talibe returned to their respective villages, they spread the good news there, and their example incited more people to go. Migration then spread to the entire Soninke homeland.[2]

When the Congo migration began, the most important religious teacher in Kungani was Fode Jomo Tanjigora (Fodé Diamou Tandjigora), or Fode

Amara Jaaxo, called more simply Seexu Jomo (Cheikh Diamou). A member of one of the two most important clerical clans in Gajaaga (the Tanjigora or Jaaxo—the other great Gajaaga clerical clan is the Darame), Seexu Jomo had been one of the closest companions of the Soninke Islamic reformer Mamadu Lamin Darame and could be considered his religious heir in the Upper Senegal region. At the beginning of the twentieth century, most of the religious teachers in Gajaaga had studied under Seexu Jomo, and his influence was noticeable as far east as the region of Kenyareme, in the northwestern part of the cercle of Nioro, and the city of Nioro itself.[3]

Islamic schools were active networks of communication because of the constant circulation of talibe between the various schools and because former students, in turn, established schools and retained ties with each other and their former master. Islamic schools were also important economic units. As we saw earlier, students owed a debt of manual labor on their teacher's farms—thus enabling members of maraboutic families to engage in full-time commercial activities. Religious schools were, so to speak, "pools of labor tied to a commercial network." The role of Islamic networks in the emergence of a modern "capitalistic" society in West Africa is well known (e.g., the Mouride brotherhood in Senegal). A recent study of industrial relations in Kano, the economic capital of Hausaland, has highlighted the role of Islamic school networks in the industrial labor market of that city.[4] The story from Kungani was not unique.

When I collected the Kungani tradition, I was told that Ba Bintu first went to work in the *Belgian* Congo.[5] But this was apparently not the case. Here is how the story was told by Al-Haj Mamadu Jaaxo (Al-Haj Majaxo n Ba Jaxo) to Adrian Adams:

> My own father began the trade of Congo-Kinshasa. It was in 1911. He had fought in the French Congo. He had been in Cameroon; he even settled as *almami [imam]* there, but they expelled all the *almami*. He had gone to Gabon; he went to take Brazza's country; he went to take the country of Bangui, Central Africa. Then he went to take the country of Fort-Lamy, Chad. Their general was named Brazza. My father himself told me all this. He went there as a soldier; that's how he was in the French Congo for the first time.
>
> My father went to take cloth in Lagos. He went with it to Congo-Kinshasa. After this first stay in the Belgian Congo, he came back with a little money; at that time [money] was [in] coins, there were no money bills. When he arrived in Kayes, he bought two horses. He bought fifteen head of cattle. He bought seven donkeys; he loaded three of these donkeys with

cola nuts, and the four others with cloth. When he arrived here, he gave to each household head a shirt and a pair of trousers. [. . .] That was how he beat the drum of Congo. After his first return here, notables from the town, Al-Haj Samba Jaaxo, Mpamara Fode, Abdu Koyta left as well.[6]

There are a number of very valuable indications in this account. We can discount the date of 1911: Brazza died in 1905. The reference to the conquest of Chad gives a more secure date: this conquest was consummated at the battle of Kousseri in 1900 with the death of Rabih.[7] In his interview with me in 1982, Al Haj Mamadu Jaaxo indicated that the Soninke began to trade cloth bought in Lagos at a time "when there was yet no [modern?] building in the village of Kinshasa" and when the future city of Kinshasa still centered around the railway station in Kintambo (one of the two African villages which later became Kinshasa, the other being Nshasha, called Kinshasa by Lingala-speakers). This would place the arrival of Ba Bintu in the Congo Free State in the first decade of the twentieth century, shortly after completion of the railway in 1897.[8]

The rest of the account is credible enough. The employment of Soninke laptots in the French Congo was a logical outgrowth of their employment as laptots in Senegal. As French colonial expansion proceeded in Africa, Senegalese laptots were recruited for military and occupation operations throughout the emerging empire. Senegalese laptots were thus used in the first Brazza missions in 1876 to 1878 and 1879 to 1882.[9] Following this, they were regularly employed in the French Congo.[10] They were also employed in the "Benin flotilla" during campaigns in Dahomey in the early 1890s, in the "Niger flotilla" at the time of the conquest of Timbuktu in 1893, and in the Monteil mission in 1893.[11] Laptots from the cercle of Kayes were even recruited to serve in Madagascar in 1895.[12] Senegalese laptots in the French Congo were often hired after their discharge from the French Navy by British (John Holt or Hatton and Cookson), German (Woermann), or French (Conquy) concerns. Already by 1883, these concerns employed about 600 people along the coast of Congo, Gabon, and Cameroon.[13] It was almost certainly to provide a religious ministry to such laptots that Ba Bintu Tanjigora went to Cameroon. It is entirely possible that his stay in the Cameroon put him in contact with laptots or commercial employees of John Holt or Woermann.[14] These contacts, in turn, may have helped him to gain information on the expanding commercial opportunities in Lagos.[15]

It is very interesting to note that Ba Bintu Tanjigora, who came from a very prominent maraboutic family, was employed for a time as a colonial soldier. This is certainly not in keeping with the traditional ideology, according to which marabouts do not fight. But there are comparable examples for that time. According to Paul Marty, a son of Seexu Jomo of Kungani, Hasan Tanjigora, worked as a laptot in Fort-Lamy (now Njamena) in Chad after returning from a twelve-year overland pilgrimage to Mecca. He then left for Benin by way of Cameroon and Nigeria, lived for a year at the home of a countryman who was a railway employee in Porto-Novo in 1911, and was arrested the following year in the Ivory Coast railway town of Dimbokro for "spreading Islamic proselytism and anti-French propaganda."[16] His occupational career, therefore, was similar to that of Ba Bintu Tanjigora, with its alternation of employment as laptot or soldier and self-employment as marabout (and probably also as merchant).

Marty indicates that Hasan Tanjigora had taken an active part in the revolt of Mamadu Lamin Darame. Following the French victory, he had wandered for a time in Soudan, come back shortly in Bakel, and finally left for Mecca in 1899. Could it be that the participation of clerics in fighting during the revolt of Mamadu Lamin Darame had made obsolete the traditional prohibition on their participation in military fighting, making it possible for clerics such as Hasan and Ba Bintu Tanjigora to become colonial soldiers? There are some indications of this. Here is what Jabe So, member of a notable family of the village of Kungani that is also a client family of the Bacili, says of Samba Hawa Tanjigora, a participant in the revolt of Mamadu Lamin Darame (the event took place some time after the revolt):

> There were no wars anymore. But Samba Hawa remained a *handsome knight*. [My emphasis; in the French language used in the interview, "un beau chevalier."] One day, Moors took a hundred cows in Jagili [Gidimaxa village across from Kungani, on the right bank of the Senegal River]. Samba Hawa went alone after the cattle thieves. He killed several, and the others ran away. Three men were guarding the cows. He tied them up and had them lead the cows back. When he arrived in Jagili [he said]: "Here are three slaves, if you want them."[17]

Such prestigious feats of arms were traditionally performed by the Bacili in Gajaaga.[18]

But, in fact, there is at least one written reference to "warrior-clerics" prior to the revolution of Mamadu Lamin Darame. In 1879, during the Baalu affair related in Chapter Three, the Bakel commandant accused the marabout of Baalu of having instigated the affair; whereupon the latter declared to interpreter Alpha Sega that "he was a warrior and he was not afraid of the

Bakel Commandant's threats."[19] In fact, the traditional separation between "warrior" aristocrats who fight and clerics who pray may have been more theoretical than real among the Soninke. It is worth noting that among the Beydan neighbors of the Soninke, there are groups such as the Ahel Sidi Mahmud or the Kunta, which are *both* clerical groups *and* warrior groups.[20] According to Abdoulaye Bathily, in a text that I have been unable to consult, there were "warrior-clerics" among the Soninke.[21] I presume that these were clients of royals.[22] On a more general plane, it is worth noting that occupational specializations in West Africa had a certain flexibility in practice: thus one finds "warrior-griots" among the Bambara, "praise singer-blacksmiths" among many Mande groups, and so forth.

We can now synthesize the above information, and give at least a plausible hypothesis about the development of the migration to the Congo Free State. Migration first developed to the French Congo as an offshoot of the traditional employment of the Soninke as laptots in Senegal. Initially, Soninke laptots in the Congo were probably predominantly from royal families and their clients. Later, either through clientage links or in the aftermath of the revolt of Mamadu Lamin Darame, marabouts also sought employment as laptots.[23] Their motivation for becoming laptots in the French Congo was not only that the occupation paid well, but that they could, after their discharge from the French Navy, minister to Senegalese migrant communities; gain employment with French, British, and German commercial houses in the area between Cameroon and Gabon; and, presumably, also engage in trade on their own. When Belgian recruiters appeared in Dakar in the 1890s, therefore, Soninke would-be migrants, especially the Soninke clerics, were already familiar with migration to the Congo. Migration, however, expanded in the first decade of the twentieth century when some migrants began to import cloth from Lagos (in fact, from Abeokuta, as we shall see later) into the Congos. The news that this trade was very profitable then spread throughout the Soninke homeland through the Koranic school network.

The "Chambres"

Family and Islamic networks were not the only Soninke networks involved in labor migration. The first direct mention of another type of migrant network is dated 1933. That year Governor Descemet of Mauritania asked in a confidential letter to the governor-general of French West Africa for information about a "Chambre du Guidimakha" founded by immigrants from this region in Dakar. He had learned about its creation from the administrator of Gidimaxa, who was concerned about political or labor union influence within this organization. The answer of the administrator of the Dakar *circonscription* was that there existed in the quarter of Niaye Thioker not one but several Chambres du Guidimakha, "thus called because they [each] house about thirty Soninkes coming from the cercle of Guidimakha." They had no political design but reflected the desire of migrants from the same village to live together and to help each other. Thus, while about half of the migrants in the *chambres* were unemployed because of the current economic depression, rent and food was paid for all by those migrants who still had work. The unemployed paid back this support by taking care of household chores.[24]

The chambre is, in fact, a fundamental institution of Soninke migration. It is called *kompe xoore* in Soninke, which can be translated "great room," hence the French translation as "chambre." But *kompe*, in fact, designates any separate inhabitation building ("hut," or *"case"* in French); thus the name could also be translated as "great building" or "great house." The chambre not only provides cheap communal housing and food to the migrants and support for the unemployed, but also an emergency fund for illness and repatriation to the Soninke homeland, a mailbox, and a place to meet, to exchange news from the village, and to hold festivities. They are a focus for the "village abroad" community.[25] We shall have more opportunities to look at this form of organization, whether in Dakar or in migrant communities abroad.[26]

The chambres had, in fact, existed in Dakar for a long time without attracting attention. According to some informants, they first appeared in Dakar at the beginning of the First World War.[27] But archival documents show that they existed before the war, as we shall see. In fact, the way in which the chambres are organized gives us a clue to their origin, which must have dated from the time of precolonial trade migrations. Each kompe xoore (or its equivalent among migrants to France today) is under the authority of the oldest man of the chiefly family who is present in the migration. This "village chief" is assisted by a member of an artisan family, which is the client of the chiefly family. The kompe xoore has a budget, fed by regular contributions of migrant villagers, which serves to rent housing for the migrants, and (in the initial stages of the migration) to feed the migrant community as well. A system of fines keeps order within the community. This succinct description reveals that the chambres were organized on the model of village youth associations.[28]

For the most part, the history of these chambres will have to be documented through oral interviews, but colonial archives give excellent information about at least one of them: the chambre of the royal village of Tiyaabu (the capital of Gwey), then situated on the Rue Thiers, in the old center of Dakar. These documents leave no doubt that already at the beginning of the twentieth century the chambres had come to play a powerful role in the traditional political life of the Soninke homeland.

Earlier, I mentioned the curious fact that the first laptots in the Upper Senegal region were apparently tunka lemmu; and there are other examples of laptots who were tunka lemmu available for the turn of the nineteenth century.[29] I have argued that the reason they entered this form of employment was the high wages offered, which enabled the laptots to make gifts to powerful elders and to compete effectively for political power. There is good evidence that this strategy was highly successful in the nineteenth century. In 1906, the old tunka of Gwey, Amadi Sumbulu, was a former laptot and so was his younger assistant (and relative) Abdul Golea, who was in charge of the collection of taxes.[30]

The office of assistant chief and tax collector was not traditional. The French administration had imposed it in order to increase the efficiency of traditional authority, which was impaired as always by Soninke gerontocracy.[31] The move was strongly resisted by the royal family of Gwey, the Bacili, and there were also protestations by Bacili in Dakar and Saint-Louis.[32] Tunka Amadu Sumbulu died in 1906. His successor, Samba Suuley, had also served as a laptot. He had even participated in the expedition of Lieutenant-Colonel Bonnier, who had conquered Timbuktu in 1893.[33] This constituted a good recommendation for the French; although Samba Suuley was younger and therefore ranked behind other candidates for kingship, the French were determined to impose a tunka who would be both efficient and loyal. According to one report, however, the selection of Samba Suuley as chief of Gwey was due to intrigues led in Dakar by his nephew, Alimana Bacili, a railway worker.[34]

Railway work was for the Soninke a logical outgrowth of their specialization as laptots. Because they were the most important group in the French station locale of the French Navy in Senegal, the Soninke had quickly monopolized all positions available in the Navy workshops.[35] In 1884, for financial reasons, the Senegalese Navy workshops were merged with the railway workshops (this was the time of steam engines on railways as well as on ships).[36] By the 1890s, railwaymen were among the best-paid in Senegal.[37] Alimana Bacili, because of his vastly superior income, probably had a prominent position in the Dakar community of migrants from Tiyaabu, which was almost certainly structured already in a chambre—hence his importance in the eyes of the French.[38]

What gives the events after the nomination of Samba Suuley as chief of Goye Indépendant a particular significance is their resemblance to the events that would lead to the tragic end of chief Ibrahima Jaaman Bacili in 1947.[39] We have seen that an essential element of the power of the precolonial tunkas was the land rights paid to them by tenant farmers. These were the basis of a public income, which was in turn redistributed down the social ladder in a hierarchy of traditional gifts. The French were by principle averse to "feudal rights," and these were even suppressed in 1888 by a Senegalese law.[40] This had not prevented the Soninke from continuing to pay land rights to their tunkas. By the beginning of the twentieth century, the French tolerated "feudal rights" in Senegal, but they refused to give them legal recognition.[41] When Samba Suuley became chief, the notables of Gwey refused to recognize his nomination—and prevented him from collecting land rights.[42] His authority being little more than a sham, Samba Suuley asked to be relieved of his functions and given a minor post in the administration (caretaker, or *planton*).[43]

His nephew, the younger and more aggressive Alimana Bacili, then lobbied the administration to allow Samba Suuley to purchase property rights to the Bacili family lands, but this was denied.[44] In 1910, faced with a virtual standstill in the administration of the Goye Annexé, the French finally decided to suppress the chiefdom altogether.[45] Alimana Bacili, undaunted, had a letter drafted by a lawyer, Paul Sabourault, and sent to Governor-General William Ponty (who was known to be more liberal toward Africans than the governor of Senegal) asking to be recognized as the rightful owner of the lands of the Bacili. The moment was well-chosen as this was a period of renewed African agitation, which a number of liberal Frenchmen such as Sabourault were abetting. The attempt failed, however, when it was shown that according to traditional custom, Alimana was not the heir of Samba Suuley, either in the latter's capacity as tunka or as a private individual.[46]

Was this episode simply an instance of the age-old family rivalries that divided the Bacili, or was it an effort by the younger Dakar migrants to reform the society of Gwey by installing a younger chief? Probably the former. What is clear, however, is that for the first time, a community of migrants had made an impact on traditional society, not by working "from the inside" through a patient build-up of influence among elders with gifts and flatteries, as was done traditionally, but by imposing a candidate from outside through the support of colonial authorities and the greater Senegalese society of which the Soninke of Gwey were now a part. The following events show that the lesson was not lost.

For several years the chiefdom of Goye Annexé was ruled directly from Bakel by the French administrator. The royal village of Tiyaabu, meanwhile, went to Samba Suuley's enemy, Demba Kona, who died two years later and was replaced by Demba Jango, another former laptot.[47] In 1912, the local administrator argued that direct administration was taking an inordinate amount of his time and, in effect, argued for a reinstatement of the chiefdom, which was effected some time later.[48] But a problem soon arose when the new tunka, Demba Jango, died. During the period in which the chiefdom of Gwey had been officially suppressed, the French, either to appease the Bacili family or to use Demba Jango's influence, had named him *assesseur* (auxiliary) to the indigenous tribunal of Gwey.[49] Demba Jango had retained this position when he had later been named tunka. After his death in 1916, the French made the mistake of giving the position to a member of a family that had been traditionally opposed to the Bacili, Fode Saalum Saaxo, the chief of the maraboutic village of Jawara.[50]

The decision brought an immediate protest from the Bacilis in Dakar, in conjunction with tunka Samba Kajata, to the governor-general of French West Africa. The administration had no difficulty in rebutting the pretensions of the Bacili, who weakened their case by arguing that they had always held the position of *cadi* (Muslim judge) in Gwey, but accusations of corruption brought against Fode Saalum Saaxo resulted in a tumultuous trial in Bakel, following which several allies of the Bacili were arrested. Samba Kajata, apparently intending to use these events as proof that the local administrator was biased toward his cause, sent in July 1918 an envoy to the Bacili of Dakar, but Gwey was then under a medical quarantine and the man was arrested on his way by the police.

The Dakar chambre soon heard of the arrest and wrote to none other than the deputy of Senegal, Blaise Diagne, the first Black African in the

French Chamber of Deputies, who was only months away from his appointment to the position of High Commissioner of the Republic for Black Troops, with a rank superior to the governor-general of French West Africa himself. Diagne wrote to the governor of Senegal asking for explanations about the arrest. There are no indications as to the fate of Fode Saalum Saaxo following this incident, but it is quite certain that the power of the tunka Samba Kajata came out enhanced by the incident.[51] The episode showed once more that the chambres had become an integral part of the political life of Gwey, but it also suggests that migrants, rather than being reformers, were people playing traditional politics in a modern context.

The Soninke Migrant Networks: Conclusions

What lessons, then, should we draw from these accounts? There is really nothing unique about Soninke migrant networks. The Islamic school network is also found, as I have noted, among the Hausa of northern Nigeria. Among the Wolof, the *dahira*, the basic structures of the Mouride brotherhood, which organized the colonization of the Senegalese New Territories and Mouride penetration of Senegalese cities in recent years, were at first village Koranic schools. The dahira still today retain symbolic ties with their villages of origin.[52] As for the chambres, except for the name, they are to be found in one form or another in all the West African cities.[53] The only difference is that the Soninke made a particularly efficient use of their networks in expanding and maintaining their migration.

There were probably contacts between the various types of migrant networks among the Soninke. Today, contacts between Soninke merchants and the Dakar chambres are commonplace; in fact, migration to France could not exist without them since merchants make the necessary arrangements for illegal migration. Contacts between the Islamic school–merchant network and the chambres, or earlier equivalents, must have existed among the Soninke from the time of their precolonial trade migration. As we have seen, relations of clientage linked the various participants (clerics, royals, artisans, slaves) in periodic trade expeditions. There is no report of organizations such as the chambres in traditional trade migration, but as we have seen, the chambres were built on the model of traditional village youth associations. In traditional migration, migrants from the same village traveled together and helped each other along the way.[54] They often resided at the home of a fellow villager (usually a marabout) who had settled abroad.[55] These settled migrants were often jatigi or commercial brokers, and some were powerful men in their new societies,[56] all the while continuing to keep in close contact with their homeland.[57] Clearly these various ties continued and developed in the modern migrations of the Soninke.

Beyond these observations, it is the greater degree of involvement of their upper classes in migration that so distinguishes the Soninke. A comparison with the geographical neighbors of the Soninke, the Fuutanke, illustrates the point. As we have seen in the 1894 Congo "samples," few migrants were from chiefly Toroodo families. What could explain this difference between two peoples in so many ways so close in customs and way of life as the Fuutanke and the Soninke? I have already discussed this question in Chapter Four, but I would like to come back to it more systematically. First, Fuuta Tooro was in a less favorable geographical position from the point of view of itinerant trade than the Soninke homeland. Fuuta Tooro is a narrow corridor between desertic areas. Unlike the Soninke homeland, it does not border well-populated regions where it is readily possible to buy desert salt and livestock brought by periodic migrants. Second, the Fuutanke maraboutic class, the Toroodo, achieved political power very early (in the eighteenth century) and thus it did not have to, as among the Soninke, transfer its energies into despised commercial activity. The Toroodo, when they did migrate, did so as preachers and militant warriors of Islam, not as traders.[58] Third, political power, although quite decentralized, was probably stronger among the Fuutanke than among the Soninke. Fourth, because the Fuutanke system of government was elective, it was necessary for potential candidates for office to remain in their villages, thus precluding their migration. Among the Soninke, on the contrary, favorable geographical factors created a long tradition of involvement in trade. The maraboutic class, being excluded from political power, became heavily involved in trade. At the same time, gerontocracy, fragmented authority, and political competition encouraged nonclerical aristocrats to take lucrative positions as agents of and workers in French commerce.

Finally, there was also probably a muted, behind-the-scenes competition between nonclerical aristocrats and marabouts among the Soninke; "warrior" (nonclerical) aristocrats must have looked upon the wealth of marabouts with some apprehension. As explained in Chapter One, such rivalry between clerical and nonclerical aristocracies should not be exaggerated; ties of clientage did link the two. But it was probably also the need to match the wealth of marabouts that led nonclerical aristocrats to participate in traditional trading migrations through clients and their own sons and, later, to monopolize positions as laptots and commercial agents in French commerce.[59] This interpretation would go a long way in explaining the scope and also the "silences" of Soninke modern labor migrations. For while migration among the Soninke often appears to have spread "from the top," it is also "shameful" and thus hidden. As the son of a prominent cleric told me in 1982: "A Darame marabout is not supposed to emigrate, he is supposed to live from the gifts bestowed on him by the Bacili."[60] This is the traditional mentality speaking here. Wealth must be redistributed from the top in a hierarchy of gifts and displays of generosity. To derive his living from a source other than the traditional political structure was for an aristocrat almost to lose face. For this reason, today migrants even of maraboutic family pretend to have left their villages to go on a pilgrimage to Mecca and only accidentally to have settled abroad to engage in trade.[61] At the same time, it was only too obvious, beginning in the nineteenth century, that migration represented the road to power. But if emigration was the road to wealth and power, there was one segment of the population that had to be barred from it: the slaves.

Slave Emancipation and Its Effects on the Soninke

Although the antislavery struggle was one of the main justifications of colonial conquest in Africa, French colonial officials had learned to compromise with traditional African slavery in order to maintain control.[62] During the conquest of the Soudan, however, the military came under virulent criticism on the part of the French abolitionist left for abuses connected with slavery, such as rewarding indigenous soldiers with slaves captured in battle.[63] In 1895, the French Parliament created the French West African federation, partly in order to bring the Soudanese military under control.[64] The Soudan was placed under the authority of the civilian administration of Senegal, whose governor headed the federation. It was in such a context that Bakel was separated from French Soudan and returned to the administration of Senegal on 1 December 1895.

Already by October 1895, it was reported that "captives from the cercle and especially in Bakel are currently in the worst kind of spirits. Many are trying to run away to be liberated in Saint-Louis." In November 1895, the new governor-general of French West Africa, Jean-Baptiste Chaudié, left for Bakel, where he declared to assembled chiefs and elders: "Freedom is good for everyone, every slave has a right to freedom: whether he is good or bad, if he runs away and wants to claim his freedom from a French official, he must be set free."[65]

Chaudié probably did not realize the impact of his speech. Slaves from Goye Indépendant who were visiting in Bakel spread the good news upon their return to their villages.[66] In the villages of Selibaby and Samba Kanji in Gidimaxa, slaves were informed by tirailleurs (African soldiers in the French army), who may have been slaves originally.[67] (The practice of buying men and turning them into soldiers in the French forces was commonplace at the time and was officially justified as a form of manumission; the Bakel region itself was an important source of slave tirailleurs.)[68] By May 1896, slaves came from Kaedi in Senegal, Kayes, Nioro, Kita, and even Sigiri in French Soudan to obtain their freedom in Bakel. Bakel's village de liberté (freed-slave village) was filled beyond capacity, and the Bakel commandant feared that the harvest was threatened in Gidimaxa. Soon, however, orders were sent to deal with the crisis: the escaped slaves' "leaders" were expelled under vagrancy laws and, in fact, turned back to their former masters. Others soon returned to captivity. About a hundred slaves had escaped to Fuuta Tooro or to the Gambia and could not be found. Sixty to a hundred who remained in the village de liberté were given freedom documents by the French.[69] This epilogue, however, only provided a temporary respite for Soninke slave owners.

The end of slavery in French West Africa began in 1905, when slaves started to flee from the Marka towns of the Middle Niger River Valley, the area that probably had the largest concentration of slaves in the entire colonial federation. The exodus spread between 1906 and 1911 to the entire French Soudan.[70] In the cercle of Kayes (Kammera and the eastern half of Gidimaxa) and in Bakel (Gwey), the exodus took place mostly in 1907, tapering off in 1908.[71] In the cercle of Nioro, the movement was delayed by administrative resistance until 1908, and it was largely over by 1910.[72] As among the Marka, the exodus was probably precipitated by food shortages in the years 1904 to 1908, as exceptionally heavy rains brought floods and the parasites that thrive in wet climates.[73]

Anthropologists Pollet and Winter have contended that the slave emancipation of 1905 to 1910 was the root cause of modern labor migration among the Soninke: overnight, the Soninke were deprived of their main source of production of "surplus value" and were forced to migrate to look for work.[74] Pollet and Winter base their view on the case of the Marka, who indeed lost most of their slaves in 1905 to 1910—although the effect of this exodus on their own migration is not discussed by Pollet and Winter.[75] But did emancipation have the same drastic consequences in the Soninke homeland as among the Marka?[76]

An examination of the numerical data casts doubt on the validity of Pollet and Winter's hypothesis. The data suggest that most Soninke slaves actually stayed in the Soninke homeland. In the administrative district of Kayes (122,000 persons in 1916), 878 slaves were liberated from 1906 to 1908.[77] "More than 600" were recorded as coming from Gidimaxa, which had a population of 14,000 at the time.[78] One-third of the population of the cercle being slaves, this would mean that about 12 percent of the slaves of the Gidimaxa of Kayes escaped. In Nioro, the colonial administration estimated the number of slave runaways from the cercle at about 3,000 in 1908.[79] The total population of the cercle was 120,000 in 1898.[80] In the cercle of Nioro, Kenyareme experienced a loss of about a thousand slaves out of a total population of 7,479 in 1908 to 1909 (600 to 650 slaves left and 350 to 450 died of famine, perhaps on the road of escape). Postulating that slaves were 60 percent of the total population in Kenyareme, as they were in neighboring Gidyume and Kingi, this would mean a loss of around 22 percent.[81] In the cercle of Gumbu, 35 percent of the slaves of the cercle either departed (6,279 departures) or left their masters to form freed-slave villages.[82] Colombani, writing after 1910, mentions that between 2,000 and 3,000 slaves left the Soninke villages of the Mauritanian cercle of Gidimaxa, and several hundreds formed freed-slave villages.[83] These would be by far the highest figure for the Soninke homeland since there were only 15,000 Soninke in Mauritanian Gidimaxa after the First World War.[84] I have no information as to the percentage of slaves in this region. Supposing it to be around 50 percent, between 28 and 38 percent of the slaves would have departed or left their masters.[85]

Although high, these figures stand in strong contrast with the available data for the Marka. By May 1906, 20,000 slaves had left from the seven Marka towns[86] situated in the cercle of Bamako, which had in 1910 a total population (including many Bambara and Malinke) of 191,000. (I have no figures for the population of the seven Marka towns alone.) In 1910, following the exodus in Beledugu, Maurice Delafosse described the villages of the Marka as "in ruins."[87] Nothing of the sort was reported for the Soninke region. In fact, a report for Kayes in 1909 mentions that "slave runaways were never very numerous" in the cercle,[88] while a report for Nioro in 1910 noted that "few [slaves] return home" and that "sedentaries appear to adapt without difficulties to the new conditions of their society."[89]

The historiography of emancipation in West Africa has traditionally asserted that slaves who escaped at emancipation were first-generation slaves, whose treatment was the harshest and who hoped to return to their regions of origin. This view finds some support in the sources. The oral testimonies collected by Adrian Adams for Gidimaxa and by Claude Meillassoux for Gumbu indicate that those who fled were especially trade slaves.[90] But it should be remembered that many trade slaves had been taken in captivity too young to remember their place of birth. Even first-generation slaves who still remembered their native land had formed sufficiently strong connections with the land of their captivity to remain there, provided a suitable compromise could be worked out with their former masters. Returning home was a dangerous enterprise, especially in this time of food shortage (many escaped slaves did die of starvation on the road). It meant to uproot children and often a wife who identified with a different ethnic background, who had never seen their father's or husband's homeland, and who may not have spoken its language. Once returned home, an escaped slave had no guarantee of finding land to cultivate. In the great turmoil of the Samorian wars, villages had been destroyed and entire populations had been moved. The village of origin may not have existed any longer, strangers may have occupied its land. For all these reasons, it was safer to stay, provided decent conditions could be obtained. This attitude was summed up very neatly by an old Marka slave acting as a spokesman for other slaves at the time of the Beledugu exodus in 1905:

> We would be only too happy if we could stay in this land, if we could work in peace and be spared the worst humiliations and the bad treatment which the Marka are constantly inflicting on us. Our wives and our children make up the homes which we have created for ourselves here, and in spite of the burning desire which we have of returning to the land of our forefathers, we know that our interest is to stay here, because we realize how difficult it would be to reconstitute our homes in our native villages.[91]

The 1909 report for Kayes made a similar point: "the majority of the individuals who were brought in as trade slaves about twenty years ago have grown roots here and, as they feel comfortable, they only wish to stay here."[92]

Colonial records for the Soninke, in fact, reveal a more complex situation than is ordinarily assumed. The 1909 report for Kayes thus argued that the slaves who escaped were, in fact, *the most well-off* among them: "It is only when [slaves] have accumulated some savings, acquired cattle, that they ask to return in the regions they came from."[93] Pollet and Winter give one example of this kind. Musa Sangare, originally a trade slave, was the head of the slaves of Bundyahala Njaay in Jafunu. He had two wives, his own hut and granary, and a horse, and (as was common practice for head slaves), the slaves of his master worked for him every day from 2:00 to 4:00 P.M. Yet:

> At the time of the liberation of slaves by the French, he had become rich. He left for Yelimane with the other slaves of his master. He also tried to leave with Bundyahala's cows but the administration only allowed him to leave if he did not take anything away from his master, not even the horse that he received from him.[94]

A 1908 report for the cercle of Kayes noted just as curiously that slaves who came to the French to ask for their liberation "*came back to their master's villages after obtaining satisfaction.*"[95] A case with similar implications is recorded in the Bakel *journal de poste* (administrative diary) in the year following the emancipation mix-up of 1896. Samba Njaay lodged a complaint against his *captifs de case* who refused to work for him. The Bakel commandant noted in amazement that Samba Njaay's slaves refused to be liberated as a settlement.[96] There can be only one explanation for these instances—and for the apparently low relative number of slave runaways: the majority of Soninke slaves was not interested in running away, but wanted to change the terms of their relationship with their master. How successful were they?

The Condition of Former Slaves after Emancipation

Contemporary French reports unfortunately have little to say about the consequences of emancipation for the slaves who stayed in the Soninke homeland. The 1910 general political report for the cercle of Nioro mentions sharecropping *(métayage)* as a basis for new relations between former slaves and their masters.[97] This, however, is doubtful since sharecropping was not part of the Western Sudanic custom (including among the Soninke). The mention probably contained a strong element of "wishful thinking" as the French administration at the time was unsuccessfully trying to replace slavery with sharecropping.[98] The report, however, may have referred to the traditional form of "serfdom" with payment of a rent in kind (see Chapter One), which may have become more frequent as a result of emancipation. Another early report is that of Colombani, writing about Gidimaxa sometimes after 1910, who indicated that Bambara "captives" (slaves) were "the cultivators of the Sarakolle [Soninke]." Custom required them to work six days a week for their owner, but "a great number have emancipated themselves, and they work only when they feel like doing so." Colombani also mentioned that "several hundred" former slaves had severed all relations with their masters and created villages in "Toubab N'Kane, Samba Kandji, and Betseida."[99]

The first detailed report about the condition of former slaves after emancipation is J.-H. Saint-Père's account of Gidimaxa. It was written around 1923, but it may reflect many elements of the situation before the First World War. According to Saint-Père, former slaves were now "servants." They worked a number of days for their masters and were remunerated with a share of the crop proportionate to the number of days of work on their master's farm. "A few intelligent and practical masters," however, lent land to their "servants" in exchange for an annual fee, which varied with the importance of the land that was rented. The male and female children of such "servants" were "domestics." They were "entrusted" to their parents' masters, who raised them along with their children, and they helped them with cultivation and household work.[100]

Saint-Père's remarks are interesting because they suggest the replacement of the older forms of slavery by an hybridization of Soninke "serfdom" and traditional hired labor contracts (nansoka). On the one hand, the prestations (communal obligations) in labor, the entrusting of children to slave masters, recall traditional forms of "serfdom." Likewise, the payment of an annual due by "servants" of "intelligent and practical masters" may have been a form of the old "serfdom" with a fixed rent in kind, although it more probably was a jakka (in principle, one-tenth of the crop), a rental payment for land obtained from the master. But the remuneration of "servants" who worked for their masters with a share of the crop strongly recalls the form of nansoka contracts. As we have seen, nansoka laborers are provided seed and are housed and fed by their employer, who also provides grain on loan to their family. In exchange, the nansoka work for their employer five mornings a week (see Chapter Four).

Gaston Boyer, writing about Kingi Jawara in the late 1940s, mentions explicitly that slaves obtained land through nansoka contracts. Landowners in this region provided their workers (who also included clients and "strangers") with a plot of land and seed. They also fed the workers. The workers cultivated the plot in two parts: three-fifths were cultivated for the master, two-fifths for themselves. Another form of provision of land mentioned by Boyer was the jakka, in which case the landowner did not give seed or food.[101]

In their examination of modern remnants of slavery in Jafunu, written in the 1960s, Pollet and Winter also described arrangements similar to nansoka for slaves who continued to reside in the masters' compounds and to work for them. Until they married, these slaves worked for their masters every morning of the week. After they married, especially after they had children, they worked for their master only *Saturday and Sunday* morning and also gave a small part of their crop.[102] These arrangements are similar to a form of the nansoka contract used in the rental of land; the most common way to rent land in Jafunu in the 1960s was to work two mornings a week, generally *Saturday and Sunday*, for the owner ("master of the land") or tenant *(te-xoore)* of the rented land. Pollet and Winter also quote an informant who had obtained land in this fashion, but in exchange for *five* mornings a week of work. Finally, land in Jafunu could also be rented through the payment of a jakka, although this was a less common occurence.[103]

What the comparison of the data from Saint-Père, Boyer, and Pollet and Winter suggests is that the crucial problem for slaves after emancipation was that they were landless. In order to obtain land to cultivate, former slaves had to accept labor "contracts" that were reminiscent of traditional "serfdom." The importance of the question of land ownership is confirmed by more recent data (1970s and 1980s) collected by Jean-Yves Weigel in Hayre-Damga and Gwey. In his study, Weigel found that *78 percent of former slaves obtained land from the family of their former owners.* Of these, slightly less than half (about 48 percent) still worked for their masters one to several mornings a week, while a little more than half (52 percent) paid only a rental payment for the land, either a jakka or a money payment, sometimes one-third of the crop on some more productive land.[104] The arrangements recorded by Weigel, therefore, reproduce in an eroded form the arrangements noted by Saint-Père, Boyer, and Pollet and Winter.

What, then, was changed in the slaves' condition? Saint-Père mentions that slaves could now go where they pleased and marry as they wished, that their children belonged to them, and that they inherited belongings and "obtained land." The last three assertions are doubtful. We have seen above what situation prevailed as to the ownership and use of land. As to children belonging to their parents, Saint-Père contradicted himself when he reported on the practice of placing children as "domestics" with former masters. Boyer mentions that customs regarding marriage and ownership of the children of slaves had not changed in Kingi Jawara in the 1940s.[105] According to Chief Ibrahima Jaman Bacili of Gwey, who wrote in the 1940s, former slaves then still worked for their masters "very often under constraint and without compensation." They were still part of dowries and inheritances. When a slave died, his master locked his granary and took possession of his belongings, giving back a portion to the widow if she was his slave also. Chief Bacili proposed that the administration draw binding contracts regulating the relationship between masters and slaves and give land to slaves.[106] This suggests that there had been almost no change at all in the condition of slaves since emancipation. But Chief Bacili's testimony was probably based mostly on the situation in his royal village of Tiyaabu. Because Tiyaabu was the seat of a regional chief and a royal family whose authority was recognized by the French (in Goye Inférieur), archaic forms of slavery probably persisted there longer than elsewhere, and the case described by Chief Bacili was perhaps exceptional, although one of my informants did mention that slaves continued to be deprived of inheritance in recent times.[107] However, both Pollet and Winter and Weigel mention that slave children continue today to work for their parents' masters. They differ, however, on who is the beneficiary of the children's work. For Weigel, children work for their *mother's* owner, thus following the traditional custom that entitled the owner of a female slave to the property of her offspring. Weigel, however, mentions at least one case of a slave who worked for his *father's* owner as well.[108] For Pollet and Winter, the children of slaves work for their *father's* owner.[109] Can we rationalize this discrepancy? In the cases mentioned by Weigel, slave parents followed tradition and sent their children to work for their "rightful owner" (owner of the mother), probably in order not to antagonize the class of former masters and thus to maintain the good relations necessary to obtain land from them. In the cases mentioned by Pollet and Winter, slave children probably worked for their father's owner in order to keep access to the lands farmed by their father. This suggests a shift from slavery to relationships of clientage.

Forms of clientage indeed did emerge with the end of slavery. In a number of cases, slaves were "adopted" by their former owners. By giving his name to a former slave, the master makes him a kind of junior member of the family. Slaves emancipated in this fashion are nevertheless not allowed to marry nonslaves.[110] Apart from such privileged relations, former slaves who have ceased to work for their former owners today still perform services for them, especially during family ceremonies (as did the komo xooro in the period before emancipation).[111] As mentioned, older slaves receive gifts from their former masters. Masters help slaves in need. They sometimes arrange the marriage of their former slaves, and slaves ask for their authorization to marry.[112]

Going back to the texts by Saint-Père and Boyer, one notes the importance of clientage in the very ambiguity of some of the descriptions. In these texts, it is not entirely clear if slaves continued to work for their former masters by virtue of contractual relationships by which their labor was actually *hired*, or whether they worked for them as a matter of traditional obligation.[113] The equivocation may, of course, be the result of the variety of situations. In some cases, slaves (in particular, second-generation "serfs") may have maintained the old forms of dependence. In others, on the contrary, they may have worked out a contractual relationship. In others still, some hybrid forms may have emerged. But the ambiguity may also come from Saint-Père and Boyer's informants. On the one hand, masters could not openly say that slavery persisted because it was officially dead. They therefore emphasized relations of clientage, referring to former slaves as their "children." For them, if slaves continued to work for them, it was due to the goodness of the traditional patriarchal system. Slaves, on the other hand, believed that they worked for their masters as hired laborers, and to a large degree, they may have been right. But they could not say this too openly: most of the good land that the slaves farmed was obtained from the families of their former owners. It was a matter of good politics, therefore, to maintain some of the outward forms of the old slave relationship. It was also a good idea to send children to work for the masters. Slave parents were rewarded to a degree for their compliance: masters made gifts (in particular, of clothing) to slave elders.[114]

To sum up, the situation probably varied in various villages and regions, but a certain pattern emerges. The worst form of chattel slavery (actual slavery of trade slaves) disappeared. (Some slaves continued to reside with their masters, but their relation with them was that of "serfs" owing a rent in labor.)[115] Although slaves still could not marry the free, they were to a degree and reluctantly admitted within the community, as evidenced by customs such as circumcision, which was now performed on slave children by the village smith, as was the case with free children, rather than by the slave master, as in the time of slavery.[116] Because slaves were landless, however, a hybrid form of exploitation somewhere in between hired labor and old forms of "serfdom" emerged, by which slaves obtained land from their former owners.

Clientage both facilitated and cemented the establishment of the new relationship between master and slave. This was to be expected, since even before emancipation the master-slave relationship already involved a considerable element of clientage. Before emancipation, slaves could hope, if they proved to be good clients, to move up from a trade slave to a "serf," and over several generations, their descendants could even attain to the freedom of the komo xooro.[117] Likewise, after emancipation, slaves who were good clients could gain access to good riverbank land; in time, they could hope to lower the number of days of labor that served as rental payment for that land. And finally, they could hope to gain access to the land through the simple payment of a jakka—something that placed them in a condition akin to that of free men of the lowest category (miskino strangers who could not become "masters of the land").

The importance of clientage explains the difference in the responses to emancipation among the Soninke and the Marka. Among the Marka, relations between masters and slaves were distant and characterized by naked exploitation. Marka slaves lived in slave villages away from the towns where their owners resided. They were visited by their masters only every two months or even less. There existed no significant difference between the condition of a trade slave and that of a woroso of the second, third, or later generation. All generations worked six or even seven days a week for their masters, whether they were first-generation slaves or woroso. Marka slave masters did not even respect their basic customary obligation to feed the slaves. When the end of slavery came, slaves attempted to work out a compromise with their masters, which would have allowed them to stay on the land and to live a reasonably decent life. Because Marka masters were absentee owners, however, they did not understand the strength of such feelings. They tried to use force and only succeeded in making things worse by kidnapping the slaves' wives and children. They told their slaves lies that were not credible, telling them, for example, that the French were about to depart.[118] They refused the honorable compromises suggested by the French. The result of all this was that dialogue became impossible, and slaves decided to move out.[119] The situation was very different among the Soninke.

The most important effect of slave liberation in the Soninke homeland, therefore, was not the kind of economic and social breakdown indicated by Pollet and Winter. Soninke slave masters retained their social dominance and much of their economic power. But Soninke slaves also gained a measure of independence and access to opportunities previously closed to many of them: a limited access to the land *and labor migration*.

A Consequence of Emancipation: Former Slaves Become Migrants

French colonial authorities strongly believed that slave emancipation had an impact on migration. The yearly report for French West Africa in 1910 reported that slaves from the western part of the Soudan departed and later *returned* (my emphasis) from the "Lower Senegal" (i.e., coastal Senegal, where peanuts were grown as a cash crop) "in numerous groups and brought back without spending any part of it, a sum of between 200 and 500 francs together with a few pieces of clothing and jewelry." The same report also noted:

> In 1910–11, we saw the former slaves of the Sahel go down in groups in Senegal, where they covered the area bordering the new railway line between Thiès and Kayes with cultivated fields; once the growing season was over, they *regained their villages* [my emphasis again], announcing their intent to return more numerous next year.[120]

These reports, it should be emphasized, do not talk about a *permanent* migration of slaves away from the regions where they had once been held in captivity, *but their entry into periodic (return or labor) migration*.

The report quoted above mentions that slave navetanes came from the western part of the French Soudan, which includes the Soninke regions in the cercles of Kayes and Nioro, or from the "Sahel," which here referred to the cercles of Nioro and Gumbu, a region of strong Soninke settlement. Reports for Nioro indicate a very rapid expansion of navetanat beginning in 1911. That year, telegraphic money orders of between 15,000 and 30,000 francs were sent home by navetanes working in the regions of Kaolack and Fatick. In 1912, money orders were sent to the cercle of Nioro for a value of 90,000 francs by navetanes working in Siin-Saalum, Bawol, and Nyani-Wuli and by laborers building the Thiès-Kayes railway line. The navetanes were estimated to be about 2,000, coming especially from the northern regions of Kingi Jawara and Kenyareme (both are Soninke regions). This estimate of 2,000 navetanes for 1912 is plausible. It would mean that navetanes in that year sent an average of 45 francs by money order. The 1910 report for French West Africa mentioned that navetanes from the western part of French Soudan brought back with them between 200 and 500 francs from their seasonal migration.[121] These were, of course, very large sums of money for the time. In 1913, the navetanes from Bawol, Siin-Saalum, Casamance, and Nyani-Wuli and the laborers building the Thiès-Kayes railway line increased the amount in money orders sent to the cercle to 120,000 francs.[122]

The years 1910 to 1912 were years of rapid expansion of peanut cultivation in Senegal due to the building of the Thiès-Kayes railway line, begun in 1907.[123] We have seen that the 1911 and 1912 reports for Nioro reported that some migrants from the cercle were working on railway premises. It is tempting to believe that migrants from Nioro gained knowledge of the new opportunities created in peanut cultivation in Senegal after being recruited to work on the railway. But, in fact, the reverse happened. The mention of migrants in Casamance for 1913 is an obvious indication that migrants from Nioro had been coming to Senegal *before* the building of the Thiès-Kayes railway.[124] The mention of migrants working in Fatick and Kaolack in the annual report for Nioro in 1911 is another such indication. In 1911, the railway spur joining Kaolack to the Thiès-Kayes line had not yet been completed (it was opened in January 1912).[125] Fatick, a port and trading post situated on a branch of the Saalum estuary, was an important center of peanut export *before* the building of the railway, exporting between 15,000 and 20,000 tons of peanuts in 1906, much of which came from Bawol.[126] The region of southern Siin where Fatick is located was originally a sparsely populated region, which was settled by migrants with the encouragement of the Buur Siin (king of Siin) Kumba Ndoffen Juuf in the years 1900 to 1910.[127] Soninke navetanes had been present in Siin-Saalum as early as the second half of the nineteenth century; a Soninke village thus adjoined the town of Nianing, an important early trading post of the peanut trade on the Petite Côte, in 1876.[128] This early presence makes perfect sense if we consider that the coast of southern Siin and the estuary of the Saalum are really geographical extensions of the Gambia (being located very close to it, with a similar climate and environment), where Soninke navetane migration had begun.[129]

It is thus plausible to argue that Soninke migrants had been present in the Siin-Saalum area before the end of slavery; later, after 1910, the building of the railway expanded the demand for navetanes in the area at a most opportune moment to provide employment for newly emancipated Soninke slaves. We have seen that many among the early Soninke migrants to the Gambia and Casamance were slaves or rather semi-emancipated "serfs" (see Chapters Two and Three). The developments of the 1910s, therefore, were a logical outgrowth of the past history of Soninke navetanat.[130]

In conclusion, emancipation transformed slaves into tenants who rented land from their former owners. Although this situation was often reminiscent of old forms of "serfdom," it gave former slaves a certain amount of freedom, allowing them to engage in periodic migration. This was due to two reasons. First, former masters continued to have power over their former slaves only because they owned the land that the slaves farmed, but they had no power over the *persons* of the slaves since slavery had lost all legal status. They could intimidate slave parents into preventing their sons from leaving the village, but they could not use violence to force a slave to stay home. Second, all slaves were now in a position reminiscent of "serfs" in the pre-emancipation era, and "serfs" in the nineteenth century apparently had the customary right to engage in periodic migration, provided that they shared their earnings with their masters. In fact, navetanes of slave status continued to give part of their earnings to their "owners" after emancipation (indeed, they were still doing so in Jafunu in the 1960s, when Pollet and Winter conducted their study).[131]

This is not to say that former masters did not put up a resistance to the emigration of their former slaves. Such resistance is exceedingly difficult to document, although it is often mentioned by informants.[132] In Gidimaxa, it was apparently not until 1960, date of the independence of Mauritania, that slaves were allowed to migrate. This happened after considerable disturbances, which saw pitched battles between "slaves" and "free men," although slavery had supposedly disappeared from the area since 1905.[133] For specific reasons, the case of Gidimaxa appears extreme, but archival and other data suggest that for most Soninke slaves true emancipation did not occur in the years 1905 to 1910, but immediately after the First World War.

The evidence on slave emancipation also suggests that *slave emancipation did not create labor migration in regions where it did not exist previously.* This was notably the case in Gumbu where labor migration began only in 1916, in spite of the very high percentages of slave runaways experienced by this region in 1908. The region of Gumbu did not traditionally send migrants to the Gambia, although it was eventually introduced to navetane migration through its contacts with the Upper Senegal Soninke.[134] The case of Gumbu suggests that a "push" factor *alone* (here, slave emancipation) is insufficient to create migration in the absence of a suitable migration network that provides information about job opportunities and support to the migrants.

Second Consequence of Emancipation: Youth Migration

Pollet and Winter were generally mistaken, therefore, when they believed that slave emancipation impoverished slave owners and forced them to migrate. But they were probably right when they hypothesized that emancipation shook the foundations of the traditional family, causing the migration of dependent males in the extended families, that is, junior brothers and young men. As shown by Pollet and Winter, the Soninke extended family was an economic unit, based on a hierarchy of labor obligations. What gave such units, which were often very large, their cohesion, was the fact that only family elders had control over the family slaves. With the transformation of slaves into tenants, the authority of elders was weakened (but certainly not destroyed).[135] It is characteristic to note that complaints by elders about the migration of the young followed each stage of slave emancipation among the Soninke. Thus, such complaints are recorded in local archives in 1897 for Bakel, following the emancipation blunder of 1895 to 1896; in 1911 in Nioro, following the emancipation of 1908; and finally, in almost all the Soninke homeland, following the First World War.[136]

Conclusion

Recent studies have explained African labor migration in terms of "relative deprivation." Some have pointed to regional poverty in Africa, sometimes accusing the colonial powers of having organized this poverty in order to create "labor reservoirs." Studies of rural poverty may throw more light on the true living conditions within the interior of West Africa than they do on the history of labor migration. The numerical importance of marabouts and tunka lemmu in migration and the clear impact of conflicts between young and old, between slave and free, all point to the importance of historical and social factors in migration.

One of the most striking peculiarities of Soninke labor migration is the downward social spread of migration I have noted in this chapter, which I shall document again in following chapters. Although traditional trade migration was practiced by all free men among the Soninke, the first proper labor migrants (i.e., wage laborers) were the laptots, who were members of the political aristocracy. Later marabouts appeared among laptots and urban migrants. In this chapter, we have likewise seen navetanat spreading from free commoners and favored "serfs" to the slaves. Later we shall see urban migration spreading from the political and religious aristocracy to the commoners and the slaves.

The peculiar position of clerics in traditional Soninke society and the fragmentation of its precolonial political system appear to explain this peculiarity of Soninke labor migration. Barred from political power, the marabouts were the first to migrate, as traders rather than wage laborers. Nonclerical aristocrats later competed with each other, and perhaps also with a growing maraboutic influence, by gaining access to the wealth released by the Europeans, tribute as well as wage labor. Later, wage labor spread to the maraboutic group, and then to the whole of Soninke society. The Soninke aristocracy, therefore, provided a role model for accession to wealth for all the Soninke, a model that, in turn, may well explain the boldness of contemporary migrations and very high rates of migration observed among this ethnic group.

Slave emancipation among the Soninke, therefore, appears to be but one episode of a downward spread of labor migration. In the nineteenth century, clerics had provoked in the Gambia the entry into navetanat of young commoners and some emancipated slaves. But the end of slavery among the

Soninke resulted in the entry of Soninke slaves into the migration movement. (It was ironic that the Soninke, who had been the most important slave owners and slave traders in West Africa, initiated a current of labor migration that ultimately spread to their own slaves.) As A. G. Hopkins wrote: the "improvement of geographical mobility" associated with the rise of a free (wage) labor force was an important stage in the "as yet unwritten labor history of Africa."[137] But emancipation brought less an exodus of slaves among the Soninke than their entry into already existing currents of labor migration.

The connection between labor migration and social change, or the transformation of African societies on a more liberal model under the impact of the modern economy, was seen by most of the scholarly specialists of labor migrations. Thus I. Schapera, in his study of Bechuanaland (now Botswana) in 1947, noted that individual or regional poverty seemed to have little impact on labor migration (which had also begun before the introduction of colonial taxation), but that the desire for independence of young men and former slaves appeared to be the cause of migration. J. Clyde Mitchell likewise described African labor migration as an element in the wider process of social change, influencing as well as influenced by this process.[138] More recently, a several-year-long study led by Gilles Sautter and commissioned by the government of Burkina Faso (formerly Upper Volta) concluded that Mossi migration, historically the most important West African labor migration, was primarily caused by the desire of young Mossi to become independent from their elders.[139]

Slave emancipation weakened patriarchal authority. From here on, the elders had a more difficult time in keeping their young at home and preventing them from migrating. They increasingly complained about this situation, and the French administration, for a number of reasons, was more and more convinced that it should listen to these complaints.

SIX

Myths and Realities of Colonial Migration

1914–1930

ALTHOUGH SONINKE LABOR migration grew rapidly after the First World War, the trend had begun before the war. What was new about the interwar period, however, was the widespread disapproval of labor migration by French colonial officials. Colonial administrators before the war had been favorable to labor migration: governors such as Clozel or Ponty played an important role in slave emancipation in West Africa, and they logically regarded labor mobility as a desirable aim.[1] By contrast, latter-day colonial writers such as Maurice Delafosse (who had been a close collaborator of Clozel) were generally opposed to labor migration.

This opposition arose from genuine concerns, but it also had ideological causes. In the first part of this chapter, I will examine the complaints of administrators, and the evidence supporting these complaints, as well as the general ideological climate among colonial administrators at the time. In the second part of the chapter, I will return to the evidence on labor migration for the 1920s, discussing the most important factors behind its expansion during this period.

French Colonial Administrators and Migration in the 1920s

First Criticisms of Migration before the First World War

There were a few occasional criticisms of migration before the First World War. The 1911 Annual Report for Nioro contains a fairly elaborate discussion of the good and bad consequences of temporary migration. Reflecting on bad crops in 1910 and 1911, the administrator expressed the concern that a level of personal taxation that was permissible in normal years might become too burdensome in bad years and might force farmers to sell their livestock capital in order to pay the tax. The administrator indicated that he had kept this point in mind when he had drawn up the tax rolls, hinting that he purposely underestimated the taxpaying population. As a result, tax was collected easily even this year. The report then moved on to temporary migration. Was it a good or a bad thing? Elders said that they were short of manpower during the growing season. Migration, however, paid taxes and bought grain during bad years. Overall, the administrator thought that temporary migration was a good thing; it brought money into the region, and it put migrants in contact with regions where French colonization was most active: "The stories that [migrants] bring back with them can only be favorable to our influence."[2] In spite of this optimistic conclusion, the report betrayed an ambiguity vis-à-vis migration: the administrator wondered if migration was not due to high taxes, and he worried about its effect on agricultural production.

Reports for the following years contain an echo of the discussion of 1911. The 1912 report reiterated concerns about the loss of manpower created by migration. However, the reports for 1913 and 1914, a tragic year of famine in West Africa, noted that migration made it possible to buy grain and thus to alleviate food shortages. By May 1914, however, grain reserves were exhausted except in Kaarta, Sanga (a Xaasonke region north of Jomboxo), and the Résidence of Yelimane (Jafunu, Gidyume, and Tiringa) and caravans no longer arrived with grain from Beledugu because grain was apparently lacking there, too. Villages in the northern parts of the cercle were deserted by their inhabitants, except for old people and invalids, and young men had gone in greater numbers than usual to Senegal. The report worried that a number of young men might not come back from Senegal in time for the cultivation of the next crop, meaning that the food deficit might persist. This fear proved unfounded; the agricultural situation returned to normal in following years, although there were problems with heavy rains in September 1914 and with grasshoppers in 1916.[3]

In spite of the alarming reports in 1914, the cercle of Nioro (and apparently other Soninke cercles as well) appears to have done relatively better than other cercles of the Western Sudan during the famine. In Bandiagara, for example, the French administrator estimated that the cercle lost *one-third* of its population as a result of the famine of 1913 to 1914.[4] Was the relatively better situation in Nioro due to the money brought back by migration (enabling the population to buy grain), as the French administrator alleged? This is possible, but the drought appears to have been less severe in the Soninke homeland than in many other parts of West Africa. The famine of 1913 to 1914, however, had an important impact on the thinking of French administrators in the Sudanic zones of French West Africa, as we shall see.

The Revival of Forced Labor in French West Africa after the First World War[5]

The fact that French colonial authorities frequently conscripted rural Africans to build roads, railways, or simply to work on private European plantations in West Africa is well-established.[6] But it would be wrong to believe that forced labor had the same impact throughout the period of French domination. Briefly summarized, the history of colonial coercion in French West Africa can be divided into three periods. Between 1881 and 1901, the military administration used forced labor in the French Soudan to build the Kayes-Bafoulabé railway or to carry supplies to French troops; yet these recruitments were not part of a planned economic design. After 1901, the civilian administration that took charge was generally opposed to coercion and took effective measures against it, although there were occasional instances of forced labor.[7]

In sharp contrast with the prewar period, the 1920s saw a spectacular revival of forced labor in French West Africa. This was the time of very large recruitments for building railways in the French Soudan and Ivory Coast, for the Office du Niger's grandiose cotton-growing project in French Soudan, and for European plantations in the Ivory Coast. Even the colony of Senegal, which traditionally had a more benevolent administration as a result of its representative institutions, was affected by colonial coercion.[8] It was only in 1930, with the coming into office of Governor-General Jules Brévié, that things began to change in French West Africa, but even the Popular Front in 1936 could not dispose of all the remnants of forced labor.

This is not the place to discuss the reasons for this widespread revival of forced labor in French West Africa in the 1920s.[9] It will be sufficient to indicate that supporters of forced labor in the colonial administration belonged to a group of "technocrats" that emerged at the beginning of the twentieth century. The "technocrats," men such as Gabriel Angoulvant (who became governor-general of French West Africa in 1918), opposed earlier colonial policies based on classical laissez-faire liberalism. They favored a voluntarist policy of large-scale government development projects undertaken through a mobilization of African labor, in particular through forced labor,[10] and the development of coastal cash-crop producing regions through migration, both definitive and seasonal.[11] In opposition to the "technocrats," "colonial humanists" such as the famous administrator-scholar Maurice Delafosse advocated small-scale projects initiated at the local level by the administration in cooperation with traditional African authorities, whom "colonial humanists" such as Delafosse were especially interested in preserving. Delafosse became the main adviser of Governor-General Joost Van Vollenhoven during his short term of office in 1917, whom he inspired with a "big program of small projects," but the replacement of Van Vollenhoven by Angoulvant in 1918 placed power into the hands of the "technocrats," who continued to have a strong influence on colonial policies until the 1930s. This larger context of widespread revival of forced labor and opposition to "colonial humanist" officials must be kept in mind while we analyze the postwar situation of the Soninke homeland.

Forced Labor in French Soudan after the First World War

The "Sarraut Plan" of development, which was partially implemented in French colonies after the war, proposed to carry out in the French Soudan a grandiose scheme of irrigated cultivation of cotton in the Niger's "interior delta," that is, Macina, roughly between Jenne and Timbuktu. The export of the cotton was to be made possible by the completion of the Thiès-Niger railway. The planned development was for the most part outside the Soninke homeland, but developers were aware of the potential of the Senegal River Valley, and the Devès and Chaumet trading company operated a concession farm near the village of Jaxandappe in Kammera, not very far from Kayes, where it established a cotton, sisal, and peanut plantation.[12]

The forced labor recruitments that took place after the First World War were important. A March 1921 report for Kayes mentions desertions of laborers on the construction sites of the Thiès-Kayes railway, but gives no numerical estimates.[13] In the cercle of Kayes, 400 men were recruited "as every year" in the third quarter of 1924 for the Kayes trading houses (probably for the unloading of river cargo).[14] Between the first day of October 1924 and the end of January 1925, 947 agricultural laborers were recruited for the plantations of the cercle (Jaxandappe).[15] In 1925, more than 1,000 harvesters were recruited for the Jaxandappe plantation and for the Kayes trading houses [in October], and 250 laborers were recruited for various public services and private enterprises.[16] In 1926, 900 men were recruited for the unloading and reloading of Kayes trading houses river transports.[17] In 1927, the French West African authorities abandoned their support to European textile fiber plantations and favored indigenous production, which meant for the local population the forced cultivation of cotton.[18]

The cercle of Nioro had lower recorded numbers of forced recruitments. But these still amounted in 1923 to more than 500 men for the Jaxandappe plantations and an additional 150 men for road building.[19] The subdivision of Yelimane, which was part of the administrative district of Nioro, had to conscript 50 men for work on the Thiès-Kayes railway in 1925.[20] The cultivation of cotton was also encouraged by the administration, with ten metric tons exported in 1924.[21] The report for the second quarter of 1926 mentioned that the chiefs of Jafunu and Gidyume indicated that the population had paid its taxes with the product of the sale of cotton in Kayes that year.[22] A report for the entire cercle of Nioro in March 1927 mentioned that the hectarage of fields planted in cotton had multiplied by ten.[23]

After 1926, recruitments in French Soudan seem to have tapered off. Although administrators in Kayes continued to complain about the heavy burden of forced labor on the populations until 1932,[24] there were in Nioro in 1927 only 115 "second-contingent" recruits (youths not drafted into the French colonial army were theoretically eligible for civilian labor service under a 1925 law).[25] In 1928, 400 men from the cercle of Nioro worked on the difficult construction of the Kayes-Nioro road.[26] In 1929, only 25 men of the "second contingent" were recruited in Nioro for additional work on the Thiès-Niger railway in 1929.[27] With the lone exception of 100 "second-contingent" laborers recruited in 1934,[28] no recruitments were recorded after 1930 until the Second World War. A report from Kayes in 1931 mentions that communal obligations (prestations) could now be redeemed with a payment in money, as had been the rule in Senegal since 1921.[29] No forced recruitments were recorded for the 1920s in the Senegalese cercle of Bakel.[30]

The largest recruitments were thus made during the period of 1924 to 1926 for the plantation of Jaxandappe and the unloading of ships in Kayes. Even during this peak period, the numbers recruited do not appear incommensurate with the populations concerned. For example, the cercle of Kayes, where recruitments were the most important, had in 1921 a population of 122,000.[31] Adding the peak figures in our list above (for the Jaxandappe plantation and the various public services and private enterprises in 1925 and the unloading of ships in 1926), we come to a maximum figure of 2,150 men recruited—about 7 percent of the adult male population of the cercle. But the recruitments for Jaxandappe and Kayes were made for periods of fifteen days only, with a rotation of laborers.[32] Taking this into account, there may have been only around 300 men (around 1 percent of the adult male population) working away from their villages at any given time that year.[33] Moreover, recruitments for Jaxandappe and Kayes were made after September, that is, after the peak period of the cultivation season (the weedings in July and August). It is unlikely, therefore, that these recruitments had a great impact on agricultural production. It is also worth noting that laborers recruited for Kayes were fed and paid 2 francs a day, which probably was close to the standard rate in regional towns in the Senegambia and Soudan.[34] Laborers for Jaxandappe were fed and paid a comparatively low 1.50 francs a day, which largely explains why so many laborers deserted the plantation during these years.[35]

The tapering off of recruitment after 1926 was partly in response to a diminished need for labor. Although archives give no reason for recruitments to unload ships in Kayes, it is clear that they were related to the temporary problems that plagued the first years of operation of the Thiès-Kayes railway between 1924 and 1926.[36] The decreased reliance on forced labor was also due to the strong resistance of the population in the cercles of Kayes and Nioro. Many, perhaps most, of the young men recruited, especially for the plantations of Jaxandappe, fled as soon as they reached their work sites. In view of this resistance, recruitments for Jaxandappe in the cercles of Kayes and Nioro were terminated after 1926.[37] After 1926, there were only relatively small recruitments for road building and railway repairing, which were mostly made during the dry season.

As for the cultivation of cotton, "encouraged" by the administration, it cannot have had very significant results. The ten metric tons exported in 1924 correspond to the production of only *ten hectares!* So we should thus take with a grain of salt the chiefs' assertion that Jafunu and Gidyume paid their taxes in 1926 with the sale of cotton. But even if this were true, it would not have amounted to much: with Jafunu and Gidyume's population of about 16,000, the two regions' tax would have amounted to 112,000 francs (16,000 x 7 francs). Considering that cotton was then worth 1 franc a kilogram[38] and that the average cotton yield in Jafunu is one ton per hectare,[39] only slightly more than a thousand hectares would have been put under cultivation to procure this result. To evaluate this performance, we should consider that in 1923 Saint-Père estimated that the Mauritanian part of Gidimaxa, with a population of about 15,000, grew 14,000 hectares in sorghum and millet, 2,000 in maize, and 1,000 in peanuts.[40] The area planted in cotton in Jafunu and Gidyume would thus have been comparable to the area planted in peanuts in Gidimaxa at the time. Moreover, the administration did not need to do much to encourage Soninke farmers to grow cotton in the period 1926 to 1927 because the price of cotton was high. When the price fell in following years, the cultivation of cotton as a cash-crop disappeared.[41]

In spite of the apparently small impact of forced labor in the Soninke homeland, the opposition of local administrators to it was widespread and vocal. One of the most articulate complaints was written by the French administrator in Nioro, Commandant Duranthon, in a series of reports from 1920 to 1922.

A Colonial Administrator's Revolt

Duranthon's first report was written at the end of 1920, a year of subsistence crisis—not an actual famine, but a difficult year for the region. Duranthon deplored the fact that there were no emergency food reserves in the cercle and that the food deficit had been made worse by administrative requisitions of cereals for two neighboring cercles.[42] Without saying so directly, Duranthon hinted that the food crisis was partly due to migration. Each year in September some 1,500 to 2,000 young men left the cercle to grow peanuts in Senegal. They left "without informing either their family heads, their village chiefs or the [administrator of the] *cercle*." In such conditions, it was difficult for the French administrator to recruit laborers or soldiers from the local population, as required by the central administration. Young men were attracted to Senegal by the greater freedom that they enjoyed there, and by easy and well-rewarded work, but, Duranthon warned, they also went to avoid labor recruitments. Duranthon asked the administration to control the migration movement—by regimenting migrants into teams with officially recognized leaders and by issuing identification cards to all migrants. Thus organized and registered, migrants would be allowed to leave only after being authorized by their village chiefs and after notifying the colonial administrator in Nioro. Duranthon pointed out that without such regulation, village chiefs had no authority over their charges: family heads themselves complained that whenever they attempted to assert control over their children, these left to become migrants. Hinting strongly that the current food crisis was the result of French reluctance to provide strong leadership, he asked how such a crisis could occur after thirty years of French domination "in a country which before our coming overflowed with millet."[43]

In 1921, as the subsistence crisis developed, Duranthon's criticisms took on a sharper tone. If a crisis had occurred, he wrote, it was because the administration had been improvident. The region was becoming drier. Irrigation should have begun more than ten years ago.[44] But no serious scheme of development could be launched without first restoring the authority of African chiefs: "Since the conquest," asserted Duranthon, "[the colonial authorities have] only been interested in politics. There has been no economic achievement. The policy implemented has been decidedly against the chiefs; it has aimed to weaken thoroughly the spirit of indigenous authority."[45] The results were complete disaffection of the population toward the chiefs, neglect of labor, insufficient crops, famines in 1914 and 1920. The tax burden had more than doubled. Military service and forced labor recruitments for public works and private concessions had been imposed. A policy that made such crushing demands on indigenous populations, without reinforcing the powers of traditional authorities, was inconsistent.[46] On the contrary, the administration punished chiefs when young people fled labor recruitments, further depreciating their prestige and influence. Recruitment gave rise to numerous incidents of resistance.[47] But "[t]his situation should not surprise: it is the consequence of the disorganization of indigenous society and the departure of all youths in Senegal."[48] Duranthon reiterated his demand that village chiefs be given the authority to regulate migration.[49] He pointed out his efforts to develop the local economy, in particular food production, by introducing wheat, encouraging the manuring of fields, and experimenting with plows. These attempts received no support from the central administration. Duranthon hinted that the same neglect was responsible for his failure to institute compulsory "provident granaries," although the central administration had long promoted the scheme. He noted that he had been successful in carrying out small-scale local development schemes, such as small dams providing drinking water for livestock, for which the chiefs had willingly provided conscripted labor—because villagers understood their importance for the local economy.[50]

One can sense Duranthon's frustration grow in these reports, and his last reports became an indictment. Forced labor recruitments, and spiraling direct taxes, which had grown from about 300,000 francs in 1916 up to 860,000 francs in 1921 without any comparable increase in the cercle's resources, had jeopardized the region's economy: "The population will soon find it impossible to pay its taxes. It gains nothing any more from agriculture. The labor that is taken away by recruitment has not been replaced by any equipment."[51] Migration had become necessary to pay local taxes. The money brought back by young migrants, however, due to the current economic crisis in Senegal, was no longer sufficient to cover local monetary needs.[52] "The cercle has been administered for thirty years," Duranthon concluded in his report for the fourth quarter of 1921; "there is nothing. Nothing has been done for the benefit of the population. The cercle pays 900,000 francs in tax. It receives nothing in return for its development."[53]

Personal files of colonial administrators for this period are still closed to the public. But the reader senses that, in view of the boldness of Duranthon's criticisms, the fact that he was allowed to stay in office for more than a year even though the governor of French Soudan, Marcel Olivier, was a partisan of forced labor and "technocratic" development in general, meant that Duranthon had influential protectors.[54] Duranthon's patrons are still unknown, but his political camp was clear. His emphasis on traditional authority and small-scale development projects was consistent with the wartime instructions sent by Governor-General Van Vollenhoven, which were inspired by Maurice Delafosse. Duranthon in Nioro thus protested the introduction of a policy inspired by the "technocrats" in a region that had been until recently immune to their actions.

The first point to note is the partisanship of some of Duranthon's remarks. An obvious instance is his assertion that the head tax tripled between 1916 and 1921 (which it did in *nominal* terms). However, the French franc (which was in use in French Africa until after the Second World War) was devalued by two-thirds from 1919 to 1920.[55] The real value of taxes in 1921, therefore, was exactly the same as in 1916. Moreover, while Duranthon assailed the 40 percent tax increase of 1921, he kept silent on the nearly equivalent tax increase of 1917, which was decided by Delafosse and Van Vollenhoven.[56]

Duranthon's successor, Administrator Blanc, evidently received instructions to verify his predecessor's allegations. Wisely, Blanc conducted a survey of the most tangible and easily accountable sign of wealth in the cercle, that is, livestock. The results were remarkable. While a similar survey in 1893 for the three Nioro provinces of Kingi, Kenyareme, and Gidyume (95,000 inhabitants) had found:[57]

3,000 cows
100,000 sheep
2,100 horses

the 1922 survey found for the cercle of Nioro proper (116,000 inhabitants):[58]

68,694 cows
50,944 sheep
66,905 goats
4,129 horses
5,837 donkeys

In the subdivision of Yélimané (25,000 inhabitants), there were:[59]

7,208 cows
1,142 sheep
10,312 goats
548 horses
642 donkeys

The disparity between the two censuses, even taking into account the devastation of the bovine plague of 1892 (see Chapter Four), is, in fact, so enormous that it is impossible that the 1893 census was not faulty.[60] However that

MYTHS AND REALITIES OF COLONIAL MIGRATION

may be, it is clear that the Soninke enormously increased their livestock after the French conquest. They were not alone in doing so; the Beydan also enlarged their herds greatly in order to respond to growing demands for meat from the rising African urban centers.[61] The Soninke were participating in this expansion.[62] The fact was not unknown to Duranthon, who drew the governor's attention to a slump in the livestock trade that had sharply reduced Soninke incomes. But there is no evidence that this was more than a temporary crisis. In 1924, the Kayes administrator reported that the completion of the Thiès-Kayes railway had brought a marked increase in the price of livestock in the cercle.[63]

What was this livestock worth, and more importantly, what income did it bring to the population of the Nioro cercle? An estimate will be found below in table form:

Table 6.1[64]

Livestock Owned by Sedentaries in Yélimané and Nioro

Type of Livestock	Unit value (in francs)	Nioro Number	Nioro Value (in francs)	Yelimane Number	Yelimane Value (in francs)
Cows	200 F	68,694	13,738,800	7,208	1,441,600
Horses	1,000 F	4,129	4,129,000	570	570,000
Donkeys	250 F	5,837	1,459,250	652	163,000
Sheep	35 F	50,944	1,783,040	1,142	39,970
Goats	35 F	66,905	2,341,675	10,312	360,920
Total			23,451,765		2,575,490

The "livestock capital" of the region's sedentaries thus amounted to 26 million francs. With a natural growth of 4 percent per year for cows, and 20 percent for sheep and goats, this meant an annual income of about 1,300,000 francs.[65] Tax for sedentaries amounted to 677,000 francs.[66] On the basis of livestock income alone, therefore, the head tax might well appear excessive. But livestock did not represent all of the region's exports. The Soninke exported large quantities of bar salt, which they obtained from the Beydan. We have figures for salt taken at the turn of the century from the three markets of Nioro, Kérané, and Tambakara, amounting to a total estimate of almost a million kilograms, or (at the postwar price) 600,000 francs.[67] These figures do not take into account all the "domestic" trade directly between farmers and nomads, and it seems safe to double this figure.[68]

The Soninke were also important producers of cotton cloth, which was in great demand in Senegal and the French Soudan.[69] Cotton cloth production is much more difficult to evaluate, and here the point is not to come to an exact figure (which is impossible due to insufficient documentation), but to come to a plausible estimate. A. G. Hopkins has showed that, contrary to common assumptions, colonization was not followed by a decline of African crafts, but by an *increase* in their production, due especially to an expanding urban demand.[70] Weaving among Soninke was a slave occupation, although other segments of the population engaged in it as well. I have made estimates on the basis of an arbitrary estimate of 7.5 percent of the adult male population of the cercle of Nioro involved in weaving, which will not appear as excessive since we know that about a third of the Soninke population was composed of slaves, even after emancipation.[71] Based on this estimate, the total production of the cercle would have come to an export value of about 3,600,000 francs a year.[72] We therefore come to a total estimated revenue of about 6 million francs of revenue every year. To this should be added the sale of other craft products, such as calabashes, baskets, ropes, raw and crafted leather, which we know the Soninke exported (as did many other West African peoples), and the sale of various agricultural products, such as shea butter and (especially in regions neighboring the railway-river network, such as Jafunu) millet and peanuts; unfortunately, there is no way to estimate the value of such exports.[73] But even on the basis of 6 million francs of revenue, a tax burden of 677,000 francs a year would represent only slightly more than 11 percent of revenue, or the equivalent of about six weeks of work per year, scarcely more that the amount of direct taxes in metropolitan France today. Of course, these are only estimates, but they at least provide an indication.[74]

The Subsistence Situation

But if taxation was not excessive, if the area was not impoverished—as Duranthon's successor asserted—how can we explain the subsistence crisis reported by Duranthon? There is no reason to doubt the veracity of Duranthon's reports on the matter, but was it *temporary*, or—as Duranthon implied —was there a *chronic* subsistence problem in Nioro?

An occasional food crisis, however severe, cannot be taken as an indication of a *chronic* subsistence problem. One of the most careful studies of rural life in West Africa, Polly Hill's study of a Hausaland village, gives us an important insight in the matter. In her study, Hill discovered wild fluctuations of cereal prices throughout the year, often doubling overnight. Hill attributed the erratic character of food prices to the poor transportation network of northern Nigeria.[75] This is, of course, the most probable explanation. Lack of transportation turns each region into an isolated market, where surpluses cannot be disposed of and where shortages cannot be alleviated. Food shortages due to poor transportation were characteristic of premodern European agricultural economies, which had a much more favorable ecological environment than their African counterparts.[76]

Food was brought by boat to the Upper Senegal region.[77] In the cercle of Nioro, and certainly elsewhere in the interior, Beydan caravans brought food from grain-producing regions to the south such as Jomboxo and Beledugu.[78] Food also seems to have been brought by train after 1925. A report from Kayes in this year mentions the bringing of relief grain (mil, i.e., millet or sorghum) from Bamako,[79] and distributions of rice (probably brought from Dakar) are mentioned in 1927 in Kayes and in 1930 in Nioro.[80] All of these forms of transportation had severe limitations. Most of the food brought by the Senegal River was probably produced in the valley itself.[81] Since climatic conditions were roughly similar throughout the valley, river transportation did not entirely shelter the Upper Senegal region from the effect of a major crisis (which was usually felt throughout the valley). Transportation by pack animals was slow and expensive.[82] And finally, transportation by train had its maximum effect in the immediate vicinity of railway stations. Elsewhere, grain had to be transported by traditional transportation (boat or pack animal); it was only with the popularization of trucks that grain could be transported rapidly and comparatively cheaply. But truck transportation did not have a serious commercial impact until the 1950s. The fact that there was a food crisis in 1920, therefore, is *in itself* no indication that there was a *chronic* agricultural problem in Nioro.

Other indications in Duranthon's report, however, point to potentially more serious problems. Duranthon mentions the apparent drying up of the region of the "Sahel" (cercles of Nioro and Nara).[83] According to George Brooks, the period 1900 to 1930 was a drier period in the history of West Africa.[84] The reports for the Soninke homeland support Brooks's findings. The adverse sequence began in 1905 to 1908 with years of exceptional rainfall, which brought floods and parasites.[85] In 1913, as we have seen, the

Soninke homeland was hit by a major drought, as was the rest of West Africa.[86] There was a lesser crisis in 1920 and then a more serious crisis in 1926 to 1927, in which 150 deaths were recorded in the cercle of Nioro.[87] In addition, there were occasional years of bad crops, which created localized food shortages without generating an overall critical situation.

Although food crises no doubt caused a great amount of suffering, especially for the poor, their impact was probably less than modern scholars have indicated. Annual pluviometric records are available for Bakel and Matam since 1922. The average annual precipitation for Bakel in 1922 to 1930 was 502 millimeters. Most years had an average above 514 millimeters, except for 1925 (496 millimeters) and 1926 (305 millimeters). Matam had a more erratic rainfall pattern, oscillating generally between 406 and 703 millimeters, with an average of 525 millimeters for the period and a low of 334 millimeters in 1926.[88] Except for 1926, these are sufficient figures to support normal agricultural production. It is true that annual rainfall does not tell the whole story; an erratic rainfall pattern one year will result in failed crops even though the overall rainfall for the year may appear as sufficient. Another useful indication is the amount of food aid provided by colonial authorities during the worst crises. These amounted to 50 metric tons of sorghum in the northern part of Gidimaxa situated in the cercle of Kayes in the second quarter of 1924;[89] 32 metric tons of sorghum sent from Bamako to Kayes in July 1925;[90] 60 metric tons of sorghum bought in Jafunu, Gidyume, and Tiringa for Kenyareme in 1926;[91] and 50 metric tons of rice in Nioro in the second quarter of 1930.[92] These are relatively small quantities: the largest (60 metric tons) would have kept alive 1,000 persons for three months, or 3,000 persons for a month (the population of the cercle of Nioro was 140,000; that of the cercle of Kayes was 120,000). Moreover, there were no indications in the reports from the cercles that these quantities were insufficient, in spite of the evident concern of administrators that local food production was insufficient during this period. The period's worst crisis, in 1926 to 1927, caused a recorded 150 deaths in the cercle of Nioro. This can be compared with the frightening death toll in Bandiagara during the famine of 1914 discussed above. In 1927, moreover, the local administrative reports contain none of the horrific descriptions of skeletal refugees that can be found in the accounts of the 1914 famine in Bandiagara or Kano, or even in the accounts of the 1858 famine in Bakel.[93] In fact, there were no descriptions of refugees from the famine in either Kayes or Nioro in 1927. What this suggests is that the 1920s were difficult years, but for most Soninke, they were not years of disaster.

Duranthon's reports raise two important questions with respect to migration. First, did migration create a labor shortage, leading to lower production and possibly a food shortage? Second, did food shortages lead to greater migration?

The first question can be at least partially answered. There were three types of migrants in Nioro.[94] The first were the navetanes proper; they left the Soninke homeland by May in order to arrive in Senegal in June at the beginning of the agricultural season. The second type of migrants are called today *firdou*, but were in the 1930s called *baranyini* (Mande for "I am looking for work");[95] they left in September and worked as harvesters of the peanut crop beginning in October.[96] The third type of migrants left after the harvest, around December, to work as temporary laborers in Senegalese harbors and trading posts, loading ships and warehouses, becoming laborers in Bamako or Kayes, or dry-season trade migrants in the traditional fashion. In 1920 to 1921, according to Duranthon, 4,000 to 5,000 migrants from the cercle of Nioro went to Senegal.[97] Of these, 1,500 to 2,000 left in September 1920 to work as harvesters.[98] In 1933, the average number of migrants to Senegal was estimated at 7,000 to 8,000 per year.[99] Of these, about 3,000 were navetanes.[100] On the basis of these numbers, it appears that the proportions of navetanes and harvesters in the cercle were roughly equal. Looking now at figures from the subdivision of Yelimane (Jafunu, Gidyume, Tiringa), which is mostly peopled by Soninke, this area sent 1,500 migrants to Senegal every year throughout the interwar period.[101] Of these, 750 would have been navetanes migrating during the entire cultivation season, or (for a population of 25,000) 12 percent of the adult male population. It is doubtful that such a migration could have had the drastic consequences alleged by Duranthon and many of his successors. Moreover, the fact that the proportion of harvesters and navetanes remained basically constant during the period 1920 to 1933 is an indication that the control of elders over the migration was more efficient than Duranthon surmised.

Turning to the second question, did occasional food crises have an effect on migration? Indeed they did, but one must distinguish very carefully what kind of migration was involved. The drought that affected the north of the cercle of Gumbu in 1899 to 1901 provides a good illustration. Inhabitants fled to the south of the cercle, where the men worked to acquire food. Some even went as far as Kita and Bamako in their search for work. By December 1902, however, things were back to normal. That month, the commandant was struck by the appearance of wealth of Soninke villages in Wagadu (traditional name of the Gumbu region).[102] The migration, therefore, had been a temporary movement *of refugees,* not a labor migration; the whole population had been involved in the migration, not simply young men, and the migration lasted only for the duration of the crisis. We must, in fact, wait until 1916 to see a mention in archival documents of a regular current of return migration from the region, in which there are also indications that Gumbu migrants were probably introduced to navetanat through contact with Soninke networks in the neighboring cercle of Nioro.[103]

Could a food crisis increase an already existing movement of temporary migration? The probable answer is that it could, but that such effect was again temporary. For example, in the cercle of Nioro, the crisis of 1926 to 1927 caused a "very important exodus *of men of all ages* [my emphasis], especially of young men going to Senegal" in the third quarter of 1926 (i.e., after the most important labor on the fields had been completed).[104] In 1928, however, once the famine was over, the "movement of navetanes [was] noticeably less important than in the previous years."[105] What these data suggest is that the crisis increased temporarily the incidence of migration, in particular by motivating the exceptional migration of middle-aged married men, but these returned to their farms once the crisis was over. Comparative data for other regions suggest similar conclusions. Paul Pélissier noted that almost all family heads who left the dry region of northern Kajoor during the drought of 1941 to 1942 eventually returned to their villages.[106]

The "Exodes"

The question remains, however, whether forced labor and military recruitments did have an impact on Soninke migration. The administrators who followed Duranthon continued to complain about forced labor. In 1923, the administrator in Nioro charged that recruitment of laborers "weighed heavily on the cercle and caused an important exodus toward Senegal."[107] At the end of the year, noting that 500 men had been recruited for the plantations of Jaxandappe, most of whom had deserted and had not returned to their villages, the administrator wondered "[who] will be left in the region if these recruitments go on for another several years." The administrator added that, in order to avoid military recruitment, young men went to the Gambia, or hid in Senegal, where they lived by "gambling or other disreputable means."[108] The administrators, however, brought up little proof or discussion of their allegations. Sometimes, they tried to support them by pointing out the migration of young men at the beginning of the dry season, when forced labor recruitments for road building were made,[109] but we know that this was also the time when migrants left to work in Senegalese and Soudanese urban centers and when traditional trade migration began.

In the beginning of the 1930s, under the liberal administration of Governor-General Jules Brévié, forced labor virtually disappeared from the Upper Senegal region. Local administrators believed that labor migration would decline from this point.[110] The situation, however, remained unchanged. Now administrators occasionally blamed military recruitment for migration. Indicative of this frame of mind, an administrator in the outlying post of Nara even reported his difficulties with military recruitment under the heading: "*Exodes*."[111]

After 1923, twenty-year-old men were recruited for a three-year-long military service. Though a relatively large number of young men were subject to the draft, only a small number were actually drafted. Although there are no figures in the local archives, there were probably around a hundred a year for each of the two cercles considered (Kayes and Nioro). The draft lasted three years, so we must multiply this figure by three to obtain the total number of draftees absent every year from each cercle.[112] The proportion of men who were drafted was less than 1 percent of the adult male population. This in itself should cast some doubt on the administrators' allegations, but we may want to investigate the question further. Let us read, for example, an eyewitness report by a French administrator on the recruiting operations of 1944: "In the villages we visited and in particular in the administrative seats of the *cantons*, we carried out a preliminary check-up of future conscripts. Most of those who were shown to us were children of twelve to sixteen. Moreover, when rolls were called, voices answered in eight cases out of ten: 'Navétane! In Senegal! In Bamako! In [French] Guinea!'" What this quotation indicates is not that young men fled to Senegal in order to avoid the draft, but rather that at the time of recruitment, most were away in Senegal or elsewhere—quite a different story.[113] Migration rates were already very high before labor or military recruitments began. For most young men, to be drafted meant losing the benefit of three of their most productive years in migration, and they simply chose to ignore the call of military authorities. Rather than resisting by "voting with their feet," young Soninke males were ignoring newly instituted "civic" duties that had no basis in local custom and contradicted a long tradition of migration.[114]

The word "exodes," which was repeatedly used by local administrators in Bakel, Kayes, and Nioro to describe labor migration throughout the interwar period, had a history in French Africa. It is well known that precolonial African populations were often very mobile. Because population density was generally low, land was widely available and extensive cultivation was common, in some cases entailing frequent relocation of villages. In the past, internecine quarrels often resulted in the breakup of family or clan units, who went elsewhere to found new villages on virgin land. Such migrations were also a familiar form of resistance to an unwelcome authority.[115] The characteristics of these population movements, which appear frequently in the French colonial archives, were that they were generally *small-scale*, involving at the most several hundred individuals; that they involved *whole family groups;* that their geographical range was *short;* and that they were *definitive*, or at any rate, that they functioned like definitive migrations because migrants went away with their dependents and belongings as if they intended to migrate forever. These migrations, therefore, had nothing in common with labor migration, which involved *very large numbers* of individuals, concerned *specific categories* of the population (young men), and were characterized by *periodic returns* to the home villages.

The French became concerned with "flight" migration very early.[116] Most relevant to us, however, are developments in the French Congo at the beginning of the twentieth century, which I shall discuss now.

Struggles in the Congo

The political rows surrounding the French Congo are essential to understand why colonial humanists such as Duranthon connected forced labor, taxation, and food scarcity with labor migration. By the turn of the nineteenth century, the "concessionary companies" (private companies in the French Congo that were granted administrative and police powers by the French state) were dominated by outspoken proponents of forced labor, such as Edmond du Vivier de Streel. Curiously, among the many writings that appeared at the time in defense of forced labor, almost none advocated the use of colonial taxation. Partisans of coercion, in fact, were more interested in establishing *direct* forms of forced labor, for example, "transitory" schemes of slave liberation involving the "renting" of slaves to European planters as indentured servants (part of the slaves' wages would have gone to their African owners as manumission payments).[117] Such suggestions had little chance of being adopted by the French Parliament,[118] but partisans of coercion apparently came close to making it a criminal offense for Africans to break a contract and giving the right to European employers to impose fines of labor on offenders.[119] If such legislation had been adopted, the result would have been the creation of a system of peonage in French colonies.

Opponents of forced labor were weakened by the difficult financial situation of the French Congo. This situation was so desperate, in fact, due to the poverty of this sparsely populated territory, that it played into the hands of the partisans of forced labor, who repeatedly called attention to the economic success of the neighboring Congo Free State, where various forms of forced labor were in place. In order to generate revenue, colonial humanists were forced to consider the establishment of a head tax. The head tax was finally introduced under the *indigénophile* Commissary-General (Governor) Henri de Lamothe in 1898.[120] As French currency was extremely rare in the French Congo, taxes were collected in kind (as was still the case in outlying areas of French West Africa). This created a problem after 1898 to 1899, when property rights over vast areas in the French Congo were granted to concessionary companies. Putting forward all products of the soil as their legal property, the companies opposed tax collection in kind by the state. The Ministry of Colonies ordered the French Congo's administration to collect taxes in money whenever possible, and in the meantime, to encourage concessionary companies to buy African products in currency.[121] The suggestion appealed very little to the companies. In a system of barter, Africans obtained European goods in concessionary company stores in exchange for goods that they could legally sell nowhere else. If currency were introduced, nothing would prevent Africans from using money earned from concessionary company stores to buy European goods from competitors (notably the British) in the region.[122]

To entice the companies, the government and some liberals apparently argued that taxation in money would encourage Africans to leave their homelands in order to look for paid employment, thus solving the "labor problem" in the Congo.[123] It is important to note that taxation (which had long been in existence in French West Africa) had been by then introduced in the French Congo, at least in principle,[124] and that the government did not intend to manipulate tax rates in order to force the Congolese to migrate. The rates adopted were those of French West Africa, and liberals in the French Parliament kept a close check on them in order to avoid excessive increases.[125] Concessionary companies, however, realized that they could use taxation to their advantage. Since the colonial state could not legally collect taxes (according to them), the companies proposed to do so on its behalf in exchange for a moderate fee. This system, inspired by the Congo Free State, was economical from a governmental point of view. For the companies, it was a way to turn tax collection into an instrument of coercion: under the guise of collecting taxes, they could legally force Africans to bring them their products.[126] The concessionary companies carried the day in the French Parliament. Soon the disastrous combination of monopoly and privatized state authority that governed the concessionary company system led to the same scandalous abuses as in the Congo Free State. In 1905, after the gruesome Gaud-Toqué affair, the former governor and founder of the colony, Savorgnan de Brazza, was sent back to the French Congo on a mission of enquiry. His instructions from the ministry were to investigate the matter of tax collection in kind by the concessionary companies.[127] By then, there already existed among more radical colonial humanists an opposition movement to direct indigenous taxes.[128]

Brazza died while returning from the Congo. His report was never published; its conclusions, however, were circulated by liberal journalists, such as Félicien Challaye, who had followed the mission as an unofficial observer.[129] Their accounts were discussed in liberal political milieux in the metropolis. In 1906, Radical party leader Joseph Caillaux claimed in the French Chamber of Deputies that there was "an indissoluble connection between the economic regime [i.e., commercial monopoly] adopted in the conventional basin of the Congo and the [current] treatment of indigenous populations."[130] By this time, the situation in the Congo basin (French Congo and Free State) had become a matter for international concern, with the emergence of the "Congo Reform Movement" led by the British journalist E. D. Morel, perhaps the first international human-rights campaign in modern history.[131] The history of French participation in this campaign is still little known, but the famous journalist Pierre Mille appears to have been in contact with Morel prior even to the Brazza mission.[132]

An important accusation made by Morel against the Free State was that forced labor policies depopulated the Congo, either because Africans died of exhaustion, because excessive work prevented them from growing enough food for their subsistence, or finally (and this is where it becomes relevant for us) because they fled en masse from Free State territory. As is well known, Morel exaggerated the impact of King Leopold's policies.[133] The density of population in the immense forested Congo basin was extremely low, and as a result, its populations were very mobile, far more than in West Africa. Villages changed location very often, either because of political disputes or because soils had become less productive and it was possible to obtain better returns by clearing virgin land. The Congo Free State regime probably increased such mobility, as villagers tended to move away from rivers, which were avenues of penetration for Free State agents, and especially from land routes, near where they might be conscripted as porters. In some areas, finally, depopulation may have occurred through disease and death, in the same fashion as in the sixteenth- and seventeenth-century Caribbean after Spanish conquerors enslaved local populations (forest populations whose diet is based on root plants and is low in protein have a low physical resistance). Such a depopulation, real or apparent, also took place in the French Congo, and members of the Brazza mission were struck by the number of village ruins encountered during their journey.

However that may be, we see that the issues raised by Duranthon and his successors—issues *of taxation, forced labor, food production, depopulation, and migration*—were already widely discussed at the beginning of the twentieth century. In fact, E. D. Morel may have made his first French contacts among West African colonial administrators, probably Governor Clozel and Maurice Delafosse, who were then in the Ivory Coast.[134] Symptomatically, it was in 1903, a year after these contacts were made, that the first mentions of the possible impact of forced labor on Soninke migration appeared in local documents.[135] Before and during the war, Delafosse charged that Angoulvant's forced labor policies in the Ivory Coast created hunger and an exodus of populations toward the neighboring British Gold Coast.[136] Betraying an even clearer influence of the Congo debates at a 1923 meeting of the Académie des Sciences Coloniales, Delafosse pledged

his strong support to the idea of solidly binding to their land the indigenous populations. He [Delafosse] especially approves the notion because [he believes] the blacks are naturally attached to it. *[The Blacks] are* [he said] *in-*

voluntary wanderers. The system of concessionary companies and of taxes in kind has driven them into this condition [my emphasis].[137]

By that time fear of depopulation in the Congo appeared to be confirmed by the 1921 census (which was, in fact, the first real census in the area since the beginning of the colonial period). Whereas the indigenous population of French Equatorial Africa (i.e., French Congo) in 1911 had been estimated at 4,280,000 persons, there were only 1,577,000 inhabitants in 1921—a loss of 63 percent in ten years.[138] Even though population decline, or stagnation, is still regarded today as probable, contemporary research has shown that such calculations were made on the basis of extravagantly high prewar population estimates.[139] But concern about the situation in the Congo certainly explains the urgency in the reports of colonial administrators such as Duranthon and many of his successors.

The Congo debates explain the widespread confusion between "exodus" and labor migration. The belief that direct taxation could force people to seek employment outside of their region of origin blurred the distinction between *a population of all ages* leaving an area *definitively* because of administrative abuses and *young men* leaving an area *temporarily* in search of paid employment. In the minds of colonial humanists such as Duranthon or Delafosse, labor migration became associated with forced labor, starvation, and oppression—a symptom of the colossal failure of a system that ignored humanitarian considerations in its relentless pursuit of economic development. But the new perception of labor migration was also the result of a new perception of traditional African society at a time when this society was challenged by rapid economic and social change.

Migration and Social Change

In an important article published in 1923, ominously called "The Dark Clouds on West Africa's Horizon," Maurice Delafosse discussed the military draft about to be imposed in Africa by the French Parliament.[140] He maintained that if such a project were carried out, the 500,000 men making up French West Africa's labor force would disappear in twenty-five years. The figures given by Delafosse were somewhat extravagant, probably purposely exaggerated in order to draw attention to a situation that worried Delafosse.[141] The article was not simply devoted to military draft, but also discussed at length the penetration in French West Africa of Black nationalist ideologies. Clearly there was a relation in Delafosse's mind between the two subjects. Delafosse opposed Black nationalists because he believed they were blind imitators of Western politics. As such, they were threats to Africa's traditional civilization. Delafosse opposed the military draft for the same reason.

The draft, wrote Delafosse, applied equally to all classes of the society, including the chiefs' own sons, and African traditional leaders regarded it as a particularly humiliating form of tribute. Military and forced labor recruitments weakened traditional African authorities. Finally, Delafosse feared that the draft (especially if conscripts were sent to France) would lead to de-tribalization:

> They complain, in our [French] countryside, that many soldiers, once freed from military duty, are reluctant to return to the plow. Yet, the change of surroundings for them was never drastic; they spent their military service among countrymen, leaves allowed them to keep in contact with their families and their soil. Such is not going to be the case with the Blacks, who will be suddenly taken to the land of the Whites. They will be completely cut off from their relatives and their familiar environment for two years, then thrown unprepared in the midst of a civilization that is wholly different from theirs. Later they will be sent back home having learned nothing of use for their future lives in their homeland, while, on the other hand, they will have forgotten almost everything of their ancient traditions.
>
> Many among them will try to stay in France, lured by the false hope of carrying on with the easy life, devoid of material preoccupations, to which their stay in the army barracks will have accustomed them. They will lead a miserable life, made of dubious experiments, of resentment, and lost illusions. Others will let themselves be repatriated but once disembarked in [an African] harbor, they will not go any further and will only swell the ranks of the useless, the dangerous idle, who already congest the great [urban] centers of Black Africa. As for the best among them, those who will choose to return to their birthland, we should fear that they will want to live "as famas" ["Bambara kings," or "powerful men"], as they say in the Sudan, i.e., as people who, being proud of their own personal value and scornful of others and of labor, are a heavy burden for the majority [of Africans] instead of helping them and who, although they have returned to their villages and families, are nevertheless lost to their own communities, from which they dissociate themselves, and lost to their soil, with which they are no longer familiar.[142]

This quotation reveals the emergence of a new perception of labor migration. For colonial humanists such as Delafosse, migration and urbanization were sinister symptoms of the demise of a traditional African society that, under the influence of metropolitan liberals and of the colonial theory of association, they were trying to preserve.[143] The danger in Delafosse's assessment, however, was that it led to considering all manifestations of social change (such as labor migration) as evil symptoms of misguided technocratic policies.

The Development of Migration in the 1920s

The reports from Duranthon and other administrators after him give the impression that the situation in the Soninke homeland, especially concerning migration, was radically different from the situation before the war. But to a historian, the continuity between the pre- and postwar periods is quite obvious. The 1920s saw the resumption and continued expansion of patterns that had begun in the years 1910 to 1913.

Those years, as we have seen in the previous chapter, had been years of considerable expansion for navetanat. Encouraged by higher prices and by the building of the Thiès-Kayes railway through Bawol and Siin-Saalum, peanut production in Senegal climbed above 200,000 metric tons in 1909 to 1914.[144] The war interrupted this progress, by causing an enormous rise in shipping rates to Europe.[145] The end of the conflict in 1918, however, brought an immediate return to prewar levels. The 1919 to 1920 season brought a price approaching 1 franc per kilogram, in comparison with which prewar prices were "derisory," commented Governor Didelot of Senegal.[146] There was a short crisis at the end of the trading season of 1920 to 1921,[147] but a clear recovery followed. The two following years were the beginning of what Philippe David calls the "golden age" of peanut production in Senegal, a period of prosperity that was interrupted only by the Great Depression.[148] In 1922 to 1923, the kilogram price of peanuts came close to the 1.0 franc mark (0.83 franc). It climbed above 1.0 franc in 1923 to 1924.[149] Responding to the price incentive, that season brought a spectacular increase of peanut exports, from about 250,000 to 300,000 metric tons in the 1918 to 1923 period to 450,000 metric tons. Following this, a price greater than 1 franc per kilogram and exports greater than 400,000 metric tons were maintained until the 1931 to 1932 season.[150] Much of this development took place in the region of Siin-Saalum. A lightly populated region before 1900, Siin-Saalum was colonized by farmers from Kajoor and northern Wolof-speaking regions who settled around the Thiès-Kayes railway line, especially around Kaolack. Kaolack, linked to the railway line in 1912, became a major exporting harbor for peanuts after the First World War.

It is easy to see how each of the successive stages of this expansion was reflected in the history of navetanat in the Soninke homeland. In 1918, the cercle of Bakel mentioned the migration of "a very large number of young men" not only toward their traditional destination of the Gambia (and the neighboring Senegalese cercle of Niani-Ouli), but toward Siin-Saalum as well.[151] The important expansion of navetanat noted by Duranthon in Nioro during 1920 to 1921 was clearly linked with the exceptionally high price for peanuts during the preceding agricultural campaign of 1919 to 1920. The movement continued in following years. In the residence of Yelimane, the estimated number of migrants to Senegal climbed from 1,300 to 1,400 in 1921 and to 1,500 in 1922.[152] In the fourth quarter of 1922, the governor of the Soudan reported numerous clandestine departures of migrants from the cercle of Kayes toward Senegal.[153] This expansion in 1922 occurred in spite of apparently good harvests in the Soudan.[154] The higher price of peanuts in 1923 to 1924 had a visible impact on migration in 1924. In September 1924 (the month when the migration of harvesters added its impact to the ongoing migration of navetanes), a report from the subdivision of Yelimane noted that "young men of age twenty to thirty-five are almost impossible to find. There are in the villages only old men, women and children."[155] It is true that grain crops that year were adversely affected by a plant disease probably due to heavy rains.[156] But the increase in migration in 1924 occurred also in the cercle of Nara (which included the Soninke area of Gumbu), where no plant disease was reported,[157] as well as the cercles of Bamako, Kita, and Bafoulabe. One additional reason for the increase, aside from the higher price of peanuts in Senegal, was the completion of the Thiès-Kayes railway in 1923, which now made it possible for navetanes to travel by train to Senegal.[158]

The popularity of peanut cultivation and navetanat is reflected in a song that appeared in the eastern Soninke region in Nioro or Nara around 1923 to 1925, and then spread to Kammera, Gidimaxa, and Gwey, where it "was the rage" for several years. The song, called *"Tiga sandan sege"* (the value—or the prestige—of peanuts is rising, which Philippe David translates as "Peanut Boom") was sung by women.

There will never be twins such as Samba Njaay's twins
The year when they went to cultivate (peanuts) has become a legend,
The lion indeed cannot grow under the canopy (of his native house).
If I had only one brother
He would go to Senegal, he would go to the Gambia
He would bring me back an undergarment cloth
A loincloth decorated with pearls which hangs to the ground
You, going to Senegal,
You are a hero like Jala Maxan
But the one who has not gone to cultivate the peanuts of Thiès Diankine,
He can mend his own trousers.[159]

By bringing back large sums of money, the migrants ensured their prestige and their manhood. This was in keeping with the nature of Soninke society, where clientage and wealth played such an important role and where notions of honor were linked with the ownership of wealth.[160]

Administrators in Nara and Nioro noted the very large sums of money that navetanes brought back or sent by money order. In 1924, the administrator in Nara reported that migrants "come back with or send to their parents each year quite important sums. I have seen several young men sending between 500 and 600 francs."[161] That same year, the administrator in Nioro mentioned that telegraphic money orders from Senegal very often amounted to 500 to 750 francs.[162] The total of money orders received from Senegal that year in Nioro was more than 100,000 francs. But, as is the case in migration to France today, the navetanes sent only small parts of their gains by money order. In 1930, Henri Labouret estimated that navetanes earned on average between 1,200 and 1,700 francs for a season in Senegal.[163] Former navetanes mention higher sums, of 2,400 to 3,000 francs, but these were probably exceptional gains.[164] Only half of the migrants to Senegal were navetanes; migrants who worked only as harvesters still made, according to Labouret, 500 francs per campaign.

In the late 1920s, perhaps 6,000 migrants left Nioro for Senegal.[165] Estimating that half were harvesters and the other half navetanes, and using Labouret's minimum figures, migrants would have earned that year:

(3,000 navetanes x 1,200 francs) + (3,000 harvesters x 500 francs) = 5,100,000 francs.

This sum would have been enough to pay for the head tax of 728,571 persons at the rate of 7 francs per person (the cercle of Nioro had a population of 142,000 in 1922), or to buy 1,700 metric tons of grain at a famine price of 3 francs a kilogram.

To what uses were put the sums earned by the migrants? Oral and written archival sources give us an idea. As we have seen, remittances by money order to the migrants' families amounted to 100,000 francs in 1924 in Nioro. A 1925 report, from Nioro, indicates that about a thousand attestations of identity were delivered this year in order to collect telegraphic money orders.[166] This would indicate that the average money order was about 100 francs.[167] Gifts were no doubt made to relatives upon the migrants' return. Migrants bought cloth for themselves and for relatives or fiancées.[168] They brought back large sums to pay for dowries; a 1933 report for the cercle of Nara (Gumbu) indicated that bridewealth was "600 to 1,500 francs among the Soninke."[169] Some migrants apparently attempted to use their incomes as capital to become traders. The administrator who preceded Duranthon in Nioro, contemptuously wrote in 1920: "Very proud, the posh Black in these parts tries to imitate the Senegalese. He dresses like him, behaves the same way, he trades wholesale. He lives from brokerage. He earns a lot of money. He lives happily."[170] Capital accumulation no doubt took place in the form of livestock, if we judge by the very important increase in the livestock capital in Nioro between 1893 and 1922 noted above. Capital accumulation also took the form of women's jewelry. Referring to the gold rings that Soninke women and girls wear in their hair, the song *"Tiga sandan sege"* thus goes:

> Salimata Dali, I take my calabash full of butter
> And I go at my aunt Njaay, Samba's daughter
> To have my hair braided
> Like a string of gold.[171]

All of these uses of the money earned in migration are very similar to the uses made of the revenues of migration today, with two exceptions: improvements to local housing (corrugated-iron roofs and cinder-block construction) were probably too costly to import in the 1920s, given the state of rural transportation, and urban real estate investments (commonplace today in Dakar and Paris) were not made, given the predominantly rural character of the migration in the 1920s.

A rare document compiled by Duranthon allows us to give at least a rough picture of the regions affected by the migration in Nioro. It was a census of migrants to Senegal who had not come back to the cercle by 1 April 1921. (Due to the lower return migration in 1920, migrants apparently lingered in Senegal that year.)

Table 6.2
Migrants from the Cercle of Nioro, 1921[172]

Ethnicity, region or place of origin	In Senegal or in Kayes		Died in Senegal Dec. 1920– Mar. 1921	Total	Percentage
SUBDIVISION OF YELIMANE (Jafunu, Gidyume, Tiringa)	1,036 (in Senegal only)	157 (in Kayes or other colonies only)	35	1,228	32.58%
SUBDIVISION OF NIORO					
Jawara	984			984	26.10%
Kenyareme	446		33	479	12.70%
Kaarta Soninke	140			140	3.70%
Youri	20			20	0.53%
Jariso	77			77	2.04%
Sangal Xaasonke	342		7	349	9.26%
Jawando	80			80	2.12%
Local Fuutanke	400		2	402	10.67%
Toronke Fuulbe	10			10	0.25%
Total				3,769	

This table demonstrates the clear dominance of the Soninke in the migration. The Soninke regions or villages in this list are Jafunu, Gidyume, Tiringa, Kaarta Soninke, Kenyareme, (Kingi) Jawara, and Youri (an important village in Kingi). Together they amounted to 75.61 percent of the total. Among the remaining migrants, moreover, 13.42 percent came from groups that are close culturally and historically to the Soninke: the Jariso, who are part Soninke and part Kagoro (another group close to the Soninke), the Jawando, and the Xaasonke.[173]

It is interesting to compare the percentages in this table with a regional and ethnic breakdown of the population of the cercle of Nioro. In Table 6.3, only the Yelimane, Kenyareme, and Toronke Fuulbe population figures are complete. For the others, I have made estimates on the basis of an incomplete census made by Duranthon in 1921. As a check on the plausibility of my estimates, I give Commandant de Lartigue's figures for 1898, which were complete figures.

Table 6.3
Population and Migration in Nioro, Early 1920s[174]

Regions	Population 1898	Population 1921–23	Percentage Population 1922	Percentage Migrants 1921
SUBDIVISION OF YELIMANE	—	26,000	18 %	32.58%
Jawara	21,650	[25,000]	18 %	26.10%
Kenyareme	—	11,057	8 %	12.70%
Kaarta Soninke	?	?	?	?
Youri	3,600	[5,000?]	[3.5%]	0.53%
Jarisso	1,900	[2,000]	1.5%	2.04%
Sanga Xaasonke	4,000	[5,000?]	3.5%	9.26%
Jawando	4,200	[3,000]	2 %	2.12%
Local Fuutanke	22,800	[15,000?]	[10.5%?]	10.67%
Toronke Fuulbe	5,400	7,154	5 %	0.25%

Again, the Soninke dominance appears very clearly. Among Soninke migrants, most came from the western region of the Xoolinbinne and Terekole valleys (Jafunu, Gidyume, Tiringa, Kenyareme). Together, migrants from this area made up 45.28 percent of the total, although the area made up only 26 percent of the population of the cercle. The incidence of migration was especially strong in the subdivision of Yelimane (Jafunu, Kenyareme, and Tiringa): 32.58 percent of the migrants came from this region, which held only 18 percent of the population of the cercle. Yet in 1921, Duranthon himself had decided to set the head tax of the subdivision of Yelimane at 7 francs instead of 6 francs as for the rest of the cercle, because its farmers "possessed a far more fertile soil and could export their products toward Kayes a lot easier."[175] Contrariwise, we note the underrepresentation of the Toronke Fuulbe (0.25 percent of migrants for 5 percent of the population). Yet according to Lartigue in 1898, the Toronke Fuulbe were "poor" and "they in general [paid] their taxes very badly," an observation that was echoed in reports for the 1920s.[176] Lartigue noted that Toronke Fuulbe refused to work for the French, according to him for religious reasons: "Fanatical Moslems, they generally refuse the work that is offered to them, and they claim everywhere that they would prefer to die of hunger rather than to work for the whites."[177] However that may be, the discussion of these figures once again makes it clear that there was no absolute correlation between poverty and temporary migration.

An important question is the relationship between migration and social change among the Soninke. Colonial administrators such as Duranthon believed that migration was both a cause and a consequence of a collapse of traditional African authority. These claims came at least in part from Soninke elders, who complained that: (1) young migrants departed without informing family heads,[178] (2) migration decreased the labor supply necessary for cultivation,[179] (3) many migrants did not come back from Senegal,[180] and (4) young men brought back a "disrespectful attitude."[181] A close examination reveals that these complaints were probably founded, but exaggerated. Definitive migration did occur. An enquiry in 1960 to 1961 revealed that there were 5,700 Soninke farms in the peanut-producing regions of Senegal (800 in Thiès, 600 in Sine-Saloum, 800 in Senegal Oriental, and 3,500 in Casamance).[182] This would correspond, according to Philippe David, to 30,000 to 40,000 persons. But we must consider that this figure represents the accumulation of migration over a period of more than a hundred years for Casamance and fifty years for the other regions, plus natural increase, and that many Soninke migrants must have married non-Soninke wives. In any given year in the 1920s, the number of migrants who established residence in Senegal is likely to have been small. Most definitive migrants, moreover, must have been grown men who had already migrated several times to Senegal since it took some time to establish a claim to a piece of land on which to settle.[183] However, it is understandable that the elders should have worried about this, especially considering that some migrants, who did not become definitive migrants, occasionally stayed for more than one season in Senegal, in particular when the price of peanuts was low and the financial return of migration was below their expectations.[184] Such migrants did not inform their families, who must have been concerned about their fate.

The fact that young migrants departed without informing family heads is often mentioned either in archival documents or by informants. According to Philippe David's informants, migrants *always* departed secretly.[185] This seems doubtful, however.[186] We have seen that the proportion of harvesters to navetanes remained constant in Nioro throughout the 1920s, a constancy that indicates a rather good control of elders over the migration. In order to migrate, a young man needed personal contacts in Senegal, which were always provided by elder brothers or relatives. Teenagers who were recently circumcised were apparently considered too young to migrate.[187] Older migrants sent home those who were considered too young. This does not mean that some young migrants did not slip through the cracks—many undoubtedly did,[188] but it is unlikely that they were the majority.[189]

The fears of elders were probably based on several real concerns: some young men migrated before their majority and without obtaining the authorization of the family head; some only sons migrated, depriving the family head of his only source of support; some migrants did not return. But I suspect that elders were perhaps less worried about the current situation than anxious about what the situation might become in the future.

Finally, one cannot discount jealousy and distrust. Throughout the world, labor migrants often return with large amounts of money, which encourage them to take on an air of independence. Migrants introduce new fashions. They are more critical of custom. This does not make them into revolutionaries, but it makes them more susceptible to envy and suspicion. In the early twentieth century, Polish migrants who returned to Poland from the United States were accused of being against the Catholic religion, while their compatriots envied their comfortable American-style homes.[190] Today, among the Soninke, migrants to France are called *"tubabs"* (whites) or *"Francemen"* and are accused of being against Islam.[191] Yet to a contemporary observer, most Soninke migrants today are very respectful of religion and of the prerogatives of elders. Much of the same may have happened in the 1920s. As we have seen, migrants from Nioro earned more than 5 million francs in 1929. This corresponded to about 3 million 1921 francs—and I have evaluated the total income of the cercle from agriculture, commerce, and craft production that year at about 6 million francs. These figures make it understandable that elders felt somewhat threatened by the wealth brought back by young migrants. However, even if the traditional family was sometimes under attack, it certainly did not collapse.

This being said, it remains plausible to argue that the Soninke patriarchal family suffered some strain during this period. This would appear to come out of this 1923 report from Nioro: "It is incredible to see the number of people today, especially women, who come to see [the administrator] in order to get a divorce: unfaithful or women who are too old, husbands who are either not trustworthy or too old."[192] Some of these divorces were probably caused by the prolonged absence of husbands as navetanes,[193] but the mention of "husbands who are too old" refers to elders, who did not migrate.[194]

Another factor contributing to the strain on patriarchal authority was the continuation from before the First World War of the process to end slavery. During the war, many, perhaps most, of the young men presented for military recruitment in French West Africa had been slaves. At their return, veterans refused to live in the same dependence on their former masters.[195] A report for Bakel in 1920 noted that Soninke veterans were former slaves who had stayed voluntarily with their former masters after emancipation, but who now left their masters, grouped together, and built separate compounds and even villages.[196] The administration supported them by giving them the use of state lands and, through the intermediary of the local Provident Society, tools and seed.[197] Adrian Adams's informers in the village of Kungani (Gwey) mentioned that it was after the First World War that "slaves began to feed their families."[198] Chief Ibrahima Jaman Bacili noted that slaves ceased to be pawned for money in 1920.[199] Although the impact of the war was important, oral and written sources leave the impression that emancipation was also a long process, which extended during the 1920s and beyond. In 1929, the administrator in Kayes reported that "[n]umerous former servants [slaves] of the Fuulbe of Nioro and of the Sarakole [Soninke] of Gidimaxa are going back to Wasulu or Sikaso from whence their parents or themselves were abducted."[200]

Slave emancipation probably contributed to increased migration. Pollet and Winter relate two cases of slaves who left after the First World War, without their master's permission, for long periods abroad as navetanes (respectively for four and fifteen years).[201] It is worth noting that both fell back under the authority of their former master or master's family after their return—one after his master found him a wife and paid the dowry (clientage) and the other apparently because he could not get any land. In contrast with these life histories, Saint-Père notes that slaves migrated in order to gain cattle and land:

> During the dry season, many slaves hire themselves abroad in Dakar, Saint-Louis and Kayes, for work on the harbor, railway building premises, etc. They use the product of their labor to buy the cattle that they need to set themselves up and their family on the land that they farm.[202]

The sources do not allow one to say whether the emancipation of slaves and young people encouraged navetanat, or the reverse. But this query reminds one of the classic nonsensical "chicken-or-the-egg" question. Slave emancipation, a certain weakening of the control of elders over family groups, and migration were mutually reinforcing processes during the interwar period.

Conclusion

Contemporary negative perceptions of Soninke labor migration owe a lot to the arguments used by colonial administrators in their struggle against partisans of forced labor at the beginning of the twentieth century. Events in the Congo helped to shape the perception of labor migration as a negative phenomenon. There, or so it seemed, traditional African societies were damaged or destroyed in order to provide exports and laborers for European plantations and businesses; and forced labor and excessive taxes caused a general decline of population and mass exodus. French colonial humanists in West Africa fought to prevent the repetition of this disaster in the territories that they saw themselves as holding in trust.

Opposition to labor migration among colonial administrators, therefore, had noble motivations. But this does not mean that these administrators were right in their appraisal of the West African situation. In fact, labor migration had little to do with flights of population. Moreover, the economic expansion following the First World War in the peanut-producing region of Senegal and the social change created in part by this expansion and in part by the war provide a much better explanation of migration than coercion and military recruitment. But colonial humanists were blind to these facts not only because of the situation in the Congo, but also because, although they paid lip service to the cause of economic and social development, they aimed to preserve traditional social structures that no longer were the only elements in the changing reality of Africa.[203]

SEVEN

The Shift to Urban Migration

1930s–1960

Soninke labor migration underwent a major transformation after the 1930s—especially during the Second World War. Previously rural and seasonal, it became urban and "pluriannual." Migration also expanded over a wider geographical area, which included West Central Africa as well as France. This period constituted the immediate background of the present Soninke migration to France. Yet in spite of this transformation, Soninke migrants remained strongly attached to the traditional society of their homeland.

Soninke Economy in the 1930s

The marginalization of the economy of the Soninke homeland, initiated by the gum crash of the 1890s, became apparent after the completion of the Dakar-Bamako railway in 1923, which finally moved the economic center of Senegal away from the river valley and into the peanut-producing regions of Bawol, Siin-Saalum, and the "New Territories." But a marginalization does not necessarily mean an *absolute* decline (a net fall in a region's volume of trade), it may mean only a *relative* decline (a drop in a region's share in the total trade of a country). A number of European and African critics in the colonial period, however, argued that the railway did cause an absolute decline for the Senegal River Valley. In the words of one Saint-Louisien in 1929, "the rail killed the river."[1] Several contemporary authors have added an anticolonial twist to this argument, suggesting that the French deliberately neglected the Senegal River Valley, which had become unprofitable to French commerce, in order to develop the port of Dakar and the peanut-exporting regions to the south, which were linked by the railway.[2] There is some truth to this argument, but the formulation exaggerates the decline of the Senegal River Valley and the Machiavellian spirit of the French.

The Senegal River was a cheap transportation route that, considered in economic terms alone, could compete advantageously with a railway.[3] A fitting illustration of this was given in 1902, when the French decided to build the Dakar-Niger railway through central Senegal. They studied a possible route for the railway in the valley between Bakel and Kayes, where the most difficult stretch of navigation on the Senegal River lay, but it was shown that even there the railway could not compete with the river.[4] The problem with the river was that it was navigable only during part of the year. In 1900, a yellow fever epidemic during the river's short period of navigability disrupted the supplying of the Soudan colony for the entire year.[5] Moreover, the Senegal River was navigable to large ships only between August and October. As a result, imports "came in during the rainy season, when farmers, having nothing to sell, could not buy them, while [agricultural] products were bought at the time when there [were] no ships [to take them]."[6] Merchandise thus had to be stocked at major cost, and much of it was spoiled by the rains as it was unloaded.[7] Finally, the river's annual flood could not be relied on every year. In 1902 it proved too small to support navigation to Kayes, and part of the supplies of the Soudan colony remained on dock in Saint-Louis.[8] These reasons led the colonial administration to favor building a railway to the Soudan.[9]

The projected railway to the Soudan could not be built along the Senegal River to Saint-Louis (as planned in the nineteenth century)[10] since, as already explained, it would have to compete with cheaper river transport. And it could not be built immediately to the south of the river through the semi-desertic Ferlo region, which would generate almost no commercial traffic.[11] The only possible course, therefore, was through the peanut-producing regions of Bawol and Siin-Saalum, then west through Nyani-Wuli, immediately north of the Gambia, where the railway could hope to divert some traffic from the British-controlled territory. Even then, the railway had to go through very sparsely populated regions in what is today Senegal Oriental, and its operation proved difficult financially. Given the problematic profitability of the railway,[12] the administration was reluctant to spend money to improve navigation on the Senegal River, which would have diverted traffic away from the railway. This neglect in the long run spelled the decline of the Senegal River trade. In order to remain operational in the modern world, the river route had to be made accessible to larger, oceangoing ships by digging canals (extremely expensive) along its course, building water locks, and removing the sand bar at Saint-Louis.[13]

The decline of the river trade, however, did not happen overnight. In 1903, the yearly traffic of the Saint-Louis harbor was only 16,000 tons. It may have climbed to 80,000 to 100,000 tons from 1907 through 1923, the peak years of the Saint-Louis harbor.[14] In 1936 to 1939, more than ten years after the railway was completed, the figure was only down to 60,000 to 70,000 tons a year.[15] This was a considerable figure since harbor traffic in Dakar (if we except coal and oil destined for the refueling of ships to South America) stood at 330,000 tons a year in 1929.[16] At the same time, the traffic of Grand-Bassam, which was the only major harbor in the Ivory Coast on the eve of the building of Abidjan, was 165,000 tons.[17] About half of the movement of the Saint-Louis harbor was composed of river traffic.[18] The ultimate decline of the Senegal River traffic was not, in fact, caused by the building of the Thiès-Kayes railway, but by the development of cheaper road transportation after the Second World War.[19]

Oral and written sources for the Upper Senegal region in the interwar period suggest that, even though the region lost its importance in the overall economy of Senegal, its agriculture still produced a surplus, some of which was marketed. In 1925, Saint-Père noted that the Soninke of Gidimaxa "preciously keep in their granaries the amounts of grain necessary for their annual consumption, plus a contingency reserve that will allow them to live without depriving themselves should the crop of the next year be deficient, . . . but they export the surplus to Senegal or sell it to the Moors."[20] The 1934 political report from Bakel mentions that monetary needs in the cercle (buying clothes and condiments for food and paying taxes) were covered by sales of cereals.[21] Adrian Adams collected similar data in oral interviews in Gajaaga. Gajaaga women in the interwar period grew peanuts for sale and bought cows with the proceeds in Bakel. In other Gajaaga villages, women grew grain for sale, using their earnings to buy thread, which they gave to weavers to make cloth that the women later sold. All the women bought gold jewelry with their earnings.[22] Men also grew peanuts for sale: in the maraboutic village of Kungani, the four hundred talibe in the renowned Koranic school of Fode Mamadu Jaaxo grew peanuts for sale in Bakel around 1938.[23] These talibe were given land by local jatigi in exchange for labor, in the same fashion as navetanes in the Gambia or Siin-Saalum.[24] These observations are probably also valid for Soninke regions to the east. Writing in the 1940s, which were in the early years a poor period for agriculture, Boyer noted that grain was the most important commercial export of the Jawara of Kingi: "they sell it to Moors against salt and to traders in Nioro against money and cloth. Their whole harvest goes to it, such is their passion for gain, and even difficult preharvest 'hungry seasons' do not make them see reason." The Jawara also sold "peanuts, beans and vegetables, which women bring for sale to the market of Nioro."[25]

The 1930s were generally a better decade for agriculture than the 1920s. For the period 1930 to 1940, annual rainfall data for Bakel, Matam, and Selibaby averaged 510, 672, and 682 millimeters, respectively.[26] There were no droughts, and rains were far above normal in 1936, resulting in a flood that year.[27] On the basis of a very thorough interview survey in the village of Kungani (which has a long history of migration and a very high migration rate today), Adrian Adams estimates that in 1938, 250 men cultivated the lands of the village, while 85 (20 percent of adult males) were away as migrants; the former cultivated at least 360 hectares in the interior lands of the jeri, harvesting a crop of at least 360 tons of grain. This estimate does not include the crop from riverbank lands (70 hectares—at least 70 tons, which would bring the total production to 430 tons). Today, the village of Kungani (with a population larger than in 1938) needs 290 tons of grain to feed itself.[28]

There is also evidence in the cercle of Bakel that new land was put under cultivation during this period. Adams mentions that a *kollengal* (a type of flood land) of about 100 hectares was opened to cultivation in Kungani in the mid 1930s; among the sixty-three families who received land, sixteen slave families were beneficiaries—this was apparently when the slave families were first granted land ownership in the village. [29] The Bakel archives show that this distribution took place after the local administration confiscated uncultivated kollengal lands in Gwey, which were declared state property, and announced that anyone could cultivate them without having to pay rent to their former owners. In this way, 500 hectares were put under cultivation in 1934 in Bakel and 1,000 hectares in villages along the river, such as Kungani, Golmi, Yaffera, and Balu.[30] The agricultural situation in the interwar period, therefore, was in no way comparable to the present situation of undercultivation and deficit in food production, which is largely due to the drought of the last two decades.

I have argued earlier that the completion of the Thiès-Kayes railway brought no *absolute* economic decline for the river valley. In fact, the railway appears to have *increased* commercial agriculture in one area of the Upper Senegal region: the cercle of Kayes, which it served—and probably neighboring areas in the cercle of Nioro (such as Jafunu) as well. The economic history of Mali (the former French Soudan) is still to be written for this period. But some fascinating data are available. Peanut exports from Soudan began to rise after the Great Depression, due to the aggressive discounting of peanut freight on the railway. In 1936, Soudan exported 90,000 tons of peanuts. In 1940, it exported 120,000 tons. These figures, of course, pale in comparison with Senegal's production, but they are remarkable when compared to figures for northern Nigeria, also a landlocked region that depended on a railway to carry its cash crops to the coast. Peanut exports in Nigeria (essentially from northern Nigeria) went above 100,000 tons in 1928 and rose to 350,000 tons in 1936, but even the pre-1928 figures were regarded as a considerable achievement.[31] In 1928, Soudanese peanut exports already amounted to 29,000 tons; around 7,000 tons, or one-fourth, came from the cercle of Kayes.[32] The Senegalese region of Bakel also participated in this expansion: Kayes trading houses opened branches in Bakel, and the villages along the river (in Gwey) exported 1,200 tons of peanuts in 1938.[33] A Soninke farmer today grows 500 kilograms of peanuts per hectare.[34] Thus 1,200 metric tons would represent the production of about 2,400 men (at one hectare each), or 4,800 women (at one-half hectare each). There were about 6,000 adult men and women in Gwey in 1937, since its total population was 12,000 persons.[35]

Yet these same regions along the railway line that were affected by the peanut expansion were also the regions from which migrants came. In 1932, for example (quite a well-documented year), out of 22,085 reported navetanes, 9,711 came from the railway-line cercles of Kayes, Bafoulabe, Kita, and Bamako, and 9,533 from the cercle of Nioro, which is not located very far from the railway.[36] Figures given by Philippe David for the following years show no decline in the trend.[37] The French colonial authorities were apparently puzzled by this phenomenon of migration from regions of export agriculture. In 1936, the cercle of Kayes made a special effort to persuade its migrants to stay at home to grow peanuts, but to no avail.[38]

The End of Navetanat

Given the continued expansion of migration from Soudan, we would normally expect that there would be no shortage of labor in the peanut-producing regions of Senegal and the Gambia in the 1930s. But, curiously enough, the reverse was true. Complaints about a decline in the numbers of navetanes were first heard in Siin-Saalum in 1927.[39] The issue was hotly discussed in commercial, political, and administrative circles in Senegal in following years. It even motivated an official intervention of Senegal's Black African deputy in the French Parliament, Blaise Diagne, in 1929.[40] After the Great Depression began, the Kaolack and Rufisque chambers of commerce and the Senegalese and Soudanese authorities jointly took measures to facilitate the coming of navetanes to Senegal. In 1932, Administrators Geismar and Duranthon were put in charge of recruiting navetanes in Senegal and the French Soudan, respectively.[41] The appointment of Duranthon was especially ironic since, as we recall, he had been such an outspoken opponent of navetanat in 1920 to 1921 in his capacity as administrator of the cercle of Nioro (see Chapter 6). In 1933, Duranthon toured the Soudan, assisted by three members of Senegal's influential Colonial Council, Amadou Duguay-Clédor, president of the Colonial Council and trusted lieutenant of Blaise Diagne, and Councilors Médoune Diouf and Babakar Ndéné Ndiaye.[42] This was to lead to the creation of an official navetane recruitment service that lasted until 1963.

Philippe David, who directed the French navetane service in the 1950s, has compiled French official figures on the migration. These figures are given below in table form. Unfortunately, no figures are available prior to 1932.

Table 7.1
Navetanes, 1932-1955 (in thousands)[43]

Year	Kayes	Nioro	Bafulabe	Kita	Bamako	Buguni	Total Soudan	Guinea
1932	1.3	6	1.5	1.1	0.9	0.4	12.3	
1936	—	—	—	—	—	—	—	35
1937	3.6	4	—	1	6.2	3	18.3	20.8
1943	3.4	5.2	2	1.7	5.9	5	—	—
1944	3.2	4.7	2.7	1.5	5.9	5.1	26.6	—
1945	2.3	3.2	1.8	1.4	4.1	3.7	17	—
1947a	1.8	1.9	1	2.5	4.5	0.4	14	5.7
1947b	1.7	2.7	1	1.4	6.6	0.4	14	—
1948	2.2	0.8	1	1.6	4.4	0.8	11.7	—
1950	1.4	1.5	0.5	0.2	8.7	0.04	12.4	—
1952	0.03	0.7	0.08	0.2	4.1	1.1	8.5	—
1955	1.6	8.5	0.9	0.6	2.1	0.2	15.3	25.5

Evaluating these figures poses some problems: different computation methods were used, the boundaries of administrative districts changed from time to time, and no administrative district was ethnically homogeneous. The figures for Kayes probably also include a significant proportion of migrants who were not from the cercle because Kayes was an important railway station for navetanes of various origins. Finally, these figures do not separate navetanes from harvesters, who were also recorded as navetanes.[44]

If we take these figures as rough estimates, however, two observations emerge. First, migrants from cercles comprising an important Soninke population (Kayes and Nioro) were the majority of the navetanes in 1932.[45] Indeed, a 1933 report from Nioro mentioned that "the cercle of Nioro is the one where the exodus toward Senegal is the most important [in Soudan]."[46] Second, the number and proportion of navetanes from Nioro and Kayes declined steadily throughout the period of 1932 to 1955, with a sharp acceleration of the decline after the Second World War (the high 1955 figure for Nioro is an oddity due to the merger of the cercle of Nioro with the cercle of Nema).[47] While Soninke navetanes became less and less numerous, French recruitment efforts in the 1930s resulted in a sharp increase in the number of Bambara navetanes from Bamako and Buguni.[48] According to Philippe David, it was in the 1930s that the Senegalese began to call navetanes "the Bambara."[49]

Taken together, quantitative and qualitative data suggest that the Soninke,

THE SHIFT TO URBAN MIGRATION

who were probably the most important group in navetanat until the late 1920s, began to turn away from this form of migration in the late 1920s and early 1930s. But we know that Soninke migration as a whole did not decrease during these years. On the contrary, local archival documents are filled with complaints from administrators and Soninke elders about the migration. Where then did Soninke migrants go?

The answer is that they were abandoning navetanat for longer-term *temporary urban* employment. This evolution comes out quite clearly in written and oral data from the Soninke homeland, particularly from Bakel. In 1925, in his monograph on the Soninke of Gidimaxa, the French administrator Saint-Père made no mention of navetanes, but he noted that migrants worked in the Dakar, Kayes, and Saint-Louis harbors and on railway building sites. However, many, but not all, of these migrants were still seasonal workers, working in town during the dry season only.[50] Reports from Bakel made no reference to Soninke navetanes in the interwar period, but beginning in the 1930s, they increasingly referred to migration to urban centers along the Senegalese railway line (probably Diourbel, Kaolack, and the smaller centers of the "peanut triangle") and to Dakar.[51] As we have seen, it was in 1933 that the French first became aware of the presence of Soninke chambres in Dakar, although these had existed at least since the First World War.[52] By 1940, the annual report in Bakel talked of "veritable Soninke quarters" in the Médina (popular African quarter) of Dakar. Conversely in 1946, a local report from Bakel mentioned the "lack of enthusiasm" (French euphemism for "dislike") of local Soninke for navetanat.[53]

Oral sources from Gwey confirm the impression given by this archival data. Galadio Tarawele from the village of Golmi migrated as a navetane for the first time in 1929 near Mbour, on the Petite Côte. He left again in 1931 and worked near Sokone in Saalum for two years. But in 1933, he left for Dakar, where he worked as a laborer until 1935.[54] Jabe So from Kungani left directly for Dakar in 1936, but he appears to have been unsuccessful in finding work there, so he went to Kaolack, where his relative, Badara Gey (the Gey are the chiefly family of Kungani), was working as a policeman. Avoiding his kinsman (who would have sent him home on account of his very young age), Jabe So went to work as a navetane near Kaolack. In 1937, after harvesting his crop in Kungani, he returned to Dakar and finally found work there in 1938 as a laborer at the Shell Company, where a kinsman of his friend and age-mate, Bakari Kamara, had already begun working in 1936.[55]

Evidence for the Soudan is less clear than for Bakel. The first mentions of urban migration date from the 1920s. They refer to seasonal (dry-season) trade migrants from the cercle of Nara who went to Bamako, where they bought hides and kola nuts.[56] Other migrants from Nara also worked during the dry season in Soudanese centers as laborers or animal drovers.[57] In Nioro, a 1925 report mentions seasonal migrants who worked in the handling and loading of peanuts in Senegalese towns.[58] A 1927 report for Nioro also mentions migrants from the cercle who were employed in "neighboring cercles," possibly in Kayes and Bamako.[59] By 1933, longer-term migration had become a major concern for elders in the cercle of Nioro when Duranthon again visited the cercle.[60] Many of these longer-term migrants may, of course, have settled as farmers in Casamance or in Siin-Saalum, but others probably followed the lead of migrants from Bakel in turning to pluriannual employment in Senegalese towns. A 1941 report from Nioro mentions migrants from the cercle in Bamako, without indication whether these were seasonal or pluriannual migrants.[61] A 1944 report, however, asserted that "whole quarters in Bamako are packed with people from Nioro."[62] The impression one retains from these data is that Soudanese Soninke were slower in making the switch to urban migration than migrants from Gajaaga and Gidimaxa. Indeed in the middle 1960s, many migrants from Jafunu were still navetanes, while navetanat had practically disappeared near Bakel.[63] When I asked Soninke informants from Gwey about navetanat, they assured me that only "the Malians" had been navetanes.[64]

Why were the Soninke leaving navetanat for employment in urban areas? The colonial scholar Labouret gave a clue in a 1930 article when he pointed out that wages paid in Dakar or on building sites in Senegal were higher than the incomes of agricultural migrants. Navetanes could earn on the average 1,200 to 1,500 francs, and sometimes up to 1,700 francs, for five months of work in a year. Africans who worked in Senegalese towns earned on average 12 to 15 francs a day.[65] Calculated over a whole year (allowing for a day a week of rest, for holidays and occasional unemployment) this amounted to at least 4,000 francs a year.[66] It will be noted that, calculated on a monthly basis, the advantage of urban work relative to navetanat appears less marked: urban workers earned 333 francs per month, while navetanes earned 240 to 340 francs a month. However, the difference was still significant, as urban work was available year round (see below). Moreover, urban wages were on an upward trend throughout much of the interwar period. In 1922, laborers in Dakar made (in 1930 francs) between 5.83 francs (beginning wages) and 7.50 to 8.33 francs a day.[67] By 1930, therefore, wages in Dakar had roughly doubled. It is also important to note that Monique Lakroum's study of wages in the port of Dakar shows that African real wages were more or less maintained at the same level during the Great Depression and began to decline only in 1937.[68]

How were the Soninke introduced to urban work? Certainly, urban migration existed among the Soninke by the end of the nineteenth century, but it was apparently an aristocratic migration of tunka lemmu and clerics.[69] At the beginning of the twentieth century, the longer-term Soninke "urban" migrants were railway workers, especially locomotive drivers and mechanics (an offshoot of employment as ship mechanics), a branch of employment that was a Soninke specialty.[70] But already by that time, many Upper Senegal Soninke migrated during the dry season to Senegambian centers, such as Saint-Louis, Bathurst, Kayes, or the trading centers of the Senegal River or the railway line, to sell cotton cloth and cattle.[71] We have seen that a similar migration was also practiced by migrants from Nara and Nioro in the 1920s. In addition, in the early 1920s, harvesters from Nioro "went, as soon as their presence was no longer necessary, to seek some employment in the handling of [peanut cargoes in Senegal], the loading of freighters, harvesting and threshing the peanuts grown by their comrades who had left earlier."[72] Such seasonal urban work was also practiced by navetanes after the harvest and probably provided the transition toward urban employment for many of them.[73] Robert Delavignette thus described the end of an agricultural season of a navetane in Senegal:

> A torrent of money, which soon will dry up, floods the shops along the rectangular market-places. . . . [The navetane] wonders at [the] flood of merchandise. He now hires out his services once more, as a day laborer this time, to build up dunes of peanuts in bulk, or forts of peanuts in sacks, before a corrugated iron store and a freighter ship. He becomes an ant in the ant-hill of the dockers.[74]

Seasonal urban employment existed for a long time in Senegal without giving rise to a longer-term migration. But during the 1920s and 1930s, urban populations in Senegal grew at an unprecedented pace. The table below gives an idea of the scale of this urban expansion. Although all Senegalese towns grew, the pace of growth was particularly sustained in the regions of Dakar and Siin-Saalum.[75]

Table 7.2
Senegal's Urban Population, 1914–1934 (in thousands)

	1914	*1921*	*1925*	*1930*	*1934*
River Valley					
Podor	2.2	—	—	1.3	—
Bakel	3.1	—	—	2.8	—
Saint-Louis	23.5	20.4	19.0	19.4	30.8
Old Peanut Basin					
Louga	1.5	3.1	3.8	6.3	3.6
Tivaouane	2.1	2.6	3.6	3.2	2.9
Thiès	3.0	6.4	6.4	12.6	15.5
Rufisque	12.9	11.3	17.1	20.0	17.6
Dakar	21.6	37.1	[40.0]	54.0	76.1
Diourbel					
Diourbel	2.2	2.5	5.9	11.3	15.4
Siin-Saalum					
Kaolack	1.5	1.5	5.7	13.3	44.2
Gossas	—	—	—	2.8	5.9
Total	73.6	84.9	[c.106.0]	147.1	212.0

This table reveals a sharp acceleration between 1925 and 1934 in the urbanization of Senegal. (While Senegal's urban population had increased by roughly 50 percent in the period 1914 to 1925, it increased by another 50 percent in the period 1925 to 1930, and by 100 percent overall from 1925 to 1934.) Was this transformation caused by the Great Depression? But we have seen that the decline of navetanat began in 1927, *before* the Depression. Rather, the phenomenon was due to the large-scale public works (essentially the building of the Dakar and Kaolack harbors) initiated in Senegal by the government-general of French West Africa after 1927.[76] These public works continued without budgetary cuts during the Depression thanks to the vote of a colonial loan by the French Parliament.[77] Historians of temporary migration in France such as Abel Chatelain or Françoise Raison-Jourde believe that one of the most important factors in the shift from seasonal rural migration to longer-term urban migration in the nineteenth century was the great public works begun in French cities at the time.[78] Likewise, Labouret believed that navetanat declined because higher-paid employment was available on construction sites in Senegal and especially in Dakar.[79] A rare note of the colonial administration in Dakar in 1932 about migrants from Gidimaxa appears to validate Labouret's opinion. Migrants from Gidimaxa in Dakar were predominantly employed on the *"Public Works building sites, the harbor Works enterprise,* or by private commercial houses for the handling of merchandise" [my emphasis].[80]

Public works (and their derivative effects on urban economies) explain in part the expansion of Soninke urban migration in the years following 1927. But the policy of great public works had also the long-term consequence of creating year-round employment in Senegalese cities. In the nineteenth and early twentieth centuries, Senegalese cities had had an essentially seasonal life; their peak activity was after the peanut harvest, when merchants bought peanuts from farmers in exchange for imported goods and the crop was loaded onto ships. But now the modern harbors built in Dakar and Kaolack employed dockers and mechanics all year. In Dakar, a petroleum harbor was built in 1926 to 1933 to fuel ships and to provision automobiles and trucks throughout Senegal; an industrial zone emerged near the harbor. Peanut oil pressing plants were created in Dakar and Kaolack. Water and electricity plants were established in all major Senegalese cities. City services were expanded.[81] This transformation is reflected in the life histories of the Soninke migrants mentioned above. Jabe So worked pumping fuel into barrels at the Shell company stockyards near the harbor in Dakar in 1938. His kinsman Badara Gey was a policeman in Kaolack.[82] Later, villagers from Kungani and Jagili (the large Gidimaxa village that faces Kungani on the other side of the Senegal River) worked at the Dakar Electricity Company,[83] at the Petersen peanut oil factory in Dakar, or in municipal services as hospital aides or gardeners.[84]

In 1938 in the maraboutic village of Kungani, 85 out of the 335 adult males (20 percent) were migrants. Of these, 35 (41 percent) were in African countries other than Senegal (Belgian and French Congos) working as traders, 19 (22 percent) were sailors, 25 (29.5 percent) were in Dakar, and only 6 (7 percent) were navetanes.[85] The high proportion of traders in the Congos is explained by the role of Kungani maraboutic families in the emergence of migration to this part of the world.[86] Most migrants to the Congos (and traders in general) were from maraboutic families, while sailors tended to be from nonmaraboutic ("warrior") free families and slaves (who were presumably clients of the former). But *three-fourths* of the migrants *to Dakar* were slaves.[87] This tends to confirm that migration to Dakar and other Senegalese urban centers emerged out of navetanat: as we have seen, Soninke navetanes tended to come from slave families.[88]

The pace of urban migration quickened during the Second World War. As French West Africa was largely cut off from Europe during the war, the French created new industries and banks in Dakar to fulfill the federation's needs. Migration to Dakar accelerated after 1943 when French West Africa joined the Allies' side, and Dakar became a strategic center in the war.[89] This expansion continued after the war.

The Soninke population in Dakar, which had probably doubled between 1930 and 1940, doubled again between 1940 and 1950,[90] an increase roughly proportional to the general population increase of Dakar.[91] On the basis of interviews collected among villagers from Jagili (Gidimaxa), Michel Samuel concluded that the Soninke colony in Dakar grew especially during the decade following the Second World War.[92] The Dakar census of 1955 recorded 4,390 Soninke residents in the city, and 448 seasonal migrants and "others."[93] Of the resident Soninke, 1,933 were adult males.[94] If we consider that the majority of Dakar migrants must have come from the Upper Senegal region (Gajaaga and Gidimaxa), which numbered around 70,000 inhabitants, the proportion of urban migrants relative to the Upper Senegal Soninke was quite high—about 11 percent of all adult males.[95]

The most important development of the postwar period was the coming of Soninke women to Dakar. According to Michel Samuel's informants, it was during this period that many migrants brought their families to Dakar.[96] This information is confirmed by the 1955 Dakar census. Of the resident Soninke, 1,933, or 44 percent, were adult males; 1,117, or 25 percent, were adult females; and 1371, or 31 percent, were children younger than fifteen.[97] This transformation was probably the cause for the relocation of Soninke chambres away from the centrally located Gambetta quarter to the "African" quarters of Médina and especially Niaye Thioker—to be closer to the downtown area (and most places of employment). This move was not due to the new housing regulations that moved much of the African population into new peripheral quarters, such as Médina, since these standards were imposed in 1914. More likely, the chambres followed the relocation of most Soninke migrants, who rented housing with their wives, away from the expensive center of town, or who lived with married relatives.[98]

Oral sources provide data on the occupations of Soninke migrants. Michel Samuel's study revealed the following occupations for retired villagers from Jagili living in Dakar: one policeman, one customs officer, two laborers at the Petersen peanut oil factory, one male nurse, one male nurse's aide, one hospital employee.[99] Adrian Adams's study reveals the following occupations for villagers from Kungani after the Second World War: one gardener's aide, one man who worked on the Dakar-Gorée boat shuttle, one laborer at the electricity company, and a number of laborers whose place of employment is not specified.[100]

A. Hauser's study of industrial workers in Dakar is an invaluable source of information on Soninke workers in this city in the 1950s.[101] Hauser found that the Soninke were "clearly over-represented" among Dakar's industrial workers, as compared with their share in the population of Senegal.[102] They were especially numerous in one peanut oil factory, most surely the Petersen factory near downtown Dakar, in which they were *more numerous than the Wolof*.[103] Soninke workers were mostly of slave status, an observation that corroborates the data collected by Adams in Kungani for the late 1930s.[104] A relatively high proportion, 51.5 percent, were unskilled laborers, but this is lower than the proportion of Fuutanke workers (57.5 percent).[105] They were usually married and lived with their wives in Dakar. Of all migrants from rural areas of Senegal (of which the largest groups were the Fuutanke and the Wolof), they were the ones who stayed in town, in the same position, for the *longest* periods of time, often for more than ten years.[106] They shared with the most skilled workers a high degree of satisfaction with their workplace.[107] However, most eventually returned to their villages, although they very often came back later for a second or a third period of employment.[108] Like other migrants of rural origin, they were often members of ethnic associations.[109] The overall impression given by Hauser's and Samuel's studies is that Soninke migration to Dakar in the period 1945 to 1960 was at a transitory stage between what Abel Chatelain, in his study of nineteenth-century migrants in France, has called *pluriannual migration* (for several years) and *"lifelong" migration* (in fact, limited to the duration of an active life, with a return to the village at retirement).[110] Such a pattern stood in contrast with that of Fuutanke migrants, who stayed for short periods of time in Dakar.

All this information may well puzzle specialists. Today the Soninke population of Dakar, apart from a small number of government employees, appears mostly composed of retirees and of wives of migrants to France, who prefer the amenities of the capital to the more Spartan life in the village. But this, of course, does not mean that such was the situation in the 1940s and 1950s. Indeed, one of Michel Samuel's informants (a woman who came to Dakar immediately after the war) noted that "there were many more villagers from Jagili [in Dakar] back then [than today]."[111]

Figures are also available for the Soninke population of Bamako for this period. In 1947, Bamako was still a small town of 37,000, with a population only twice as large as Kayes (19,000), the second city in Mali.[112] Five percent of Bamakois at the time were Soninke.[113] In following years, Bamako grew very rapidly, to 76,000 in 1958 and 128,000 in 1960.[114] The proportion of Soninke in its population grew to 10.6 percent in 1960.[115] However, because the Soninke in Mali were recorded together with the Mande-speaking Marka of the Middle Niger Valley, it is almost impossible to translate these figures into a proportion of the Malian Soninke who lived in Bamako, as I just did for Upper Senegal Soninke in Dakar.[116]

Dakar and Bamako were not the only urban destinations of Soninke migrants in the 1950s. In her 1961 study of the Damga village of Hamadi-Wunare (Amadi-Ounaré), whose population is half Soninke, half Puular-speaking Fuutanke, and which had a very high migrant population (60 percent of adult males), Colette Le Blanc noted that although Dakar was the first destination of most migrants, only 11 percent found work there. Those migrants who had been unsuccessful in finding work in Dakar had to go to less preferred destinations.[117] A large number continued to go to urban centers in the peanut-producing region of Senegal: 41 percent of the migrants from Hamadi-Wunare thus went to Diourbel and Kaolack. Such migrants were either weavers or petty traders *(bana-bana)*.[118] Adrian Adams likewise noted migrants from Kungani living in Tambacounda,[119] Koungheul,[120] Thiès,[121] and especially Kaolack.[122] In addition, the migration of Soninke traders to the Gambia and Casamance also continued during these years.[123]

Another important migration that developed especially after the war was toward urban centers in the Ivory Coast. This migration is less documented than others. The northwestern region of the Ivory Coast was a destination of trade migrants in the precolonial period, who bought kola nuts in exchange for salt, cattle, and cotton cloth.[124] The majority of these migrants probably came from eastern Soninke regions, such as Gumbu, Kingi Jawara, and even Jafunu and less so from Gajaaga and Gidimaxa, which were situated too far for seasonal migrants.[125] Some Soninke migrants settled in the northern Ivory Coast at an early date.[126] For example, the most renowned Islamic leaders of the Korhogo region at the beginning of the twentieth century were descendants of Ibrahima Suumare, born "near Bakel" around 1836, who had first come to the area as a trader.[127] The Soninke migration of traders continued in the colonial period. Archival documents from the cercle of Nioro and Nara mention the movement of kola nut traders between these cercles and the Ivory Coast.[128] The migration of Soninke traders probably expanded in the wake of the larger movement of Mande traders, who penetrated forest areas that had been closed to them in the precolonial period, settling in the new centers created by colonial authorities.[129] Soninke migration probably also developed from the migration of Soninke employed on the Ivoirien railway line which reached the interior town of Bouaké in 1913.[130] Migration to the Ivory Coast apparently picked up in the 1930s, as Ivoirien cities grew.[131] By 1961, 30 percent of the migrants from Hamadi-Wunare migrated to the Ivory Coast. These migrants were either weavers or banabana selling cotton cloth in Ivoirien centers, especially in Bouaké, which was the second most important urban center in the Ivory Coast until independence.[132] In her surveys of migrants from Kungani, Adrian Adams also noted the presence of a small number of wage laborers among the migrants to the Ivory Coast, most of whom were merchants.[133] Finally, there were smaller numbers of Soninke migrants in Guinea, some of whom worked as traders in the capital, Conakry.[134]

Soninke Migrants in the French and Belgian Congos

We have seen the beginnings of Soninke migration in the French and Belgian Congos. After the completion of the Matadi-Kinshasa railway, Soninke migrants reverted to trade. In Lagos, which was one of the ports of call on their way to the Congos (or rather according to one oral report, in the neighboring market town of Abeokuta),[135] Soninke migrants bought low-priced indigenous Yoruba cloth and imported Dutch "wax" cloth. These types were much in demand in West Africa, but even more so in the Congos, where (according to Soninke informants) most indigenous people initially did not wear cotton clothes. Soninke migrants established residence in Kinshasa and Brazzaville, and later in provincial towns of the Belgian and French Congos. Their operations were generally modest, carried out as itinerant merchants on bicycles who radiated from an urban center into the surrounding countryside. In time, some migrants came to own stalls in urban marketplaces. Soninke cloth traders sold as retailers and also to local women traders.[136]

In the initial stages of the migration, when women were few, migrants apparently lived in communal housing.[137] As in Dakar (the chambres) and in France, migrants from the same village pooled their resources in a mutual aid fund for emergencies,[138] and they recognized as their chief the oldest man present among the members of the chiefly family of the village.[139] Wealth-ier migrants, usually from well-known maraboutic families, began to buy houses in Kinshasa before the First World War.[140] One informant, a reli-gious leader, was quick to point out that houses were bought not to be rented but to provide hospitality to relatives and other migrants.[141] This was, in-deed, what was expected of a marabout, whose reputation (and eventual sta-tus as a patron) was based on his generosity.[142] But other migrants appeared to have bought houses as investments and in order to rent them. In fact, it would be wrong to view hospitality as incompatible with investment and renting.[143] As Sandra Barnes has shown in her Lagos study, African land-lords often act as patrons for their tenants.[144] Conversely, the provision of hospitality enhanced the prestige of a landlord in his community. By the 1930s, communal housing had disappeared; new migrants lived at the homes of their relatives, and women had begun to appear among the migrants. Mean-while, commercial operations were becoming more sophisticated.[145] Some Soninke traders began to deal in commodities other than cloth, such as peanuts, dried fish, and kola nuts—the latter imported from the Ivory Coast by Soninke migrants.[146]

Former migrants recall as an important moment their building of a mosque in Kinshasa in "1910."[147] The Soninke in the Belgian Congo were part of a wider West African Muslim migrant community, comprising Fuu-tanke, Wolof, and especially Hausa, whose identity centered around Islam in this predominantly animist country. Islamic communities in Kinshasa and Brazzaville were organized around their *imams* and especially their *cadis* (Is-lamic judges).[148] The cadis, who were the true chiefs of Muslims, were al-ways Soninke.[149] As we have seen, the migration was believed to have begun in the Koranic school of the village of Kungani. The first cadi of Kinshasa, Mamadu Jaaxo, was the younger brother of Ba Bintu Tanjigora ("Laji Gile," or the giant), who reportedly began the migration among the talibes of Seexu Jomo Tanjigora around the turn of the nineteenth century. After Mamadu Jaaxo's death, Ba Bintu's son, Al-Haj Mamadu Jaaxo, succeeded him as cadi of Kinshasa.[150] Other maraboutic families also came to the area. Particularly worth noting were the Darame, who held the office of cadi in Brazzaville, on the other side of the Malebo Pool.[151] These families gained dominance among non-Soninke Muslims because of their religious prestige, knowledge, and training, which other West African migrants (for example, Wolof artisans and Fuutanke fishermen) did not have.

In the 1960s, there were perhaps two thousand Soninke in urban centers in Zaire (the former Belgian Congo).[152] The Islamic community in Kinshasa (which was dominated by the Soninke) was then described as "an exceedingly prosperous group."[153] Although most Soninke traders in Zaire continued to be petty traders, astounding success stories were recorded by Samir Amin in his meticulous 1969 study of Senegalese business. In the 1960s, some of the most successful migrants (about a hundred of them) came back to their villages with fortunes of 5 to 50 million CFA francs, or about $20,000 to $200,000 at the prevailing exchange rate. Amin estimated the volume of yearly monetary transfers from Zaire to Senegal at about 500 million CFA francs, or $2 million. This capital was invested in housing in Dakar or the home villages of the migrants or in cattle. (Village funds also were used to build mosques and to create Koranic schools in the Soninke homeland.)[154] But even larger sums were invested in Zaire and in the (French) Congo by the migrants, who bought movie theaters, stores, and large agricultural plantations.[155] Commercial operations had by then become so intricate that retail shops were created in Dakar to train young migrants for future trading in Zaire and the Congo or the Ivory Coast.[156] A small minority of marabouts amassed very large fortunes of 100 to 200 million CFA francs (between $400,000 and $800,000).[157]

Informants' interviews suggest that migration to the Congos was longer-term, pluriannual, or "lifelong" (returning to the village upon retirement), and a trend toward definitive migration was visible by the 1960s. Ties with the Soninke homeland, however, were strong. Children born in the Congos were systematically sent back to be raised in the Soninke homeland so that they would speak Soninke, learn Soninke customs, and grow up in a predominantly Muslim society. This policy, however, created problems for the many migrants who had married Congolese wives, as they resisted being separated from their children. They were supported in their resistance by young Soninke of the second generation, who, of course, had a stronger bond with the Congos, where they were born. Such conflicts apparently played a role in the emergence of the "Wahabiyya" Islamic movement in the Congos. The "Wahabiyya," which shares only its name with the historic Saudi Arabian movement, is an Islamic reformist movement noted for its opposition to magical practices and is well-represented in Mali among generally well-to-do merchants. In the Congos, the "Wahabiyya" especially appealed to young, reform-minded second-generation Soninke.[158]

Soninke Sailors in Dakar and in France

Sailing was a prestigious occupation among the Soninke. As we have seen, this preference went back very far in time. Laptot wages eroded at the turn of the nineteenth century, but the creation of an international harbor in Dakar enabled Soninke laptots to change to oceangoing sailing. An important port of call on international shipping lines between Europe and South America, Dakar provided employment on the great ocean liners. In 1920, the French administrator in charge of maritime employment in Senegal estimated the total number of registered African sailors in Dakar at 3,000.[159] Eighty percent of these men were from the cercles of Matam and Bakel and from French Soudan and Mauritania, that is, they were mostly Soninke.[160]

Some Senegalese sailors had already been to French harbors in the nineteenth century but only for passing visits. In the several years preceding the First World War, Senegalese sailors began to visit Marseilles more regularly. Most were apparently Wolof *originaires* from the Four Communes.[161] The First World War changed the situation entirely. As French sailors were mobilized, French shipping companies began to recruit colonial sailors. The demand was such that the companies usually disregarded the requirement that sailors produce a regulatory maritime registration booklet.[162] A *fascicule* could be obtained in Senegal after three years of employment in local coastal navigation *(cabotage)*,[163] but as such opportunities were very limited, African sailors obtained employment in Marseilles with dubious registration papers or no papers at all. Many, in fact, reached Marseilles as stowaways.[164] Although data on the origins of migrants is lacking for this period, subsequent information suggests that most of these undocumented sailors were Soninke.

After the war, French sailors were progressively demobilized and demanded their old jobs back. While stowaways continued to flow from Dakar to Marseilles[165] there were conflicts between Africans and French sailors' unions.[166] Wolof sailors in Marseilles, who were mostly French citizens from Saint-Louis, created the Amicale des Originaires de l'AOF, which functioned as an unofficial African sailors' union and opposed the coming of Soninke undocumented workers. These efforts notwithstanding, there seems to have been a marked increase in the number of stowaways from Senegal after 1925.[167] In 1925, the Chargeurs Réunis and Sud-Atlantique companies disembarked 154 stowaways in Bordeaux alone.[168] Stowaways slipped aboard ships in Dakar by passing as porters or dockers, with or without the complicity of dockers or sailors.[169] Most reportedly were Soninke from the cercles of Bakel and Selibaby (Mauritanian Gidimaxa).[170] A traffic developed in sailors' registration documents. Sailors who retired or went on leave usually passed on their fascicule to relatives.[171] Villagers from Jawara in Gwey obtained their documents through the intermediary of Musa Saaxo, a member of the village's chiefly family, who was employed as a planton at the Dakar sailors' registration office.[172] Others had to pay handsome sums to intermediaries in Dakar, such as the famous Magatte Louis N'Diaye, who created a sailors' union in Dakar in the early 1920s.[173] This traffic also took place in Marseilles. In 1926, the Ministry of Colonies even started an inquiry about its own representative in Marseilles, Louis Josselme, a former colonial administrator who headed the local branch of the C.A.I. (the colonial ministry's surveillance organization, which watched over colonial subjects residing in France), whom it suspected of selling provisional registration documents to undocumented African sailors.[174]

By 1930, the Soninke were "numerically the most important African group in Marseilles."[175] In the Upper Senegal region, oceangoing sailing had become the most popular occupation among young Soninke.[176] According to one informant, it was only when one did not succeed in becoming a sailor that one went to the Congos.[177] It is easy to understand why: the beginning wages of a sailor in 1930 were 420 francs a month (5,020 francs a year). A stoker earned 585 francs a month (7,020 francs a year).[178] At the same time, a navetane earned 1,200 to 1,500 francs in a yearly agricultural season.[179] Chief Ibrahima Jaman Bacili described the excitement of village youths upon the return of a "navigator" with 200,000 francs in savings and luggage bursting with goods and gifts.[180] The popularity of the sailing occupation was reflected in the 1920s in the already quoted song *"Tiga sandan sege"* ("Peanut Boom") celebrating navetanat:

> Mamadu the wealthy sailor has come back home
> Suuleyman the wealthy sailor has come back home
> Can the little birds serve as food to bats?
> Listen all
> And you the leaders of prayer
> Listen

Our father Mamadu Konte, the chief of sailors has come back home and
Jama Majigi who has come down from the ships to see again his
mother Jele Salu and his aunt Awa Samba[181]

As with navetanes, young men considered too young to migrate occasionally defied their parents' opposition and left secretly to become sailors.[182]
Older migrants, however, controlled employment and solidarity among
sailors. Younger migrants obtained employment in Dakar or Marseilles
through older patrons, the *caporals*,[183] who introduced them to shipping
companies.[184] Soninke sailors in Marseilles, and presumably elsewhere, had
village mutual aid associations, which were similar in organization to the
Dakar chambres.[185] Sailors generally kept to themselves in French ports, living and socializing in the same hotels and *"bars"* (a bar is a small cafe in
modern French language).[186]

African sailors in France were strongly solicited by Paris-based African
nationalist organizations during the 1930s.[187] In 1930, the activist and then
Communist sympathizer, Tiémokho Garan Kouyaté, attempted to create a
branch of the Ligue de Défense de la Race Nègre among African sailors in
Marseilles, but Soninke sailors refused to support him.[188] During the Great
Depression, however, many African sailors became unemployed and were
deported back to Africa. To avoid this fate, many went to French harbors of
the Atlantic coast, where Africans were less controlled than in Marseilles.[189]
Parisian African activists appear to have been more successful at enlisting
the support of such sailors in Le Havre, the Atlantic harbor closest to Paris.
By late 1931, the Ligue de Défense de la Race Nègre, now controlled by Gar-
veyists under the leadership of the Saint-Louisien intellectual, Emile Faure,
had a branch or affiliated union in Le Havre composed of African sailors.[190]
It is worth noting that the treasurer of Emile Faure's LDRN was a Soninke,
Amadi Diara, born in Mannayel (Gwey) in 1895.[191] This ethnic connection
may have played a role in bringing unemployed Soninke sailors to the Ligue.

However that may be, a fresh interest in politics, or rather in political patronage, became visible among Soninke sailors after the election of Galandou
Diouf as deputy of Senegal in 1934. Galandou Diouf, a somewhat neglected
figure in Senegalese political history, appears to have had a greater concern
than his predecessor Blaise Diagne for the non-Wolof rural groups of Senegal.[192] Diouf was also connected, partly for electoral reasons, with Emile
Faure's Garveyist Ligue de Défense de la Race Nègre in Paris.[193] In October

1934, a large group of sailors in Dakar sent a letter to Diouf, referring to themselves as his "Sarakole [Soninke] admirers." The letter demanded the right for documented sailors in Dakar to seek employment in Marseilles.[194] In 1934 also, a group of African sailors in Le Havre, most probably the Ligue's branch discussed above, wrote to Diouf asking him to intercede on behalf of African sailors in France. Diouf accepted.[195] In November 1935, a deputation comprising delegates of African sailors from Marseilles, Bordeaux, Le Havre, and Dunkerque went to see the minister of merchant marine in Paris. The African sailors were introduced to the director of the cabinet of the minister by Galandou Diouf. The move was a resounding success since the minister soon afterwards urged shipping companies that contracted with the French government to hire more Senegalese sailors.[196]

The minister's intervention had very important consequences. By 1937, the government-controlled Messageries Maritimes company operated a veritable ethnic quota system in its employment of African sailors in the machine rooms of its ships. In Marseilles, for example, five ships were reserved for Senegalese sailors, six for Arab sailors from Aden, and two for sailors from the French Côte des Somalis (Djibouti).[197] The employment of Arab sailors from Aden is worth a short digression. Aden Arabs first gained employment on French ships in the 1920s in much the same way as the Soninke, by using documents that were not theirs or falsified documents.[198] Ironically, Senegalese sailors (including the post-1938 Amicale, where the Soninke were represented) fought throughout the interwar period against the employment of these "foreigners," or "Arabes anglais"![199] In the "ethnic quota system" in use on the ships of the Messageries Maritimes (and companies that contracted with it), the positions reserved for Senegalese sailors were filled in Marseilles through recommendation by the conservative Amicale des Originaires de l'AOF. For the time being, this ensured the continued dominance of Saint-Louisien sailors since they dominated the Amicale.[200] But this situation did not last.

A newly formed group, the Comité de Défense des Travailleurs de la Mer Originaires d'Outre-Mer des Bouches-du-Rhône, had mandated two Marseilles sailor delegates to Paris in 1934.[201] These delegates were Auguste Guèye, the president of the conservative Amicale des Originaires de l'AOF, and a former sailor from French Soudan, Tumaani (François) Sangare. Sangare was the owner of a "bar" on 26, Rue Puvis de Chavannes, which was described as the "usual meeting place of the Sarakole [Soninke]."[202] According to French surveillance reports, Sangare was planning to create a new organization of African sailors in Marseilles.[203] In 1938 Auguste Guèye was ousted from the presidency of the Amicale by a coalition of younger men, many of whom had received their political education in the cafe of Pierre Mbaye, who was Kouyaté's contact in Marseilles in 1930, but who had maintained contact with the rival Ligue of Emile Faure in following years.[204] One of the rebels, Abdulay Njaay, had played a role in the creation of the Comité de Défense des Travailleurs de la Mer and had been in contact with Tuumani Sangare in 1935.[205] Another, Amadu Njaay, may have been an official of the Ligue's branch or union in Le Havre in 1931.[206] Although many of these men were Wolof, the bureau of the renewed Amicale was composed of equal numbers of representatives of all the ethnic groups among the African sailors in Marseilles. Thus the dominance of Saint-Louisiens over African sailors in Marseilles now came to an end.[207]

It was at about that time also that Soninke sailors began to join French sailors' unions. In the wake of the Popular Front, the reunified C.G.T. (the main French union, with ties to the socialists and communists) opened its doors to foreign workers in France.[208] Colonial workers apparently took advantage of this liberalization of union policy. In 1937 and 1938, the colonial administration in the Mauritanian part of Gidimaxa noted that Soninke sailors were now registered members of the C.G.T.'s sailor branch union. This worried the French at first but, as they soon realized, the Soninke remained uninterested in French politics.[209] Through this move, however, Soninke sailors had completed their penetration of the Marseilles labor market.

The Wolof almost completely disappeared among African sailors after the Second World War.[210] Soninke sailors now clearly dominated the African community in Marseilles, but this community was smaller than before the war. This was due to the shift from coal to diesel power on French liners after the war, which considerably reduced available employment for sailors, especially for Africans, who were generally employed as stokers or mechanics.[211] Although this point needs confirmation, it was probably during the postwar period that Soninke sailors began to gain employment as *postals*, that is, waiters or orderlies. By the 1970s, all Soninke sailors employed by French companies were postals.[212]

In 1948, three Soninke sailors, Jabe So, Ja and Samba Suumare, founded the Foyer du Marin Sénégalais (Senegalese Sailors' Hostel), which the prewar Amicale had unsuccessfully tried to create in the 1920s. The Foyer provided lodging, food, and laundry to new migrants, as well as a focal point for the Senegalese sailor community. It was the culmination of an associational effort that had begun well before the war. Soninke migrants in Marseilles, as mentioned, were organized in village associations. Each of these associations had its treasury, which covered the costs associated with sickness or deaths among its members and also served to repatriate undesirables. Village funds also covered the expenses of feeding and housing migrants in Marseilles. In other words, these associations were identical to the Dakar chambres and to village mutual funds in the Congos. In addition, the village funds pooled their resources into a common treasury in certain cases. This common treasury, like the village associations, was created before the war, but it ceased to function during 1940 to 1945.

A number of Soninke sailors appreciably improved their position in the postwar years. In 1949, the companies declared their best sailors *"titulaires."* The beneficiaries gained paid holidays, retirement pensions, security of employment, and free return tickets to Africa, and housing was found for those who did not have any. The often relaxed relations between African sailors and shipping companies are illustrated by the circumstances of the creation of the sailors' Foyer, which was bought by representatives of the sailors for 3 million francs. Jabe So recalls: "I went to see Roland Frayssinet. He handed me the three million directly without a receipt. I went then to see a real estate representative, who bought the premises in the name of our association." I have no information as to whether the "ethnic quota system" of the prewar period was maintained after 1945, but it is quite probable that something of the sort was in operation. In the 1970s, Soninke sailors were employed by French shipping companies by virtue of agreements negotiated between African governments and the French government, which guaranteed African sailors the same level of employment as had prevailed during the period of French colonization.[213]

A number of Soninke sailors began to acquire property in Marseilles in the form of hotels after the Second World War. Hotels and small cafes made a lot of sense as profitable investments for sailors, who found a ready-made clientele in their workmates since hotels and cafes were the only "homes" of sailors on solid land.[214] In 1948, only three Senegalese and two Malgaches owned hotels in Marseilles. In later years, although it is impossible to give a figure, hotel and cafe ownership became more common among former sailors. Many of these hotels were bought with profits from smuggling.

Smuggling had always been a lucrative activity for some Soninke sailors, but conditions were especially favorable to this form of "trade" in postwar Marseilles. Soninke sailors smuggled coffee for the black market, gold, silver coins; they also smuggled opium for a time in New York (where there is a small Soninke community.) They exported expensive manufactured products (such as watches) from France to foreign countries and imported objects from Japan, such as prints and small tables. Soninke sailors also "traded" with the Congo basin area, where many had relatives. Smuggling went together with a certain amount of contact with the underworld.[215] To temper the damaging aspects of this information for Soninke sailors, it should be said that practically all categories of sailors in Marseilles were involved in smuggling and that the Marseilles underworld had acquired at the time a manner of respectability by refraining from violent crime in favor of the *père tranquille* activities of smuggling and prostitution.[216]

Because migration as sailors was so prestigious among the Soninke, it was generally a "lifelong" migration—a *métier* according to one informant.[217] But Soninke sailors continued to maintain contact with their villages. Some took extended leaves of absence (one to three years) to "cultivate their fields" back home. Even some of the most successful hotel owners in Marseilles wished to return home eventually. A few Soninke, however, established permanent residence in France,[218] apparently because they valued the independence that their life abroad gave them vis-à-vis the demands of their extended family.[219]

Chief Ibrahima Jaman Bacili: Failure of a Modernizing Attempt

The story of Chief Ibrahima Jaman Bacili (Ibrahima Diaman Bathily) provides fascinating insights into the society of the Soninke homeland during the period considered in this chapter. This society, when Ibrahima Jaman Bacili was named head of the small canton of Goye Inférieur (Gwey) in the cercle of Bakel after the Second World War, was still "feudal" in spite of decades of migration and French rule. With great dedication, Chief Bathily attempted to reform it. However, he received no help from the very people from whom he had expected support, the French, the young, and the migrants, who did not back him in his struggle against his conservative opponents.

Chief Ibrahima Jaman Bacili's story was that of an educated man pitted against a society of illiterates. Until at least the Second World War, the Soninke, partly for religious reasons, had refused obstinately to send their children to the "Nazarean" (Christian) French schools. Students in the Bakel school were more or less conscripted by the local administrator, but at the first opportunity, they found a way to slip back to their villages.[220] In contrast, Ibrahima Jaman Bacili had received an exceptional education for the times. His father, Jaman Demba Bacili, was first a marine in the colonial army and then an interpreter.[221] Born in the 1890s, Ibrahima Jaman received a primary education in the French Soudan, then continued with secondary schooling at the famous School of the Sons of Chiefs in Saint-Louis. He then graduated from the Ecole Normale (Teachers' College) of Gorée in 1917 and taught in primary schools for twenty-seven years, mostly in the Soudan, where he married and where his children were born. In 1942, Ibrahima Jaman asked to be sent as a schoolteacher to or near Bakel, so as to be near his homeland. He was appointed principal of the primary school of Pout in Senegal in 1942. Soon after his return to Senegal, Ibrahima Jaman became involved in the political situation of Gwey.[222]

The French had always been trying to do away with gerontocratic control in Soninke society. With little success, they had tried to bring in younger men at the head of the chiefdoms. In the small canton of Goye Inférieur (the former Goye Indépendant—"Independent" Gwey), after the failure of the experiment with Samba Suuley described in Chapter Five, French administrators had reverted to the old expedient of appointing a younger councilor to assist the tunka. In so doing, the French had tried to give some form of legality to what was only an informal custom imposed out of necessity.[223] Thus in 1932, we find an official act bearing the signature of Konko Golla as official representative of the tunka of Gwey. This tunka was Samba Kajata, whom we have seen earlier soliciting the Senegalese Deputy Blaise Diagne through relatives in Dakar.[224] In 1935,[225] Konko Golla was appointed chief of Gwey by the French in replacement of Samba Kajata, either through his successful manipulation of the French or more simply because the French had decided to put an end to the intrigues developing around a senile Samba Kajata's potential succession. The process was almost repeated at Konko Golla's expense.[226] Konko Golla became blind and senile by 1938 and the French solved the problem by relying on Tambo Bacili, the man who had the most influence on him at the time.[227] But after 1941, Tambo Bacili either died

CHAPTER 7

[204]

or was pushed aside, and intrigues resumed among the Bacilis. In 1944, Konko Golla, who perhaps was not as senile as it was believed, succeeded in ousting a certain Papa Bacili, who evidently wanted to take Tambo's place.[228] It was in reaction to this situation that the French decided once again to by-pass custom and to name a younger chief. In 1944, Ibrahima Jaman Bacili was named chief of Goye Inférieur in replacement of Konko Golla, who kept the honorary title of canton chief.

It is important at this point to note that there had been discussions be-tween the French and the Bacilis, during which at least a section of the clan had expressed the desire of seeing Ibrahima Jaman "serve as their interme-diary between them and the administration."[229] Apparently, a number of people in the traditional elite realized the increasing sophistication of ad-ministration and the need to put an educated man in charge of their relations with the colonial authority. One of the reasons behind this belated awaken-ing was most certainly the fact that in 1939 Bakel had ceased to be the *chef-lieu* (chief town) of the cercle, when the cercle was split between the subdivision of Goudiry (cercle of Tambacounda) to the south and the cercle of Matam, downstream on the Senegal River.[230] The coalition of Bunduke and Soninke aristocrats that had until then ruled the cercle of Bakel found its voice drowned by other ethnic groups. The Soninke watched in dismay as Muslim Bunduke lost influence to Malinke, who not so long ago had been in their eyes pagans and infidels, while they themselves lost to the Puular-speaking Fuutanke of Damga and Bosseya. The groups that gained influence (this is more evident in the case of the Malinke in Goudiry than in that of the Puular-speaking Fuutanke in Matam) did so not so much because of their numerical importance as their greater level of education. In Gwey, there were only *six* men who had as much as a primary education. Only two of them lived in Gwey, and one of them was Ibrahima Jaman Bacili.[231]

The traditional elites that asked Ibrahima Jaman to come to Tiyaabu (the royal village) saw him as a subordinate in a political design. But in a classic development, Ibrahima Jaman saw his nomination as an occasion to bring badly needed reforms to Soninke society. During his life in the French Soudan, Ibrahima Jaman had become a member of the influential French Socialist party (S.F.I.O.), which was then very active in Africa. The postwar period was a period of rising hopes for reform-minded Africans, as political rights were granted to the whole of French Africa in recognition of its role in the liberation of France. In this period of colonial liberalism, Ibrahima

Jaman may, in fact, have presumed too much of the support that the French were willing to give him.

Ibrahima Jaman, like French colonial humanists such as Delafosse or Robert Delavignette, was no adversary of traditional authority per se. But the two institutions that Chief Bacili intended to discard, slavery and gift giving, were essential to traditional society. Slavery was the traditional basis of the power of Gwey's aristocracy. The testimony of Ibrahima Jaman's papers on its persistence in Gwey was appalling. It makes a contemporary observer realize how limited the authority of the French colonial administration could be. Slaves, wrote Ibrahima Jaman, were bought and sold as late as 1910. In 1920, they were still pawned for debts. In the mid 1940s, slaves were still given as dowry and included in inheritances. Children of slaves were deprived of their parents' inheritance, which according to custom went to their masters. Ibrahima Jaman wanted land to be granted to slaves or at least that the conditions of their employment by free men be formalized in contracts with legal sanctions.[232]

The second institution Ibrahima Jaman wanted to suppress was the practice of extravagant spending at funerals or harvests. A funeral could waste the savings of a lifetime, he wrote, reducing a family to misery and forcing its sons to emigrate. At harvests, young men went from farm to farm providing token amounts of "help," for which they expected to be lavishly fed and entertained by their hosts.[233] That these customs were giving rise to a considerable amount of waste and parasitism was not in doubt, but by attacking them, Ibrahima Jaman was also attacking a foundation of traditional politics. In traditional society, as we have seen, successful men were the most generous. An essential element of popularity derived from giving gifts to griots. Praise-singers kept alive family rivalries, and the need to save face led to further competition in gifts and extravagant spending, and ultimately to renewed tension within an already segmented and "anarchical" Soninke society. To this picturesque but wasteful and divided society, Ibrahima Jaman wanted to substitute a disciplined, efficient organization, more adapted to the modern world, the model of which he apparently saw in traditional village youth associations, with their semidemocratic character, their strong discipline, and their orientation towards collective effort and solidarity.[234]

Thus the attempt made by Ibrahima Jaman Bacili at reforming Gwey was essentially political, yet he was probably the first Soninke to voice concern about the economic condition of Bakel. The redistricting of the cercle of

Bakel was in a sense the consequence of its continuing economic decline since the gum crisis. This was clearly perceived by Ibrahima Jaman. The remedies he wanted to apply were those which had been advocated by the various French administrations, and in particular by French colonial humanists. He tried to introduce new cultivation techniques (perhaps the plow)[235] and to enforce regulations on emergency granaries.[236] Finally, Ibrahima Jaman was concerned about the level of migration in Gwey. He wrote that no development could take place around Bakel unless the migrants first came home.[237] Chief Bacili believed that this was possible if local agriculture was modernized, local transportation improved, and new activities were created in the area.

The returned migrants, especially sailors, in theory could have been good supporters for Chief Bacili. We have seen that there was no educated elite in Gwey in 1945; however, the returned sailors had traveled, most by this time having lived in France for shorter or longer periods, and thus they could be expected to have a broader experience and a more open mind than the majority of their compatriots. But this support did not materialize. Indeed the sailors—or "navigators," as they were called—were either indifferent or, more probably, hostile to Chief Jaman's reforms.[238]

We have seen that from the days of French penetration in the interior of West Africa the chiefs in Gajaaga and Gidimaxa had often been former sailors. The highly advantageous wages paid in this form of employment had made "navigation" particularly attractive to the upper strata of Soninke society, in particular the sons of chiefs and the members of the royal clan of the Bacili, who appear to have maintained a dominance over this form of employment.[239] The attraction of high wages was not simply a function of money, but of what it could achieve in Soninke society. In Soninke society, becoming a sailor was for an aristocrat a way to build up influence and popularity through a careful display of generosity dispensed adroitly to clients and strategically placed elders, without neglecting the griots, those influential praise singers, intelligent counselors, and confidants.

The Bakel archives give some idea of the rivalries, the struggles for influence that went on among these men as they competed to become respected elders, notables, and chiefs, many hoping to become the chief counselor of the tunka and perhaps, one day, the tunka himself. For colonial administrators, Bakel was the cercle of the "navigateurs," turbulent and hard to govern. The French explained this unruliness by the influence of new ideas picked up along the sailors' peregrinations all around the world, which brought them in conflict with the unchanged society of their homeland. But the navigators were not reformers. They wanted to achieve success in their traditional society, and this is why their attitude appeared so unruly to the administration, for the money they brought back from their migrations heightened their rivalries.[240] It was no surprise that the result was confusion in local authority, a weakening of its control in a region where authority had never been very strong in the first place.[241] This competition explains why Chief Ibrahima Jaman found so little enthusiasm among returned sailors for the reform of a traditional political system they all hoped to manipulate to their own benefit.[242]

Chief Ibrahima Jaman's ultimate downfall, however, was brought about by the economic underpinnings of the traditional political system. As Chief Samba Suuley before him, Chief Ibrahima Jaman's nomination had been largely due to the will of the colonial administration, and the Soninke transferred to him none of the essential prerogatives of the tunka's authority. Although Ibrahima Jaman was for the French the only legal chief in Gwey, to the Soninke the "honorary chief" Konko Golla was still the tunka, and the villagers continued to pay him the jakka, and other traditional land rights. Ibrahima Jaman appears to have remonstrated about this to the administration, but the French, because they had always refused to recognize "feudal rights" while balking at their suppression for fear of a revolt of the traditional authorities (which were the only channels of French authority in the area),[243] were powerless to act. The French also did not immediately realize the seriousness of Chief Bacili's situation. In 1945, the Bakel administrator doubted the reality of a "plot" against Chief Bacili—a real enough coalition of various enemies of which the French administrator was informed by Chief Bacili himself.[244] Ibrahima Jaman had to compete with Konko Golla solely with the help of the meager financial resources provided by his administrative salary. The struggle was unequal. The final blow probably came from the young people in whom Chief Ibrahima Jaman had so much faith. The political agitation so characteristic of French West Africa after the Second World War finally reached Bakel, but this agitation took the form of a rejection of all authority, which ultimately meant also the authority of the liberal chief Ibrahima Jaman Bacili.[245] Attacked from all sides, deprived of any meaningful support from the French, Chief Ibrahima Bacili committed suicide in 1947.

Conclusion

The period 1930 to 1960 thus saw a shift not only from *rural-rural* migration (navetanat) to *urban* migration, but also from seasonal to *pluriannual* and even *lifelong* migration, with a return to the village upon retirement (the trend toward the latter form of migration being especially visible by the end of the period). Yet Chief Bacili's tragic story showed that the reorientation of Soninke migration toward the African cities and the lengthening of the periods of time spent in the migration resulted in no "penetration of city values" among migrants.[246] As in the nineteenth century when the ambition of all migrants (including slaves) was to save enough money to buy slaves, who would give them both economic security and status in their home villages, the greatest desire of many migrants apparently still was to become village notables, and they had no inclination to challenge traditional society. Through migration, a young man could obtain a measure of emancipation from the traditional society simply by living abroad with independent financial resources, but these financial resources also allowed him to build up influence within his home society as the years went by. When he became old, he would return to his village and become a respected elder himself.[247]

They are many similarities in this respect between Soninke migration and the French migrations described by specialists such as Abel Chatelain or Françoise Raison-Jourde.[248] In the late nineteenth century, temporary migrants who had migrated as seasonal workers, some of them for centuries, such as the Auvergnat and the Creusois, began to take longer-term employment in French cities. Many of these urban migrants returned to their villages only upon their retirement.[249] Yet the main ambition of most urban migrants was *not* to settle in the cities but to obtain a better life eventually *in their villages,* by acquiring land. Even migrants who spent all their occupational career in the city came back to spend their retirement near their home village, generally in a small, neighboring country town, living as local notables. The persistence of rural ambitions among migrants was, in fact, so strong that it has persisted *until today, even among second- or third-generation migrants.* Jean-Luc Chodkiewickz has described how second- or third-generation migrants from Auvergne, who were born in Paris (but often raised in the "home" village by retired grandparents) continue to own land in "their" villages, participating fiercely in the local electoral campaigns, during which they clash with villagers "who have stayed *au pays,*" and who have different economic preoccupations.[250] The data on European labor migration, briefly summarized here, suggest that a number of traditional assumptions about African labor migration should be revised. African migration specialists have argued that temporary migrations have persisted for so long in Africa because African wages were too low and discouraged migrants from bringing their families to the towns.[251] In order to verify this hypothesis, one would need to have proof that the migrants really wanted to establish residence in the towns. Examination of the Soninke and French data in fact suggests no evidence of such an inclination.[252] In the French case, it took almost three hundred years, and in some cases longer, before the seasonal and temporary migrations of old were transformed into the *exode rural* of the 1950s.[253]

It could be argued, of course, that it took that long for suitable employment opportunities to develop in the French cities. But a detailed examination of labor migration from individual French regions shows that migrants continued to return even when such opportunities were available. Corsica, like the Soninke homeland, was for centuries a land of both emigration and immigration. In Corsica until not so long ago, migrants from the Italian city of Lucca did most of the agricultural work, while the native ideal was that of the idle country gentleman. To realize their patriarchal ideal, Corsicans were ready (in spite of their proverbial reputation for laziness) to accept the hardest types of work abroad. In the nineteenth century, however, Corsican migrations became increasingly long term, as migrants took comparatively well-paying and secure minor government jobs. Yet the migrants continued to retire in their villages, even though this often proved difficult when they had married non-Corsican women abroad. Today the attachment of Corsicans for their homeland still proves extremely strong, even among second-generation Corsicans born "on the continent."[254] Some authors have spoken about "reluctant farmers" in the case of African city-bound migrants, but in fact, it appears that often the formulation should be reversed and one should speak about *"reluctant urbanites."*[255]

This reluctance to move to cities, and this attachment to traditional values, should not be castigated as a "backward mentality," but recognized as an implicit will to perpetuate the home society. The paradox of temporary migration, however, is that it eventually evolves into a situation in which the return of the migrant becomes more and more problematic. During the period 1930 to 1960, Soninke migration became increasingly longer term, although only a minority of migrants became definitive migrants.

Other important changes were in the making during this period. Urban migration expanded over a wider and wider geographical area, which included not only Dakar, Kaolack, or Bamako, but Bouaké and Abidjan in the Ivory Coast; Kinshasa, Brazzaville, and Lubumbashi in the Congos; and Marseilles, Bordeaux, and Le Havre in France. Overall, Soninke migration in the 1950s appeared poised for further expansion. Soninke migrants possessed remarkable institutions of solidarity: a tradition of communal housing in the initial stages of migration, village mutual funds, and the chambres. Settled migrants provided new migrants with hospitality and contacts in the employment market. More remarkable even, the networks of solidarity of migrants in different geographical areas were linked. In a single village, it was not rare to find relatives going to Dakar, the Ivory Coast, and the Congos as well as France. To illustrate this "overlapping" or interconnectedness of migrants' networks with a striking example, Jabe So, the founder of the Foyer du Marin Sénégalais in Marseilles, was a relative by marriage of Al-Haj Mamadu Jaaxo, the cadi of Kinshasa.[256] As the West African population expanded, an increasing number of young migrants appeared on the labor market. All that was needed for the migration to expand was an increased demand for labor in Dakar, in the Congos—or in France.

Conclusion

THIS STUDY ENDS in 1960, as Soninke migration to France began in earnest. One of the most important developments since this date has been the Sahelian drought, which has very severely and perhaps permanently damaged agricultural production in the Soninke homeland. The drought may have left few other options to the Soninke apart from migration, unless or until successful irrigation schemes are set up, preferably by the Soninke themselves.[1] It is important to remember, however, that the drought began in 1968 to 1972, at a time when migration to France was already quite well established, and thus it cannot be considered the original cause of migration.

In this final chapter, I will first give a brief outline of the emergence of Soninke migration to France, and I will attempt to assess, of necessity tentatively, the course of Black African migration to France in the last decades and to forecast its future. Finally, I will gather the various threads followed in this study and propose some directions for placing Soninke labor migration within the larger context of labor migration history.

Epilogue—Soninke and African Migration to France

Journalistic and other sources often give the impression that African migration to France began around 1958 or 1960.[2] As we shall see, there was probably an increase of African migration to France during these years. But already by 1956, African workers in France officially numbered 15,000 (versus only 2,000 in 1953).[3] In 1963, when African migration caught the attention of the French press, migrants officially numbered 22,000. This suggests that the migration began earlier than is usually presumed, in the early or middle 1950s.[4]

In contrast with other European countries, France had almost no foreign workers (as opposed to colonial workers) until the late 1950s. The reason was not slower growth, for the French economy began to gather speed in the early 1950s, but the long and cumbersome immigration procedures adopted by the postwar Office National de l'Immigration, which alone had the authority to recruit workers abroad.[5] Although French government circles realized the need to attract migrants in this period of reconstruction, the French public, which faced a dramatic housing crisis, was generally hostile to it.[6] Ironically, it was this opposition to foreign migration that led to the recruitment of migrants in France's colonial African territories. French colonial subjects in Africa (Algerians and French West Africans) were legally French citizens after 1946, hence there were no legal obstacles to their employment. This explains not only the massive increase of Algerian immigration after the war, but also the timid emergence of Black African migration in the mid 1950s.

The Algerian war accelerated the pace of Black African migration to France. In 1956, in an attempt to curb the spread of terrorism on metropolitan soil, the government imposed entry visas for Algerians, which were only suppressed in 1962 by the Evian accords.[7] Because most Algerian migrants were temporary migrants who traveled back and forth between France and North Africa, the effect of this measure was dramatic. Entries of Algerians in France fell from 194,000 in 1955 to 79,000 in 1956, and the balance of entries over departures fell from about 25,000 per year between 1950 and 1955, to only one thousand in 1956. In 1958, the year of the European settler revolt in Algiers, departures from France of Algerian workers exceeded arrivals by 14,000.[8] There is an obvious connection between this fall in the number of Algerian workers in France from 1956 to 1958 and the increase in the number of Black African migrants noted during or immediately after these years.[9] Longer-term factors also increased this impact. The period of the Algerian war witnessed a considerable increase in the number of Algerian *families* living in France[10]—a development that was connected with the promotion of Algerian migrants to higher skilled jobs. Whereas in the early 1950s, these had been mostly employed in unskilled manufacturing jobs, in the late 1950s and early 1960s many began to move toward somewhat more skilled occupations in the building trades.[11] Becoming settled, they brought their families to live with them in France. This meant that there was an even greater need for unskilled laborers in France.

These trends and events created a critical situation for French employers. The labor shortage that prevailed from 1956 to 1962, during the most dynamic period of French economic expansion, actually shattered the official immigration system. With the end of the Algerian war in 1962, thousands of Algerian migrants were allowed back in France, but the coming of more than a million French Algerian settlers to France created a boom in construction, which stimulated the French economy and increased the demand for migrant workers. In the period from 1955 to 1965, around one million foreign workers entered France. The overwhelming majority (79 percent in 1965) were "regularized" (a euphemism for the pardoning of workers who had entered the country illegally) by the Office National de l'Immigration.[12] In this situation of complete breakdown of official control, French enterprises ran their own recruitment abroad with total impunity.[13]

According to Jabe So, one of the founders of the Hostel of Senegalese Sailors in France in the 1950s (see Chapter Seven)—whose account is corroborated on many points by other sources—during the Algerian war, all the major French automobile factories in Paris, such as Renault and Simca, and even the sanitation services of the City of Paris (a stereotypic employer of Algerian migrants) sent labor recruiters to Marseilles, perhaps to other French harbors as well, where they knew that Black Africans were employed.[14] One may marvel at the City of Paris or the state-run Régie Renault endeavoring to hire workers in semiclandestine fashion (for these employers never admitted to having organized these recruitments, and even denied for a long time that they employed large numbers of Africans). But, in fact, these attempts may have been made precisely in order to avoid recruiting illegal aliens, for the employment of migrants from the former French West African territories remained unrestricted until 1963, although these territories had become independent in 1960.[15]

Migration to France: An Extension
of Urban Migration in Africa

Why did recruiters for French enterprises try to recruit Black Africans in Marseilles? They may simply have heard that Black Africans lived there, and they may have assumed that, as "colonial" migrants, they would be just as willing as Algerians to take low-paying jobs disdained by the French. But it is perhaps worth noting that by 1953 a number of Africans in Marseilles were employed in local factories already.[16] Some may have found industrial work through African hotel and cafe owners, who acted as intermediaries for local factories.[17] These early African industrial workers in Marseilles were probably not Soninke, but the existence of a small African industrial labor network in Marseilles may have been one of the reasons for the coming of labor recruiters to Marseilles.

According to Jabe So, labor recruiters went to African cafes in Marseilles, where they tried to recruit Soninke sailors. The sailors told the recruiters that they already had satisfactory jobs, but that they could send for relatives. Migration to France from that point on spread in an informal fashion through Soninke family networks.[18] Persistent rumors, however, which were relayed by French and African journalists in the 1960s, refer to a more elaborate recruitment effort. According to these, French enterprises sent labor recruiters to Dakar and other African harbors to enlist workers for French enterprises.[19] One report even mentions that the recruiters were African sailors, who had contacts with members of the Marseilles underworld, who themselves acted as intermediaries for Parisian enterprises.[20] These reports are not entirely implausible (we have seen that there were contacts between former sailors and the Marseilles underworld), but even if such recruitments did take place, their impact was probably exaggerated with a view to dramatizing these journalistic accounts.[21]

More intriguing is the information that that the chambre of Muderi (Gwey), was at some point involved in the recruitment of Soninke migrants to France.[22] The chambres, like African bars and hotels in Marseilles, were meeting places for migrants in Dakar, and places where information about employment opportunities was exchanged. They almost certainly served to make contacts for the migration of stowaways, which had continued into the 1960s and beyond.[23] We have seen also that there were contacts between African sailors in Marseilles and Dakar in the interwar period.[24] It would have been quite logical for Soninke in Marseilles to pass on information about the new factory jobs in France to fellow villagers in Dakar, where, as we have noted, many Soninke migrants went to seek work in the 1960s (very often unsuccessfully) and, furthermore, where a number of Soninke already worked in factories (see Chapter Seven).

However that may be, all available information concurs that the earlier Soninke industrial workers in France had first been migrants to Dakar. According to various sources consulted by Souleymane Diarra, African migrants until 1956 to 1957 had all lived for a time in an African harbor.[25] According to an unnamed automobile plant executive in Paris (almost certainly from the Renault factory in Billancourt), Africans who sought employment in the plant until 1956 to 1957 either came from Dakar or had lived there a number of years.[26] Adrian Adams likewise collected oral testimonies in the village of Kungani indicating that the first migrants from the village to France had lived several years in Dakar prior to their migration in the early 1960s.[27] Finally, Souleymane Diarra noted during his inquiry in 1963 that 35.7 percent of a representative sample of 1,500 migrants in Paris spoke enough French to be able to communicate. He added: "These are migrants who have lived in an [African] city for some time . . . ."[28] These reports should not surprise us: migrants who had worked in Dakar already had an experience of work in the city—for some, of *industrial* work (see Chapter Seven)—and some knowledge of the French language. Hence, they had a better chance to "make it" in France (that is, to be hired, to find housing, and so forth) than migrants who came directly from the village. This means that *migration to France was initially the continuation of the urban migration that had begun among the Soninke in the interwar period*. However, once migration had become established in France (that is, after it had established its networks of solidarity, such as village mutual funds and communal housing), it spread to younger Soninke who had not migrated anywhere previously. In the late 1960s, Soninke migrants went directly from their villages to France.[29]

That African migration to France began among *urban* migrants (to an African city) is interesting in view of the later evolution of the migration. In the 1970s, African migration to France spread to geographical neighbors of the Soninke such as Puular-speakers (Fuutanke or Fuulbe), Beydan, or Bambara. But this spread was limited. OECD statistics for 1979 estimated the number of *Senegalese* residing in France at about 80,000 persons. Of these migrants, 22 percent came from the Fleuve region and 17 percent from Sénégal Oriental, that is, predominantly Soninke and Fuutanke regions.[30] Eighteen percent came from Casamance; the dominant group among them, the Manjak, have a history of employment as sailors that is very similar to the Soninke. But the last important group of Senegalese in France (15 percent) was the Wolof of the Cap Vert region, in other words, from Dakar.[31] Any encounter with such migrants makes it clear that these are urbanized migrants, who have lived at least several years in Dakar prior to coming to France.[32] If one now considers *Black Africans* as a whole, and not simply the Senegalese, the evolution in the last decades is even more striking. It is not only that the Soninke are now a *minority* among African migrants, but migrants from Senegal, Mauritania, and Mali comprised in 1981 *less than half* of Africans in France (students not included).[33] Although West Africans still predominate, there are relatively large and growing groups from Cameroon and the Congo basin. African migrants to France are increasingly diverse in both their occupational makeup (from factory worker to high-fashion model) and their ethnic origins (from almost all Francophone African countries, and even from Anglophone countries such as Ghana). They are members of groups that either have long histories of migration comparable to the Soninke (such as the Hausa or the Mossi) or whose homelands are *in the vicinity of large African cities* (such as the Wolof).[34] In other words, *African migrants to France are members of groups affected by urban migration;* African migration to France *is an extension of the process of (temporary) migration to African cities.*

The Soninke, therefore, appear to have been the vanguard of a larger movement of intercontinental migration from urban Black Africa. Considering the range of their migrations, it is not surprising that they should have played such a role. It is, in fact, possible to trace this "vanguard role" of the Soninke through their connections with other African groups. The case of the Hausa is the most conspicuous. As is well known, the Hausa, whose homeland is on the desert edge, played in the Central Sudan a role of itinerant traders similar to that of the Soninke. Moreover, the known history of the Hausa begins before the fifteenth century with the coming of the "Wangarawas," that is, of Soninke, Wangara, or Gangara from the Tagant region in Mauritania, an area that was originally peopled by Soninke agriculturalists.[35] The influence of the Soninke on the Hausa is still visible today: like the Songhay, the Hausa have traditional songs that comprise parts sung in the Soninke language.[36] In the Congos, the Soninke and the Hausa met for the second time in their history, and both formed the nucleus of an Islamic community in Kinshasa and Brazzaville (see Chapter Seven). As a consequence of contacts with the Soninke in these cities, Hausa migrants came to Dakar after the Second World War.[37] Most certainly as a result of this recent history, there are today Hausa migrants in Paris, who share common village funds with the Soninke.[38] Likewise, the growing number of migrants from the Brazzaville-Kinshasa area to France must bear some relation to the historical presence of the Soninke in this region.[39]

A similar story may be detected in the history of other well-known international migrations. Migration from Algeria to Europe, for example, began among the Kabyle of the Djurdjura mountains. The Djurdjura are covered with heavy snow in the winter, and like the Auvergnat or the Savoyard, the Kabyle migrated in order to make the best of the long winter season of agricultural inactivity.[40] In the 1870s, Kabyle began to migrate to France as petty traders, selling indigenous crafts such as carpets. By the turn of the century, they worked as temporary migrants in the mines and factories of northern France. At the time, they also made up a significant proportion of the urban population of Algeria. Following the Kabyle, and presumably through contacts with them, migrants to France then came from *urban* areas in Algeria; many were skilled workers from cities such as Algiers. From that point, migration tended to spread, through the agency of rural-urban migrants in Algeria, *back to rural areas*.[41] A similar pattern of international migration beginning in urban areas has been identified for migration from Italy, Yugoslavia, and Turkey within and to Europe,[42] and for nineteenth-century migration from Europe to the United States. Recent research on "Atlantic migration" indeed suggests that migration to the New World in the nineteenth century was an offshoot of temporary migration to European *cities* (even though it eventually developed into definitive migration).[43]

The comparison with Algerian migration may give an indication about the future of Black African migration to France. The Black African community in France is expanding extremely rapidly: around 60,000 in the early 1970s, 120,000 in 1981, and 660,000 now, according to the latest French census (1992).[44] This enormous expansion is all the more remarkable considering the long-standing problem with unemployment in France (unemployment has been running at more than 10 percent of the labor force for nearly two decades). One wonders how large African migration will become once the French employment market recovers from its currently depressed situation. Black Africa is experiencing a dramatic process of urbanization; in some countries one-third of the population already lives in urban areas (as compared with one-tenth or less twenty years ago), and the process of rapid urban growth show no signs of abating.[45] If indeed African migration to France is an offshoot of African urban migration, this means that it will probably grow in the coming decades. A massive migration from Africa would affect not only France, but neighboring European countries as well. (Growing numbers of Black African migrants have been reported in Italy and Spain in recent years).[46] Furthermore, it is fallacious to believe that this migration will not become permanent. The case of Algerian migrants in France illustrates the trend: in the 1950s and 1960s, Algerian migrants were mostly male, temporary migrants who lived in hostels and were almost completely separated from the French population. Today in the 1990s, most Algerians in France live in families among French and other immigrant families, and their main problem is the integration of their children, who are born in France and generally do not speak Arabic, but who are still perceived as "foreign" by the French. I was scolded by a reviewer of an earlier version of this study for writing that Soninke migration to France would eventually become permanent. Yet, at the time when this comment was made, I had attended a Soninke festival in Paris, which was attended mostly by young Soninke families, whose children spoke only French, despite the fact that the event was organized by the Association for the Preservation of the Soninke Language! But today, the fact that Soninke migration to France is becoming permanent is no longer in doubt.[47] This discussion suggests that the French, and southern Europeans in general, should be prepared to see African migration grow in the coming decades and should also be prepared to tackle the problems posed by the integration of large numbers of Africans in their population.

General Conclusion

Throughout this study, I have spoken about *a* Soninke labor migration, but this expression is to some degree misleading; in fact, as we have seen, there was not one but *several* Soninke labor migrations. Considering these from a geographical vantage point, there were migrations from the "western" Soninke region (the Upper Senegal) and migrations from the "eastern"

Soninke region (Nioro and Nara). The Soninke from the Upper Senegal region were the first to become navetanes and the first to migrate to Dakar and Senegalese cities; they were the only ones to migrate as sailors; and they were the first to migrate as industrial workers to France. Conversely, the Soninke from the eastern region tended to migrate to Kayes, Bamako, and the Ivory Coast. Considering migration from a social point of view, the migration of sailors, long the preserve of "warrior" aristocrats, should be distinguished from the migrations of merchants, which were dominated by marabouts, and from the migration of navetanes (and its continuation, the migration of laborers and industrial workers to Dakar), which was dominated by slaves and by poor commoners.

This being said, however, all Soninke migrations eventually spread beyond their initial geographical or social sphere to gain a wider impact. Navetanat spread from Gajaaga and Gidimaxa in the western region to Jafunu, Gidyume, and Kingi probably by the end of the nineteenth century, and to the Gumbu-Nara region around the First World War. Likewise, migration to France began among the Upper Senegal Soninke, but by the 1970s, its center of gravity had shifted eastward toward the Xoolinbinne River Valley, and migrants came from as far as Nara. In the late nineteenth century, the migration of laptots spread from "warrior" aristocrats to at least some clerics and slaves. Migration to the Congos, at first essentially a migration of royal aristocrats and clerics, eventually spread to all classes in Soninke society. Although the evolution of the social composition of the migration to France is unknown, migrants to France today come from all classes of society, except perhaps Bacili royals from Gajaaga (who apparently shun factory work, although they have continued to be strongly represented in the sailing occupation.)[48]

Historically, several factors have tended to give some unity to Soninke migration. First, there were numerous ties between the various Soninke polities. Clan ties linked one region to another (for example, the Jawara clan, based in Kingi Jawara, is also found in Gidimaxa and other regions), joking relationships linked ruling families (the Bacili of Gajaaga and the Suumare of Hayre-Damga), and joking relationships could even link the entire populations of two neighboring regions (Gidimaxa and Jafunu). Second, in precolonial trade migration, all classes of society participated, even slaves (although "actual slaves" could not migrate), and although the western Soninke tended to migrate to the Gambia while the eastern Soninke tended to migrate to the Ivory Coast, such regional specializations were not absolute. Furthermore, still in precolonial migration, the maraboutic networks of clerical clans, jatigi, and religious schools crisscrossed the map of the various Soninke polities. Relations of clientele, family, and clan alliances helped the spread of migration from one social group to the other; for example, the migration of laptots spread from warrior aristocrats to their maraboutic, casted, and slave clients. Competition or emulation between classes (for example, between warrior aristocrats and clerics, between free and slave) also encouraged the spread of migration. As a result, it is possible *today* to speak about *a* Soninke labor migration, although it should be understood that this unity is the outcome of an initial diversity and, just as importantly, that the ethnic boundaries of this migration were and remain fluid: Islamic and merchant networks linked Soninke, Jaxanke, and Mande in precolonial times, and clan ties often extend to other ethnic groups.[49]

This presentation reveals the important role played by "traditional" factors (clan ties, traditional trade migration) in the emergence and development of labor migration. This affirmation contradicts both a certain colonial historiography, which opposed the "traditional" to the "modern" as mutually exclusive terms, and Marxist historiography, which emphasized the historical break of proletarianization. The history of Soninke labor migration, like the history of labor migration in Europe, reveals on the contrary a fundamental historical continuity. Premodern trade migration helped to pave the way for migration to regions of commercial agriculture, which then developed into rural-urban migration. Such transformations occurred through the agency of "traditional" institutions, for example, in the Soninke case, clans, joking relationships, clientage, and youth associations (remodeled into chambres and migrants' mutual funds). Rather than being obstacles to historical change, "traditional" links and social structures were, in fact, its vectors.

It could be contended that focusing on traditional trade migration, clans, traditional clientage, and so forth, teaches us a great deal about the *channels* taken by migration, but not much about its *causes*, which upon analysis must be found to be economic. In the case of African labor migration, it has been argued that although traditional trade migrations facilitated the emergence of modern labor migration, colonial taxes and rural poverty were its main causes. We have seen what we should think of the taxation explanation as concerns the Soninke. As for poverty, we saw that the Soninke homeland was comparatively prosperous in the nineteenth century, but that this did not prevent migration from expanding. It is true that the economy of the Soninke homeland has steadily declined since that time, although this decline has often been exaggerated. Looking back at quantitative evidence, however, we cannot help but be struck by the fact that temporary migration was always important among the Soninke. From 1885 to 1986, as we have seen, about 10 percent of the male active population in the Upper Senegal region had worked for the French as laptots or urban laborers,[50] a figure that did not include those who migrated as navetanes or as traditional trade migrants, whose combined numbers were presumably greater than those of laptots and urban workers. In 1912, a colonial administrator in Bakel, reporting on a tour of the five Soninke villages of Goye Annexé, noted that "ten to twenty" young men in each village migrated each year as navetanes and that men also migrated seasonally to the Gambia in order to exchange locally produced cloth for kola nuts; to the Gambia and Siin-Saalum to sell horses, cows, and donkeys; to various parts of Senegal to work as laptots, sailors, houseboys, and workers on the Thiès-Kayes railway; or to the Belgian Congo to work on the railway.[51] Since the five villages in question had in 1904 about 1,800 inhabitants,[52] 12 to 25 percent of their active male population migrated as navetanes each year, and it is not unreasonable to think that, in addition, an equivalent number also migrated as laborers and trade migrants. On the basis of detailed oral interviews, Adrian Adams has established that in 1938 in the Goye Annexé village of Kungani, out of 335 adult males, 85 were away as migrants, or again about 25 percent.[53] Colonial sources give an even higher figure: a verification of lists of reservists effected this year in the cercle of Bakel revealed that two-fifths of the men (around 40 percent) were absent.[54] Comparing such figures with contemporary figures is interesting. In the 1970s, it was estimated that 35 percent of the active male population in Gwey and riverine villages in Gidimaxa was away as migrants in France. To this, it is true, should be added less than 5 percent away in African countries other than Senegal and an indeterminate number away in Senegal itself.[55] These numbers suggest that even though migration has increased over the years, in particular in recent years, it was very important in the past, at a time when the economic situation of the Soninke homeland was considerably better than today.

In the popular view of migration, labor migration is easily explained as a movement from a "poorer" to a "richer" region. It is true that labor migrants migrate because they find an economic advantage in their migration. But this observation is trivial. As was noted previously, it does not indicate if it is poverty that pushes migrants away from their homeland or wealth that attracts them to cities and other places of employment. More interestingly, a comparative approach uncovers facts that appear completely at variance with a purely economic approach. The following observations were made in this study, which are as relevant to the Soninke as other groups in Africa or in Europe:

There are comparatively poor regions that *do not* send migrants, while comparatively richer regions *do*.

Likewise, some regions send much "bolder" migrations than other regions whose economic conditions are *similar*.

A region may become richer, and export more products, *without* seeing its migration diminish or stop.

Some of the first modern migrants came from the *upper* classes.

Many regions are *at the same time* regions of out-migration and regions of in-migration. (In other words, one person's "poorer" region is another's "richer" region.)

To call attention to these "oddities" of labor migration is to point to several observations (with which I am sure that most economists would agree). First, economics cannot be separated from the society in which they operate. Clearly, the temporary migration of members of upper classes makes more sense in the history of African societies than in that of most Western societies, where membership in the upper social echelons gave a person individual wealth and power. In Soninke society, where wealth was owned by the family group, authority was gerontocratic, succession to political office was not automatically regulated by patrilineal filiation, and polygyny gave aristocrats very large numbers of offspring, it made sense for young aristocrats to migrate with a view to build up resources that would later make them influential elders, and eventually chiefs or kings, at home. Second, although modern labor markets are in theory open to all, in practice, we know that there are reasons of historical opportunity that make certain groups aware of potentially attractive job opportunities before others, and that in some cases enable them to maintain a monopoly over them. With respect to the Soninke, we noted the following:

The location of the Soninke in an important zone of desert-side trade allowed them to participate in trade migration from precolonial times.

Precolonial trade migration (to the Gambia) made the Soninke aware of labor opportunities created by peanut export production (navetanat) before other ethnic groups.

Trade contacts with the French (which were an offshoot of the precolonial history of trade among the Soninke) led to the employment of Soninke aristocrats as laptots.

The migration of laptots later led to the employment of some Soninke in Senegalese cities in the nineteenth century.

It also led to the specialization of the Soninke as seagoing sailors in the first decades of the twentieth century.

The employment of Soninke as sailors led to their coming to France.

The seasonal employment of navetanes in Senegalese towns in the dry season later led the Soninke to take longer-term urban employment when Senegal's cities began to expand in the 1930s.

The employment of some former navetanes as factory workers in Dakar prepared them for employment as factory workers in France.

To look at such historical circumstances is to realize that they, and the social networks that made them possible, were much more than *channels* that led migrants toward certain particular occupations and locations. They were also *causes* of migration: precolonial migrations, ties with French commerce, clerical networks, family connections, and so forth, made the Soninke aware of comparatively well-paying work opportunities abroad before other groups, and therefore, they were *causes in their own right*. Without such historical and social connections, Soninke migration could have followed other "scenarios." In the nineteenth century, the Soninke could have stayed at home producing cereals for the Beydan, or peanuts for the French, instead of becoming laptots and navetanes. In the twentieth century, they could have remained navetanes and urban migrants in Senegal and Mali, instead of spreading all over West Africa, the Congos, and France as sailors, merchants, and industrial workers. None of these conservative scenarios prevailed, although they did among other ethnic groups in the area, whose economic situation was similar to the Soninke's.

Should we say then that it is impossible to generalize about Soninke labor migration because its causes are historical and therefore entirely contingent? We have seen, however, that there are characteristics of Soninke migration that appear to be found quite generally among contemporary labor migrations worldwide. The social networks that make migration possible—such as kinship networks, clerical networks, chambres—are common in Africa and have equivalents in Europe. The emancipatory role of labor migration for lower classes and subordinate groups (slaves and younger people in Africa) is also a common phenomenon. We have also seen that Soninke labor migration has tended over time to evolve from seasonal rural-rural migration into pluriannual urban migration, and finally into lifelong and eventually permanent urban migration. This historical pattern has been general in Europe. It closely parallels, and in fact it is the result of, the evolution of the modern economy—where the expansion of commercial agriculture has preceded the expansion of cities and where casual and temporary labor in the cities has preceded the emergence of permanent (and increasingly skilled) urban occupations. This discussion reveals that labor migration is a transitional stage between the premodern peasant world, where activity revolved around the seasonal rhythms of agriculture, and the modern world of cities, where occupations are year-round and increasingly more varied and specialized.

In this book, I have made frequent comparisons between the Soninke and groups well known for the "boldness" of their migrations, such as the Auvergnat and the Limousin in France or the Kabyle in North Africa. All of these groups have a long history of premodern migration, which seems to be rooted in a fragmented political structure and in a geographical environment characterized by long periods of agricultural inactivity and the proximity of an ecological frontier (desert-side frontier or mountain-plain frontier). Because these migrations are so old, the migration networks of these groups have had the time to develop over very wide geographical areas. Also because they are so old, these migrations are characterized by strong communal solidarity, social conservativeness, and communal monopolies over certain occupations (all are typical features of premodern societies). Men migrate rather than women, who are left behind under the control of elders, to raise the children in traditional values. There is little interest in modern education or in integration to the host society—neither of which were open options in premodern times when the migration began, and neither of which are necessary today since communal solidarity and occupational specialization are sufficient strategies to provide migrants with jobs. Finally, because communal solidarity is so strong and the aspiration to integrate the host society is generally lacking, the desire to reintegrate into the home society at least upon retirement is very strong. In sum, these migrations are *old migrations*, which continue to have features of premodern migrations.

Not all modern migrations, of course, are of that type, although I have by necessity focused on such examples for the purpose of this study. In high contrast with the Soninke or the Auvergnat, the migrations of the Sereer in Senegal or the Breton in France are *young migrations* (they began at the beginning of the twentieth century for Breton and around the 1960s for the Sereer).[56] With some exceptions, the Sereer and the Breton in premodern times were stereotypical "sedentary peasant" societies, which traditionally did not engage in trade migration. Their modern migrations have been generally timid, operating at a close geographical range. These groups have not clustered into certain particular occupations to the same degree as other groups. Also in contrast with the Soninke or the Auvergnat, groups that live in the vicinity of towns or big cities, such as the Wolof in Senegal or migrants from Lower Burgundy or the Parisian basin in France, have not gone through the stages of seasonal rural-rural, pluriannual urban, lifelong urban, and definitive migration, but instead have moved from a short initial period of seasonal migration directly into lifelong and definitive migration to the city. Such groups, because they migrate at close range and share basically the same culture as people in the city, generally assimilate very rapidly and do not form ethnic associations. Among other groups, which need to be studied in more detail, female migration has been very important, and occasionally it has occurred earlier and has been more important numerically than male migration. Others still, such as the Corsicans and migrants from Aquitaine or, more recently, French West Indians, have made education the engine of their migration and tend to cluster in government jobs.[57] Finally, for certain groups, migration has been the occasion of important social transformations; such has been the case in Africa for the Wolof or the Bambara, who by migrating to Dakar or Bamako have often gained access to superior educational and occupational opportunities.

In making such comparisons, I am not suggesting that historians develop a "science" of migrations, for there are as many migrations as there are historical situations, but a historical *typology* of migrations would certainly be very useful. This typology would place African labor migration in a global perspective through comparisons with other forms of migration worldwide, but it would also enable one to define an *African* typology of migration. The history of African labor migration has its own characteristics, which distinguish it from migration on other continents. Premodern seasonal trade migration was probably far more important in the tropical regions of Africa, particularly Sudanic Africa, than in Europe because of the prevalence of decentralized political structures and the existence of a very long period of dry-season agricultural inactivity. A vast amount of information is available about precolonial migration in Africa, both from primary and secondary sources, yet historians have given no more than perfunctory attention to the link between them and modern migrations. The role of Islamic networks in urban migration has attracted some attention.[58] The importance of clan ties and interclan ties is well known in African studies in general, but it has received no application to the study of labor migration, although David Robinson and Jean Schmitz have called attention to its importance in the emergence and development of the Fergo Umar, the religious migration of Fuutanke followers of Al-Haj Umar Tal to Kaarta and Segu.[59] The study of clientage is becoming increasingly more important in political science studies, but it is not yet used in migration studies. Finally, Ken Swindell was the first to call attention to the historical links between labor migration and the slave trade (both the European slave trade and the internal African slave trade), but he has had few followers. Recognizing the distinctive character of African migrations, incidentally, is not to close the door on comparisons with other parts of the world. Islamic and clan networks, for example, are also likely to be found in Asia, with which the African case could be fruitfully compared.

Notes

Introduction

1. Elliot J. Berg, "The Economics of the Migrant Labor System," in Hilda Kuper, ed., *Urbanization and Migration in West Africa* (Berkeley; Los Angeles: University of California Press, 1965), pp. 161–162.

2. Souleymane Diarra, "Les travailleurs africains noirs en France," *Bulletin de l'IFAN*, Série B, vol. 3, 1969, pp. 884–1004. See also Adrian Adams, *Le long voyage des gens du fleuve* (Paris: Maspéro, 1977); Michel Samuel, *Le prolétariat africain noir en France* (Paris: Maspéro, 1978).

3. Interview of "Kissinger," a Soninke merchant in Bamako, by Sylviane Kamara, "Analphabètes mais millionaires," *Jeune Afrique*, no. 989, 19 Dec. 1979, p. 60.

4. Elliot J. Berg, "Backward Sloping Labor-Supply Functions in Dual Economies: The Africa Case," *Quarterly Journal of Economics*, vol. 75, 1961, pp. 468–492.

5. J. Clyde Mitchell, "The Causes of Labour Migrations," *Bulletin of the Inter-African Labour Institute*, vol. 6, no. 1, 1959, pp. 12–47.

6. J. Van Velsen, "Some Methodological Problems of the Study of Labour Migration," *Urbanization in African Social Change*, Proceeding of the Inaugural Seminar, Centre for African Studies, University of Edinburgh, [c. 1961], pp. 34–42.

7. Berg, "Backward Sloping Labor-Supply Functions;" "Economics of the Migrant Labor System."

8. The relevant literature is immense and cannot be quoted in its entirety. Some influential works are Samir Amin and Daryll Forde, eds., *Modern Migrations in Western Africa* (London: Oxford University Press, 1974), pp. 3–126; Mitchell, "Causes of Labour Migrations"; Elliott P. Skinner, "Labor Migration among the Mossi of Upper Volta," in Hilda Kuper, ed., *Urbanization and Migration*, pp. 60–84, see esp. pp. 62–65; Immanuel Wallerstein, "Migration in West Africa: The Political Perspective," ibid., pp. 148–159, see pp. 151–152.

9. In this study, I will generally use the terms "Fuutanke" to describe the ethnic group, which used to be called "Tukulor" in colonial scholarship. The name Tukulor was used to describe speakers of Puular (also called Fulfulde or Fulani) in the region of the Middle Valley of the Senegal River (called Fuuta Tooro), who are not Fuulbe (Fulani) pastoralists. The term Tukulor has fallen into disuse because it is not used by the people concerned, who prefer the terms "Halpuularen" ("those who speak Puular") or "Fuutanke" (the people who inhabit Fuuta Tooro). The term Fuutanke is increasingly replacing Tukulor in the current literature, but it occasionally creates problems since there are inhabitants of Fuuta Tooro whose primary language is not

Puular (there are significant Wolof and Soninke minorities in Fuuta Tooro). In this paragraph, where I refer to both Puular-speaking and non-Puular-speaking (Soninke) Fuutanke, I have avoided the geographical term.

10. As one goes downstream towards the middle valley in the districts of Kanel and Ourossogui, they decline to about 5 to 8 percent.

11. Francine Kane and André Lericollais, "L'émigration en pays soninké," *Cahiers de l'ORSTOM*, Série sciences humaines, vol. 12, no. 2, 1975, pp. 178–179.

12. Oscar Handlin, *The Uprooted* (Boston; Toronto: Atlantic-Little, Brown, 1973.) See the criticism of this Pulitzer Prize-winning book, first published in 1951, by Charles Tilly and C. Harold Brown, "On Uprooting, Kinship and the Auspices of Migration," *International Journal of Comparative Sociology*, vol. 8, 1967, pp. 139–164.

13. Literature in English on the subject of modern migration includes the important article by Tilly and Brown, "On Uprooting, Kinship and the Auspices of Migration"; Lynn Hollen Lees, *Exiles of Erin, Irish Migrants in Victorian London* (Ithaca, N.Y.: Cornell University Press, 1979); Barbara A. Henderson, *Internal Migration during Modernization in Late Nineteenth-Century Russia* (Princeton: Princeton University Press, 1980); Leslie Page Moch, *Paths to the City, Regional Migration in Nineteenth-Century France* (Beverly Hills; London; New Delhi: Sage, 1983); William H. Sewell, *Structure and Mobility: The Men and Women of Marseille, 1820–1870* (Cambridge: Cambridge University Press; Paris: Maison des Sciences de l'Homme, 1985); Nancy L. Green, *The Pletzl of Paris: Jewish Immigrant Workers in the Belle Epoque* (New York; London: Holmes and Meier, 1986).

I have made extensive use of the very large body of French scholarly literature on the subject, which has largely inspired the present literature in English. See Louis Chevalier, *La formation de la population parisienne au XIXe siècle* (Paris: P.U.F., 1950); Philippe Pinchemel, *Structures sociales et dépopulation rurale dans les campagnes picardes de 1836 à 1936* (Paris: A. Colin, 1957); Jean Pitié, *Exode rural et migrations intérieures en France: l'exemple du Poitou-Charentes* (Poitiers: Nevers, 1971); Alain Corbin, "Migrations temporaires et société rurale: le cas du Limousin," *Revue Historique*, no. 500, September–December 1971, pp. 293–334; and *Archaïsme et modernité en Limousin au XIXe siècle, 1845–1880* (Paris: Marcel Rivière, 1975), 2 vols.; Françoise Raison-Jourde, *La colonie auvergnate de Paris au XIXe siècle* (Paris: Ville de Paris, Commission des Travaux Historiques, 1976). The outstanding reference work on the history of French labor migration is Abel Chatelain, *Les migrants temporaires en France de 1800 à 1914* (Lille: Publications de l'Université de Lille III; C.N.R.S., 1976), 2 vols.

For a fuller bibliography of the enormous literature on this subject published in recent years, see the references in the introduction and bibliography of Sewell, *Structure and Mobility*.

14. On the debate concerning "substantivist" economic theory, see Karl Polanyi, "The Economy as an Instituted Process," in Karl Polanyi, Conrad M. Arensberg, and Harry W. Pearson, eds., *Trade and Markets in the Early Empires* (Glencoe, Ill.: The Free Press; Falcon's Wings Press, 1957), pp. 243–269; E. E. Le Clair, Jr. and Harold K. Schneider, eds., *Readings in Economic Anthropology: Readings in Theory and Analy-*

sis (New York: Holt, Rinehart and Winston, 1968); for a recent assessment of the debate about substantivism, see Sutti Ortiz, ed., *Economic Anthropology, Topics and Theories* (Lanham, Md.; New York; London: University Press of America; Society for Economic Anthropology, 1983); Peggy F. Barlett, ed., *Agricultural Decision Making, Anthropological Contributions to Rural Development* (New York; London, etc.: Academic Press, 1980), esp. pp. 7–9; Rhoda H. Halperin, "Polanyi, Marx, and the Institutional Paradigm in Economic Anthropology," *Research in Economic Anthropology*, vol. 6, 1984, pp. 245–272, see pp. 245–246. Of particular relevance to this study are the remarks on the debate by Philip Curtin, *Economic Change in Precolonial Africa, Senegambia in the Era of the Slave Trade* (Madison: University of Wisconsin Press, 1975), pp. 235–237; 257.

15. See in particular Samir Amin's introduction to Amin and Forde, *Modern Migrations*.

16. Elliot J. Berg, "The Development of a Labor Force in Sub-Saharan Africa," *Economic Development and Cultural Change*, vol. 13, 1965, pp. 394–412, quotation, p. 400 (my emphasis).

17. Curtin, *Economic Change*, p. 197. In the same vein, see also A. G. Hopkins, *An Economic History of West Africa* (New York: Columbia University Press, 1973), p. 6; pp. 8–77. Yves Person, who accepted the concept of subsistence economy, argued that it was inapplicable to West Africa, except for a limited area of the coastal forest zone; Yves Person, *Samori, une révolution dyula* (Dakar: IFAN, 1968–[1975]), vol. 1, pp. 69–75.

18. Such was the case of the famous Glen-Gray act of 1894 in South Africa, designed to create labor migration through a manipulation of tax rates. See *John X. Merriman, Paradoxical South African Statesman* (New Haven, N.J.; London: Yale University Press, 1982).

19. Timothy C. Weiskel, *French Colonial Rule and the Baule Peoples: Resistance and Collaboration, 1889–1911* (Oxford: Clarendon Press, 1980), pp. 159; 204; see also p. 81.

20. A. G. Hopkins, *Economic History*, p. 219.

Chapter 1

1. The reference work on the Soninke is Eric Pollet and Grace Winter, *La société soninké (Diahunu, Mali)* (Brussels: Editions de l'Institut de Sociologie, 1971). Other relevant works are quoted in this chapter.

2. Curtin, *Economic Change*, p. 197; quoted in Introduction.

3. The main difficulty is that the Marka (see below), who are Soninke in origin, but who no longer speak Soninke, have been recorded as Soninke in Malian censuses; Pollet and Winter, *Société soninké*, p. 33. My estimate roughly agrees with Pollet and Winter, and Souleymane Diarra; "Travailleurs africains noirs en France," p. 903.

4. This assertion was made to me by a number of scholars, both specialists and nonspecialists of the Soninke.

5. On these regions, see Paul Pélissier, *Les Paysans du Sénégal: les civilisations agraires du Cayor à la Casamance* (Saint-Yriex, France: Imprimerie Fabrègue, 1966).

6. P. Bradley, C. Raynaut, J. Torrealba, *Le Guidimakha mauritanien: Diagnostic et propositions d'action* (London: War on Want, 1977), p. 11 (see also Senegalese rainfall map on p. 6); Gaston Boyer, *Un peuple de l'ouest soudanais: les diawara* (Dakar: I.F.A.N., 1953), p. 59; Pollet and Winter, *Société soninké*, p. 89.

7. *Jeri* agriculture, whose yields have fallen drastically, is being progressively abandoned; Adrian Adams, *La terre et les gens du fleuve. Jalons, balises* (Paris: L'Harmattan, 1985), pp. 67–92; and Lucie Steinkamp-Ferrier, "Sept villages du Guidimakha Mauritanien face à un project de développement: l'histoire d'une recherche," Doctorat de Troisième cycle, Ecole des Hautes Etudes en Sciences Sociales, 1983.

8. Bradley, Raynaut, Torrealba, *Guidimaka Mauritanien*, pp. 91–96.

9. My special thanks to James Webb for helping me to sort out the information on the effects of drought on agriculture.

10. Steinkamp-Ferrier, "Sept villages du Guidimakha mauritanien," pp. 184–185 and passim; Monique Chastanet, "Cultures et outils agricoles en pays soninke (Gajaaga et Gidimaxa)," *Cahiers ORSTOM, sér. Sci. Hum.*, vol. 20, 1984, p. 455.

11. ANS 13 G 171, Bakel, BAC August 1872, No. 25.

12. Pollet and Winter, *Société soninké*, p. 95.

13. Adams, *Terre et gens du fleuve*, p. 97 and passim.

14. Boyer, *Un peuple de l'ouest soudanais*, p. 98; Adams, *Terre et les gens du fleuve*, p. 103 (two metric tons 100 kilograms for a field in the *jeri* in the 1930s).

15. The operation of the most important salt-mine of the desert, Ijil, is documented from only the eighteenth century, although it may have begun much earlier; Ann McDougall, "The Ijil Salt Industry: Its Role in the Pre-Colonial Economy of the Western Sudan," Ph.D. thesis, University of Birmingham (Great Britain), 1980.

16. Al-Bakri and Al-Idrisi quotes in J. F. K. Hopkins and N. Levtzion, eds. *Corpus of Early Arabic Sources for West African History* (Cambridge: Cambridge University Press, 1981), pp. 81; 77–78; 107.

17. Pollet and Winter, *Société soninké*, pp. 19–34; 36–85; Abdoulaye Bathily, *Les Portes de l'or. Le royaume de Galam (Sénégal) de l'ère musulmane au temps des négriers (VIIIe–XVIIIe siècle)* (Paris: L'Harmattan, 1989); Nehemia Levtzion, *Ancient Ghana and Mali* (London: Methuen, 1973).

18. Compare Pollet and Winter, *Société soninké*, and Bathily, *Portes de l'or*, with Charles Monteil, *Les Bambaras du Ségou et du Kaarta* (Paris: Larose, 1924); and Carleton T. Hodge, ed., *Papers on the Manding* (Bloomington: Indiana University Press, 1971).

19. These existed even in "stateless" Soninke polities, for reasons explained below. The singular is *tunka lemme*.

20. Some of these slaves were also owned by village chiefly families and were employed in village community service. Pollet and Winter, *Société soninké*, pp. 240–243.

21. Jean-Loup Amselle, *Logiques métisses. Anthropologie de l'identité en Afrique et ailleurs* (Paris: Payot, 1990), especially Chapter 4, "L'Etat et le segmentaire"; E. R.

Leach, *Political Systems of Highland Burma: A Study of Kachin Social Structure* (London: Athlone Press, 1st ed., 1954).

22. This is what Aidan Southall has called a "segmentary state," i.e., an intermediary form between a state and a stateless "segmentary" society; Aidan Southall, *Alur Society: A Study in Processes and Types of Domination* (Cambridge: W. Heffer, 1953).

23. Pollet and Winter, *Société soninké*, pp. 62-67.

24. Monique Chastanet, "De la traite à la conquête coloniale dans le Haut Sénégal: l'Etat soninké du Gajaaga de 1818 à 1858," *Cahiers du C.R.A.*, No. 5, October 1987, pp. 371-425. The civil war between Gwey and Kammera was already in the making in the eighteenth century; see Bathily, *Portes de l'or*, pp. 253-353.

25. On Gidimaxa, Jean-Hubert Saint-Père, *Les Sarakollé du Guidimakha* (Paris: Larose, 1925), pp. 1-8; 14-16; on Gajaaga, Bathily, *Portes de l'or*, pp. 79-166; on Kingi, Boyer, *Un peuple de l'Ouest Soudanais*.

26. This rule is still in use in some Soninke villages, Pollet and Winter, *Société soninké*, p. 277. It follows the normal rule of devolution of power within Soninke households.

27. Pollet and Winter, *Société soninké*, pp. 276-277; Bathily, *Portes de l'or*, p. 193.

28. S. N. Eisenstadt and Louis Roniger, "Patron-Client Relations as a Model of Structuring Social Exchange." *Comparative Studies in Society and History*, vol. 22, no. 1, 1980, pp. 42-77.

29. Abdoulaye Bathily, "Imperialism and Colonial Expansion in Senegal in the Nineteenth Century; with Particular Reference to the Economic, Social and Political Development of the Kingdom of Gajaaga (Galam)." Ph. D. dissertation, Centre of West African Studies, University of Birmingham, U.K., 1975, pp. 330-332.

30. Bathily, *Portes de l'or*, p. 40.

31. Bathily, "Imperialism," Chapter 4.

32. Claude Meillassoux, Lassana Doucouré, Diaowé Simagha, *Légende de la dispersion des Kusa* (Dakar: IFAN, 1967), pp. 13-14.

33. Bathily, *Portes de l'or*, pp. 334; 210-211.

34. "The office of the Tunka was so lucrative that every *tunka lemme* regarded it as the fundamental goal of his life." Bathily, "Imperialism," p. 341. As mentioned, the king was supposed to be the eldest man of the royal clan, but in the absence of birth records, age was a matter for debate.

35. "During official ceremonies, and in particular the *kafundo* (general assemblies of the royals), casted groups received *kuye* ("gifts") from royals. The prestige, even the wealth of each royal, depended of his generosity with casted men." Bathily, *Portes de l'or*, p. 224

36. Bathily, *Portes de l'or*, p. 130.

37. (The enumeration runs for several pages in the written transcript of the oral text.) Meillassoux, Doucouré, and Simagha, *Légende de la dispersion des Kusa*, pp. 37-43. On this form of gift, see also Bathily, *Portes de l'or*, p. 137.

38. Bathily, *Portes de l'or*, p. 150

39. Ibrahima Diaman Bathily, "Notices socio-historiques sur l'ancien royaume

Soninké du Gadiaga," *Bulletin de l'IFAN*, B, vol. 21, 1969, pp. 76–79; Pollet and Winter, *Société soninké*, pp. 261–265; also Boyer, *Un peuple de l'ouest soudanais*, p. 76. I have also drawn on my recollections from conversations with youngsters of the village of Kungani (Upper Senegal) in 1982.

40. It is sometimes said that "all villagers are relatives." Pollet and Winter, *Société soninké*, p. 175.

41. Pollet and Winter, *Société soninké*, pp. 334–345. Archival material relative to Gajaaga are filled with data on litigations about land.

42. F.-M. Colombani, "Le Guidimakha, étude géographique, historique et religieuse." *Bulletin du Comité d'Etudes Historiques et Scientifiques de l'Afrique Occidentale Française*, vol. 14, 1931, pp. 428–432 and pp. 409–410.

43. Bathily, *Portes de l'or*, p. 119. On the claimed origins of the Saaxo-Wakkane, ibid., pp. 118–120; and Charles Monteil, "La légende du Ouagadou et l'origine des Soninké," in Monteil, Charles, *Mélanges ethnologiques*, Mémoires de l'I.F.A.N., no. 23 (Dakar: I.F.A.N., 1953), p. 378.

44. Excellent discussion of the literature in J. Davis, *People of the Mediterranean: An Essay in Comparative Anthropology* (London: Routledge, 1977), pp. 89–101; also J. K. Campbell, *Honour, Family and Patronage: A Study of Institutions and Moral Values in a Greek Mountain Community* (Oxford: Clarendon Press, 1964); and J. Pitt-Rivers, "Honour and Social Status," in G. Perestiany, ed., *Honour and Shame. The Values of Mediterranean Society* (London: Weidenfeld and Nicolson, 1965), pp. 19–78.

45. Bathily, "Imperialism," pp. 320–322; also Saint-Père, *Sarakollés du Guidimakha*, pp. 21–22.

46. The social taboos concerning the *nyaxamala* sometimes bear a resemblance to the Indian caste system; Pollet and Winter, *Société soninké*, pp. 218–220.

47. Pollet and Winter, *Société soninké*, pp. 145–148.

48. Pollet and Winter, *Société soninké*, pp. 418–428. My estimates are made on the basis of the average pay for local wage labor given in pp. 142–145, and of wage labor in Malian state rice and cotton plantations, p. 140.

49. Saint-Père, *Sarakollé du Guidimakha*, p. 107. Dowries were announced at the village mosque during the Islamic marriage ceremony. This was a way to provide witnesses for the marriage contract, but a very small dowry no doubt must have been a cause for shame. See ibid., pp. 113–114.

50. Boyer, *Un peuple de l'ouest soudanais*, p. 79.

51. "But sometimes," adds Saint-Père mischievously, "it happens that the wind lifts the cloth that covers one of the baskets, and one sees that it is empty—fortunately for the vanity of the women, such an incident is rare." Saint-Père, *Sarakollé du Guidimakha*, p. 32.

52. Saint-Père, *Sarakollé du Guidimakha*, pp. 89–91. For Saint-Père, "these jewels are a way for women to save earnings they do not invest in cattle." This is indeed true, but some of the jewelry was offered by husbands, and jewelry was inferior to cattle as an investment, in the sense that it was unproductive. Saint-Père also described the elaborate silver jewelry and decorated daggers worn by men, ibid., pp. 90–91.

53. Pollet and Winter, *Société soninké*, p. 410.

54. Bathily, "Islam and Colonial Expansion," p. 324; Pollet and Winter, *Société soninké*, p. 246; Bathily, "Islam and Colonial Expansion, p. 324; Charles Monteil, "Fin de siècle à Médine (1898–1899)," *Bulletin de l'I.F.A.N.*, vol. 28, série B, nos. 1–2, 1966, p. 117; Claude Meillassoux, "Etat et condition des esclaves à Gumbu (Mali) au XIXe siècle," in Claude Meillassoux, ed., *L'esclavage en Afrique précoloniale* (Paris: Maspéro, 1975), p. 229.

55. See in particular Bathily, *Portes de l'or*, pp. 190–202.

56. Mungo Park, *The Travels of Mungo Park* (London: J. M. Dent; New York: Dutton, 1910), pp. 49ff.

57. On such raids, see Jean Bazin and Emmanuel Terray, eds., *Guerres de lignages et guerres d'Etats en Afrique* (Paris: Editions des archives contemporaines, 1982). Among Soninke-speaking peoples, the Kaagoro were an exception; see Claude Daniel Ardouin, "Une formation politique précoloniale du Sahel occidental malien: le Baakhunu à l'époque des Kaagoro," *Cahiers d'Etudes Africaines*, vol. 28, nos. 111–112, 1988, pp. 463–483.

58. Bathily, "Imperialism," p. 350. Like the French *taille*, the Gajaaga wartime tax *(sagalle)* was not paid by aristocrats (tunka lemmu and their clients, *mangu*, Darame and Jaaxo [Tanjigora] marabouts, and casted artisans. For a good overview of taxation in prerevolutionary France, see François Hincker, *Les français devant l'impôt sous l'Ancien Régime* (Paris: Flammarion, 1971.)

59. Pollet and Winter, *Société soninké*, pp. 311–345.

60. See oral traditions collected by Adriam Adams, *Terre et gens du fleuve*, pp. 9–92; and Bathily, "Imperialism," pp. 128–133. See also Monteil, "Fin de siècle," pp. 101–102; and J. Y. Weigel, *Migration et production domestique des Soninké du Sénégal* (Paris: O.R.S.T.O.M., 1982), pp. 63–68.

61. Adams, *Terre et gens du fleuve*, p. 29; Bathily, *Portes de l'or*, p. 200.

62. Steinkamp-Ferrier, "Sept villages," pp. 103; 132–133. Fragmentary information in Saint-Père, *Sarakollé du Guidimakha*, pp. 166–169.

63. Boyer, *Un peuple de l'ouest soudanais*, p. 78.

64. Steinkamp-Ferrier, "Sept villages," p. 184.

65. Weigel, *Migration et production domestique*, p. 66; Steinkamp-Ferrier, *Sept villages*, p. 133.

66. Bathily, "Imperialism," Chapter 4, passim; and *Portes de l'or*, passim, e.g., p. 224.

67. See Malian transhumance routes in G. Doutressoule, *L'élevage au Soudan français* (Algiers: E. Imbert, 1952), and Rokiatou N'Diaye Keita, *Kayes et le Haut-Sénégal* (Bamako: Editions Populaires, 1972), pp. 117–120.

68. The following description is mainly taken from Claude Meillassoux, "Le commerce pré-colonial et le développement de l'esclavage à Gumbu du Sahel (Mali)," in Claude and Daryll Forde ed., *The Development of Indigenous Trade and Markets in West Africa* (London: International African Institute; Oxford University Press, 1971), pp. 182–195. Additional references are given below. On the trade of the Marka, who

are ethnic relatives of the Soninke, see Richard Roberts, "Long-Distance Trade and Production: Sinsani in the Nineteenth Century," *Journal of African History*, vol. 21, 1980, pp. 169–188.

69. Claude Meillassoux, who was probably the first to call attention to the desert-side trade in West Africa, speculated that these symbiotic relations between Soninke farmers and desert nomads were at the origin of the *jatigi* middleman system of the great trading cities of the Sudan. Meillassoux, "Commerce et esclavage à Gumbu," p. 189; on this institution, see Polly Hill, "Landlords and Brokers: A West African Trading System," *Cahiers d'Etudes Africaines*, vol. 26, 1966, pp. 349–366.

70. I am very grateful to James Webb for his clear and concise description of the physiological need for salt intakes in hot climates, which I paraphrase here.

71. Raymond Mauny, *Tableau géographique de l'Ouest Africain au Moyen Age* (Amsterdam: Swets and Zeitlinger N.V., 1967), pp. 321–322; Curtin, *Economic Change*, pp. 224–228.

72. French official figures of 1896 quoted in Pollet and Winter, *Société soninké*, p. 117; also Emile Baillaud, *Sur les routes du Soudan* (Toulouse: Privat, 1902), pp. 36; 40–42ff., 143–144; Roberts, "Long-Distance Trade: Sinsani."

73. Mauny, *Tableau géographique*, pp. 275–291.

74. Curtin, *Economic Change*, pp. 211–215; Meillassoux, "Commerce et esclavage à Gumbu," p. 193; "Etat et condition des esclaves," pp. 249–250. According to Bathily, there originally existed in Gajaaga a caste of professional spinners (and weavers?) called *maabu*, who went from town to town performing their craft, but these disappeared in the nineteenth century due to the large-scale import of slaves in the area. Bathily, "Imperialism," Chapter 3.

75. For Gumbu, Meillassoux, "Commerce et esclavage à Gumbu," esp. pp. 186–187 (salt, horses, cotton cloth traded in Banamba, Segu, Nyamina, "rarely further"; the main import was slaves); for the Jawara of Kingi, Boyer, *Un peuple de l'ouest soudanais*, p. 110 (salt, horses, mats, pottery, and calabashes traded on the Niger bend, also kola nut trade in the Ivory Coast and Guinea); for Jafunu, Pollet and Winter, *Société soninké*, pp. 116–117; also 114–115 (salt, livestock, cotton cloth, sold in the Ivory Coast and Guinea, kola nut trade from these areas); for Gajaaga, Bathily, "Imperialism and Colonial Expansion, pp. 206–230ff. (cattle trade toward Saint-Louis and Bure; slave imports from Kita; annual trading expeditions to Médine, and less frequently to Segu, through Banamba and Nyamina, or to Sikaso through Kita and Buguni); also Raffenel, *Voyage dans l'Afrique occidentale . . . exécuté en 1843 et 1844* (Paris: A. Bertrand, 1846), p. 449 (hides exported presumably from Gajaaga to the Gambia, imports of salt); Jean-Baptiste Durand, *Voyage au Sénégal fait dans les années 1785 et 1786* (Paris: Dentu, 1807), p. 221 (trade of salt for iron, shea butter, and gold, from Soninke settled in Bundu and presumably to Bambuxu); ANS 2 D 4–12, Etude sur la formation historique et ethnique des provinces qui constituent le cercle, par Maubert, administrateur-adjoint, Monographie, Bakel, Mar. 6, 1904 (livestock and cotton cloth taken from Gwey to urban centers along the Senegal River and the Dakar-Saint-Louis railway line); for Kammera (Gajaaga), ANS K 14, Capitaine Mazillier, Rapport sur la

captivité dans le cercle de Kayes, July 8, 1894 (trade with Sikaso ["les états de Tiéba"], with Bambuxu); Saint-Père, *Sarakollé du Guidimakha*, p. 51. This reference list is not exhaustive.

76. Curtin, *Economic Change*, pp. 75, 230; Bathily, "Imperialism," Chapter 3; and Raffenel, *Voyage*, p. 449.

77. "The credit of having organized long-distance trade amidst communities that were structured until then as narrow and closed communities is due to [the Soninke]. The dominance of [Soninke] *jamu* [clan names] among the *jula* is a sure indication of this fact." Yves Person, *Samori, une révolution dyula* (Dakar: I.F.A.N., 1968–1975), vol. 1, p. 95; see also p. 108.

78. Person, *Samori*, pp. 95–98.

79. Roberts, *Warriors, Merchants and Slaves*.

80. Bathily, *Portes de l'or*, p. 99; Thomas Hale, *Scribe, Griot and Novelist: Narrative Interpreters of the Songhay Empire* (Gainesville: University of Florida Press / Center for African Studies, 1990), in particular pp. 175–176.

81. Personal communication, Lanciné Kaba, Chicago, 1991.

82. Lamin O. Sanneh, *The Jakhanke* (London: International African Institute, 1979), pp. 219–240; Pollet and Winter, *Société soninké*, p. 491.

83. Bathily, "Imperialism," pp. 234–236. As if to emphasize this similarity, Soninke clerics called commercial success *baraka*, which may be translated as "grace of God."

84. Bathily, *Portes de l'or*, pp. 332–333.

85. Ibid., pp. 335–336.

86. Nehemia Levtzion, "Merchants vs. Scholars and Clerics in West Africa: Differential and Complementary Roles," in Nehemia Levtzion and Humphrey J. Fisher, eds., *Rural and Urban Islam in West Africa* (Boulder, Colo.: Lynne Rienner, 1987), pp. 21–37.

87. Interview and personal conversation, Professor Xadi Darame, Bamako, Mali, 1 September 1982.

88. Meillassoux, "Commerce et esclavage," pp. 187, 189–190; Pollet and Winter, *Société soninké*, p. 118.

89. See also a similar conclusion for different Soninke regions in Meillassoux, "Commerce et esclavage," p. 193 (Gumbu region); and Pollet and Winter, *Société soninké*, p. 228.

90. ANS K 18, Cercle de Bakel, "Questionnaire au sujet de la captivité," 1904 (35,000 slaves in the *cercle*, including the Puular-speaking region of Bundu, or two-thirds of the population); K 14, "Etude sur la captivité dans le cercle de Nioro," n.d. (number of slaves was "less than that of free men"); ANS K 14, "[Rapport sur la captivité par le] Capitaine Mazillier," Kayes, 8 July 1894 (36 percent of slaves among the Soninke of the cercle, but Mazillier noted that the number of slaves recorded was probably underestimated since family heads did not report many of their slaves in order to pay fewer taxes). Pollet and Winter also quote Mazillier's figures for Kingi and Gidyume, amounting to 60 percent of the population for these regions; *Société soninké*, p. 238. Meillassoux gave a figure of 1,000 to 1,500 slaves for a total population

of 5,200 in the town of Goumbou before the French conquest, i.e., a proportion of 20 percent to 30 percent of the population in "Commerce et esclavage," p. 193; but he revised his estimate upwards in "Etat et condition des esclaves" (p. 225), where he wrote that the most conservative estimate would be 2,000 slaves or about 40 percent of the total population. In this source, Meillassoux also quotes the French official report ANS K 19, "Rapport sur l'esclavage dans le cercle de Sénégambie-Niger," which gave a proportion of 50 percent for the cercle of Gumbu.

91. ANS K 27, Captivité et repression de la traite au Sénégal 1902–1907, rapport transmis par lettre No. 39, Résident du Baol oriental à Administrateur du cercle de Thiès, Diourbel, 10 May 1902.

92. Pollet and Winter, *Société soninké*, pp. 237–261; Meillassoux "Etat et condition des esclaves," in particular p. 235.

93. For example, ANS 13 G 198, Ct. Bakel to Gov. Senegal, No. 68, 5 May 1896.

94. Xadi Darame, Bamako, 1 September 1982; Bathily, "Islam and Imperialism," p. 213.

95. There was one exception, Gumbu, which adopted the slave village system from the neighboring Marka in the late nineteenth century. Meillassoux, "Etat et condition," pp. 245–246. On slavery among the Marka see Richard Roberts, *Warriors, Merchants and Slaves: The State and the Economy in the Middle Niger Valley, 1700–1914* (Stanford: Stanford University Press, 1987).

96. Pollet and Winter, *Société soninké*, p. 238.

97. Pollet and Winter, *Société soninké*, p. 239.

98. Bathily notes that it was considered a dishonor for tunka lemme to touch a *tonge* (hoe); the same was more or less true of the mange; Bathily, "Imperialism," p. 264.

99. Ibid.

100. Pollet and Winter, *Société soninké*, pp. 245–246; Meillassoux, "Etat et condition des esclaves," p. 235.

101. Bathily, "Imperialism," p. 213.

102. This field may be not one but several plots, situated on different soils; see Steinkamp–Ferrier, "Sept villages," p. 182.

103. Pollet and Winter, *Société soninké*, pp. 377–397. See also Weigel, *Migration et production domestique,* pp. 71–73; Steinkamp-Ferrier, "Sept villages," pp. 182–215; ANS 13 G 195, Organisation foncière des indigènes dans le cercle de Bakel, 1894.

104. Steinkamp-Ferrier reports that in the riverbank villages of Gidimaxa where she did her field study, women's fields are like the salumo situated on the periphery of the great field. Steinkamp-Ferrier, "Sept villages," pp. 281–286.

105. Adams, *Terre et gens du fleuve*, pp. 9–31; Weigel, "Migration et production domestique," pp. 48–56; Monique Chastanet, "Cultures et outils agricoles," pp. 453–454; Saint-Père, *Sarakollé du Guidimakha*, pp. 33–36, 168–169; Raynaut, Bradley, Torrealba, *Guidimakha mauritanien*, p. 107; Steinkamp-Ferrier, "Sept villages," pp. 281–286; Pollet and Winter, *Société soninké*, pp. 395–397.

106. Adams, *Terre et gens du fleuve*, pp. 74–75; Steinkamp-Ferrier, "Sept villages," p. 210.

107. Weigel, "Migration et production domestique," p. 50 (average areas: 7 hectares cultivated by family group—4.8 by men and 2.2 by women).

108. James Searing, "Aristocrats, Slaves, and Peasants: Power and Dependency in the Wolof States, 1700–1850," *International Journal of African Historical Studies*, vol. 21, no. 3, 1988, pp. 475–503; Peter Kolchin, *Unfree Labor: American Slavery and Russian Serfdom* (Cambridge, Mass.; London: Belknap Press of the Harvard University Press, 1987).

109. Bathily, "Imperialism," pp. 322–323; ANS K 14, Capitaine Mazillier, Rapport sur la captivité dans le cercle de Kayes, 8 July 1894; Saint-Père, *Sarakollés du Guidimakha*, p. 24; Colombani, "Le Guidimakha," p. 412.

110. Pollet and Winter, *Société soninké*, p. 244.

111. Meillassoux, "Etat et condition des esclaves," p. 234.

112. Bathily, "Imperialism," p. 323.

113. An unfortunate result of the confusion between slave conditions and their generational status is that these slaves are usually called "household slaves" in the literature (because they were born in their master's household), while their main characteristic is *that they did not live within their master's household.*

114. Bathily, "Imperialism," p. 325; Pollet and Winter, *Société soninké*, p. 250; Saint-Père, *Sarakollé du Guidimakha*, p. 250; Meillassoux, "Etat et condition," p. 227.

115. Bathily, "Imperialism," p. 323.

116. ANS 13 G 195, Desmarets, Rapport sur la captivité dans le cercle de Bakel, 26 May 1894; Charles Monteil, "Fin de siècle," p. 114; Meillassoux, "Etat et condition," p. 227.

117. Pollet and Winter, *Société soninké*, p. 251 (curiously, Jafununke at the time of this study had no precise recollection of the details of the condition of woroso slaves); on kome woroso in Gumbu, see Meillassoux, "Etat et condition des esclaves," p. 237.

118. ANS 13 G 195, Desmarets, Rapport sur la captivité dans le cercle de Bakel, 26 May 1894 (four days); Bathily, "Imperialism," p. 323 (five days; the mention is for first-generation slaves who were married and had formed an independent household).

119. ANS K 14, Captain Mazillier, Rapport sur la captivité, 1894.

120. Meillassoux, "Etat et condition des esclaves," p. 234; on slavery in Beledugu, Roberts, *Warriors, Merchants and Slaves.*

121. The report added that during the dry season, these slaves worked only until noon for their master. This would perhaps suggest a reference to serfs rather than actual slaves. K 14, Rapport sur la captivité dans le cercle de Nioro, n.d. [1894].

122. ANS 13 G 195, Desmarets, Rapport sur la captivité dans le cercle de Bakel, 1894; see also Meillassoux, "Etat et condition," p. 233. All slaves made cloth, including those who owed a rent in kind; see ibid., p. 238.

123. Meillassoux, "Etat et condition des esclaves," pp. 236–238. On the *mudd* (which varied from region to region, and even from family to family), see Curtin, *Economic Change*, p. 239, note 6; Pollet and Winter, *Société soninké*, p. 93.

124. Pollet and Winter, *Société soninké*, p. 239; Meillassoux, "Etat et condition des esclaves," p. 240.

125. Monteil, "Fin de siècle," p. 113. There are only indications of this slave status in other sources. Saint-Père and some informants of Pollet and Winter mention the payment of rents in kind by some former slaves after the slave emancipation of 1905 to 1910; Saint-Père, *Sarakollé du Guidimakha*, pp. 182–183; Pollet and Winter, *Société soninké*, p. 261. The rent in kind is also reported in the 1890s for some *women* slaves in Bakel who paid a rent of two guinée cloths a year to their owners; see ANS 13 G 195, Desmarets, Rapport sur la captivité dans le cercle de Bakel, 26 May 1894.

126. Meillassoux, "Etat et condition," p. 236.

127. ANS 13 G 195, Rapport sur la captivité, Bakel, Desmarets, 26 May 1894; ANS K 14, Capitaine Mazillier, Rapport sur la captivité dans le cercle de Kayes, 8 July 1894; Meillassoux, "Etat et condition," p. 238; Bathily, "Imperialism," p. 323.

128. Meillassoux, "Etat et condition," p. 236.

129. Ibid., p. 238 makes no mention of slaves of the other categories accompanying caravans. Other sources are imprecise on this point.

130. Ibid.

131. ANS K 14, Etude sur la captivité dans le cercle de Nioro, [1894]; Capitaine Mazillier, Rapport sur la captivité, Kayes, 8 July 1894.

132. Pollet and Winter, *Société soninké*, pp. 243–244; see also testimony of former slave, p. 249. Meillassoux mentions that "[w]omen [slaves] worked on the fields like the men," "Etat et condition," p. 235.

133. Pollet and Winter, *Société soninké*, p. 244; also Adams, *Terre et gens du fleuve*, p. 28.

134. Bathily, "Imperialism," p. 233.

135. Martin A. Klein, "Women and Slavery in the Western Sudan," in Claire Robertson and Martin A. Klein, *Women and Slavery in Africa* (Madison: University of Wisconsin Press, 1983), p. 85.

136. In the cercle of Nioro in 1894, adult males sold for 18 pièces de guinée and adult females sold for 20 pièces. ANS K 14, Etude sur la captivité dans le cercle de Nioro, 1894. In the cercle of Kayes, adult males sold for 20 pièces, or about 200 francs, while a young female thirteen to fourteen years of age, "good-looking according to [local] standards," sold for 250 to 300 francs. ANS K 14, Capitaine Mazillier, Rapport sur la captivité dans le cercle de Kayes, 8 July 1894.

137. Klein, "Women and Slavery," pp. 82–83.

138. Monteil, "Fin de siècle," pp. 113, 115; also indications in Pollet and Winter, *Société soninké*, p. 257.

139. In Gajaaga, all slaves born in servitude (i.e., all serfs, whatever their category) apparently could own slaves; see Bathily, "Imperialism," p. 325; Monteil, "Fin de siècle," p. 114. Meillassoux (for Gumbu) and Saint-Père (for Gidimaxa) mention only great slaves as owning slaves, "Etat et condition," p. 240; *Sarakollé du Guidimakha*, p. 22. There are no reports of female slaves owning slaves.

140. Monteil, "Fin de siècle," p. 113. This, however, was advantageous only if the wife had no children or children below the age of five; ANS 13 G 195, Desmarets, Rapport sur la captivité dans le cercle de Bakel, 1894.

141. Monteil, "Fin de siècle," pp. 113–114; ANS 13 G 195, Desmarets, Rapport sur la captivité dans le cercle de Bakel, 1894; ANS K 14, Capitaine Mazillier, Rapport sur la captivité dans le cercle de Kayes, 8 July 1894; Saint-Père, *Sarakollé du Guidimakha*, p. 23; Bathily, "Imperialism," p. 325.

142. However, Boyer mentions a low price of 84 mudd in Kingi Jawara, *Un peuple de l'ouest soudanais*, p. 74.

143. Pollet and Winter, *Société soninké*, pp. 245–246; Bathily, "Imperialism," p. 325. Paraphrasing conversations with informants, Monteil indicated that "it is a very bad thing to let slaves buy themselves back, because it reduces the patrimony." "Fin de siècle," p. 114.

144. Saint-Père, *Sarakollé du Guidimakha*, pp. 21–23; Bathily, "Imperialism," pp. 318–323; Pollet and Winter, *Société soninké*, pp. 241–242; Meillassoux, "Etat et condition," pp. 238–240; Monteil, "Fin de siècle," pp. 113–114; Boyer, *Un peuple de l'ouest soudanais*, p. 73.

145. Meillassoux, "Etat et condition," p. 237.

146. This was a general feature of slave systems in the Western Sudan; see Klein, "Women and Slavery," pp. 73–76.

147. See Chapter Five.

148. P. Lovejoy and S. Baier, "The Desert-Side Economy of the Central Sudan," *International Journal of African Historical Studies*, vol. 7, 1975, pp. 551–581; Richard Roberts, "Long-Distance Trade: Sinsani," pp. 169–188. Philip Curtin has called attention to the desert-side trade as a worldwide phenomenon; see *Cross-Cultural Trade in World History* (Cambridge: Cambridge University Press, 1984).

149. Mossi and Fuutanke trade migrations are not very well known. My references come from colonial writers. For the Mossi, Baillaud, *Sur les routes du Soudan*, pp. 240–241ff.; and for the Fuutanke, Louis Tautain quoted in Pollet and Winter, *Société soninké*, p. 113.

150. See the excellent special issue on nineteenth-century French migrations of *Ethnologie française*, vol. 10, no. 2, 1980; in particular Françoise Raison-Jourde, "Endogamie et stratégie d'implantation professionnelle des migrants auvergnats à Paris au XIXe siècle," ibid., pp. 153–162; and Alain Corbin, "Les paysans de Paris: histoire des Limousins du bâtiment au XIXe siècle," ibid., pp. 169–176. The reference work on French temporary migration is Abel Chatelain, *Migrants temporaires en France*. See also Raison-Jourde, *Colonie auvergnate de Paris*.

151. Raison-Jourde, *Colonie auvergnate de Paris*, pp. 70–71.

152. Emmanuel Terray, "Commerce noncolonial et organisation sociale chez les Dida de Côte d'Ivoire," in Meillassoux and Forde, *Development of Indigenous Trade and Markets*, pp. 145–152.

153. I have discussed this point in "The Patriarchal Ideal of Soninke Labor Migrants: From Slave Owners to Employers of Free Labor Migrants." *Canadian Journal of African Studies*, vol. 23, 1989, pp. 106–125.

154. Ivor Wilks, *Asante in the Nineteenth Century: The Structure and Evolution of a Political Order* (Cambridge: Cambridge University Press, 1975).

155. James Lee, "Migration and Expansion in Chinese History," in William H. Mc-Neill and Ruth S. Adams, *Human Migration: Patterns and Policies* (Bloomington: Indiana University Press, 1978), pp. 28 and 34.

156. See Alain Corbin on the traditionally migrating society of Limousin, where Africanists will easily recognize the main features of a segmentary society; *Archaïsme et modernité en Limousin au XIXe siècle, 1845–1880* (Paris: Marcel Rivière, 1975. 2 vols), pp. 298–299; or again the description of Corsican migration in Chatelain, *Migrants temporaires en France*, pp. 978–988.

157. Timothy C. Weiskel, "The Precolonial Baule: A Reconstruction," *Cahiers d'Etudes Africaines*, 1978, vol. 18, no. 72, pp. 503–560.

Chapter 2

1. André Delcourt, *La France et les établissements français au Sénégal entre 1713 et 1763* (Dakar: IFAN, 1952), p. 92.

2. The following account is based on the excellent article by Xavier Guillard, "Un commerce introuvable: l'or dans les transactions sénégambiennes du XVIe au XVIIIe siècle," *Cahiers du C.R.A.* [Centre de Recherches Africaines, Université de Paris I Sorbonne], no. 5, 1987, pp. 31–75.

3. Bathily, *Portes de l'or*, p. 174.

4. Delcourt, France et établissements français; Bathily, "Imperialism," pp. 32–74; Curtin, *Economic Change* (see slave trade figures in Supplement, p. 68); James L. A. Webb, Jr., *Desert Frontier: Ecological and Economic Change along the Western Sahel, 1600–1850* (Madison: University of Wisconsin Press, 1995), p. 107; Abdoulaye Bathily, "La traite atlantique des esclaves et ses effets économiques et sociaux en Afrique: le cas du Galam, royaume de l'hinterland Sénégambien au dix-huitième siècle," *Journal of African History*, vol. 27, 1986, pp. 269–293.

5. Bathily, "Traite atlantique"; and André Delcourt, ed., of Pierre David, *Journal d'un voiage fait en Bambouc en 1744* (Paris: Société française d'histoire d'outre-mer, 1974), pp. 247–253.

6. Georges Hardy, *La mise en valeur du Sénégal de 1817 à 1854* (Paris: Larose, 1921); Paul Marty, *Etudes sénégalaises* (Paris: Leroux, [ca. 1925]); Curtin, *Economic Change*.

7. Hardy, *Mise en valeur*, p. 70. On the Waalo scheme, see Hardy and Boubacar Barry, *Le royaume du Waalo: le Sénégal avant la conquête* (Paris: Maspéro, 1972).

8. Webb, *Desert Frontier*, pp. 97–131; Curtin, *Economic Change*, pp. 215–218.

9. Hardy, *Mise en valeur*, p. 255.

10. Ibid., p. 295.

11. ANS 13 G 165, Commandant [Administrator] Bakel to Director of Internal Affairs, 3 March 1847.

12. See esp. (source of quote) ANS 13 G 165, [Mutilated document], Ct. Bakel [probably Hyacinthe Hecquart], 20 July 1847.

13. Ibid.

14. Edouard Bouët-Willaumez, *Commerce et traite des noirs aux côtes occidentales d'Afrique* (Paris: Imprimerie Nationale, 1848), p. 33; identical statement on p. 30.

15. Personal communication, based on book manuscript, July 29, 1992.

16. Richard Roberts, "Long-Distance Trade: Sinsani," pp. 169–188; *Warriors, Merchants and Slaves;* Webb, *Desert Frontier;* McDougall, "Ijil Salt Industry"; John Henry Hanson, "Umarian Karta (Mali, West Africa) during the Late Nineteenth-Century: Dissent and Revolt among the Futanke after Umar Tal's Holy War," Ph.D. dissertation, Michigan State University, 1989.

17. Webb, *Desert Frontier,* pp. 3–14.

18. Ibid., passim.

19. Such transactions, which were conducted in the countryside, generally went unrecorded in French documents. But scattered direct and indirect references to the exchange of guinées for grain exist: lower valley, early nineteenth century, René Caillié, *Travels through Central Africa to Timbuctoo* (London: F. Cass, 1968; reprint of London: Henry Colburn and Richard Bentley, 1830), vol. 1, p. 78; lower valley—escale du Coq, mid nineteenth century, ANSOM Senegal XIII, Conseil d'administration, meeting of 14 May 1850; Matam, 1870s, 13 G 171, Bakel, BAC, No. 17, February 1871; Médine, 1885, ANS 13 G 185, Médine, Commercial report, 1st quarter 1885; Gidimaxa, 1893, 13 G 193, Bakel, Pol. report, May 1893; Nioro region, ca. 1900, Baillaud, *Routes du Soudan,* p. 35. The Beydan also bought grain and dates from oases in the Adrar with guinées; Caillié, *Travels,* pp. 99–100.

20. Baillaud, *Routes du Soudan,* p. 35; De l'Orza de Reichenberg, "Autour de Nioro," *Revue de Géographie,* vol. 29, 1891, p. 226.

21. ANS 13 G 166, Ct. Bakel to Gov. Senegal, No. 13, 25 August 1851; No. 9, 25 April 1853.

22. Raffenel, *Voyage,* pp. 241–242.

23. Bouët-Willaumez, *Commerce et traite,* p. 37.

24. ". . . deux cent milliers de gommes . . . ."

25. ANS 13 G 164, Rapport demandé par M. le Gouverneur du Sénégal et Dépendances au Commandant de poste de Bakel, sur les inconvénients et les avantages qu'il y aurait sur les propositions de l'almami du Bondou, Sambala et Caya, chef du Kasso à l'effet de détruire le village de Makana (Toubaboukany—demeure des blancs—Samba Yacine dans le Camera haut Galam), 17 August 1842.

26. ANS 13 G 165, [No. 9], 10 Mar. 1850, [Commandant Bakel] to Governor Senegal. On Ahmed Taleb, see Georges Poulet, *Les Maures de l'Afrique occidentale française* (Paris: Challamel, 1904), p. 94.

27. Poulet, *Maures,* pp. 80; 82; McDougall, "Ijil Salt Industry," pp. 257–259; Paul Marty, *Etudes sur l'Islam et les tribus du Soudan,* Vol. 3, *Les tribus maures du Sahel et du Hodh* (Paris: Ernest Leroux, 1921), p. 387; Lanrezac, "Cercle de Nioro," p. 244; Mariella Villasante Cervello, "Collectivités tribales, restructuration des stratégies sociales de reproduction et de pouvoir. Quelques aspects du système foncier dans la

région de l'Assaba, République islamique de Mauritanie," unpublished thesis, Université de Genève, Institut Universitaire d'Etudes du Développement, Mémoire no. 46, 1989, pp. 219–222, 250–253, 271.

28. Poulet, *Maures*, p. 109.

29. ANS 13 G 184, Bakel, Bulletin agricole, commercial et politique, July 1884. On relations between the Idaw Aish, Sidi Mahmud, and Kunta, see Poulet, *Maures*, pp. 87–88, 93.

30. ANS 13 G 185, Bakel, Rapport commercial, 2d quarter 1885.

31. The Meshduf developed in the second half of the nineteenth century, especially at the expense of the Awlad Mbarek. By their victory, they gained the allegiance of the latter's tributary and maraboutic subjects; see Marty, *Etudes sur l'Islam et les tribus du Soudan*, Vol. 3, pp. 131–132, 387–388.

32. Marty, *Islam et tribus du Soudan*, Vol. 3, p. 365.

33. McDougall, "Ijil Salt Industry."

34. On this trade (the "petite traite"), see Bouët-Willaumez, *Commerce*, pp. 29–30, 35, 38; Webb, *Desert Frontier*, pp. 117–119 (Webb noted: "This trade in grain on the lower Senegal intensified during the 1830s, when European demand for gum doubled"). On the problems of agriculture in the lower valley, see J.-L. Boutillier et al., *La moyenne vallée du Sénégal (étude socio-économique)* (Paris: P.U.F.; République Française; République Islamique de Mauritanie; République du Sénégal, 1962); C. C. Stewart, *Islam and Social Order in Mauritania: A Case Study in the Nineteenth Century* (Oxford: Clarendon Press, 1973), pp. 115–116.

35. Bouët-Willaumez, *Commerce et traite*, p. 30.

36. References: capacity—Stewart, *Islam and Social Order*, p. 162; weight in sorghum *(mil)*— ANS 13 G 181, Bakel, *Bulletin agricole et commercial, May;* September 1881.

37. A straightforward calculation would amount to about five tons, but we must allow for the space not used for commercial purposes.

38. Pollet and Winter, *Société soninké*, p. 239.

39. Gwey (without Bakel): 5,000, ANS 13 G 199, Bakel, Rôle de l'impôt, 1896. Kammera: 6,700; Soudan part of Gidimaxa: 14,000; ANS 1 G 310, Renseignements historiques, géographiques sur le cercle de Kayes, [c. 1902]. The Mauritanian part of Gidimaxa had roughly the same population as its Soudan part: 14,000. Jafunu: 7,500, Lartigue, "Notice géographique." The population of Xaaso cannot have been greater than that of Gajaaga; guesswork: 10,000. David Robinson gives a figure of 25,000 for Damga at the beginning of the twentieth century, based on French sources, *Chiefs and Clerics*, p. 185. David Robinson's estimate of 50,000 for Gajaaga is clearly too high; *The Holy War of Umar Tal: The Western Sudan in the Mid-Nineteenth Century* (Oxford: Clarendon Press, 1985), pp. 150–152.

40. Among them: average production figures for the nineteenth century were probably higher than the twentieth-century figures calculated by Pollet and Winter; first-generation female slaves participated in the production of sorghum; and because slaves had few children, a greater surplus could be extracted from them.

41. ANS 13 G 164, Ct. Bakel to Gov. Senegal, No. 49, 12 January 1837; Rapport du Ct. de poste et du gérant principal de la . . . [Compagnie du Galam] à M. le Gouverneur du Sénégal . . . , 7 April 1837 (buying of grain in Kungani and Jagili); ANS 13 G 165, Ct. Bakel to Dir. Aff. Ext., 16 January 1849 (comptoir of the Compagnie du Galam in Jagili); Curtin, *Economic Change*, supp., p. 15 (comptoir of the famous French trader Duranthon in Kungani); ANS 13 G 165, Ct. Bakel to Gov. Senegal, No. 25, 15 February 1847 (unsuccessful attempt by the French merchant Zeller to establish a comptoir in Balu, at the mouth of the Falemme river); Ct. Bakel to Dir. Aff. Ext., No. 146, 16 January 1849 (navire, i.e., comptoir flottant (floating trading post), of Creole merchant Charles d'Erneville in Jogunturo, Gidimaxa); 13 G 166, Ct. Bakel to Gov. Senegal, No. 7, 5 March 1851 (Zeller had a navire in Jogunturo and another in Sollu, Gidimaxa; other petits comptoirs mentioned, unspecified); information on the trade of the petits comptoirs in ANS 13 G 165, Ct. Bakel to Gov. Senegal, 10 March 1850. More on the comptoirs in the following chapter.

42. On European trade in the region above Bakel, see Curtin, *Economic Change*, pp. 140–152; Hardy, *Mise en valeur*, esp. pp. 296–297. See also Abdoulaye Bathily, "La conquête française du haut-fleuve (Sénégal), 1818–1887," *Bulletin de l'IFAN*, B, vol. 34, 1972, pp. 67–112.

43. ANS 13 G 166, No. 23, 1 August 1854, Traitants of Bakel, forwarded to Gov. Senegal by Joris, Ct. Bakel. Twenty-five years later, Gallieni estimated the quantities of peanuts produced in the region between Medine and Bafoulabe (Logo and Niataga) to be *"considérables"* (very important); ANS 1 G 41, Gallieni, Mission de Bafoulabé, 17 November 1879. See also ANS 13 G 169, Ct. Bakel to Gov. Senegal, No. 77, 19 March 1864.

44. Grain and peanuts were also carried to the Senegal River from distances sometimes greater than 100 kilometers on pack animals (local or provided by the Beydan); see ANS 13 G 164, Ct. Bakel to Gov. Senegal, No. 49, 12 January 1837; Paul Soleillet, *Voyage à Ségou, 1878–79* (Paris: Challamel, 1887), pp. 22–223; ANS 13 G 168, Ct. Bakel to Gov. Senegal, No. 44, 7 October 1863; ANS Q 51, Sénégambie et Niger, Cercle de Kayes, Rapport commercial, 2d quarter 1904; Meillassoux, "Commerce et esclavage"; and more generally for Senegal, see Frédéric Riembau, *De Dakar au Niger. La question du chemin de fer et la mise en valeur des territoires de la Sénégambie et du Niger* (Paris: Challamel, 1908), p. 39.

45. Paragraph's quotes: 13 G 166, Ct. Bakel to Gov. Senegal, No. 8, 10 March 1851; No. 13, 29 May 1851; No. 4, 9 February 1853.

46. Frédéric Carrère and Paul Holle, *De la Sénégambie française* (Paris: F. Didot, 1855), pp. 382–393; Leland Conley Barrows, "The Merchants and General Faidherbe: Aspects of French Expansion in Senegal in the 1850s," *Revue française d'histoire d'outre-mer*, vol. 61, no. 223, 1974, pp. 250–51, 254–55.

47. Curtin, *Economic Change*, supp., pp. 74–77.

48. Monique Chastanet, "L'état soninké du Gajaaga de 1818 à 1858 face à l'expansion commerciale française au Sénégal," Mémoire de maîtrise, Université de Paris I Sorbonne (Centre de Recherches Africaines), 1975–1976; "De la traite à la conquête";

Bathily, "Imperialism," pp. 371–425; and "La conquête française du haut-fleuve (Sénégal), 1818–1887. *Bulletin de l'I.F.A.N.*, vol. 34, Série B, 1972, p. 65; Raffenel, *Voyage*, pp. 292–293.

49. See the useful chronology of Gajaaga in Curtin, *Economic Change*, supp., pp. 16–17.

50. ANS 13 G 166, Ct. Bakel to Gov. Senegal, No. 9, 25 April 1853.

51. ANS 13 G 166, Lettre des traitants à M. Hilaire Maurel, à St. Louis, June 22, 1853. The observation was accurate, as one can verify in Curtin, *Economic Change*, supp., p. 77.

52. Governor Protet to Minister, 8 November 1852, quoted in Yves St. Martin, *L'Empire toucouleur et la France. Un demi-siècle de relations diplomatiques (1846–1893)* (Dakar: Université de Dakar, Publications de la Faculté des lettres et sciences humaines, 1967), pp. 61–62. In 1854, Governor Faidherbe wrote: "Trade in the Upper Senegal [region] is today, I believe, almost equal to that of the lower valley." Letter of 22 December 1854, quoted in Hardy, *Mise en valeur*, p. 355. Exports from regions other than the Senegal River Valley were at the time of little importance in the economy of Senegal; see Curtin, *Economic Change*, supp., pp. 61–72.

53. Webb, *Desert Frontier*, p. 130; also Hardy, *Mise en valeur*, pp. 317–22; Stewart, *Islam*, pp. 92–93.

54. ANSOM Senegal XIII, 10c, letter from Captain Pontac, enclosed in Note for the Direction of Colonies from director of personnel, Register of Sailors [bureau de l'inscription maritime], No. 575, 17 February 1855.

55. Curiously, they are not mentioned in the Bakel archives, but they are clearly mentioned in other sources; see Louis Faidherbe, *Le Sénégal: la France dans l'Afrique occidentale* (Paris: Hachette, 1889; Nendeln: Klaus reprints, 1974), pp. 58–59; Joseph Simon Gallieni, *Deux campagnes au Soudan français, 1886–1887* (Paris: Hachette, 1891), p. 164; Riembau, *De Dakar au Niger*, pp. 154–155; I. D. Bathily, "Notices," p. 97.

56. The reference work on navétanat is Philippe David, *Les navétanes* (Dakar; Abidjan: Nouvelles Editions Africaines, 1980). On the history of the term, see pp. 46–47 and 166. See also Ken Swindell, "Serawoolies, Tillibunkas and Strange Farmers: The Development of Migrant Groundnut Farming along the Gambia River, 1848–95," *Journal of African History*, vol. 21, 1980, pp. 93–104.

57. Curtin, *Economic Change*, p. 75; Bathily, "Imperialism," p. 81; Raffenel, *Voyage*, pp. 449–483.

58. Curtin, *Economic Change*, pp. 171, 230–231. According to a sample of purchases on the Gambia River made by the British Royal African Company in 1684 to 1688, 20 percent of the cost of slaves for European traders "went for agricultural provisions to feed slaves waiting shipment and to store ships for the Atlantic crossing"; ibid., p. 230. Similar evidence in Bathily, "Traite atlantique."

59. Curtin, *Economic Change*, p. 230.

60. M. Vène, "Rapport sur les établissements anglais de la Gambie et les comptoirs français d'Albréda et de Casamance," *Annales maritimes*, vol. 82 (November 1837), n.p., quoted in Amédée Tardieu, *Sénégambie et Guinée* (Paris, 1847), p. 113; and Tardieu, ibid., p. 116.

61. George E. Brooks, "Peanuts and Colonialism: Consequences of the Commercialization of Peanuts in West Africa, 1830–70," *Journal of African History*, vol. 16, 1975, pp. 29–54.

62. David, *Navétanes*, pp. 12–15.

63. Martin Klein, *Islam and Imperialism, Sine-Saloum, 1847–1914* (Stanford: Stanford University Press, 1968), pp. 177–178 (apparently a better quote than Swindell, "Serawoollies," p. 94).

64. Estimate by Governor MacDonnell, Curtin, *Economic Change*, p. 231.

65. Swindell, "Serawoolies," p. 94.

66. David, *Navétanes*, pp. 12–19.

67. E. Bertrand-Bocandé, "Carabane et Séhiou," *Revue coloniale*, vol. 15, 1856, p. 412.

68. David, *Navétanes*, pp. 166–206.

69. Swindell, "Serawoolies," pp. 97–102.

70. In an earlier article, I postulated that the British commitment to ending the slave trade and their willingness to give asylum to escaped slaves made it risky for slave traders to come to the Gambia. Specialists, however, have pointed out to me that slaves were extensively sold in the Gambia, especially during the troubled 1850s and 1860s (the decade of the Marabout wars) and were widely used in local peanut production. Martin Klein, personal correspondence, 1990; see also Paul Lovejoy, *Transformations in Slavery: A History of Slavery in Africa* (Cambridge: Cambridge University Press, 1991), pp. 189–190; Charlotte A. Quinn, *Mandingo Kingdoms of the Senegambia* (Evanston, Ill.: Northwestern University Press, 1972), passim; Peter M. Weil, "Slavery, Groundnuts, and European Capitalism in the Wuli Kingdom of Senegambia, 1820–1930," *Research in Economic Anthropology*, vol. 6, 1984, pp. 77–119.

71. David, *Navétanes*, pp. 188–191; see also G. Rocheteau, "Société wolof et mobilité," *Cahiers de l'ORSTOM*, ser. sc. hum., vol. 12, no. 1, 1975, pp. 3–18.

72. Bertrand-Bocandé, "Carabane et Séhiou," p. 412.

73. ANS 13 G 195, Desmarets, Rapport sur la captivité dans le cercle de Bakel, 26 May 1894.

74. Bathily, "Imperialism," p. 323.

75. In my earlier article about the origins of navetanat, I had speculated that many migrants may have been talibe, or students of Koranic schools. Although my hypothesis rested on a faulty reading of Raffenel (relying on faulty notes, I wrote that Raffenel saw a "large number of talibes" on the road to the Gambia; this was, in fact, incorrect), the hypothesis remains plausible. As is well known, professional traders in West Africa were generally from clerical families. Clerics were also, according to all major sources, heavily involved in the slave trade. On the other hand, religious leaders from clerical families ran religious schools. These talibe were young unmarried men who needed money for bridewealth and other marriage expenses. In addition, the talibe were required by custom to give their teachers a graduation gift of a value equal to at least one slave. The talibe, therefore, were young men with important monetary needs who worked for families that were heavily involved in trade—especially the slave trade. For all these reasons, it would have been natural for talibe to be the first to

hear about the new employment opportunities in the Gambia. We shall see later an example of an Islamic school functioning as a network of information about employment opportunities. See Chapter Five.

76. Bertrand-Bocandé, "Carabane et Sédhiou," p. 412.

77. Abdon M. Eugène Mage, *Voyage dans le Soudan occidental (Sénégambie-Niger) 1863–1866* (Paris: Hachette, 1868), pp. 106–107.

78. Martin Klein, "Slave Resistance and Slave Emancipation in Coastal Guinea," in Suzanne Miers and Richard Roberts, eds., *The End of Slavery in Africa* (Madison: University of Wisconsin Press, 1988), pp. 203–219.

79. Klein, *Islam and Imperialism*, p. 119. I do not have Gambian peanut prices for this period, but peanut prices were a function of the world market and, therefore, were roughly similar at different areas of the Senegambian coast.

80. Pollet and Winter, *Société soninké*, p. 99.

81. Swindell, "Serawoolies," pp. 98–99. Twelve shillings is an 1893 figure (there are apparently no earlier figures for the Gambia); conversion table of pounds to francs, Curtin, *Economic Change*, supp., p. 56. "Customs" payments by navetanes in neighboring Sine-Saloum in the 1890s were up to 20 francs; Klein, *Islam and Imperialism*, pp. 177–178; see also David, *Navétanes*, pp. 24–26. On areas planted by navetanes and the yields of their personal plots, ibid., pp. 197–205.

82. I have no price for grain for this period, but since it stayed quite steadily around 0.10 francs a kilogram for the whole of the second half of the nineteenth century (except in bad years), this figure may be used for an estimate. Reference: ANS 13 G series.

83. Swindell, "Serawoolies," pp. 94–95.

84. David, *Navétanes*, pp. 18–19.

85. Pollet and Winter, *Société soninké*, pp. 137–138. Pollet and Winter note that in practice this is rarely the case today.

86. Saugnier, *Relation de plusieurs voyages à la côte d'Afrique . . .* (Paris: Geffier jeune, 1791), p. 215; see also p. 228.

87. Soleillet, *Voyage*, p. 326, note.

88. See, e.g., Curtin, *Economic Change*, pp. 114, 279.

89. Slave laptots were generally employed in boat-building during the slack season.

90. James F. Searing, *West African Slavery and Atlantic Commerce: The Senegal River Valley, 1700–1860* (Cambridge: Cambridge University Press, 1993), pp. 93–128.

91. Searing, *West African Slavery*; and Malcolm Thompson, "In Dubious Service: The Recruitment and Stabilization of West African Maritime Labor by the French Colonial Military, 1659–1900," Ph.D. thesis, University of Minnesota, Minneapolis, 1989.

92. Searing, *West African Slavery*, pp. 124–125.

93. On this military lifestyle, see Bathily, "Imperialism," p. 278. It is probable, moreover, that Soninke laptots worked in teams that included only their countrymen, a practice that reduced their contact with the slave laptots.

94. Swindell, "Serawoolies," p. 95; Charlotte Quinn, "Mandingo States in Nine-teenth Century Gambia," in Hodge, *Papers on the Manding*, pp. 212–213; also Quinn, *Mandingo Kingdoms*, pp. 27, 42, 49, 69, and 171.

95. Bathily, *Portes de l'or*, pp. 127–166.

96. Thompson, "In Dubious Service," p. 89, note 48.

97. Searing, *West African Slavery*, pp. 93–128.

98. Curtin, *Economic Change*, p. 279.

99. Ibid.

100. Ibid., supp., p. 83 (use conversion tables on p. 56 to obtain figures in French francs).

101. The early laptot was a jack-of-all-trades, in turn a "house servant, shop em-ployee, gardener, male nurse, spahi [native soldier], soldier in a river outpost." Anne Raffenel, *Nouveau voyage au pays des nègres* (Paris: Chaix, 1856), p. 179. Part of the laptots' wages, at least until 1848, was paid in kind, enabling them to trade on their own; see Abbé P. D. Boilat, *Esquisses sénégalaises* (Paris: P. Bertrand, 1853), p. 441. In 1724, a certain "Aly Mody," a laptot, ran a trading post in the royal village of Lagny (Kammera); Curtin, *Economic Change*, p. 114.

102. Saugnier, *Relation*, pp. 214–215.

103. ANS 13 G 166, Ct. Bakel to Gov. Senegal, 5 March 1851; see also 13 G 166, Re-port Dudras, director Affaires Extérieures, following a journey to Bakel, October 1851; both references quoted by Chastanet, "Etat soninké du Gajaaga," pp. 216, 220. Barka Bacili, chief of Maxanna and de facto tunka of Kammera, controlled many of the laptots, "who could only hire themselves out to Saint-Louisian traders with his permission," Thompson, "In Dubious Service," p. 89, note 44 (the archival reference is ANSOM, Senegal IV, 19, Conseil d'administration, séance, 30 August 1852, No. 19).

104. Soleillet, *Voyage*, pp. 326–327; Yves Saint-Martin, *Une source de l'histoire colo-niale au Sénégal: les rapports de situation politique (1874–1891)* (Dakar: Université de Dakar, Publications de la faculté des lettres et sciences humaines, 1966), p. 97; Bathily, "Imperialism," p. 282. On Samba Njaay and Tambo Bacili's diplomatic role, see Saint-Martin, *Empire toucouleur*, pp. 150–156.

105. Curtin, *Economic Change*, pp. 235–237.

106. In time, some migrants became full-time traders: the wealthy Auvergnat mer-chants in Spain, whose associations dominated the hierarchy of Auvergnat migrants in the seventeenth and eighteenth centuries, could be compared to the Soninke jula of precolonial Sudanic cities. See Raison-Jourde, *Colonie auvergnate*, pp. 67–71.

107. Chatelain, *Migrants temporaires*, especially Vol. 1, pp. 386–395, 434–453.

108. Stefano Fenaltoa, "Migration," unpublished presentation to the Banca d'I-talia, November 1991. My special thanks to the author for letting me quote this pre-liminary study.

109. Bertrand-Bocandé, "Carabane et Séhiou," p. 412.

110. Warren Dean, *Rio Claro: A Brazilian Plantation System, 1820–1920* (Stanford: Stanford University Press, 1976).

111. Manchuelle, "The Patriarchal Ideal of Soninke Labor Migrants," pp. 106–125; and "Slavery, Emancipation and Labor Migration in West Africa: the Case of the Soninke," *Journal of African History*, vol. 30, 1989, pp. 89–106.

Chapter 3

1. Robinson, *Holy War of Umar Tal*, p. 161.

2. Ibid., pp. 233–234.

3. Calculation based on the sterling price per metric ton in Curtin, *Economic Change*, supp., p. 101 (Table A 15.9); currency conversion table, p. 56. A similar calculation for 1824 to 1826 (Table A 15.5, p. 97) gives a similar price of 1.85 francs. In 1845 to 1846, the price was 2.20 francs a kilo; Henri Zion, "Le poste de Bakel à l'époque du gouverneur Faidherbe, 1855–1865," Mémoire de maîtrise, Université de Dakar, Faculté de lettres et sciences humaines, 1968, p. 186. The price of 2 francs a kilo was mentioned in the deliberations of the 11 October 1859 meeting of the *Conseil d'administration* of Senegal, discussed immediately below.

4. Zion, "Poste de Bakel," p. 186.

5. ANSOM Senegal XIII, 33a, Minister of marine to minister of agriculture and commerce, 27 December 1839.

6. Proceedings in ANS 3 E 28, Conseil d'Administration, Meeting of 11 October 1859, Deliberation No. 19.

7. Hardy, *Mise en valeur*, pp. 323–326. Barrows,"Merchants," pp. 247–249; Johnson, *Emergence*, esp. pp. 38–47; François Zuccarelli, "Les maires de St. Louis et Gorée de 1816 à 1872," *Bulletin IFAN*, B, 1973, pp. 551–573.

8. Paul Leroy-Beaulieu, *De la colonisation chez les peuples modernes*, vol. 2 (Paris: Alcan, 1908), pp. 570–594.

9. While the move was clearly in the interest of the Saint-Louis and Bordeaux commercial houses, it was also not unlike the proposal made not so long ago by the Nigerian economist Adebeyo Adedeji to increase direct taxes after the price of one of Nigeria's main exports, cocoa, experienced a continued downward trend. In fact, during the recent world recession, many African economists, such as Adedeji, have been critical of indirect forms of taxation such as import, export, and excise duties, which put national economies at risk without any promise of greater fiscal justice, and very much in favor of direct taxes, in particular of personal taxes. Adebeyo Adedeji, "The Future of Personal Taxation in Nigeria," in Milton C. Taylor, ed., *Taxation for African Economic Development* (London: Hutchinson International, 1970), pp. 257–278; and contributions by other authors in the same source.

10. Henry Laufenberger, *Histoire de l'impôt* (Paris: P.U.F., 1954), esp. pp. 39–57; and Marcel Marion, *Histoire financière de la France depuis 1715*, 6 vols. (Paris: Rousseau, 1914–1931). This position recalls that of some contemporary African economists—see note immediately above.

11. Hardy, *Mise en valeur*, pp. 341–342ff.

12. The personal tax in Senegal was established by Imperial Decree of 4 August

1860. The *arrêté* of the governor on 9 August 1861 set its amount. See ANSOM Senegal IX, 14a.

13. ANS 13 G 167, N'Diaye Sow to the Dir. Aff. Ext., 29 May 1859. Famine was apparently due to a combination of floods (ANS 13 G 167, Bakel, 14 February 1859) and pilfering of the fields, most probably by passing refugees (ibid., 10 February 1859).

14. ANS 13 G 167, Ct. Bakel to Governor Senegal, No. 2, December 26, 185[9 or 8?].

15. Robinson, *Holy War of Umar Tal*, pp. 233–241.

16. See, e.g., ANS 13 G 168, Ct. Bakel to Gov. Senegal, No. 4, 25 March 1860.

17. Zion, "Poste de Bakel," pp. 72–74; Bathily, "Conquête," p. 91; Robinson, *Holy War of Umar Tal*, p. 240.

18. Bathily, "Conquête," p. 95. Bathily gives Zion ("Poste de Bakel," pp. 105–109) as his reference, but Zion noted that emigration preceded taxation by several years and that taxation was "very modest." There is no mention in Zion (nor apparently in the Bakel documents) of migration to the Niger River Valley.

19. ANS 13 G 168, Ct. Bakel to Gov. Senegal, 20 May 1862. Robinson notes that 5,000 persons took refuge in the Gambia from the Upper Senegal in 1859; Robinson, *Holy War of Umar Tal*, p. 239; in 1860, a French administrator noted the return of inhabitants of Bundu who had taken refuge in the Gambian kingdom of Wuli; see ANS 13 G 168, Ct. Senoudebou to Gov. Senegal, 21 April 1860.

20. 13 G 169, 3 January 1864. The first recorded tax census dates from December 1863 (ANS 13 G 168, Ct. Bakel to Gov. Senegal, No. 56, 2 December 1863), but there apparently was an earlier census or census estimate in 1862; referred to in 13 G 168, Ct. Bakel to Indigenous Affairs, 5 June 1862.

21. ANS 13 G 168, Ct. Bakel to Gov. Senegal, Indigenous Aff., No. 14, 5 June 1862.

22. ANS 13 G 168, Ct. Bakel to Gov. Senegal, Indigenous Aff., No. 21, 20 August 1862; Zion, "Poste de Bakel," p. 108.

23. ANS 13 G 168, Ct. Bakel to Gov. Senegal, Indigenous Aff., No. 14, 5 June 1862; No. 21, 20 August 1862; No. 25, 13 September 1862.

24. ANS 13 G 168, Ct. Bakel to Gov. Senegal, No. 45, 11 October 1863.

25. The arrest of the chiefs in 1862 was the only incident of this period. Bathily's assertion that there was unrest in 1863, 1864, and 1865 is based on an unclearly worded sentence in Zion, "Poste de Bakel," p. 107.

26. A. S. Kanya-Forstner, *The Conquest of the Western Sudan: A Study in French Military Imperialism* (Cambridge: Cambridge University Press, 1969), pp. 33–34. This was due to the American Civil War, which created a worldwide shortage of cotton after unionist forces blockaded the southern confederacy.

27. ANS 13 G 168, in particular "Rapport sur la situation générale de l'Arrondissement de Bakel 1862" [to the governor, dated 27 November 1862]; Ct. Bakel to Gov. Senegal, 25 January 1862; 20 May 1862; No. 36, 26 November 1862; "Rapport sur la situation commerciale à Bakel," 22 February 1863; Aff. Indigènes, No. 6, 5 April 1863; No. 8, 5 May 1863. On Pineau's troop movements ("Vous me reprochez, M. le Gouverneur, de mettre trop souvent mes troupes en mouvement: permettez-moi de vous dire que

c'est à mes continuelles courses que je dois le résultat que le commerce constatera cette année"), ANS 13 G 168, Indigenous Aff., No. 5, 4 March 1862. Jauréguiberry had requested suggestions three months before on how to increase the cultivation of peanuts and cotton; ANS 13 G 168, Gov. Senegal to Ct. Bakel, 25 January 1862.

28. Hardy, *Mise en valeur*; Barry, *Royaume du Waalo*. Curtin notes that the Compagnie du Galam lost 18 percent of its capital trying to run a plantation it was required to maintain in Waalo, Curtin, *Economic Change*, p. 133.

29. ANS 13 G 168, "Rapport sur la situation générale de l'Arrondissement de Bakel 1862," Ct. Bakel to Gov. Senegal, dated 27 November 1862.

30. Figures in Zion, "Poste de Bakel," pp. 203–204. See also the shrewd utilization of floods by the Gwey populations: in 1862, a flood allegedly destroyed all the crops in the immediate vicinity of the Senegal River; while peanut production was maintained, almost the entire cotton crop was "lost"; see ANS 13 G 168, Ct. Bakel [de Pineau] to Gov. Senegal, 25 January 1862. The peanut price estimate is from the tables (mostly based on information in the ANS series 13 G) in the Appendix of my doctoral dissertation, "Background to Black African Emigration to France: The Labor Migrations of the Soninke, 1848–1987," University of California, Santa Barbara 1987; see also Klein, *Islam and Imperialism*, p. 119 note.

31. Zion, who has seen some documents I have not been able to review (in particular the file ANSOM Sénégal I, 48d), says that the tax was payable either in money or in cotton; Zion, "Poste de Bakel," p. 106.

32. Quoted in Zion, "Poste de Bakel," p. 109.

33. In the same fashion, the *Journal de Bordeaux* likened direct taxation of the indigenous population to the tributes formerly paid by French merchants to local African chiefs. Ibid. On nineteenth-century French liberal perceptions of colonization in Algeria, see François Manchuelle, "Origines républicaines de la politique d'expansion coloniale de Jules Ferry (1838–1865)," *Revue française d'histoire d'outre-mer*, vol. 75, no. 279, 1988, pp. 185–206.

34. Zion, "Poste de Bakel," pp. 108–109; Barrows, "Merchants and General Faidherbe," pp. 276–277. Barrows noted that prominent merchants such as Marc Maurel, who had supported the personal tax under Faidherbe, were the ones who most opposed it under Jauréguiberry. Ibid.

35. ANS 13 G 168, Ct. de Pineau to Gov. Senegal, Military Affairs, No. 10, 19 May 1863; Ct. Bakel to Gov. Senegal, Indigenous Aff., No. 14, 30 June 1863; and 5 August 1863.

36. Tax census for 1863: Baalu: 15 taxpayers; Arundu: 25; Yaafera: 25; Golmi: 25; Kungani: 40; total—125 taxpayers. ANS 13 G 168, Ct. Bakel to Gov. Senegal, No. 56, 2 December 1863. Amount actually paid: 12 *pièces de guinée conjon*, valued at 16 francs each by the commandant; ANS 13 G 169, Ct. Bakel to Gov., 3 January 1864. I lack demographic information on Goye Annexé for the 1860s, but I have available a probably underestimated 1888 census and an apparently better census for 1891. The first yielded a figure of 1,240 inhabitants for the five villages of Goye Annexé and the second 1,554

inhabitants. These figures were given as figures for the whole population, male and female, including small children, who did not have to pay the tax. ANS 13 G 189, Rapport du Capitaine Darr, Commandant le poste de Bakel sur la perception de l'impôt personnel pour l'année 1889, 7 November 1888; ANS 13 G 191, Cercle de Bakel, Impôt personnel, 1891.

37. ANSOM IX, 14a.

38. Zion, "Poste de Bakel," pp. 105–106; ANS 13 G 174, "Instructions générales...," left by the Bakel commandant to his successor in 1878 (no other date).

39. ANS 13 G 174, Poste de Bakel, Perception de l'impôt personnel pour l'année 1877 (add figures for the five villages of Goye Annexé). It is probable that the French applied taxation only to *family heads*. An 1891 document mentions that only family heads paid the tax until 1890, when taxation was extended to all (all adults) first in Kammera, then later in Gwey. ANS 13 G 191, Bakel, No. 404, 10 August 1891. Some women, however, paid tax in 1877; see Table 3.2 below.

40. ANS 13 G 168, Bakel to Gov. Senegal, No. 56, 2 December 1863.

41. On Bundu at the time, see Robinson, *Holy War of Umar Tal*, pp. 219–220.

42. *Feuille officielle du Sénégal*, No. 199, 20 October 1863, quoted in Zion, "Poste de Bakel," p. 204. Export figures in Zion, "Poste de Bakel," p. 204; prices in ANS 13 G 168, Ct. Bakel to Gov. Senegal, No. 25, 18 August 1863. On the basis of these figures, the Bakel region would have exported 452,631.56 francs. References on the weight of a *barrique* (capacity measure for peanuts and grain): (for peanuts) ANS 13 G 169, Ct. Bakel to Gov. Senegal, AP 108, 18 June 1872 and 13 G 171, Bakel, Agr. and comm. bulletin, No. 4, September 1872; (for sorghum), ANS 13 G 181, Bakel, Agr., comm. and pol. bulletin, May 1881. Gum was briefly back this year to its pre-1859 level of one franc a kilogram, but the gum trade continued to be disrupted by bad relations between the French and the Umarians, and only 183,533 kilograms were exported in 1863. Zion, "Poste de Bakel," p. 204.

43. In fact, in 1863 a caravan came from Konyakari in Kaarta, some 200 kilometers away, with eight elephant tusks, about forty cowskins, and ten barrels of peanuts (about 1,200 kilograms). ANS 13 G 168, Ct. Bakel to Gov., No. 44, 7 October 1863. Such an event was probably exceptional (this one was an attempt of Umar's son Ahmadu to reestablish relations with the French in order to obtain firearms). Better relations between the French and the Umarian empire followed the important negotiations of 1860; see Robinson, *Holy War of Umar Tal*, pp. 241, 251.

44. My estimate of 200 villages is generous but perhaps plausible. Under colonial administration, Gidimaxa was split in two halves (Mauritanian and Malian) with about equal population. Saint-Père estimated the number of villages in the Mauritanian half at fifty; *Sarakollé du Guidimakha*, p. 17. Assuming that the French traded with an equal number of villages on the northern and southern bank, 200 appears acceptable, but I have not taken into account the fact that villages above the Falemme confluence (i.e., about a hundred) traded with Médine rather than Bakel after 1855.

45. Kanya-Forstner, *Conquest of the Western Sudan*, pp. 45–50.

46. ANS 13 G 170, Ct. Bakel to Gov. Senegal, Political Affairs, No. 11, 3 February 1866; and Pol. Aff., [No.] 20, 19 March 1866.

47. ANS 13 G 170, Ct. Bakel to Gov. Senegal, Pol. Aff. No. 25, 4 April 1866.

48. ANS 13 G 170, Ct. Bakel to Gov. Senegal, [No.] 61, 8 November 1866.

49. Ibid.

50. Tax apparently was not connected in Goye Annexé between 1865 and 1876. Two documents mention that tax was collected in Goye Annexé in 1870, but the context suggests that tax may have been collected in the town of Bakel only that year. ANS 13 G 171, No. 5, December 1870; ANS 13 G 172, Instructions générales laissées à mon successeur . . . [n.d., early 1873]. Between 1865 and 1876, Goye Annexé was mentioned only with reference to its refusal to pay tax. Each time, the governor recommended patience to the commandant. In 1873, the Bakel commandant described the population of Gwey as divided between "N'Diayankés" (Njaay, founding family of Bakel) and slaves, thus betraying his complete lack of knowledge of the Soninke outside Bakel; ANS 13 G 172, Instructions générales laissées à mon successeur . . . [n.d., early 1873]; and ANS 13 G 169 to 172.

51. ANS 13 G 170, Letter Abdoulaye Dieye, 19 June 1868; and Pol. Aff. 28, 1 July 1868.

52. See "Bulletins agricoles et commerciaux" in files of ANS 13 G series after 1863.

53. For the detail of Upper Senegal trade figures (guinées, gum, peanuts, cereals), see Manchuelle, "Background," pp. 618–668.

54. Roger Pasquier, "Villes du Sénégal au XIXe. siècle," *Revue française d'histoire d'outre-mer*, vol. 47, 1960, p. 405.

55. ANS 13 G 168–171. One document lists the tonnage of *chalands* anchored in Bakel as six to thirty-two nautical tons; 13 G 171, Bakel, Agr. and Comm. Bulletin, January 1869. Reference to tugs in ANS 13 G 171, Bakel, Agr. and Comm. Bulletin, No. 4, October 1872.

56. Henri Frey, *Campagne dans le Haut Sénégal et le Haut Niger (1885–1886)*, (Paris: Plon, 1888), p. 45. Contrast with Carrère and Holle's description in 1855: ". . . boats. . . which have to be towed by human strength, [which] take thirty-five to forty-five days to cross a distance of a hundred and fifty leagues [the distance between Saint-Louis and Bakel.]" Carrère and Holle, *De la Sénégambie française*, p. 385. The cost of carrying freight from the Upper Senegal fell dramatically, from 45 francs per nautical ton in 1855 to 19.50 francs a ton in 1868. Carrère and Holle, ibid.; ANS 13 G 170, Bakel, Agr. and Comm. Bulletin, November 1868.

57. ANS 13 G 169, No. 93, 19 April 1864; No. 119, 2 July 1864; 13 G 170, No. 18, 15 April 1867; Pol. Aff. No. 28, 1 July 1868; 13 G 171, No. 33, 29 February 72; Bull. Agricole & Commercial, No. 75, May 1871; 13 G 172, Aff. Pol. No. 20, 14 February 1873; 13 G 173, 22 March 1876.

58. ANS 13 G 169, Bakel, No. 119, 2 July 1869.

59. ANS 13 G 172, Bakel, AP No. 20, 14 February 1873. See also ANS 13 170, Ct. Bakel to Gov. Senegal, No. 18, 15 April 1867; 13 G 173, Bull. agricole, commercial et politique, Nov. 1875.

60. ANS 13 G 170, Bakel, No. 4, 1 May 1868; 13 G 172, Bakel, Bull. agricole, com-

mercial et politique, No. 43, March 1873; 13 G 173, Bakel, Bull. agricole, commercial et politique, November 1875; Soleillet, *Voyage à Ségou*, p. 149; 108; ANS 13 G 184, Bakel, Rapport trimestriel prescrit par la circulaire du 4 Avril 1884, 10 October 1884.

61. ANS 13 G 170, Ct. Bakel to Gov. Senegal, No. 18, 15 April 1867; Pol. Aff. 58, 18 October 1867; 13 G 171, Pol. Aff. No. 7, 1 February 1869. Several *traitants* dealt "almost exclusively" in peanuts in 1873. ANS 13 G 172, Bakel, Bull. agricole, commercial et politique, May 1873.

According to Monique Chastanet, there was a "famine" in the agricultural year 1866 to 1867, and a "great famine" in 1867 to 1868 and 1868 to 1869, which she believes to have been due to French taxes and forced labor; Monique Chastanet, "Les crises de subsistances dans les villages soninke du cercle de Bakel, de 1858 à 1945," *Cahiers d'Etudes Africaines*, vol. 23, no. 89–90, 1983, p. 27. The only evidence for this appears to be a request for a tax exemption in April 1868 from the Soninke chief of Bakel, who argued a bad crop that year (but the Bakel commandant noted that Bakel villagers appeared to "exaggerate a bit their misfortune," suggesting they intended to avoid paying tax and thus be like "Goye Annexé"), and the May 1868 report that mentioned that *mil* was becoming rarer in Bakel. Yet later reports mention no deaths or famine. (Contrast with the data for 1859, where famine appears very clearly.) ANS 13 G 170, Ct. Bakel to Gov. Senegal, No. 12, 1 April 1868; and No. 18, 1 May 1868. Note this answer by the Bakel commandant in 1867 to a request from the governor that he recruit *tirailleurs* (indigenous soldiers) in Bakel: "I doubt that the recruitment you are asking me to do for the *tirailleur* battalion will meet with any success here. *The region has become rich, the sarrakholes [Soninke] accept employment only on steam boats*," ANS 13 G 170, Ct. Bakel to Gov. Senegal, Pol. Aff. No. 35, 1 July 1867 [my emphasis] .

Chastanet's method of accepting as evidence of subsistence crises local requests for tax exemptions ("Crises," p. 17) ignores the possibility that such requests may have been fabrications, destined to get rid of French control in the region.

62. ANS 13 G 171, Ct. Bakel to Gov. Senegal, No. 33, 29 February 1872.

63. 13 G 169, No. 203, Ct. Bakel to Gov. Senegal, 5 June 1865.

64. Xavier Guiraud, *L'arachide sénégalaise* (Paris: Librairie technique et économique, 1937) p. 163; Louis Faidherbe, *Le Sénégal: la France dans l'Afrique occidentale* (Nendeln: Klaus reprints, 1974; 1st ed., Paris: Hachette, 1889), p. 105.

65. Source: tables in appendix, Manchuelle, "Background" (source: mostly ANS 13 G).

66. Carrère and Holle, *Sénégambie française*, pp. 12–13.

67. François Zuccarelli, "Le régime des engagés à temps au Sénégal (1817–1848)," *Cahiers d'Etudes Africaines*, no. 7, 1962, p. 445.

68. Carrère and Holle, *Sénégambie française*, pp. 345–347.

69. This is indeed the mechanism that created a demand for African workers (North Africans and Black Africans) in France in the second half of the twentieth century.

70. I have consulted the archives of the famous Devès métis family in the National Archives of Senegal. They contained very little information on laptots.

71. ANF CC 3 1183, [Captain Rebel], Note sur le personnel de la Subdivision du Sénégal, Sep. 1872.

72. ANF CC 3 1182, Rapport de la commission sur le recrutement des matelots indigènes au Sénégal [September 1877].

73. ANF CC 3 1182, Senegal, Etat-major to Minister of Marine, No. 224, 29 April 1877.

74. ANF CC3 1183, Ministry of Marine and Colonies, Direction of colonies, 2d bureau, No. 3, [1880], Recrutement des laptots au Sénégal.

75. There are mentions of laptots or Soninke-speaking French (a sure evidence of laptot service in the French Navy for the vernacular in Saint-Louis was Wolof) for the villages of Gumal (Damga) [Soleillet, *Voyage*, p. 77]; Muderi (Gwey) [ibid., p. 84]; Golmi (Gwey) [ANS 13 G 184, Ct. Bakel to Gov. Senegal, 10 April 1884]; Yaafera (Gwey) [ANS 13 G 182, Bulletin Commercial, Agricole et Politique, January 1882]; Tanbunkaani (Kammera) [ibid.]; Muusala (Kammera) [ibid., pp. 136–137]; Ganyi (Gidimaxa) [Soleillet, *Voyage*, p. 148]; Somankidi (Gidimaxa) [ibid., p. 149]; Sebeku (Gidimaxa) [ibid., p. 110]. All the Gajaaga villages mentioned are either maraboutic (Muderi, Tanbunkaani, Yaafera) or royal villages (Golmi and Muusala); see Chastanet, "Etat"; three (Muderi, Yaafera, Muusala) were represented in the 1894 Congo migration (in addition Somankidi in Gidimaxa was also represented); see Chapter Four.

76. ANF CC 3 1183, Division navale de l'Atlantique Sud, Personnel, Equipages de la flotte, Rapport d'inspection générale de la subdivision du Sénégal in 1881, Recrutement et avancement des marins indigènes, 8 May 1881.

77. ANS, Series L [this series was being reclassified when I was given access to it], [Gov. Senegal to Chief of the Service de l'Intérieur], 3 March 1878.

78. These were *common* wages in Saint-Louis at the time. In rush periods, commercial houses paid higher wages. ANF CC 3 1183, Recrutement des laptots au Sénégal, 1880.

79. Henri Sée, *Histoire économique de la France* (Paris: A. Colin, 1942), pp. 332–337.

80. Compare with farm incomes (grain farmer in Bakel and navetane in the Gambia) in Chapter Two.

81. Numerous examples in ANF CC 3 1182 and 1183; e.g., report by Captain Rebel, quoted above; CC 3 1182, Commandant de la Marine et de la subdivision navale to Gov. Senegal, No. 21, 12 April 1877.

82. Walter Elkan, *Migrants and Proletarians: Urban Labor in the Economic Development of Uganda* (London: Oxford University Press, 1960); and "Migrant Labor in Africa: an Economist's Approach," *American Economic Review*, May 1959, pp. 188–202.

83. ANF CC 3 1183, Rapport de la commission sur le recrutement des matelots au Sénégal, September 1877.

84. Frey, *Campagne*, p. 239.

85. Frey, *Campagne*, pp. 238–239.

86. ANF CC3 1183, Note sur l'organisation des laptots au Sénégal, [n.d.]

87. See his fascinating description of the "dream of a Soninke," *Voyage*, p. 77.

88. It would be useful to find evidence for this period of intrafamily conflict over

migration earnings (which, once again, belonged to family heads), but archival texts offer no evidence of the kind. Judiciary records are not helpful because the French administrator in Bakel until 1879 apparently dealt only with litigation between Saint-Louisien traitants and the local population, and he left the internal administration of justice to the chiefs and the *cadis* (Islamic judges). Later documents, however, show evidence of such conflicts between family heads and younger men.

89. Soleillet, *Voyage*, p. 77.

90. Frey, *Campagne*, p. 239.

91. ANS K 14, Capitaine Mazillier, Rapport sur la captivité dans le cercle de Kayes, 8 July 1894.

92. Given the generally gerontocratic character of traditional African society, the desire for independence from family elders must have been a fairly frequent motivation for the migration of young men, although it has only recently come to the attention of scholars. See Guy Rocheteau, "Société wolof et mobilité," *Cahiers de l'ORSTOM*, ser. sc. hum., vol. 12, 1976, pp. 3–18. For a fuller discussion of the issue see Chapter Four.

93. See Chapter Two.

94. ANS 13 G 182, Bakel, Comm., agr. and pol. report, January 1882.

95. Soleillet, *Voyage*, p. 149.

96. Ibid., pp. 136–137; for the status of the village, refer to Chastanet, "Etat soninké du Gadiaga," Appendix.

97. See Chapter Five. Available lists of laptots often carry the name Bacili (royal family of Gajaaga, i.e., Gwey and Kammera); see, e.g., "Médailles commémoratives de l'expédition du Dahomey déposée dans les bureaux du Commandant de la marine au Sénégal et destinées à des marins indigènes du Sénégal et dépendances congédiés," *Journal Officiel du Sénégal*, 1894, pp. 95 and 105.

98. See the data on migrants to the Congo Free State in 1894 and 1897 in Chapter Four. See also 1851 quotation on laptots in Chapter Two.

99. "Often [laptots] re-enlist, but not in this or that service indifferently, but in such or such a ship in particular. A matter of parish, of cousins!" ANF CC 3 1182, Rapport au Commandant de la Marine au Sénégal, 2e. fascicule: Personnel, mouvement des Etats-Majors, Direction du personnel, [section] Laptots, 3d quarter 1885; see also CC 3 1183, Rapport de la Commission sur le recrutement des matelots indigènes au Sénégal, September 1877.

100. Ronald W. Davis, *Ethnohistorical Studies on the Kru Coast* (Newark, Del.: Liberian Studies, 1976), p. 39.

101. There is a wonderful description of such tactics in the partly nonfictional novel by the great Francophone African writer Amadou Hampate Ba, *L'étrange destin de Wangrin, ou les roueries d'un interprête africain* (Paris: Union générale d'éditions, 1973), pp. 25-58.

102. "Soninke" in this context means "pagan," that is, non-Muslim.

103. David, *Navétanes*, pp. 15–19.

104. ANS 13 G 175, Copie du registre [du] journal [de poste] du 1er au 30 juin 1879, 9 [June]; 9 July; 1 October; 2 October; 29 [n.d.—probably December]; and 13 G 175,

Directeur des Affaires politiques Gallieni to Gov. Senegal, No. 2, Medine, 14 September 1879; and No. 5, 3, 17 October 1879.

105. ANS K 14, Captain Mazillier, Rapport sur la captivité dans le cercle de Kayes, 8 July 1894.

106. ANS 13 G 200, Bakel, Copie du journal de poste, June 1897.

107. ANS 13 G 200, Bakel, Copie du journal de poste, June 1897.

108. ANS 13 G 170, Ct. Bakel to Gov. Senegal, [No] 18, 4 March 1866.

109. Yves St. Martin, "Les relations diplomatiques entre la France et l'Empire Toucouleur de 1860 à 1887," *Bulletin de l'IFAN*, ser. B, vol. 27, 1965, p. 186.

110. The taxation effort during these years was probably related to the civil war that erupted in 1870 between Ahmadu and his brothers Habib and Moktar; see Robinson, *Holy War of Umar Tal*, p. 199. I am grateful to Professor David Robinson for pointing this out to me.

111. My estimate of the actually paid *ʒakkat* is guesswork but probably a minimum on average. Pollet and Winter simply say that the *ʒakkat* was one-tenth of the harvest, *Société soninké*, p. 69. Lartigue, however ("Notice historique," pp. 89–90), wrote that its value was rarely an exact one-tenth and implied that the actual amount was negotiated between each village and the Umarian state. A 1932 French document, referring to the *ʒakkat (assaka)* still paid to the tunka of Gwey, mentioned that it was "in principle" one-tenth, but that there were "generous arrangements" between the parties; ANS 2 D 4/21 (12), Inspector of Adm. Affairs to Gov. Senegal, No. 119, 13 October 1932. Contemporary *ʒakkat*-type payments (which are land-rent payments rather than taxes) are often symbolic, but this must have been rarely the case in precolonial times when traditional authorities were still strong.

112. The Umarians may have demanded at first as much as 200 "of each" (on traditional gift giving in the Senegambia, see Curtin, *Economic Change*, p. 288). They later reduced this to 100, then finally to 80 of each after the Gidimaxa population threatened war; see 13 G 169, Ct. Bakel to Gov. Senegal, No. 193, 12 May 1870; Bulletin agricole et commercial, No. 4, September 1872; No. [4?], Oct. 1872; ANS 13 G 171, Ct. Bakel to Gov. Senegal, No. 74, 16 November 1872. On the Umarian tax system, see Commandant de Lartigue, "Notice historique," pp. 89–101. On the taxation system of the ancien régime, see Hincker, *Français devant l'impôt*.

113. ANS 13 G 191, Cercle de Bakel, Impôt personnel, 1891 (a better census estimate than the underestimated ANS 13 G 189, Rapport du Capitaine Darr, Commandant le poste de Bakel sur la perception de l'impôt personnel pour l'année 1889, 7 November 1888).

114. Cereal price based on figures in ANS 13 G series.

115. ANS 13 G 171, Ct. Bakel to Gov. Senegal, 29 February 1872. Bambara taxes in Gidimaxa, which the Umarians probably continued after bringing them into some conformity with Islamic law, were "never collected in *mil* [sorghum], because of the difficult transportation of this food product." Colombani, "Le Guidimakha," p. 414. The Umarians did sell grain coming from the taxes of Jomboxo in Médine; Hanson, "Umarian Karta," pp. 134–135. But villages neighboring Bakel were very much on the outskirts of their domain.

116. Horse price in Nioro in 1892 (at the time of French conquest) in Pollet and Winter, *Société soninké*, p. 118; see also ANS 13 G 195, [Bakel] Bulletin agricole et commercial, February 1894, which gives a similar price. The rifle price is for a double-barreled (luxury) gun, but given for 1829, Curtin, *Economic Change*, p. 324 (use the conversion table into francs in supp., p. 93). The Umarians asked for double-barreled guns, but it is not clear if they got them. The guinée price is a median figure between two prices given in 1876; ANS 13 G 173, Gov. Senegal to chiefs of Gwey, 18 August 1876; and Ct. Bakel to Gov. Senegal, no. 35, 24 August 1876. None of these figures are contemporary but the guinée and horse price appear quite plausible; information on the arms trade is exceedingly difficult to obtain and figures are entirely lacking in ANS 13 G.

117. 13 G 170, Ct. Bakel to Gov. Senegal, No. 21, 19 March 1870. The quotation is from ANS 13 G 169, Ct. Bakel to Gov. Senegal, No. 119, 2 July 1864. Colombani has frightening information on Beydan oppression in Gidimaxa after 1870, "Guidimakha," pp. 415–416. However, his annual figure of 30,000 mudd (67,500 kilograms) of grain appears far too high if it was for each village. According to Pollet and Winter, the yearly surplus of one man was 100 mudd; *Société soninké*, p. 239. The average Gidimaxa villages contained 400 to 600 persons. Colombani may have taken his information from the village of Sélibaby, where he was based as a colonial administrator, which had 2,145 inhabitants in the late nineteenth century. ANS 13 G 199, Cercle de Bakel, rôle de l'impôt, 1896. In 1847, the Gidimaxa villages were said to pay an equivalent of 70 guinées each (part in guinées, part in cereals) to the Idaw Aish, but we do not know if this was a regular amount of tax, ANS 13 G 165, Ct. Bakel to Gov. Senegal, 3 May 1847.

118. ANS 13 G 189, Rapport sur la situation politique . . . , 25 April 1889. These villages had paid the 1889 French tax by the time when this report was written.

119. See Chapter Four.

120. ANS 13 G 169, Notes laissées à mon successeur, enclosed in Ct. Bakel to Gov. Senegal, No. 116, 13 July 1865. The Bakel commandant proposed in 1864 the building of a tower on the north bank, with a garrison of ten men to protect from Beydan raids the Gidimaxa population and "notre commerce qui a une foule d'établissements dans les villages Guidimakhas," 13 G 169, 9 July 1864.

121. Yves Saint-Martin, *L'empire toucouleur et la France: un demi-siècle de relations diplomatiques (1846–1893)* (Dakar: Université de Dakar, Publications de la Faculté des lettres et sciences humaines, 1967), p. 129 ff.

122. ANS 13 G 171, Ct. Bakel to Gov. Senegal, 2 August 1872.

123. ANS 13 G 172, Cercle de Bakel, Instructions laissées à mon successeur . . . , n.d. but easily identifiable as an early 1873 document; see also Ct. Bakel to Gov. Senegal, A.P. [No.] 65, 15 May 1873.

124. ANS 13 G 172, Ct. Bakel to Gov. Senegal, P[ol.] A[ffairs], No. 52, 21 December 1874.

125. The following paragraphs are based on ANS 13 G 172 and 173.

126. Curtin, *Economic Change*, supp., p. 14; Marty, *Etudes sénégalaises*, pp. 166–172.

127. ANS 13 G 173, Procès-verbal du tribunal de 1ere instance de Bakel, n.d. [ca. 1875]. Most of the families who lost their lands emigrated with Umar, but they appar-

ently had local allies and their grievances reportedly played a role in the events of 1873 to 1875.

128. Bathily asserts that the shots were fired *on* the village of Yaafera ("Conquête," p. 103), whereas a later French administrator asserted they were fired purposely *over* it; ANS 13 G 181, Ct. Bakel to Gov. Senegal, 12 April 1881; ANS 13 G 173 contains virtually no information on the actual events of Brière's visit, but I believe that the second assertion (shots fired over the village) is more probable. The lack of concern evinced by Governor Brière over the prospect of losing money on taxes paid in guinées instead of currency and his remark about the purpose of taxation (see immediately below) indicate that the French did not intend to be harsh.

129. The tax census of April 1876 (in fact, an estimate, since Soninke chiefs still refused to carry out any census) came to 460 francs. Yaafera was to pay 80 francs, and the other villages between 60 and 120 francs. ANS 13 G 173, Ct. Bakel to Gov. Senegal, Pol. Affairs [No.] 18, 26 April 1876. Bathily mentions that Yaafera's fine was four times the amount of the tax; "Conquête," p. 103. The ten guinées fine to the brother of the chief of Yaafera is mentioned in ANS 13 G 173, Letter Gov. Senegal to chiefs of Gwey, 18 August 1876. This would mean a total of 96 guinées. A total of 85 guinées was paid in August 1876, but this did not include the tax of the village of Arundu, which had been paid a month earlier. ANS 13 G 173, Ct. Bakel to Gov. Senegal, No. 35, 24 August 1876. Adding the 80 francs (8 guinées) for Arundu, I come to a total figure of 93 guinées, only slightly below 96 guinées. Guinées were then accepted at a value of 10 francs each (ibid.) in payment of the tax and fines, but they may have been worth more. ANS 13 G 173, Gov. Senegal to chiefs of Gwey, 18 August 1876, mentions a price of 15 francs. I have taken a median figure of 12.5 francs (also the price of guinées in 1879; see ANS 13 G 175, Ct. Bakel to Gov. Senegal, No. 37, 29 January 1879) as the actual price of guinées.

130. ANS 13 G 174, Poste de Bakel, Perception de l'impôt personnel pour l'année 1877.

131. ANS 13 G 173, Ct. Bakel to Gov. Senegal, Pol. Affairs [No.] 18, 26 April 1876.

132. ANS 13 G 173, Gov. Senegal to chiefs of Gwey, 18 August 1876.

133. Brière de l'Isle, note in the margin of ANS 13 G 175, Ct. Bakel to Gov. Senegal, No. 37, 29 January 1879. The guinée price had been fixed in 1876 by Brière de l'Isle at fifteen francs for personal tax collection. (ANS 13 G 173, Gov. Senegal to chiefs of Gwey, 18 August 1876.) In 1879, according to the commandant, its value was 12.50 francs.

134. ANSOM Senegal IX, 14a, No. 188, 13 May 1874.

135. Frey, *Campagne*, p. 242. I was tempted at first to reject Frey's account because of his role in the repression of Mamadu Lamin Darame's revolt in 1886. (Sharply attacked for his handling of the military campaign, Frey may have been tempted to paint a more rosy picture of the situation.) However, the French traveler Soleillet in 1878 to 1879 also noted the greater appearance of wealth of the Soninke villages, which sharply contrasted with sluggish economy of the Fuutanke villages in the middle valley. (See, e.g., *Voyage*, p. 77.) The economic data I have presented above also support these testimonies.

136. Frey, *Campagne*, p. 249; Capitaine Brosselard, Rapport sur la situation dans la vallée du Sénégal en 1886. Insurrection de Mamadou Lamine, quoted in Bathily, "Imperialism," p. 458.

137. Population figure based on roughly contemporary French censuses. The Bakel figure does not include traitants, French employees, or the village de liberté (in all only about 400 people in 1896). I roughly estimated the able-bodied male population to be one-fourth of the total population. Censuses (which were made for tax purposes) may have been underestimated by one-third (this was suggested by ANS 4 G 132, Ct. Bakel to Gov. Senegal, No. 42, 11 September 1912), in which case the adult male population may have been as high as 14,000 persons; thus the proportion of laptots would have been between 9 and 11 percent. Census references: ANS 13 G 189, Cercle de Bakel, Nov. 7, 1888, Rapport du Capitaine Darr, Commandant le cercle de Bakel sur la perception de l'impôt pour l'année 1889; 13 G 191, Cercle de Bakel, impôt personnel, 1891; 13 G 199, Cercle de Bakel, impôt personnel, 1894; 13 G 199, Cercle de Bakel, Rôle de l'impôt, année 1896; 1 G 310, Renseignements historiques, géographiques et économiques sur le cercle de Kayes [1902].

138. Abdoulaye Bara Diop, *Société toucouleure et migration (enquête sur l'immigration toucouleure à Dakar)* (Dakar: IFAN, 1965); Boutillier et al., *Moyenne vallée.*

139. For a comparison with other non-European societies, see George Dalton, "The Impact of Colonization on Aboriginal Economies in Stateless Societies," *Research in Economic Anthropology*, vol. 1, 1978, pp. 131–184.

140. See, in particular, Chatelain, *Migrants temporaires en France;* and Raison-Jourde, *Colonie auvergnate de Paris.*

141. Chatelain, *Migrants temporaires en France*, pp. 978–980.

142. John N. Andromedas, "The Enduring Urban Ties of a Modern Greek Folk Sub-Culture," in Perestiany, *Contributions to Mediterranean Sociology*, pp. 269–278.

143. Ibid.; compare with the description of the "segmentary states" of the Soninke in Chapter One.

Chapter 4

1. Bathily, "Conquête," pp. 105–107.

2. The record of forced labor for the period is as follows: 200 men were promised by the tunka of Wey in December 1879, but he later evaded his promise. Laborers recruited in Goye Annexé refused to go further than three Bambara villages near Bakel and deserted. Kammera refused to provide laborers (ANS 13 G 175, No. 62, 24 December 1879). 110 laborers from Goye Annexé left for Médine in January 1880 (13 G 175, journal de poste, January 1880). Laborers from Goye Annexé disbanded for the second time in January 1880 (13 G 175, No. 63, 4 January 1880). 47 laborers were sent to Médine on April 7 1880 (13 G 175, journal de poste, 7 April 1880). The telegraph line was completed on 27 April 1880 (13 G 175, journal de poste, 4 May 1880). For the unloading of coal, 110 laborers were employed on 15 September 1880, 115 on 16 September, 100 on 17 September (13 G 175, journal de poste, 15; 16; 17 September 1880). In January 1881,

Upper Senegal chiefs meeting in Daramanne swore that they would not provide one laborer to the French (13 G 181, No. 3, 27 January 1881). Nevertheless, discussions were carried out in Tiyaabu (capital of Gwey) to obtain 20 men to carry telegraph poles in February 1881 (13 G 181, No. 13, 7 February 1881). In March 1881, the tunka secretly offered laborers to the commandant for work on the telegraph line (13 G 181, No. 8, 9 March 1881). In April 1881, Goye Indépendant, which had promised 300 laborers, sent 54 "who loitered in Kayes for as little time as possible" and returned to their villages under various pretexts (13 G 181, 12 April 1881, Report Ct. Bakel to Gov. Senegal). In May 1881, the tunka refused to provide men for pulling barges (13 G 1881, Bulletin commercial, agricole et politique, May 1881). In August 1881, the tunka "gave a slight proof of his loyalty" by providing laborers to unload a barge in Bakel (13 G 1881. Bulletin commercial, agricole et politique, August 1881). In December 1881, "Gwey [was] beginning to understand its interests," and the commandant was able to send a detachment of laborers headed by a notable from Tiyaabu in the Upper Valley (13 G 182, December 1881). In June 1883, when a barge ran aground near Golmi (Gwey), the European commanding it gave the village the order to send several men to help the crew; the village chief replied that the villagers "were not the slaves of the whites" (13 G 182, 28 June 1883). I discuss the question of the pulling of barges in note 5 below.

3. Agricultural work in the Upper Senegal is mostly done between mid May and mid December (flood land cultivation, in mid September to mid April, is far less important to the local economy than rainy season cultivation). See Monique Chastanet, "Les crises de subsistances dans les villages soninké du cercle de Bakel. Problèmes méthodologiques et perspectives de recherches," *Cahiers d'Etudes Africaines*, vol. 23, nos. 89–90, pp. 18–19. Hence, with the exception of the unloading of coal in September 1880, recruitments were always done during the slack season. The French were well aware of the agricultural season and the fact that recruiting during this time would have adverse effects on agricultural production. (See ANS 13 G 175, No. 63, 4 January 1880.)

4. A letter of Commandant-Supérieur Borgnis-Desbordes to the Bakel Commandant Laude in 1881 reprimanded him for "not always regularly" paying recruited laborers ("*hommes de corvée*"). (ANS 13 G 181, Ct. Sup. Borgnis-Desbordes, Order of 29 May sent to Ct. Bakel.) In 1881, Soninke inhabitants of Bakel wrote to complain of Commandant Laude. One of the complaints dealt with the payment of requisitioned laborers for the "Upper Valley works." Bakelois wrote that they had been offered 3 cubits of guinée a day (1.50 franc) by Commandant-Supérieur Boilève. They had accepted only 2 cubits "by patriotism" but were paid only 1 cubit by Commandant Laude. ANS 13 G 181, Plainte des habitants de Bakel contre M. Laude, commandant de Bakel, 7 November 1881. In fact, 1 cubit (0.50 franc) was the standard pay of laborers outside Saint-Louis. Later records of payment of laborers in the Upper Senegal (see below) show that they were paid 1 to 2 cubits a day.

5. An 1889 document mentions that it was customary for villagers to help stranded barges and receive "gifts" in payment. A list of such payments, given at difficult points

in Fuuta, ranged between 4 and 14 cubits of guinée (2 to 7 francs), 8 cubits on average. Forty laborers had to help at the "dam" of Muderi (Gwey), but the context indicates that this must have been an exceptional occurrence. ANS 13 G 188, [letter by *patron* of (unnamed) barge], 16 May 1889. One cubit (0.50 franc) being the standard pay of a laborer outside Saint-Louis, on the basis of a twelve-hour work day, 14 cubits would have paid forty persons for four hours and twenty minutes of work. But some villagers were obviously paid above market price. The document mentions that one laborer hired to retrieve several baskets of grain that had fallen from the barge near Wawunde (Damga) was paid 1 guinée, or about 12.50 francs!

Stranded barges were apparently quite common in the period of low waters (February through June). The cultivation period begins at mid May, but the most important agricultural work takes place from July to August. A Kayes political report blamed work to help stranded barges for the high rate of navetane migration from Kammera in 1903. (By that time, a special official posted on government barges made sure that villagers were paid, but commercial barges were accused of not respecting agreements; ANM 1E 44, Kayes, yearly pol. report, 1903.) However, if the impact of such work had been important, first, it would have caused a *permanent* migration *inland* of whole families, not a temporary migration of young men. (I discuss the issue of permanent flight migration versus temporary labor migration in Chapter Five.) This did not occur. Second, it would have caused subsistence crises. Yet in 1902, the cereal production of riverbank villages was reported as "very superior" to the needs of its population and giving rise to "very important [commercial] transactions." (ANS 1 G 310, Renseignements historiques . . . sur le cercle de Kayes, [1902]. See also ANM 1E 44, Kayes, Pol. reports, March, April and July 1900.) Finally, two of the most difficult "dams" (shoals) were by the villages of Tanbunkaani and Jaxandape (Kammera), but there is no indication that these villages had a higher rate of migration; in fact, there is no indication that they migrated at all.

6. ANS 13 G 181, Ct. Bakel to Gov. Senegal, No. 9, 1 April 1881. The nonpayment of livestock and pack animals was not mentioned in the letter of complaint of the inhabitants of Bakel in 1881; ANS 13 G 181, Plainte des habitants de Bakel, 7 November 1881. The Bakel commandant in 1881 supplied 295 donkeys, 30 harnessed horses, and 107 oxen. ANS 13 G 181, Ct. Bakel to Gov. Senegal, No. 3, 27 January 1881. This represented a value of about 40,000 francs. See for livestock prices, ANM 1E 60, Pol. Agr. and Comm. Report, Nioro, 30 August 1892; similar price available for oxen in 1885 (but not surprisingly, higher price for donkeys) in ANS 13 G 185, Bakel Comm. report, 1st quarter 1885.

7. Frey, *Campagne*, pp. 246–249; also ANS 13 G 181, Ct. Sup. Borgnis-Desbordes, Order of 29 May 1881 sent to Ct. Bakel.

8. Even Krumen from the Guinea Coast were recruited. From 1883 to 1884, there were from 1,200 to 1,700 Moroccan and 900 to 1,000 indigenous laborers employed in Upper Senegal. Documents suggest that the latter were not recruited in the Bakel region (they probably came from Bambara or Malinke regions between Senegal and Niger); ANS 1 B 42, Ministry of Marine, Direction des Colonies, Bureau du Haut

Senegal, no. 1213, 4 September 1883; Service des Travaux du Haut-Fleuve, no. 1077, 5 September 1883; no. 1247, 5 October 1883; Bureau du Haut-Senegal, 3 November 1883; Service des Travaux du Haut-Senegal, 18 September 1884 (this document quotes a letter by Commandant Superior Borgnis-Desbordes pleading against a Senegalese government proposal to reduce the number of Moroccans, arguing that "serious work" would be impossible without them). The 160 Chinese were skilled workers (masons, etc.); Bathily, "Imperialism," p. 442.

9. Reports came back to Bakel that the donkeys had been sold by the chief of Golmi. In addition, the inhabitants of Golmi feasted on stolen cattle. ANS 13 G 181, Ct. Bakel to Ct. Sup., no. 5, 17 January 1881; No. 7, 25 January 1881; and ANS 13 G 181, 12 April 1881. In the last document Commandant Laude complained, "if I had the least support, [the chief of Golmi] would be quickly put under lock and key in Bakel."

10. "Governor Brière de l'Isle sent [to the tunka] a letter of threats and reproach, to which he never replied." Bathily, "Conquête," p. 106.

11. Daniel Nyambarza, "Le Marabout El Hadj Mamadou Lamine d'après les archives françaises," *Cahiers d'Etudes Africaines*, vol. 9, no. 33, 1969, pp. 124–145; Humphrey Fisher, "The Early Life and Pilgrimage of al-Hajj Muhammad al-Amin the Soninke," *Journal of African History*, vol. 11, 1970, pp. 51–69; Abdoulaye Bathily, "Mamadou Lamine Dramé et la résistance anti-impérialiste dans le Haut-Sénégal (1885–1887)," *Notes Africaines*, no. 125, January 1970, pp. 20–32; "Imperialism," pp. 426–486; Sanneh, *The Jakhank*, pp. 67–93; Ivan Hrbek, "The Early Period of Mahmadu Lamin's Activities," in John Ralph Willis, ed., *Studies in West African Islamic History, vol. 1, The Cultivators of Islam* (London: F. Cass, 1979), pp. 211–232; B. Olatunji Oloruntimehin, "Muhammad Lamine in Franco-Tukulor Relations, 1885–1887," *Journal of the Historical Society of Nigeria*, vol. 4, 1968, pp. 375–396. There is interesting information on how the Umarians viewed Mamadu Lamin in David Robinson, *Chiefs and Clerics: Abdul Bokar Kan and Futa Toro, 1853–1891* (Oxford: Clarendon Press, 1975), pp. 145–148. There is useful oral information on the revolt and repression in Jafunu under Umarian domination in E. Blanc, "Contributions à l'étude des populations et de l'histoire du Sahel soudanais," *Bulletin du Comité d'Etudes Historiques et Scientifiques de l'Afrique Occidentale Française*, vol. 8, no. 2, 1924, pp. 258–319, see pp. 305–314. An important primary source on the revolt is Frey, *Campagne*. Gallieni's account *(Deux campagnes)* is considered unreliable for the events of the revolt in Gajaaga and Gidimaxa (which Gallieni did not witness personally) by Hrbek; see discussion of sources in "Early Period," pp. 231–232.

12. The tunka lemmu who supported El Haj Umar in 1855 did so for local political reasons connected with the civil war between Gwey and Kammera. Bathily, "Imperialism," pp. 413–421. But Islam progressed rapidly in the general population. In 1873, the Bakel commandant, angered by the "insolence" of Bakel talibes, called for a "system of secret persecution of marabouts." ANS 13 G 172, Bakel, Instructions générales laissées à mon successeur . . . [1873].

13. This rather extraordinary information about the causes of the 1881 riot was given to me by Malcolm Thompson, who was then completing his Ph.D. thesis on the history of Senegalese laptots. The information comes from oral sources. The episode

may not have actually happened, but Soninke laptots were clearly perceived as "pagan" drinkers. Malcolm Thompson, conversation at Queen's University, Kingston, Canada, 14 May 1988. For an archival record of the mêlée, ANS K 30, Ct. Sup. Borgnis-Desbordes to Gov. Senegal, 5 October 1881.

14. Frey, *Campagne*, p. 249; also 399, 403, 412; Capitaine Brosselard, Rapport sur la situation dans la vallée du Sénégal en 1886. Insurrection de Mamadou Lamine, quoted in Bathily, "Imperialism," p. 458.

15. See Robinson, *Holy War of Umar Tal*.

16. Frey, *Campagne*, pp. 312, 414, 435n.

17. Bathily, "Mamadou Lamine," p. 30.

18. ANM 1E-60, [Cercle de Nioro], Bulletin politique et militaire, July 1893. Livestock prices on the market in Nioro; ANM 1E 60, Nioro, Pol., agr. and comm. report, 30 August 1892; and (sheep price, also on the market in Nioro, 1892), Pollet and Winter, *Société soninké*, p. 118.

19. There were 95,000 inhabitants in Kingi, Kenyareme, and Gidyume in 1893. ANM 1E-60, [Cercle de Nioro], Bulletin politique et militaire, July 1893. There were around 18,000 inhabitants in both Gweys and Kammera (8,500 inhabitants in Gwey, 3,200 in Bakel, and 6,700 in Kammera; see ANS 13 G 199, Cercle de Bakel [tax census], 1894, and 1 G 310, Renseignements historiques, géographiques et économiques sur le cercle de Kayes, [1902]) and around 28,000 inhabitants in Gidimaxa (13,746 in the half of this region situated in French Soudan; 1 G 310, Renseignements historiques . . . sur le cercle de Kayes, [1902]).

20. ANS 13 G 189 [Ct. Bakel to Ct. Sup.], Rapport sur la situation politique . . . , 25 April 1889. The village of Bakel in 1890 owned more than 2,000 cows—then equivalent to 80,000 francs (the price of cows was low that year, 40 francs—the price in regular years was around 100 francs). (ANS 13 G 190, 12 March 1890; 1890 cattle price in 13 G 190, 15 February 1890.) It is true that Bakel fought on the side of the French during the rebellion of Mamadu Lamin; they thus kept and actually increased their cattle by participating in the war. But the wealth in cattle for the whole cercle is mentioned in 13 G 192 [Ct. Bakel to Ct. Sup.], No. 98, 28 March 1892. In 1890, Beydan raiders reportedly stole 80 cows from the village of Golmi (Goye Annexé) or 3,200 francs (8,000 francs in regular years). (ANS 13 G 190, Ct. Bakel to Ct. Sup., 28 October 1890.) See also ANS 13 G 190 [Ct. Bakel to Ct. Sup.], 1 May 1890, mentioning the particularly easy collection of tax.

21. ANSOM XIII, 32a, [Ministry of] Marine and Colonies, Service des Colonies, 2eme. sous-direction, 4eme. Bureau, 27 March 1884, Renseignements sur le marché de la gomme, Senegal, [addressed] to MM. Laroche Joubert et Cie. in Angoulême.

22. See Table 4.1.

23. ANS 13 G 190 [Bakel], Comm., agr. and pol. bulletin, January; May; July 1890. The expansion of grain production in the Upper Senegal and Niger Valley that accompanied the French conquest has been noted by Richard Roberts, *Warriors, Merchants and Slaves*, see pp. 135–173; "Long-Distance Trade: Sinsani," pp. 169–188; and Hanson, "Umarian Karta."

24. The record of forced labor after 1886 is as follows. Kammera had to clear a

12- to 15-meter-wide road along the telegraph line, give help to stranded barges, and plant trees along the riverbank between Jaxandappe and Kayes (about 20 kilometers). (ANS 13 G 187, Convention with Kammera, quoted in Instructions for Mr. Largeau, Ct. cercle, in charge of the mission of Kammera.) These were rather heavy obligations, but it is not certain that the road was actually cleared. At the commandant's orders, 152 porters from seven villages in December 1887 and 137 porters from ten villages in January 1888 carried products to Bakel's new monthly market. (ANS 13 G 187, Report Captain Darr, Ct. Bakel on the monthly market of December 1887; and 13 G 188, January 1888.) Again, it is not certain that the scheme was actually followed up (it probably was not). Moreover, this was not during the cultivation season. There were also recruitments during military campaigns. In October 1890, the tunka of Gwey "keenly insisted" on providing 150 men and Goye Annexé provided an additional 150 men. (ANS 13 G 190, Ct. Bakel to Gov. Senegal, 28 October 1890.) In May 1894, the brother of the chief of newly conquered Selibabi (Gidimaxa) was given thirty lashes in reprisals for the village's alleged resistance to providing 60 porters to carry supplies to the post (Sélibaby?); 20 porters and 20 donkeys were eventually provided. (ANS 13 G 195, Lieutenant commandant les tirailleurs, Sélibaby, to Ct. Bakel, 14 May 1894.) Finally, in March to April 1894, inhabitants of Gidimaxa were building a road to Tagant (north of the region, in the desert), taking turns in teams of 70 men. (ANS 13 G 202, Ct. Bakel to Gov. Senegal, No. 37, 29 May 1894.) There are lists of names of laborers in 13 G 192 and 13 G 196, but these were probably free laborers. They were paid from 0.50 (1894) to 1 franc (1892) a day. Most worked for short period of time of three to four days.

25. ANS 13 G 186, Comm., agr. and pol. bulletin, December 1886.

26. Jacques Méniaud, *Les pionniers du Soudan* (Paris: Société des publications modernes, 1931), vol. 1, p. 507; the data provided by Méniaud on forced recruitment of porters after 1888 concern only non-Soninke regions east of Kayes; ibid., vol. 1, p. 451.

27. See the treaties with Gwey and Kammera, *Journal Officiel du Sénégal*, 13 September 1888.

28. ANS 13 G 189, Report of Capitaine Darr, Ct. Bakel, on the collection of personal tax for the year 1889, No. 783, 7 November 1889.

29. Frey, *Campagne*, p. 320.

30. See the electoral platforms of the Senegalese candidates to the French legislative elections of 1893, Alfred Gasconi and Jean Crespin, *Journal Officiel du Sénégal*, pp. 299–301. The desire to give French Soudan an outlet to the sea was probably the reason for the policy of expansion toward French Guinea advocated by Gallieni during his term as Commandant-Supérieur in 1886 to 1888; A. S. Kanya-Forstner, *The Conquest of the Western Sudan: A Study in French Military Imperialism* (Cambridge: Cambridge University Press, 1969), p. 153.

31. Gallieni, *Deux campagnes*, pp. 620–625; Kanya-Forstner, *Conquest*, pp. 84–173.

32. *Journal Officiel du Sénégal*, 21 June 1888; and Conseil Général, 6e séance, 25 June 1888.

33. Total revenue: 2,782,474 (1889 Budget, *Journal officiel du Sénégal*, supplement of 27 December 1888).

34. Until 1889, in fact, only family heads paid tax. (The Senegalese law specified that every man and woman between age fifteen and sixty-five had to pay tax; see Chapter Three.) The new policy on tax collection was introduced after an experiment in Kammera (in 1889?) (ANS 13 G 191, Ct. Bakel to Ct. Supérieur, No. 504, 10 August 1891); it had been prepared in Bakel already in 1888 (ANS 13 G 189, Rapport du capitaine Darr . . . , No. 783, 7 November 1888).

35. ANS 13 G 191, Ct. Bakel to Ct. Sup., No. 504, 10 August 1891; 13 G 189 [Bakel], Etat des recettes, Impôt personnel, January 1890.

36. An ox valued 40 francs in guinées suddenly cost 30 francs in currency; ANS 13 G 190, Ct. Bakel to Ct. Sup., No. 80, 15 February 1890.

37. ANS 13 G 193, Cercle de Bakel, Impôt 1893.

38. Data from ANS 13 G series. See the detail in Manchuelle, "Background," Appendix. All these figures are more or less incomplete and should be taken as indications rather than exact figures. The price of 1 franc a kilo in 1892 is from ANS 13 G 195, Agr. and comm. report, March 1894.

39. For the complete Senegalese export figures at the time, see J. Mavidal, *Le Sénégal, son etat présent et son avenir* (Paris: Duprat, 1863), p. 169.

40. Excellent description of the gum trade credit system in 1898 by Baillaud, *Routes du Soudan*, pp. 35–42.

41. For this reason, it would be useful to have detailed trade figures for 1893. Unfortunately, the Bakel records give complete detailed figures only for 1894.

42. ANS 13 G 192 [Ct. Bakel to Ct. Sup.], No. 98, 28 March 1892. The disease (simply described as *peste bovine)* destroyed 80 to 85 percent of the herds in certain areas of Senegal. See the speech of the Governor of Senegal at the opening session of the General Council of Senegal in 1892, Senegal, Conseil Général, *Procès-Verbaux des Séances*, 8 December 1892.

43. ANS 13 G 192, Bakel, No. 98, 28 March 1892; April 1892, Report on the political, commercial, and agricultural situation of the cercle of Bakel. Deaths by cholera are mentioned in ANS 13 G 193, Bakel, No. 488, 4 September 1893; and ANS 13 G 195, No. 2334, 30 May 1894.

44. This incident is discussed in Chapter Five.

45. ANS 13 G 200, Bakel, No. 127, Quarterly report, July–August–September 1897; and Bakel, No. 85, Political, Agricultural and Commercial Report, 2d quarter 1897.

46. ANS 13 G 200, Copie du journal de cercle, year 1897.

47. ANS 13 G 200 [Ct. Bakel to Governor Senegal], Quarterly report July–August–September 1897, No. 127, 1 October 1897.

48. ANS 13 G 201.

49. ANS 13 G 203, "Political, Economical, Public Works and Schools Report of the Cercle of Bakel until 31 August 1900," No. 715, 1 September 1900.

50. Riembau, *De Dakar au Niger*, p. 76.

51. ANS 2 D 4/12, Bakel, Monographie, Etude sur la formation historique et ethnique des provinces qui constituent le cercle, par Maubert, administrateur-adjoint, 16 March 1904.

52. 13G 201, No. 1, December 1898, Rapport politique, commercial et agricole; ANS 2 D 4/12, Bakel, Etude . . . , Maubert, 16 March 1904; 2D 4–9, Bakel, Rapport de l'administrateur Gaillardon, tournée effectuée dans le Goye supérieur en février et mars 1912.

53. ANS 2 D 4/12, Bakel, Etude . . . , Maubert, 16 March 1904; Riembau, *De Dakar au Niger*, pp. 78–79.

54. ANS 2 D 4/9, Bakel, Rapport de l'Administrateur-adjoint Gaillardon, tournée effectuée dans le Goye supérieur en février et mars 1912. These canoe owners participated in the supplying of Kayes and took peanuts on their way back to Saint-Louis.

55. Régine Van Chi-Bonnardel, *Vie de relations au Sénégal* (Dakar: I.F.A.N., 1978), p. 372.

56. ANS 2 D 4/12, Bakel, Etude . . . , Maubert, 16 March 1904.

57. See the table of exports from French Soudan in Baillaud, *Routes du Soudan*, p. 30. In 1893, the Nioro region exported 500 tons of gum and its total exports came to a value of more than a million francs. See table in ibid., p. 36.

58. ANM 1E 44, Kayes, Pol. reports, March; April and July 1900. Trade between Africans (agriculture and artisan products) in the cercle was estimated at 2,500,000 francs annually ca. 1902. ANS 1 G 310, Renseignements historiques. . . sur le cercle de Kayes [ca. 1902].

59. ANM 1E 44, Kayes, Pol. report, January 1910. I compare Soudanese and Nigerian peanut exports in Chapter Seven.

60. See in particular ANM 1E 44, Kayes, Pol. report, March 1899; Yearly pol. report, 1903.

61. ANM 1E 44, Kayes, Periodic report for 1892–1893.

62. The French called "Sahel" regions which are part of the hydrographic system of the Xoolinbinne, thus of the Senegal River (such as Jafunu and Kenyareme), as well as what I defined in my introduction as the eastern Soninke region (Kingi, Baaxunu, Wagadu, Soxolo).

63. See quote from Keyes commandant above.

64. Bakel guinée figure; ANS 13 G 193, Bakel, Impôt 1893. I do not have contemporary figures for Kayes, but figures for Kayes around 1900 are very comparable (6.50 to 8 francs). ANS 1 G 310, Renseignements historiques, géographiques et économiques sur le cercle de Kayes [1902]. The sorghum *(mil)* price for Bakel is an estimate based on prices for the 1890s from ANS 13 G; see tables in Appendix, Manchuelle, "Background." Nioro figures; ANM 1E 60, Nioro, Pol., agr. and comm. report, 30 August 1892.

65. Estimate of yearly commercial production in Pollet and Winter, *Société soninké*, p. 239.

66. ANS 13 G 195, Desmarets, Rapport sur la captivité dans le cercle de Bakel, 26 May 1894; Bulletin agricole et commercial, April 1894.

67. The policy had a precedent in French administrative practice: Faidherbe's confidential circular of 14 November 1857 on indigenous slavery specified that fugitive slaves coming from states that were at peace with the French would be expelled from

French outposts under vagrancy laws, but that "a decision of the governor would indicate whether fugitives [from states at war with the French] would be accepted in our settlements where they will be granted their freedom." ANS 13 G 195, appendix to Rapport sur la captivité, Bakel, Desmarets, May 1894.

68. On slave liberations in Gidimaxa, see ANS 13 G 186, Bakel, No. 217, 17 May 1886; No. 655, 31 August 1886; 13 G 188, Agr., comm. and pol. bulletin, April 1888; 13 G 189, Report on the political situation on 25 April 1889; 13 G 190, 28 October 1890. On the political background of Gidimaxa's annexation, see Méniaud, *Pionniers du Soudan*, vol. 1, p. 272; Kanya-Forstner, *Conquest*, pp. 134–136, 143–144; see also Chapter 7, pp. 174–214.

69. ANS 13 G 190, 28 October 1890.

70. Monteil, "Fin de siècle," p. 105.

71. See David, *Navétanes*, pp. 24–27.

72. The other (payment of daily wages) is surely modern and may be ignored here.

73. Pollet and Winter, *Société soninké*, pp. 142–143; see also arrangements between nansoka and their employers in Kingi Jawara in Boyer, *Un peuple de l'ouest soudanais*, pp. 98–99.

74. See Chapter Six.

75. Boyer, *Un peuple de l'ouest soudanais*, p. 98. Although published in 1953, Boyer's work was completed between 1946 and 1951; see p. 17. Note also the description of the labor arrangements of young talibe (Koranic school students) in the village of Kungani in 1938 by Adrian Adams. These laborers cultivated peanuts for sale, had a jatigi who housed them and fed them, and generally worked under arrangements reminiscent of navetanat. *Terre et gens du fleuve*, pp. 74–75.

76. Kane and Lericollais, "Emigration en pays soninké," p. 186; Weigel, *Migration et production domestique*, p. 49; André Guillebaud, "De la brousse aux bidonvilles," *Le Monde*, 18–21 May 1973; Steinkamp-Ferrier, "Sept villages," pp. 83, 88–89. According to Dr. Manthia Diawara (from Kingi Jawara), many "Bambara" working in the Soninke regions of Mali are in fact Malinke from the Kita area; Dr. Manthia Diawara, personal conversation, Santa Barbara, California, February 1988.

77. Pollet and Winter, *Société soninké*, p. 144.

78. Roberts, *Warriors, Merchants and Slaves*, pp. 201–203. I have discussed the implications of the phenomenon of "immigration in a land of emigration" in Manchuelle, "The Patriarchal Ideal of Soninke Labor Migrants."

79. Boyer, *Un peuple de l'ouest africain*, p. 63. The Jawara also are represented in Sanga (Xaasonke region from which many navetanes came in the twentieth century; see Chapter Six), Kaarta (Bangasi), the cercles of Bafoulabe (Diala) and Buguni, Fuuta Tooro and Bundu, the cercle of Buguni, and the Gambia. Ibid. Saint-Père also mentions Jawara in Buli in the Mauritanian Gidimaxa, *Sarakollé du Guidimakha*, p. 13.

80. Pollet and Winter, *Société soninké*, passim; see in particular pp. 46–51.

81. Pollet and Winter, *Société soninké*, p. 183.

82. As a striking illustration, the Soninke minorities in the region of Kaedi (Mauritania; Middle Senegal River Valley) classify themselves into *Baalunko* (those from

Baalu, a village that, according to oral tradition, was destroyed four times; the first location of the village may have been in Kingi; today two villages of that name are located respectively in Gidimaxa and Gajaaga), *Jaahunanko* (people from Jafunu), *Gidin'manko* (people from Gidyume), *Konciganko* (People from Konciga, perhaps in Jafunu), *Jaaxalinko* (people from Jaaxali, an important maraboutic village of old Gajaaga, in Kammera), *Jaaranko* (people from Jara, in Kingi Jawara), *Karo* (people from Kaarta). Ousmane Moussa Diagana, *Chants traditionnels du pays soninké (Mauritanie, Mali, Sénégal)* (Paris: L'Harmattan, 1990), p. 17.

83. See Chapter Three.

84. See Chapter Three.

85. On the events surrounding the migration to the Congo Free State, see François Zuccarelli, "Le recrutement de travailleurs sénégalais par l'Etat Indépendant du Congo (1888–1896)," *Revue française d'histoire d'outre-mer*, vol. 47, 1960, pp. 475–481. Zuccarelli consulted only the French archives and thus did not discuss the documents analyzed below, which are kept in the Senegal Archives. To obtain the full picture of the "Laplène affair," see in addition to ANSOM XIV, 27 and 26 discussed by Zuccarelli; ANS K 31; K 397 (132).

86. ANS K 31 [Depositions of laborers engaged by Laplène, addressed to Gov. Senegal by Delegate of Interior in Dakar], 27 February 1894.

87. On navetane migration to Saalum, see David, *Navétanes*, pp. 20–27; and Klein, *Islam and Imperialism*. Professor Klein wrote me that he was struck to note, while researching on the history of Siin-Saalum in the late nineteenth and early twentieth centuries, that many migrants to Siin-Saalum appeared to come from well-off regions, and therefore it appeared that migration was motivated by a search for higher incomes rather than by poverty in the region of origin of the migrants. (Personal correspondence, September 1985).

88. My special thanks to Professor Abdoulaye Bathily for drawing my attention to this crucial fact. Dakar, 1978.

89. Bathily, "Imperialism," pp. 91–92.

90. For information on the social status of villages in Gajaaga (Gwey and Kammera), see Chastanet, "Etat soninke du Gajaaga," Appendix.

91. The Jawara of Tiyaabu are a lineage of shoemakers. They are apparently quite close to their patrons. Abdoulaye Bathily mentions that his informant Dogo Jawara from Tiyaabu in his youth considered the elder Bacili of the village as "his father's equals." Bathily, *Portes de l'or*, pp. 21–22.

92. ANS 2 D 4/21 (9) [may be reclassified under a different number at the present—Cercle de Bakel Archives], Bakel—affaires des Bathily—Réclamation d'un groupe de Bathily de Dakar Samba Diama et consorts et de Samba Kadiata, chef du Goye Inférieur contre l'assesseur du tribunal Fodé Saloum de Tuabo—Correspondance—Rapports—1917–1918.

93. Bathily, *Portes de l'or*, pp. 245, 334. Note also in the list, the presence of a Jallo in the village of Yellingara. However, I have no information about the Jallo in this particular village.

94. Bathily, "Imperialism," pp. 330–332.

95. The Fofana were one of clans of the original masters of the land of Gajaaga, but were reduced to slave status by the Bacili at the time of their conquest. Bathily, *Portes de l'or*, pp. 202–203.

96. ANS K 397 (132) List of emigrants from Bathurst to [the] Congo Per S.S. "Eduard Bohlen," Bathurst, J. Brown, Superintendent of [illegible] [sent to the Senegalese administration by the French Consul in Bathurst, Gambia], 18 March 1897.

97. Bathily, *Portes de l'or*, p. 334.

98. Bathily, *Portes de l'or*, p. 227.

99. Bathily, *Portes de l'or*, pp. 19–20.

100. Jean Schmitz, December 1991. I am responsible for the interpretations of the material suggested below.

101. A total of 37 migrants in an overall total of 68 came from this area—from the villages of Dioudé-Diabe, Diaranguel, Diongui, Pete, Mbolo-Birane, Dirimbodia, Diaba, Baladyi, Orefonde, Asnde-Bala, Ouro-Mollo, [Aniam-]Tiodaye, Barga, Tilogne, Goudoude, Dabia, Boki-Diave, Doumga, Sedo, Ndiafane, Belinabe, Kaedi, Silanage, Dondou, Ali-Ouri.

102. Raffenel, *Voyage*, pp. 36–37, 41, 54.

103. Out of 68 migrants, almost half came from Cuballo and Ceddo villages: 9 came from Cuballo villages—Ndormbos (1 migrant), (Halaybe), Ndiafane (2) [also a Toorodo village] (Booseya), Dondou (2), Ali Ouri (2) (Ngenaar), Diela (4) (Damga); 23 came from Ceddo villages—Ndioum (2) (Toro), Aere-Lao (1) [also a Toorodo and Fuulbe village], Dioude-Diabe (1) (Laaw), Dirimbodia (1) (Yirlaabe), Kaedi (1), Silanabe (1) [also a Toorodo village], Orefonde (1) [also a Fuulbe village] [Aniam-Barga] (1), Tilogne (1) [also a Toorodo village] (Booseya), Sedo (1) [also a Wolof village], Sintiou-Garba (11) [also a Denyanke village] (Ngenaar); Barkevi (1) [also a Denyanke village] (Damga). Of the thirteen family names identifiable by social class, five are Ceddo.

104. The name of one village in the sample reflects this strategic location at a ford: Dioude-Diabe *(juuwde* = the ford). It is also interesting to note that the only mention of the clan name Kan is for the village of Mbolo-Birane, where the district chief, the Alkati Mboolo, who was chosen among this family, collected dues on river crossing.

105. The near-absence of the prominent Toroodo chiefly family the Kan (only one occurrence in Mbolo-Birane, Yirlaabe) is glaring, in contrast with the presence of the Bacili royals in the Soninke sample. There is, however, one interesting exception. No less than 11 migrants came from the village of Sintiou-Garba, a village of Koliabe-Denyanke, that is, of remnants of the old Denyanke dynasty and their warrior followers (the Koliabe), who took refuge in Damga after the successful Islamic revolution of Abd-al-Qadir in the mid eighteenth century. The Koliabe-Denyanke have historical connections with the Bacili ruling family of Gajaaga, see Bathily, "Imperialism," p. 330; Adams, *Terre et gens du fleuve*, pp. 48–49.

106. Personal conversations and correspondence, 1992.

107. It is interesting to note from a comparative point of view that the societies

most traditionally affected by migration in Europe were often gerontocratic societies (this was the case of the Corsican and the Auvergnat, and generally of European mountain societies).

108. I am quoting here from the comments made by an anonymous reader on a previous version of the present study, who based his argument on the article by John Hanson, "Islam, Migration and the Political Economy of Meaning: *Fergo* Nioro from the Senegal River Valley, 1862–1890), Journal *of African History*, vol. 35, no. 1, 1994, pp. 37–60.

109. John Salt and Hugh Clout, eds. *Migration in Post-War Europe: Geographical Essays* (London: Oxford University Press, 1976), p. 163.

110. Ibid.; and Momar Kebe Ndiaye, "Mamadou au pays des ritals," *Jeune Afrique*, No. 1098, 20 January 1982.

111. Chatelain, *Migrants temporaires en France*, pp. 979–980 ff.

112. Jean-Pierre Chauveau, "Notes sur les échanges dans le Baule precolonial," *Cahiers d'Etudes Africaines*, vol. 16, no. 68, 1977, pp. 567–601.

113. Yves Marguerat, "Des ethnies et des villes. Analyse des migrations vers les villes de Côte d'Ivoire," *Cahiers de l'ORSTOM*, Serie sciences humaines, vol. 18, 1981–82, pp. 303–340.

114. Ibid.; see also Yves Marguerat, *Analyse numérique des migrations vers les villes du Cameroun* (Paris: ORSTOM, 1975), (Travaux et documents de l'ORSTOM, No. 40).

115. Arthur Redford, *Labour Migration in England, 1800–1850*, 2d ed. (Manchester: Manchester University Press, 1964); see also J. D. Chambers, "Enclosures and Labour Supply in the Industrial Revolution," *Economic History Review*, ser. 2, vol. 4, 1953, pp. 319–343.

116. See the special issues of *Ethnologie Française* (1980) and *Cahiers d'Etudes Africaines* (1983) on migration and urbanization, in particular, Françoise Raison-Jourde, "Endogamie et stratégie d'implantation professionnelle des migrants auvergnats à Paris au XIXe. siècle," *Ethnologie Française*, vol. 10, no. 2, 1980, pp. 153–162; Michel Agier, "Etrangers, logeurs et patrons. L'improvisation sociale chez les commercants soudanais de Lomé," *Cahiers d'Etudes Africaines*, vol. 21, no. 81–83, 1981, pp. 251–266; and Gerard Salem, "De la brousse Sénégalaise au Boul'Mich: le système commercial mouride en France," ibid., pp. 267–288; Paul M. Lubeck, "Islamic Networks and Urban Capitalism: An Instance of Articulation from Northern Nigeria," ibid., pp. 67–78.

Chapter 5

1. ANS K 397 (132), Delegate Interior du Laurens to Dir. Interior, 2 August 1896.

2. Interviews conducted at the *Chambre de Koungany*, Dakar, Senegal, of Lasana Jaaxo (nephew of the first Soninke *cadi* (Moslem judge) of Kinshasa, Zaire), 13 December 1979; 24 January 1980; Lasana Ndaw, 17 December 1979; and in Kungani, Senegal, of Al-Haj Mamadu Jaaxo, last Soninke *cadi* of Kinshasa and son of Ba Bintu Tanjigora, 13 August 1982.

3. Paul Marty, "L'Islam en Mauritanie et au Sénégal," *Revue du monde musulman*, vol. 31, 1915–1916, pp. 322–323; *Etudes sur l'Islam au Sénégal* (Paris: Leroux, 1917), pp. 128–129; 128; *Etudes sur l'Islam et les tribus du Soudan*, vol. 4, pp. 27–33, 214, 239–240. One of the most important battles (which was lost by the French) during the revolt of Mamadu Lamin Darame was fought near Kungani, where Mamadu Lamin was based at the time when the hostilities began; Bathily, "Mamadou Lamine Dramé," p. 24.

4. Paul M. Lubeck, "Islamic Networks." See also J. S. Hogendorn, "The Origins of the Groundnut Trade in Northern Nigeria," in Carl K. Eicher and Carl Liedholm, eds., *Growth and Development of the Nigerian Economy* ([East Lansing]: Michigan State University, 1970), pp. 30–51.

5. Lasana Jaaxo, Dakar, 13 December 1979; 24 January 1980. This informant mentioned that Ba Bintu had originally worked on the building of the Matadi-Kinshasa railway. Another informant mentioned that he had first gone as a *tirailleur*, without specifying where he had served, but the context of the interview suggested the Belgian Congo. Lasana Ndaw, Dakar, 17 December 1979.

6. Adams, *Terre et gens du fleuve*, pp. 77–78. I interviewed Al-Haj Mamadu Jaaxo in 1982, who told me a short version of his father's story. Because I was under the impression of earlier interviews, I wrongly assumed that when he talked about his father having been a soldier in the Congo, he was talking about the Belgian Congo.

7. Catherine Coquery-Vidrovitch, *Cambridge History of Africa*, vol. 6 (Cambridge: Cambridge University Press, 1985), p. 303.

8. Al-Haj Mamadu Jaaxo, Kungani, 14 August 1982. On the beginnings of Kinshasa, see Patrick Manning, *Francophone Sub-Saharan Africa, 1880–1985* (Cambridge: Cambridge University Press, 1988), pp. 187, 190–191.

9. ANS 1B 31, fol. 235, Comptoir du Gabon, 21 August 1877; ANS 3B 16, No. 132, 1 May 1880; ANF CC3 1183, Recrutement des laptots au Sénégal, No. 3 [1880]; Extrait d'un rapport de M. le Commandant du Gabon en date du 23 Décembre 1880; ANS 1B 30, No. 3394, 10 November 1880.

10. ANS 1 B 30 No. 230, 1 April 1882; 6 G 12, 1 March 1885; 1V 49, 2 March 1885; 1B 44, 27 February 1886; 1B 55, 16 August 1886; 20 August 1886; 1B44, 2 July 1887.

11. Monteil mission: ANS 3B 99, No. 6, 8 June 1893; "Flottille du Bénin": ANS 1B 62, 31 May 1892; 10 July 1890; "Flottille du Niger": ANS 1B 62, 22 February 1895 (Dead from Timbuktu "events" of 1893); 9 December 1896.

12. 1E-44, Kayes, Pol. report, March 1899.

13. Coquery-Vidrovitch, *Cambridge History of Africa*, p. 300.

14. There were literate Wolof commercial employees in the Congo. Interviews, Lasana Ndaw, Mamadu Jaaxo.

15. It was in 1894 that Elder Dempster and Woermann, which had been increasingly important in the trade of Lagos, formed the first West African shipping conference. Charlotte Leubuscher, *The West African Shipping Trade, 1909–1959* (Leyden: A. W. Sythoff, 1963), p. 15.

16. Marty, *Etudes sur l'Islam au Sénégal*, pp. 128–129.

17. Adams, *Terre et gens du fleuve*, p. 58.

18. Bathily, "Imperialism and Colonial Expansion," pp. 266–267.

19. ANS 13 G 175, Médine, 14 September 1879, No. 2, Gallieni, Directeur des Affaires Politiques to Gov. Senegal.

20. Georges Poulet, *Les Maures de l'Afrique occidentale française* (Paris: Challamel, 1904).

21. Information given by Professor Samba Traoré of the Université de Saint-Louis, Saint-Louis, December 1992. I was unable to obtain a copy of this thesis.

22. Their presence on the battlefield may have been initially welcome because of their magical knowledge and expertise.

23. There is an irony in the fact that marabouts who had fought *against* the French in the revolt of Mamadu Lamin Darame (e.g., Hasan Tanjigora) later fought *for* the French as laptots. This fact casts some doubt on explanations of the revolt as antiimperialist.

24. ANS 9 G-86, Gov. Mauritania to Gov. general FWA, [Telegram], No. 122/AP.CF., 16 May 1933 (confidential); Secretary for Gov. general to Administrator of the *circonscription* of Dakar, [No.] 673 AP/I, 26 May 1933; Gov. general to Gov. Mauritania, No. 376 APA, 30 June 1933.

25. Fuutanke migrants have a comparable form of organization, called *suudu*, which is a Puular equivalent of *kompe*. Diop, *Société toucouleure et migration*, pp. 155–158; p. 75, note 2. It is interesting to note that the French name *chambre*, or *chambrée*, refers to a similar form of migrant organization, which reached its highest point in the years 1800 to 1850 in southern France, in particular in Provence. The origin of the word, according to Maurice Agulhon, was the room *(chambre*, or *chambrée)* rented collectively by migrant laborers. See Maurice Agulhon, "Un problême d'ethnologie historique: les chambrées en Basse-Provence au XIXe siècle," in Maurice Agulhon et al., *Ethnologie et histoire: forces productives et problêmes de transition* (Paris: Editions sociales, 1975), pp. 539–560. A tempting hypothesis is that the Soninke adopted the French name (an approximative equivalent of *kompe)* from French Navy sailors at the very beginning of their migration to Senegal's cities (i.e., Saint-Louis) around 1850. On similar associations in mid 19th-century Toulon, then a major naval base in relation with Senegal, as well as a working-class town and a focus for migrations from the Provençal interior, see Maurice Agulhon, *Une ville ouvrière au temps du socialisme utopique. Toulon de 1815 à 1851* (Paris; The Hague: Mouton, 1970).

26. See Chapter Seven.

27. Bakeli Jabira and Wadi Fili (Gay) Jabira, Kungani, Senegal, 17 August 1982 (the information was specifically about the chambre of Kungani).

28. See Chapter One. My description of the chambres is based mostly on the well-documented organization of contemporary migrant communities in France, since there are no early detailed descriptions of chambres. But early chambres cannot have been much different. In Chapter Seven, I describe "village abroad" organizations in the Congo and Zaire and in France in the interwar period, which were very similar.

29. See "Médailles commémoratives de l'expédition du Dahomey déposées dans les bureaux du Commandant de la marine au Sénégal et destinées à des marins indigènes du Sénégal et dépendances," *Journal Officiel du Sénégal*, 1894, pp. 95, 105; see also the lists of unclaimed inheritances of Senegalese who died in the Congo Free

State and French Congo, in which one Bacili is listed as *milicien* (policeman)—a clear outgrowth of previous occupation as a laptot; *Journal Officiel de l'Afrique Occidentale Française*, 1898, pp. 70; 110. In the 1894 Congo migrant sample, the only migrant (identifiable by last name) who declared he was a laptot was a Bacili.

30. ANS 13 G 202, Ct. Bakel to chief of cabinet of Gov. Senegal, No. 237, 19 March 1906.

31. It is worth noting, however, that the French to a degree followed an *informal* Soninke custom since very old tunkas generally had a chief counselor who had the real authority. Pollet and Winter, *Société soninké*, pp. 296–297.

32. ANS 2 G 6/3, Senegal to French West Africa, Pol. report, 1st quarter 1906.

33. ANS 2 G 6/4, Bakel, Monthly political report, April 1906.

34. ANS 4 G 120, Rapport d'inspection relatif aux cercles du fleuve, 1909.

35. In 1864, European mechanics were replaced by Senegalese, who were organized in a Compagnie Indigène des Mécaniciens; see ANF CC3 1182, Pièces diverses concernant les ateliers de la marine à Saint-Louis et le personnel ouvrier qui y est employé. I have related earlier the 1881 riot between the Soninke personnel of the Navy workshops and the Wolof population of Saint-Louis; Chapter Four.

36. ANS 1 B 47, Direction des colonies, 7th Bureau, Haut-Sénégal, No. 209, 19 July 1884.

37. Railway mechanics were paid up to 260 to 280 francs a month in 1896; ANS K 397 (132), pièce 31, Mission report, Administrator Superville to Gov. general FWA, 4 August 1896.

38. This importance may have been electoral as well. Some Soninke who had lived a long time in the "Four Communes" were French citizens; for example, see "Lettre de Boubou Soulé N'Diaye" [a Soninke French citizen], Senegal, Conseil General, procès-verbaux, 4 December 1897, p. 121; see also ibid., 11 December 1893, p. 49; and *Journal officiel de l'Afrique Occidentale Française*, 1899, p. 358. Later developments (see immediately below) suggest that some Bacili in Dakar had contacts with Senegal's urban political class. (One should also note that the 1890s Congo migration was organized by Justin Devès, one of the most important Senegalese métis politicians of the time; see Chapter Four.) It is worth noting that 1906 was a high point in the offensive led by Governor Camille Guy against the Senegalese political franchise; see Idowu, "The Conseil General of Senegal, 1879–1920," Ph.D. dissertation, University of Ibadan, 1966, pp. 364–365.

39. See Chapter Seven.

40. Senegal, Conseil General, Procès-verbaux, 25 June 1888.

41. See ANS 2 D 4/21 (12), which is for a later period (1931 to 1932) but gives insights on the earlier period.

42. ANS 2 D 4/21 (2), Réclamation du nommé Aly Bathily mécanicien au chemin de fer Dakar-Saint-Louis contre Demba Kona de Bakel au sujet de 480 hectares de terre en bordure du fleuve Sénégal, Correspondance 1908–1910.

43. ANS 4 G 120, Rapport d'inspection relatif aux cercles du fleuve, 1909.

44. ANS Fonds Sénégal, 2 D 4/21 (2).

45. ANS Fonds Sénégal, 2 D 4/9 c, Ct. Bakel to Gov. Senegal, April 29, 1910.

46. ANS Fonds Sénégal, 2 D 4/21 (2). On Sabourault, see Johnson, *Emergence*, pp. 119ff., 136ff., 147.

47. ANS Fonds Sénégal, 2 D 4/9 c, Ct. Bakel to Gov. Senegal, 29 April 1910. ANS 4 G 132, No. 49, Bakel, 11 September 1912. Demba Kona had been sentenced in 1906 to six months in prison for allegedly slandering Samba Suuley, the cercle's interpreter and the commandant. ANS 2 G/3, Senegal, Pol. Report, 3d and 4th quarter 1906.

48. ANS 4 G 132, No. 49, 11 September 1912. Demba Jango was named chief of Goye Inférieur on 15 November 1913; Marty, *Etude sur l'Islam au Sénégal*, p. 127.

49. For a description of the indigenous court system in French West Africa, see Raymond Leslie Buell, *The Native Problem in Africa*, vol. 1 (London: Frank Cass, 1965; 1st ed., Cambridge, Mass.: Bureau of International Research of Harvard University, 1928), pp. 1005–1020.

50. Bathily relates the story of a civil war between Jawara and the village of Tiyaabu ca. 1820 to 1828, which resulted in the execution of seventy clerics and the dispersion of the villagers of Jawara; "Imperialism," pp. 303–308. Events of this period still fed family vendettas in 1947; I. D. Bathily, "Notices," p. 62. I had the feeling, during interviews in Dakar in 1979 to 1980, that villagers of Jawara and Kungani (whose main maraboutic family is traditionally the client of the Bacili) viewed each other with defiance.

51. ANS Fonds Sénégal 2 D 4/21 (9), Bakel, Affaires des Bathily—Réclamation d'un groupe de Bathily de Dakar Samba Diama et consorts et de Samba Kadiata chef du Goye Inférieur contre l'assesseur du tribunal Fodé Saloum de Tuabo [*sic*]. Correspondance—Rapports. 1917–1918. (The letter by Blaise Diagne to the Governor of Senegal is pièce No. 7, 30 July 1918.) See also ANS 2 G 18/25, Monthly reports, Ct. Bakel to Gov. Senegal, 1918. Administrator Colombani (who strongly opposed Samba Kajata from 1917 to 19) mentioned to an official enquiry in 1922 that after his departure from the cercle "ses successeurs MM. Saint-Père et Taity se sont trop reposés sur les chefs du soin de diriger le pays." ANS 4 G 163, Rapport d'inspection concernant le cercle de Bakel, January 1922.

52. M. C. Diop, "Fonctions et activités des *dahira* mourides."

53. See, e.g., Michael Banton, *West African City* (London: Oxford University Press, 1957).

54. Roberts mentions that participants in Marka caravans were usually kinsmen and close friends from the same town; Roberts, *Warriors, Merchants and Slaves*, p. 64.

55. Pollet and Winter, *Société soninké*, p. 118.

56. See one such example in Bathily, "Imperialism," pp. 230–231, 228–229.

57. Ibid., pp. 232–233.

58. Diop, *Société toucouleure et migration*, pp. 15–16; 49–50.

59. On the curious relationship between marabouts and royals (Bacili) in eighteenth-century Gajaaga, see Curtin, *Economic Change*, pp. 72–74, and references quoted in notes; useful information also on occasional *armed* conflicts between marabout and Bacili villages in "Chronological outline of Gajaaga (Galam or Gadiaga)," ibid., supplement, pp. 10–21.

60. Xadi Darame, son of the last Soninke cadi of Brazzaville, Congo; from Tafasiriga, Kamera; interview, Bamako, 1 September 1982.

61. This claim was made to me by a very important figure of Soninke emigration in the Congos, whose name I prefer to withhold here. There are two similar examples in the work of Paul Marty: Hasan Tanjigora (Seexu Jomo's son), who took six years to go to Mecca around 1900 and lived five years in Chad, Dahomey, and the Ivory Coast on his return, Marty, *Etudes sur l'Islam au Sénégal*, p. 129; and Yekunda Njaay, brother of the important religious leader Ibrahima Njaay of Somankidi (Gidimaxa), who left for Mecca in 1903 "but stopped on the way and ended up in Congo," *Etudes sur l'Islam au Soudan*, p. 34.

62. François Renault, *L'abolition de l'esclavage au Sénégal, l'attitude de l'administration française, 1848–1905* (Paris: Société française d'histoire d'outre-mer; Librairie orientaliste Paul Geuthner, 1972); Suzanne Miers and Richard Roberts, eds., *The End of Slavery in Africa* (Madison: University of Wisconsin Press, 1988).

63. Kanya-Forstner, *Conquest*, esp. pp. 200–201, 228, 249, 272–273, and 215–236.

64. C. W. Newbury, "The formation of the Government-General of French West Africa," *Journal of African History*, vol. 1, 1960, pp. 111–128.

65. ANS 13 G 198, Ct. Bakel to Gov. Senegal, Pol. Report, 1895. Chaudié had just received instructions from the French Ministry of Colonies to observe the 1892 Brussels Convention on the slave trade; Martin A. Klein, "Slavery and Emancipation in French West Africa," Colloquium Paper, History, Culture and Society Program, Woodrow Wilson International Center for Scholars, Washington, D.C., 5 June 1986.

66. They must have been *sarido* (second-generation slaves) who were allowed to travel.

67. On the involvement of indigenous soldiers, 13 G 197, Ct. Bakel to Gov. Senegal, No. 74, 20 May 1896; No. 135, 17 June 1896. On the involvement of Bakel slaves, ANS 13 G 198, Ct. Bakel to Gov. Senegal, Pol. Report, 1895.

68. Myron Echenberg, "Slaves into Soldiers: Social Origins of the Tirailleurs Sénégalais," in Paul E. Lovejoy, ed., *Africans in Bondage: Studies in Slavery and the Slave Trade* (Madison: University of Wisconsin Press, 1986), pp. 311–333. Gidimaxa slave owners whose slaves were requisitioned as porters in 1894 complained that these were not returned. ANS 13 G 195, Ct. Bakel to Gov. Senegal, March 1894.

69. ANS 13 G 197; Denise Bouche has related the whole episode in *Les villages de liberté en Afrique noire française, 1887–1910* (Paris: Mouton, 1968), pp. 94–96.

70. Richard Roberts and Martin Klein, "The Banamba Slave Exodus of 1905 and the Decline of Slavery in the Western Sudan," *Journal of African History*, vol. 21, 1980, pp. 375–94; Klein, "Slavery and Emancipation."

71. ANM 1E-44, Kayes. ANS 2 G-10, Senegal, Pol. report, 1st quarter 1908; 4 G 117 1–4 Rapports d'inspection concernant le cercle de Bakel.

72. ANM 1E-61, Nioro.

73. These food shortages did not bring famine, except perhaps in the eastern Soninke region (where most of the dead appear to have been fugitive slaves on the road, who apparently had not brought enough food with them). ANS 2 G 4 G 117 14,

Rapport d'inspection du cercle de Bakel passée du 5 au 10 Août 1908; ANM 1E-44, Kayes, Rapport de l'Administrateur-adjoint Dubosq à M. l'Administrateur Commandant le cercle de Kayes, sur la tournée effectuée dans le Guidimakha, du 10 Avril au 21 Mai 1907; 1E-61, Nioro, Yearly Report 1908. On the Marka, Roberts, *Warriors, Merchants and Slaves*, p. 184. Similar climatic conditions prevailed at the time in the West African "Sahel"; Nicholson, "Methodology of Historical Climate Reconstruction."

74. Pollet and Winter, *Société soninké*, pp. 127, 371, and 529.

75. There is no evidence that the Marka slave exodus was followed by the migration of Marka slave owners.

76. Pollet and Winter seem to contradict themselves when they show that there are many descendents of slaves in Jafunu today and that many continue to work for their masters. *Société soninké*, pp. 256ff.

77. ANM 1E-44, Cercle de Kayes, Rapport de l'administrateur adjoint Duboscq, à M. l'administrateur commandant le cercle de Kayes, sur la tournée effectuée dans la province du Guidimakha du 10 avril au 21 mai 1907; and periodic reports, March; April 1908.

78. Population figure: ANS 1 G 310, Renseignements historiques, géographiques et économiques sur le cercle de Kayes [ca. 1902].

79. ANM 1E-61, Nioro, yearly report 1908.

80. Commandant de Lartigue, "Notice géographique sur le Sahel," *L'Afrique française, renseignements coloniaux*, 5, 1898, p. 123.

81. ANM 1E-61, Cercle de Nioro, Commissaire des Affaires indigènes Passant à M. l'administrateur commandant le cercle de Nioro, 20 April 1909. See references on Soninke slave populations in Chapter One.

82. Richard Roberts, "The End of Slavery in the French Soudan, 1904–1914," in Suzanne Miers and Richard Roberts, eds., *The End of Slavery in Africa* (Madison: University of Wisconsin Press, 1988), p. 291. The number of runaways from the town of Gumbu (as opposed to the cercle, which counted many non-Soninke areas) may have been higher. Meillassoux quotes a French report (probably 1894) estimating slaves to be 50 percent of the population of Gumbu. In the 1960s, their descendents were 22 percent of the population. Meillassoux, "Etat et condition des esclaves," pp. 225, 246.

83. Colombani, "Guidimakha," p. 412.

84. Saint-Père, *Sarakollé du Guidimakha*, p. 19.

85. To obtain the pre-emancipation population, one must add to the post-emancipation figure of 15,000, the 2,000 to 3,000 slaves who departed, and the "several hundred" who went to freed-slave villages (let us say 500). The total population of 17,500 to 18,500 is divided by two, to give a pre-emancipation slave population of 8,750 to 9,250.

We could also suppose that slaves were one-third of the population as in Gajaaga. The pre-emancipation slave population would have been 5,833 to 6,166 and the percentage of those who departed from the cercle or went to freed-slave villages would have been 42 to 56 percent, leaving only 2,666 to 3,333 slaves, 18 to 22 percent of the Soninke population of the cercle. This, however, does not agree with Colombani's post-emancipation observation that slaves in Gidimaxa (excluding those in freedmen villages) were "very numerous." The observation agrees more with a pre-emancipation proportion of 50 percent, which would leave a post-emancipation remainder of 38 to 41 percent of slaves in the total population. French reports indicating that Gidimaxa had a more intense agricultural activity than Gajaaga (see Chapters Two and Three), as well as reports that slaves were more harshly treated in Gidimaxa (Monteil, "Fin de siècle," p. 114), suggest that Gidimaxa had more slaves than Gajaaga.

86. Roberts, *Warriors, Merchants and Slaves*, p. 192. From the estimates given by Roberts, it would seem that the population of Beledugu was far inferior to that of the cercles of Kayes and Nioro; see ibid., pp. 119–120.

87. Maurice Delafosse, "Monographie du cercle de Bamako," *Renseignements coloniaux. Afrique française*, 1910, p. 67 (population figure for the cercle p. 58). See also Roberts, *Warriors, Merchants and Slaves*, p. 200.

88. ANM 1E-44, Kayes, March 1909.

89. ANM 1E-61, Rapport sur la politique générale, 1910.

90. Adams, *Terre et gens du fleuve*, pp. 69–71; Meillassoux, "Etat et condition des esclaves."

91. Quote from the archival file on the Banamba incidents kept at the Institut des Sciences Humaines in Bamako, Mali, in Pollet and Winter, *Société soninké*, p. 254.

92. ANM 1E-44, Ct. Kayes to Gov. Soudan, May 1909.

93. ANM 1E-44, Ct. Kayes to Gov. Soudan, May 1909.

94. Pollet and Winter, *Société soninké*, p. 246.

95. ANM 1E-44, Ct. Kayes to Gov. French Soudan, 4th quarter 1908.

96. ANS 13 G 200, Bakel, Copie du registre des réclamations pour le mois de Novembre 1897.

97. ANM 1E-61, Nioro, Rapport sur la politique générale, 1910.

98. Richard Roberts, "End of Slavery in French Soudan," pp. 290–291.

99. Colombani, "Guidimakha," p. 412 (Colombani's text was published in 1931, but it was written some time after 1910; see p. 430).

100. Saint-Père, *Sarakollé du Guidimakha*, pp. 182–183.

101. Boyer, *Un peuple de l'ouest soudanais*, p. 98.

102. Pollet and Winter, *Société soninké*, p. 257.

103. Ibid., pp. 323–324.

104. Weigel, *Migration et production domestique*, pp. 75–77, 66–67.

105. Boyer, *Un peuple de l'ouest soudanais*, pp. 73–74.

106. I. D. Bathily, "Notices," pp. 86–87.

107. Xadi Darame, Bamako, September 1982.

108. Weigel, *Migration et production domestique*, pp. 75–76.

109. Pollet and Winter, *Société soninké*, pp. 257–258.

110. Ibid., pp. 256–257.

111. Ibid., p. 257.

112. Ibid., p. 258.

113. Compare in particular Boyer, *Une société de l'ouest soudanais*, pp. 98 and 74.

114. Pollet and Winter, *Société soninké*, pp. 256–257.

115. Ibid., pp. 256–257.

116. Ibid., p. 255. I am grateful to Martin Klein for drawing my attention to this important point.

117. See Chapter One.

118. Pollet and Winter, *Société soninké*, p. 254 note (testimony of Marka slave quoted above).

119. On Marka slavery and emancipation, see Roberts and Klein, "Banamba Slave Exodus"; Roberts, *Warriors, Merchants and Slaves;* "End of Slavery in French Soudan"; MacDougall, "Ijil Salt Industry," pp. 263–309.

120. David, *Navétanes*, pp. 123–124; 34.

121. Ibid., p. 123.

122. ANM 1E-61, Nioro, Annual reports, 1911, 1912, 1913.

123. Paul Edward Pheffer, "Railroads and Aspects of Social Change in Senegal, 1878–1933," Ph.D. dissertation, University of Pennsylvania, 1975, p. 238.

124. Soninke migration to Casamance emerged in the middle of the nineteenth century. See Chapter Two.

125. Pheffer, *Railroads*, p. 257.

126. Pheffer, "Railroads," p. 285, note 84; Klein, *Islam and Imperialism.*

127. Pélissier, *Paysans du Sénégal*, pp. 205–206.

128. David, *Navétanes*, p. 453. On the peanut trade at Nianing, Klein, *Islam and Imperialism*, p. 115.

129. On the environment of the region, Pélissier, *Paysans du Sénégal.*

130. It is true that French colonial reports from the cercle of Nioro for the 1910s make no explicit references to the impact of the end of slavery on navetanat, while reports from the cercle of Kita make such references. David, *Navétanes*, pp. 126–127. But that is easily explained: the only migrants from Kita before 1908–1910 had been jula. After emancipation, however, a migration of navetanes developed rapidly between the cercle and Senegal. The connection between navetanat and slave emancipation in Kita was, therefore, obvious. It was less obvious in Nioro, where French administrators were aware of the existence of labor migration prior to emancipation.

131. Pollet and Winter, *Société soninké*, p. 257.

132. It was mentioned to me by Professor Xadi Darame, personal conversation, Bamako, September 1982; it was also mentioned by numerous Soninke informants of Catherine Quiminal, personal conversation, Paris, July 1992.

133. Emile Le Bris, Pierre-Philippe Rey, Michel Samuel, *Capitalisme négrier, la marche des paysans vers le prolétariat* (Paris: Maspéro, 1976), pp. 110–111. Professor Xadi Darame alluded to this incident in a personal conversation with me, Bamako, September 1982.

134. The local administrator in Gumbu noted in 1916 the numerous military recruitments of "young people from the *cercle* made either in Senegal or in neighboring districts notably *in Nioro*." (My emphasis.) ANM 1E-38, Cercle de Goumbou, January 1916. This was the first report of this kind for Gumbu, while similar reports for the

neighboring region of Nioro, conversely, had been numerous for the period preceding the First World War. I have emphasized the mention of Gumbu migrants in Nioro, which indicates that migrants probably first sought employment in Nioro before being made aware of opportunities further afield in Senegal and the Gambia. In the cercle of Nioro itself, the districts from which most migrants came at the beginning of the century were the Soninke-speaking districts of Kenyareme and Kingi Jawara, which were introduced to navetanat probably as a result of their migration to Gidimaxa in 1892–1893 (see Chapter Three). See ANM IE-61, Cercle de Nioro, Rapport annuel pour 1912 [dated 1913].

135. For a reassessment of Pollet and Winter on this point, see Weigel, *Migration et production domestique*, pp. 44–48.

136. ANS 13 G 200, Bakel, Copie du journal de cercle, 6 February 1897; ANM 1E-61, Nioro, Yearly report, 1911; and Chapter Six.

137. *Economic History*, p. 225.

138. I. Schapera, *Migrant Labour and Tribal Life* (London: Oxford University Press, 1947); J. Clyde Mitchell, "Causes of Labour Migrations." See also Margaret Read, "Migrant Labour in Africa and Its Effects on Tribal Life," *International Labour Review*, vol. 45, no. 6, June 1942, pp. 605–631; P. H. Gulliver, "Nyakusa Labour Migration," *Rhodes-Livingstone Journal*, vol. 21, 1957, pp. 32–63; A. W. Southall, "Population Movements in East Africa," in R. Mansell Prothero and Kenneth Michael Barbour, *Essays on African Population* (New York: Praeger, 1961), pp. 157–192; J. Clyde Mitchell, "Wage Labour and African Population in Central Africa," ibid., pp. 193–248.

139. Gilles Sautter, "Migrations, société et développement en pays mossi," *Cahiers d'Etudes Africaines*, vol. 20, no. 79, 1980, pp. 215–253.

Chapter 6

1. For example, see Clozel's "Circulaire au sujet de la règlementation de la main d'oeuvre indigène et du régime du travail," Dakar, 6 March 1912, *Journal Officiel de l'A.O.F.*, 1912; in ANS K 398 (132).

2. ANM 1E-61, Kayes, Annual Report, 1911.

3. ANM 1E-61.

4. E. Bernus and G. Savonnet, "Les problèmes de la sécheresse dans l'Afrique de l'Ouest," *Présence africaine*, 1973, p. 113.

5. This section is a very short summary of François Manchuelle, "Forced Labor in French West Africa, 1881–1946: A Reappraisal." Presentation at the annual meeting of the (U.S.) African Studies Association, Denver, Colo., 22 November 1987 (unpublished).

6. Jean Suret-Canale, *Afrique noire occidentale et centrale* (Paris: Editions sociales, 1964); see vol. 2, esp. pp. 288–298, 310–327; Crowder, *West Africa under Colonial Rule*, pp. 184–187; Buell, *Native Problem*, vol. 1, pp. 1037–1045; vol. 2, pp. 27–30. There are

few case studies of forced labor in French West Africa; Dennis Cordell and Joel W. Gregory, "Labour Reservoirs and Populations: French Colonial Strategies in Koudougou, Upper Volta, 1914 to 1939," *Journal of African History*, vol. 23, 1982, pp. 205–224; Oussouby Touré, "Le refus du travail forcé au Sénégal Oriental," *Cahiers d"Etudes Africaines*, vol. 24, no. 93, 1984, pp. 25–28; also on another area of French Africa, Jane I. Guyer, "The Food Economy and French Colonial Rule in Central Cameroons," *Journal of African History*, vol. 19, 1978, pp. 577–597.

7. There was an important exception: the Ivory Coast after 1908 under Governor Gabriel Angoulvant, which presaged the forced labor policy of the 1920s. On the period after 1901, see Manchuelle, "Forced Labor in French West Africa."

8. See Buell, *Native Problem*, vol. 2, p. 27; Senegal, Conseil Colonial, *Procès-verbaux des séances*, October 1923, pp. 48–53; and session extraordinaire, November 1926, pp. 56–67; also Touré, "Refus du travail forcé au Sénégal Oriental."

9. I have discussed the matter in "Forced Labor in French West Africa, 1881–1946." I will be preparing a fuller version of this presentation for later publication. For information in support of the explanation presented here, see the memoirs of colonial governor Louis Sanmarco, *Le colonisateur colonisé* (Paris: Favre, 1983).

10. See, e.g., Gabriel Angoulvant, "L'Afrique occidentale française," *Le monde colonial illustré*, no. 5, February 1924, p. 98.

11. See Angoulvant's plan for the Senegalese peanut economy, David, *Navétanes*, p. 44.

12. Babacar Fall, "Une entreprise agricole privée au Soudan français: la Société anonyme des cultures de Diakandape (Kayes), 1919–1942," in Catherine Coquery-Vidrovitch, ed., *Entreprises et entrepreneurs en Afrique au XIXe et XXe siècle*, Vol. 1 (Paris: L'Harmattan, 1983), pp. 335–350.

13. ANM 1E-19, Kayes, Telegram-letter, March 1921.

14. ANM 1E-19, Administrator Kayes to Gov. French Soudan, Pol. report, 3d quarter 1924.

15. ANM 1E-19, Kayes, telegram-letter, No. 217, 2 February 1925.

16. ANM 1E-19, Adm. Kayes to Gov. Soudan, 4th quarter 1925.

17. ANM 1E-19, Adm. Kayes to Gov. Soudan, Pol. report, 30 September 1926.

18. "Les indigènes cultiveront le coton parce que j'ai donné l'ordre d'en faire; mais le peu qui sera ensemencé le sera par crainte de représailles." ANM 1E-19, Adm. Kayes to Gov. Soudan, 2d quarter 1927.

19. ANM 1E-36, Adm. Nioro to Gov. French Soudan, Rapport politique, 2d quarter 1923; and 4th quarter 1923. The recruitment for Jaxandappe appears to have been set at 100 men originally, but most of the men recruited escaped, and four successive recruitments had to be made, only to end up with the same results.

20. ANM 1E-36, Adm. Nioro to Gov. Soudan, Pol. report, 1st and 2d quarter 1925 (one report).

21. ANM 1E-36, Nioro, Yelimane, September 1924.

22. ANM 1E-36, Nioro, 2d quarter 1926.

23. ANM 1E-36, Nioro, No. 37, 14 March 1927.

24. ANM 1E-19, Adm. Kayes to Gov. Soudan, Pol. report, July 1929; 3d quarter 1932.

25. ANM 1E-36, Adm. Nioro to Gov. Soudan, 3d quarter 1927.

26. ANM 1E-36, Adm. Nioro to Gov. Soudan, 1st quarter 1928.

27. ANM 1E-36, Adm. Nioro to Gov. Soudan, 3d. quarter 1929.

28. ANM 1E-19, Adm. Kayes to Gov. Soudan, 1st quarter 1934.

29. ANM 1E-19, Adm. Kayes to Gov. Soudan, 10 October 1931.

30. Philippe David mentions that some "second-contingent" laborers were recruited "quite late" (1930s?) to work as stokers on the Dakar-Niger railway. David, *Navétanes,* p. 118.

31. Marc Michel, *L'appel à l'Afrique. Contributions et réactions à l'effort de guerre en A.O.F. (1914–1919)* (Paris: Université de Paris I-Panthéon Sorbonne, Institut d'histoire des relations internationales contemporaines, 1982), p. 481.

32. With transportation to and from the working premises, however, the time spent away from the laborers' villages was greater. Fall believes it to have been between twenty-five and thirty days, but this seems unlikely for laborers recruited in the cercle of Kayes, who could come to Kayes in one or two days by boat. Fall, "Une entreprise," p. 340.

33. The unloading of ships in Kayes lasted three months. Thus there were six successive shifts: 900 ÷6 = 150 laborers per shift. The harvesting in Jaxandappe lasted four months, thus eigth shifts: 125 laborers per shift.

34. In 1922, ordinary laborers were paid beginning wages of 3.50 francs a day in Dakar, and 3 francs in Saint-Louis. That same year, the labor tax (prestations) was redeemed at the rate of 2 francs a day in Bakel. Sénégal, Conseil Colonial, *Session ordinaire,* November 1922, 4 November 1922, p. 80; 24 November 1922, p. 49.

35. Fall, "Une entreprise," p. 342; laborers were also physically abused, and exploited, ibid., pp. 342–344.

36. Pheffer, "Railroads and Social Change," pp. 248–250.

37. Fall, "Une entreprise," p. 341.

38. Jean Suret-Canale, *French Colonialism in Tropical Africa, 1900–1945* (New York: Pica Press, 1971), p. 222.

39. Pollet and Winter, *Société soninké,* p. 99.

40. Saint-Père, *Sarakollé du Guidimakha,* p. 33.

41. ANM 1E-36, Official telegram, 2 May 1931; see also Suret-Canale, *French Colonialism,* p. 222.

42. Responding to Duranthon's pleas in 1921, Governor Olivier of French Soudan identified one of these cercles, by indicating that he would no longer require Nioro's participation in supplying Nema (a desert cercle, today in Mauritania). ANM 1E-36, No. A. 195, 9 May 1921, Gov. Soudan to Adm. Nioro.

43. ANM, 1E-61, Adm. Nioro to Gov. Soudan, Pol. report, 3d quarter 1920.

44. ANM 1E-36, Nioro, Tour report No. 35, Duranthon, 6 February 1921.

45. Governor Olivier or one of his aides underlined this last sentence and wrote in the margin an indignant: "This is untrue."

46. ANM 1E-36, Nioro, 2d quarter 1921.

47. Unfit men were presented, and it was necessary to threaten people with jail terms in Kenyareme, Kingi Jawara, and Masasi and to send the *gardes cercle* (local police force) to the Fuulbe and local Fuutanke.

48. ANM 1E-36, Nioro, 1st quarter 1921.

49. ANM 1E-36, Nioro, 2d quarter 1921.

50. See ANM 1E-36, Adm. Nioro to Gov. Soudan, 2d quarter 1921; and 4th quarter 1921.

51. ANM 1E-36, Nioro, 2d quarter 1921.

52. ANM 1E-36, Nioro, 3d quarter 1921; see also 2d quarter 1921.

53. ANM 1E-36, Adm. Nioro to Gov. Soudan, 4th quarter 1921.

54. We shall see that Duranthon, though transferred from his post in 1922, came back to Nioro in 1932 in charge of one of the most important official missions in the history of labor migration in French West Africa. See Chapter Seven. On Olivier's interest in forced labor, see Marcel Olivier, *Six ans de politique sociale à Madagascar;* book prefaced by Albert Sarraut (Paris: Grasset, 1931); biography of Olivier in *Hommes et destins,* vol. 3.

55. See François Caron, *An Economic History of Modern France* (New York: Columbia University Press, 1979), p. 249. After the devaluation of the franc, direct taxation in *metropolitan* France also tripled in nominal value between 1920 and 1925; ibid., p. 251.

56. Michel, *Appel à l'Afrique,* pp. 442–443. Another inconsistency was Duranthon's remark about a "general flight of all youth" taking place during the *dry season*, at the time of labor recruitment, while in the same report he mentioned that departures toward Senegal took place every year in *September* (the rains stop by September or October, but humid conditions persist until December or January), ANM 1E-61, Nioro, 3d quarter 1920.

57. ANM 1E-60, Nioro, Pol. and military report, July 1893.

58. ANM 1E-36, Nioro, Yearly report, 1922, No. 22, 30 December 1922. These figures are for sedentary populations only.

59. Ibid.

60. Even accounting for a loss of 80 to 85 percent during the bovine plague of 1892, there would have been only 15,000 to 20,000 cows in the region prior to the plague.

61. Thus creating the severe problems of overgrazing, which are in part responsible for the present desertification of Mauritania. Charles Toupet, *La sédentarisation des nomades en Mauritanie centrale sahélienne* (Lille: Atelier de reproduction des thèses, 1977), passim.

62. Pollet and Winter, *Société soninké,* p. 124; Boyer, *Un peuple de l'ouest africain,* p. 97 (includes figures); ANM IE-61, Annual report 1913. See also Saint-Père, *Sarakollé du Guidimakha,* pp. 38, 51.

63. ANM 1E-19, Delegate Kayes to Governor French Soudan, Télégramme-lettre, No. 922, 28 May 1924; and 1E-36, Rapport politique, 1st quarter 1924, reporting about the "worrisome" high local price of cattle in Nioro.

64. Livestock figures from ANM, 1E-36, Nioro, Rapport Annuel 1922, No. 22, 30

December 1922. It is not easy to obtain local prices for livestock at this precise time. My estimates are based on the following: ANM 1E-19, Delegate Kayes to Gov. Soudan, No. 922, 28 May 1924 [cow 200–400 francs; horse 700–2,000 francs; donkey 250–350 francs; sheep 20–35 francs; goat 20–35 francs]; 1E-36, Nioro, Pol. report, 1st quarter 1924 [cow 200 francs; pack ox 350 francs; donkey 310 francs; sheep 25, 50, and 75 francs]; Saint-Père, *Sarakholés du Guidimakha*, p. 51 [horse 700 francs in Gidimaxa, 1,500 to 2,000 francs in the Gambia; donkey 100 francs in Gidimaxa, 300, 350, and 400 or even 500 francs in the Gambia—these prices are ca. 1923.]

65. The French parliamentarian Henri Cosnier, who traveled in French West Africa on an economic mission after the war, estimated on the basis of a 1912 census the annual proportion of cattle available for sale in Senegal at one birth per two females, of which two-thirds would survive and half would be males salable for meat, that is, about 8 percent. Henri Cosnier, *L'Ouest africain français* (Paris: Larose, 1921), pp. 100–107. Samir Amin, however (who worked in the administration of Mali, the former French Soudan), estimates that the growth rate in the French Soudan prior to the 1930s was 4 percent for bovines and 20 percent for sheep and goats, Amin, *Trois experiences africaines de développement: le Mali, la Guinée et le Ghana* (Paris: P.U.F., 1965), p. 26. Samir Amin's more conservative estimates for cattle have been preferred here. I have no figures for horses, but I assumed a natural growth similar to that of cattle. At the time when I wrote this chapter, I had not yet read the reference work by Gudrun Dahl and Anders Hjort, *Having Herds: Pastoral Herd Growth and Household Economy* (Stockholm: Department of Social Anthropology, University of Stockholm, 1976). These authors quote various sources giving a proportion available for slaughter of 8 percent for cattle (p. 168) and 20 to 30 percent for sheep and goats (p. 208).

66. In 1921, the total direct tax (nomads and sedentaries) amounted then to 860,000 francs. See ANM 1E-36, Nioro, Rapport politique, 3d quarter 1921. In 1924, nomads paid a *zakkat*, or cattle tax, of 134,265 francs. There is thus a slight discrepancy between the 1921 and 1924 figures (134,265 + 677,000 = 811,265), which is probably due to the fact that the 1921 figures also included the tax levied on itinerant traders, the *patente*.

67. Baillaud gives yearly sales figures for the three markets of Nioro, Kerane, and Tambakara, all located in the cercle of Nioro, amounting to a total of 97,060 kilograms of loose salt and 35,101 bars of salt; *Routes du Soudan*, p. 36. These bars were probably Ijil bars of 25 kilograms (see Curtin, *Economic Change*, pp. 225–226.) The total would be 974,585 kilograms. Salt sold in 1925 in Kayes for 0.60 francs a kilogram. (ANM 1E-19, Delegate Kayes to Gov. Soudan, No. 1247, 24 July 1925.) The total value would be 584,751 francs.

68. This should not be seen as an exaggeration: official trade figures were always underestimated. Moreover, Pollet and Winter give a 1896 French estimate of 1,354,303 francs for salt imported in the Soudan by way of the "Sahel" region (Nioro and Nara) for a total of 2,320,760 francs for the whole of the French Soudan, corresponding to 3 million kilograms—thus the "Sahel" region imported 1,750,680.5 kilograms or at the 1925 Kayes price, 1,050,408.3 francs. See *Société soninké*, p. 117.

69. ANS 13G 201, No. 1, December 1898, Rapport politique, commercial et agri-

cole; ANS 2D 4–12, Maubert, 1904; ANS 2D 4-9, Bakel, Rapport de l'administrateur Gaillardon, tournée effectuée dans le Goye supérieur en février et mars 1912; Saint-Père, *Sarakollé du Guidimakha*, p. 51; reports for all regions regularly mention dry-season migrations of itinerant traders.

70. Hopkins, *Economic History*, pp. 250–251; also Richard Roberts, "Women's Work and Women's Prosperity: Household Social Relations in the Maraka Textile Industry of the Nineteenth Century," *Comparative Studies in Society and History*, vol. 26, 1984, pp. 229–250.

71. Unlike the Fuutanke, the Soninke have no weaver caste. Seven and a half percent of the Soninke population of the cercle of Nioro represents only 2,625 persons. (There were 140,000 sedentaries in the cercle in 1922; ANM 1E-36, Nioro, Pol. report, No. 22, 30 December 1922—one-fourth [35,000] is the usual estimate for adult males.) The proportion of 7.5 percent is a conservative arbitrary choice on my part due to the absence of firm data on the proportion of Soninke occupied in weaving. There are indications, however, that this proportion was much larger. In 1909, the Soninke region of Kenyareme in Nioro was reported as a "large producer of cotton. In almost all the villages and especially in Bougoudri, Korompo, [and] Ouainkanou, every compound is a small factory, where people are making thread, weaving and dyieng cloth. Indigo *(gara)* is cultivated on a large scale." ANM 1E-61, Nioro, Commis des Affaires Indigènes Passant to Ct. Nioro, 20 April 1909. In the early 1960s, in Amadi-Ounaré, a Damga village peopled by an equal number of Puular-speaking Futanke and Soninke, half of the villagers reportedly engaged in craft production, which provided one-third of the village's income. Weaving predominated among the various crafts. Colette Le Blanc, "Un village de la vallée du Sénégal: Amadi-Ounaré," *Cahiers d'Outre-mer*, vol. 17, no. 66, 1964, p. 142.

72. Production figure based on Meillassoux, "Commerce," p. 193; corrected in "Etat et condition des esclaves," pp. 249–250; Saint-Père, *Sarakollé du Guidimakha*, pp. 42–43, 51.

73. On other Soninke exports, see Saint-Père, *Sarakollé du Guidimakha*, p. 51; also ANM 1E-36, Nioro, 1st quarter 1923.

74. My predicament is similar to that of historians of taxation in ancien régime France. Although the available evidence indicates that tax rates were by no means excessive (ancien régime direct taxes appear to have been three times lower and indirect taxes four times lower than today's French taxes), it is still insufficient to prove this with absolute certainty; Hincker, *Français devant l'impôt*, pp. 39–54. In 1966, the French state levied in direct taxes the equivalent of twenty-six days out of the labor of an average French wage earner (and about forty-five days in indirect taxes); ibid., p. 42. I have made my Soninke estimate on the basis of a six-day work week, without counting religious holidays.

75. Polly Hill, *Rural Hausaland: A Village and a Setting* (Cambridge: Cambridge University Press, 1972), pp. 128–132.

76. Subsistence crises in France disappeared after the completion of the French railway network in the middle of the nineteenth century. On what was probably the last subsistence crisis in France, see Toshio Horii, "La crise alimentaire de 1853 à 1856

et la Caisse de la Boulangerie de Paris," *Revue Historique*, no. 552, October–December 1984, pp. 375–401.

77. Monique Chastanet reports that the 1913 to 1915 crisis was called *Baani dulle* by Gajaaga Soninke, after the name of the boat *(Bani)* that brought food relief to the area. Chastanet, "Crises de subsistence," p. 22.

78. ANM 1E-61, Nioro, May 1914; 1E-36, Nioro, 2d quarter 1926.

79. ANM 1E-19, Kayes, Telegramme-lettre, No. 1247, 24 July 1925.

80. ANM 1E-19, Kayes, 2d quarter 1927; 1E-36, Nioro, 2d quarter 1930.

81. Although Indochinese rice and Soudanese sorghum were brought by ships to the Upper Senegal region at an undetermined period, probably between 1900 and 1945; I. D. Bathily, "Notices socio-historiques," p. 72. There were probably emergency deliveries of such grain during the First World War; 1914 was called *Hitande Marodyi*, "the year of the *rice* distributions," by the Fuutanke; André Lericollais, "La sécheresse et les populations de la vallée du Sénégal," in Colloque de Nouakchott, 17–19 Décembre 1973, *La désertification au sud du Sahara* (Dakar; Abidjan: Nouvelles Editions Africaines, 1976), p. 111.

82. Early twentieth-century reports for the cercle of Bamako indicated that it cost *six times* more to move a metric ton of grain by caravan than by water. Roberts, *Warriors, Merchants and Slaves*, p. 166.

83. ANM 1E-36, Nioro, Tour report No. 35, 6 February 1921.

84. George E. Brooks, *Landlords and Strangers: A History of Western Africa, 1000–1630* (Boulder, Colo., 1992), Chapter 1.

85. This is consistent with a drier period, which is usually signaled by a greater irregularity of rains, which can be too heavy at times, although the trend over the long term is toward a decline.

86. Bernus and Savonnet, "Problèmes de sécheresse."

87. ANM 1E-36, Nioro, 3d quarter 1927.

88. Bradley et al., *Guidimakha mauritanien*, p. 144.

89. ANM 1E-19, Kayes, 2d quarter 1924.

90. ANM 1E-19, Kayes, No. 1247, 24 July 1925, Telegram-letter.

91. ANM 1E-36, Nioro, No. 93, Pol. report 1926.

92. ANM 1E-36, Nioro, 2d quarter 1930.

93. See Chapter Three. For a description of famine in Kano in 1913 to 1914, see A. T. Grove, "A Note on the Remarkably Low Rainfall of the Sudan Zone in 1913," *Savanna*, vol. 2, no. 2, December 1973, p. 135.

94. Four if we count pluriannual *urban* migration, but this type of migration was not prevalent until the end of the 1920s to the beginning of the 1930s (see Chapter Seven). For a description of the various types of migration from Nioro in the 1920s, see in particular ANM 1E-36, 1st and 2d quarters 1925.

95. Henri Labouret, *Paysans d'Afrique Occidentale* (Paris: Gallimard, 1941), p. 225.

96. The migration of the firdou has been neglected by scholars, but it was very important. In the early 1930s, there were no less than 40,000 firdou every year in Senegal, for 50,000 navetanes; Henri Labouret, "La grande détresse de l'arachide," *L'Afrique française*, 1932, pp. 732-733.

97. ANM 1E-36, Nioro, 3d quarter 1921.

98. ANM 1E-61, Nioro, 2d quarter 1920.

99. ANM 1E-36, Nioro, 1st quarter 1933.

100. ANM 1E-36, Nioro, Extrait du rapport politique, 2d quarter 1933.

101. See Pollet and Winter, *Société soninké*, pp. 129–130.

102. See ANM 1E–38, Political reports, Goumbou, 1899–1902.

103. It was then noted that many young men from the cercle were drafted in Senegal or in neighboring cercles, especially Nioro. ANM 1E-38, Goumbou, Pol. report, January 1916. The mention of migrants in Nioro is interesting: the Soninke from Gumbu must have been introduced to navetanat through a first migration in Nioro, just as migrants from Nioro were probably introduced to navetanat through their migration to Gidimaxa in 1892 to 1893 (on this migration, see Chapter Four).

104. ANM 1E-36, Nioro, 3d quarter 1926.

105. ANM 1E-36, Nioro, No. 37, 14 March 1927.

106. Pélissier, *Paysans du Sénégal*, pp. 181–182.

107. ANM 1E-61, 3d quarter 1923.

108. ANM 1E-36, Nioro, 4th quarter 1923.

109. For example, see ANM 1E-36, 1st quarter 1930.

110. ANM 1E-19, Adm. Kayes to Gov. Soudan, 3d quarter 1932.

111. ANM 1E-32, Nara, Pol. report, 4th quarter 1931; 1st quarter 1932; see also 1E-36, Nioro, 1st quarter 1930; 3d quarter 1935; 1942; Télégramme-lettre No. 499, 17 October 1944; 1E-44, Yélimané, 1943, Rapport de tournée No. 8 effectuée les 8–30 Octobre 1943 par le chef de subdivision de Yélimané dans le canton du Kéniarémé.

112. The only indication provided by local reports was for Nioro in 1927. It indicated that the Soudanese central administration this year had an objective of 145 recruitments per cercle, but the commandant in Nioro stated that he hoped to recruit mostly among the *bons absents* of previous years, for example, the young men who were absent at the time of the draft. ANS 1E-36, Adm. Nioro to Gov. Soudan, 4th quarter 1927. According to Buell, there were 2,700 men recruited for military service in Senegal and Soudan in 1928. This was out of a total population of 3,662,818 (Cosnier, *Ouest Africain Français*, p. 199; I have used Cosnier's figure rather than Buell's, which includes the Upper Volta in the Soudanese figure). Thus, recruitments amounted to 1 in 1,200 persons. In Nioro, the sedentary population (no military recruitments were made among nomads) was about 140,000, so there were about 116 draftees a year, 350 away every year. For Kayes, with a population of 122,000, the figures come to 90 draftees and 270 away every year. Using annual recruitment reports in the French West African Archives, Myron Echenberg came to almost identical estimates for the interwar period of 114 annual recruits for Nioro, and 90 for Kayes. *Colonial Conscripts: The Tirailleurs Sénégalais in French West Africa, 1857–1960* (Portsmouth, N.H.: Heinemann, 1991), figure 4.1, pp. 52–57.

113. ANM 1E-36, Nioro, Rapport de tournée effectuée du 21 Septembre au 17 Octobre 1944 par M. Cancel Jean, administrateur adjoint des Colonies, Adjoint au Commandant de cercle de Nioro. See also ANM 1E-36, Nioro, 4th quarter 1924; and

Rapport de tournée, Youri, Sandaré, Samantara, Lakamané, Sanké, Sambadigané, Diéma, Fougoune, Tinkaré, 31 December 1941.

114. The same observation can be made about forced labor recruitments. It is worth noting that "second-contingent" laborers were instructed *to remain in their villages at the disposal of the authorities for three years.* Not surprisingly, the administration had little success in enforcing this excessive regulation. ANM 1E-36, Nioro, 3d quarter 1929.

115. For example, there was in 1907 a migration of about a thousand persons from the Gidimaxa of Kayes (Soudan) to Northern Gidimaxa in Mauritania, probably because of the more tolerant attitude of the French administration there toward slavery. See ANM 1E-44, Kayes, Rapport de l'Administrateur adjoint Duboscq à M. l'Administrateur commandant le cercle de Kayes, sur la tournée effectuée dans la province du Guidimakha du 10 avril au 21 mai 1907.

116. In 1888, Fuulbe emigration from Walo to the Umarian state (this was, in fact, the *Fergo Umar,* a movement of religious emigration) was explained by a desire to evade allegedly excessive French taxes. (This was highly unlikely as the tax then was only 3 francs per head, and the Fuulbe possessed large herds of cattle whose meat was no doubt in high demand in Saint-Louis—I have discussed the political motives underlying the affair in my article "Métis et colons.") The same year General Gallieni was accused by liberal critics of "depopulating" the French Soudan through forced recruitments for the construction of the Kayes-Niger railway. See Méniaud, *Pionniers du Soudan*, Vol. 1, pp. 319–320.

117. Catherine Coquery-Vidrovitch, *Le Congo au temps des grandes compagnies concessionnaires, 1898–1930* (Paris; The Hague: Mouton, 1972), pp. 103–103ff.; [Lucien-Auguste] Aspe-Fleurimont, *La Guinée française* (Paris: Challamel, 1900), pp. 122–127; Capitaine Renard [secretary-general of the Union congolaise française, which was largely the concessionary companies' syndicate], *La colonisation au Congo français* (Paris: Kugelmann, 1901), pp. 59–61; Henri Cuvillier-Fleury, *La mise en valeur du Congo français* (Paris: Larose, 1904), pp. 218–221; Leroy-Beaulieu, *Colonisation chez les peuples modernes*, p. 584 (quoting the economic nationalist Augustin Bernard on the necessity "de ménager la transition entre l'esclavage et la liberté).

118. Cuvillier-Fleury noted that such ideas were completely foreign to the French political tradition, *Mise en valeur du Congo*, pp. 218–221.

119. Aspe-Fleurimont, *La Guinée française*, pp. 127–128; Capitaine Renard, *Colonisation au Congo français*, pp. 53–64; Cuvillier-Fleury, *Mise en valeur du Congo*, pp. 82, 73–103, 226–228.

120. Because the French Congo was only very marginally under French control, tax collection was at first an experiment. The policy, however, continued under Lamothe's successor, Albert Grodet (also a liberal), under specific orders from the ministry. See Coquery-Vidrovitch, *Congo au temps des compagnies concessionaires*, pp. 117–141.

121. Jules Lefébure, *Le régime des concessions au Congo* (Paris: "L'université de Paris," 1904), pp 122–148.

122. Capitaine Renard [president of the Union Congolaise], *Colonisation au Congo français*, p. 25; also Aspe-Fleurimont, *La Guinée française*, pp. 144–155.

123. The idea was probably inspired by reports about the South African Glen-Grey Act of 1894, one of the first instances of tax manipulation for the purpose of creating labor migration. In 1898, Gallieni experimented with taxation rates in Madagascar in order to provide laborers for French colonists. Manchuelle, "Forced Labor in French West Africa."

124. The principle of direct taxation in the French Congo had been in place since 1894; see Coquery-Vidrovitch, *Congo au temps des compagnies concessionnaires*, p. 119. (Coquery-Vidrovitch adds that its creation had been decided in 1897 "pour pallier aux difficultés de la crise financière dans laquelle se débatait la colonie." It was finally imposed in the most loyal areas in 1900.)

125. See, for example, the reports on the budget of French colonies in the French Senate; *Annales du Sénat*, 1903; 1905; 1906.

126. Coquery-Vidrovitch, *Congo au temps des compagnies concessionnaires*, pp. 132–135.

127. *Quinzaine coloniale*, vol. 16, 1st semester 1905, pp. 216–218.

128. Comité de défense des indigènes, "Lettre à Vigné d'Octon," *Le Temps*, 7 November 1899. Compare with Mary Kingsley, *West African Studies* (New York: Barnes and Noble, 1964; 1st ed. 1899), esp. pp. 294, 313, 317, 332.

129. Some of Brazza's papers and letters were published in 1906; see P. Savorgnan de Brazza, *Lettre à M. Paul Bourde écrite de Brazzaville à la veille de son retour en France sur les impressions et les conclusions de l'enquête qu'il vient de terminer au Congo (24 Août 1905)* (Paris: L. de Soye, 1906); Amédée Britsch, *Pour le Congo français: la dernière mission Brazza d'après le registre de correspondance inédit de P. Savorgnan de Brazza, extrait du Correspondant, le 10 janvier 1906* (Paris: L. de Soye, 1906); see also Félicien Challaye, *Le Congo français: la question internationale du Congo* (Paris: F. Alcan, 1909).

130. Interpellation of February 22, 1906, quoted by Challaye, *Congo français*, p. 193 note. See also Joseph Caillaux, *Agadir* (Paris: Albin Michel, 1919), pp. 55–56.

131. Louis and Stengers, *E. D. Morel's History of the Congo Reform Movement;* Catherine A. Cline, *E. D. Morel, 1873–1924* (Belfast: Blackstaff Press, 1980).

132. Louis and Stengers, *E. D. Morel's History of the Congo Reform Movement*, p. 97; see also pp. 79–81; Pierre Mille, *Le Congo Léopoldien* (Paris: Cahiers de la Quinzaine, 1905), p. 41. Morel, whose real name was Edmond Pierre Morel de Ville, was of French origin. He spoke French fluently and must have been quite at ease in liberal French circles that shared his belief in free trade and humanitarianism.

133. Critical debate of this question in Louis and Stengers, *E. D. Morel's History of the Congo Reform Movement*, pp. 252–256.

134. Morel, *The British Case in the French Congo* (New York: Negro University Press, 1969; 1st ed. London: Heinemann., 1903), p. 214. Clozel and Delafosse's names appear in Morel's *Affairs of West Africa* (London: Heinemann, 1902), pp. 171–173, 273. This book is an apology for the French methods of administration in West Africa. Morel translated and published two of Delafosse's articles in his newspaper the *West African Mail* in 1904 ("The Mystery of the Fulani" and "Where the Natives Build

Castles of Clay," January and September–December 1904, reference in E. Joucla, *Bibliographie de l'Afrique Occidentale française* (Paris: Société d'éditions gégraphiques, maritimes et coloniales, 1937), p. 291.

135. A report from Kayes expressed the opinion that the high frequency of migration among the Soninke of Kamera was due to the fact that villagers were constantly requisitioned to aid stranded vessels on the Senegal River. ANS 1E-44, Kayes, Yearly political report, 1903. I have discussed this question in Chapter Four.

136. Maurice Delafosse, "Sur les routes," article apparently published between 1912 and 1913 in *Dépêche coloniale*, republished in *Broussard ou les états d'âme d'un colonial* (Paris: Larose, 1922), pp. 197–203; Louise Delafosse, "Comment prit fin la carrière coloniale de Maurice Delafosse," pp. 107–108.

137. Académie des Sciences Coloniales, *Compte-rendu des séances, communications*, vol. 2, 1923–1924, p. 29 (meeting of 8 November 1923).

138. Camille Guy, "L'avenir de l'Afrique Equatoriale Française," *L'Afrique française*, January 1926, p. 10.

139. Gilles Sautter, *De l'Atlantique au fleuve Congo, une géographie du sous-peuplement. République du Congo. République Gabonaise* (Paris; Hague: Mouton, 1966), p. 982.

140. Maurice Delafosse, "Les points sombres de l'horizon en Afrique occidentale," *L'Afrique française*, no. 6, June 1922, pp. 271–285.

141. Delafosse argued as follows: The sedentary population of French West Africa amounted to 12 million persons. (For a variety of reasons, nomads were not subject to the draft; Buell, *Native Problem*, vol. 2, p. 12.) The number of adult males among them was about 2,730,000. Since military recruitments during the war had shown that 75 percent of young males in French West Africa were physically unfit, there were really only 622,500 able-bodied men susceptible to the draft. Current projects aimed to draft some 60,000 men per year. Since recruitments were for a period of three years, some 180,000 men were to be away from their farms at all times, leaving only 500,000 to tend the fields. One of the projects then under review in the French Parliament called for African conscripts to serve in France. Delafosse estimated that if such a project were carried out, some 20,000 draftees would either die every year or stay on in the metropolitan territory. As a result, in twenty-five years the 500,000 men making up French West Africa's labor force would disappear!

But Delafosse's figures were exaggerated. The proportion of men declared unfit for military service during the First World War, which Delafosse put at 75 percent *minimum*, was estimated by Marc Michel at about 30 percent *on average*. Moreover, the high percentages of physically unfit among potential draftees during the First World War probably resulted from draft evasion, as cripples and old men were deliberately presented to the draft. Delafosse, who was a high official in French West Africa during the war, cannot have been unaware of these facts. The number of 2,700,000 adult males he gives for a population of 12 million is also too low (it is less than one-fourth). Finally, the estimate of a loss of one-third of the African contingent in France, even counting the men who would simply stay in France (how did Delafosse expect to calculate this?), is certainly extravagant; Professor Marc Michel estimated *wartime* losses among Africans in France (during the First World War) to be one-fifth of the contingent, including, of course, loss of life on the battlefield and loss of life due to emergency wartime living conditions among the soldiers (Michel, *Appel à l'Afrique*, p. 472). Delafosse's exaggeration was perhaps deliberate: Delafosse himself admitted in one earlier writing that he deliberately exaggerated certain facts in order to draw attention to trends he thought were dangerous. Delafosse, "Sur les routes," pp. 202–203.

142. Delafosse, "Points sombres," p. 277 [my translation].

143. Michel, "Un programme réformiste en 1919," pp. 325–326; Louise Delafosse, "Comment prit fin la carrière coloniale de Maurice Delafosse," pp. 107–108.

144. See slightly different figures in Guiraud, *Arachide sénégalaise*, p. 37; Pheffer, "Railroads and Social Change," p. 513 (Source: Senegalese customs); David, *Navétanes*, p. 464 (Sources: various contemporary administrative reports, Chamber of Commerce meeting 1929; Portères report 1952). Note that the figures in David are dated by the year of their production and commercialization in Senegal, while figures in Guiraud and Pheffer are dated by the year of their export. Export figures are dated one year later than production figures since peanuts were harvested at the end of the year and exported at the beginning of the following year.

145. David, *Navétanes*, pp. 42–44.

146. Ibid., p. 45.

147. It was the one mentioned by Duranthon in his reports, see above.

148. David, *Navétanes*, p. 54.

149. Guiraud, *Arachide sénégalaise*, p. 37.

150. David, *Navétanes*, p. 57. Production and export figures in ibid., p. 464; Guiraud, *Arachide sénégalaise*, pp. 37–38; Pheffer, "Railroads and Social Change," p. 513.

151. ANS 2 G 18/25, Bakel, Political situation during the month of February 1918.

152. Pollet and Winter, *Société soninké*, p. 129.

153. David, *Navétanes*, pp. 54, 490, note 35.

154. The year 1922 was a very good one in Nioro. ANM 1E-36, No. 22, Nioro, Annual report 1922. There are no mentions of bad crops in the periodic reports from Kayes. And it was a good year in Senegal; David, *Navétanes*, p. 54.

155. ANM 1E-36, Yelimane, September 1924.

156. ANM 1E-36, Nioro, 1st quarter 1924. A similar problem affected the north of Gidimaxa in the cercle of Kayes. ANM 1E-19, Kayes, 2d quarter 1924.

157. The first mention of navetanes for the 1920s in the cercle of Nara dates from that year. ANM 1E-32, Nara, 3d quarter 1924.

158. ANM 1E-19, Kayes, No. 922, 28 May 1924.

159. David, *Navétanes*, pp. 118–120.

160. See Chapter One.

161. ANM 1E-32, Nara, 3d quarter 1924.

162. ANM 1E-36, Nioro, 1st quarter 1924.

163. These figures are discussed in Chapter Seven.

164. David, *Navétanes*, p. 122; Adams, *Terre et gens du fleuve*, p. 101.

165. I have used a median figure, between the 4,000 to 5,000 migrants mentioned by Duranthon in 1921 and the 7,000 to 8,000 reported in 1933.

166. ANM 1E-36, Nioro, 3d and 4th quarter 1925.

167. It is interesting to note that the annual amount of telegraphic money orders in Nioro (100,000 francs) was the same in 1924 as in 1912, even though the franc was now worth three times less. But transportation was much faster with the completion of the Thiès-Kayes railway in 1923, and Soninke migrants, who are still today suspicious of banks and government institutions (with some reason, as they are often cheated by corrupt employees), apparently preferred to entrust their remittances to Soninke traders or returning migrants. Lassana Diakho, interview, Dakar, 13 December 1979.

168. See testimony of Galadyo Tarawele, from Golmi (Gwey), who migrated as a navetane and a laborer in Dakar between 1929 and 1936, in David, *Navétanes*, p. 122. Also testimony of Jabe So, from Kungani (Gwey) who migrated as a navetane in 1936, Adams, *Terre et gens du fleuve*, p. 101.

169. ANM 1E-32, Nara, No. 550, 24 May 1933.

170. ANM 1E-61, Nioro, 2d quarter 1920.

171. David, *Navétanes*, p. 120.

172. ANM 1E-36, Nioro, Etat des hommes partis au Sénégal et non rentrés à la date du premier Avril 1921, joint au rapport No. 40.

173. The Jawando are a casted group of Fuulbe praise singers, but a branch of the Bacili family today renowned for its commercial success in Mali called Bacili jagoranu—"jogorane" is the Soninke equivalent of Jawando—allegedly once ruled "the territory around the city of Nioro," Bathily, *Portes de l'or*, p. 196. On the Jawando and Jariso, see Lartigue, "Notice géographique," pp. 118, 121.

174. Sources: the 1898 figures are from Lartigue, "Notice géographique"; the 1921 to 1923 figure for the subdivision of Yelimane comes from the 1922 census in ANM 1E-36, Nioro, Annual report 1922; the 1921 to 1923 figure for Kenyareme is calculated from data in ANM 1E-36, Nioro, 1st quarter 1923; the other figures come from an ongoing and therefore incomplete census made by Duranthon in 1921, ANM 1E-36, 3d quarter 1921.

175. ANM 1E-36, Nioro, 3d quarter 1921.

176. Lartigue, "Notice géographique," p. 120; ANM 1E-36, Nioro, 1st quarter 1923; ANM 1E-36, 1st quarter 1921.

177. Lartigue, "Notice géographique," p. 120.

178. ANM 1E-61, 3d quarter 1920; ANS 4 G 163, Bakel, Inspection report, January 1922.

179. ANM 1E-61, Nioro, Annual report 1911; ANS 4 G 163, Bakel, Inspection report, January 1922.

180. ANM 1E-36, Nioro, Extrait du rapport politique, 2d quarter 1933; 1st quarter 1933.

181. ANM 1E-36, Yelimane, September 1924.

182. David, *Navétanes*, p. 460.

183. On the process of settling in peanut-producing regions of Senegal, see Gabriel Rocheteau, "Société wolof et mobilité," *Cahiers de l'O.R.S.T.O.M.*, Série sciences humaines, vol. 12, 1975, pp. 3–18.

184. David, *Navétanes*, pp. 204–205; Pollet and Winter, *Société soninké*, pp. 260–261; ANM 1E-61, Nioro, 1st and 2d quarter 1925.

185. David, *Navétanes*, p. 120.

186. I did not get this impression from my informants.

187. Saint-Père relates that newly circumcised *(girikuto)* made themselves a pair of trousers and a smock. They were considered *girikuto* until these clothes were worn out. "As long as they are *girikuto* [young men] are not allowed to travel and to engage in trade; they must stay at home and work on the farm. If they ignored this prohibition, God would give them the idea of settling abroad, and they would never come back to their country." *Sarakollé du Guidimakha*, p. 80. In Jafunu, navetanes became migrants for the first time after the ceremony of the "taking of trousers," which occurs some time after circumcision and marks a young man's coming to adulthood. Pollet and Winter, *Société soninké*, p. 134.

188. See the case of Jabe So in Adams, *Terre et gens du fleuve*, pp. 99–100.

189. There is a compelling argument against the disorganization of Soninke families as a result of migration in the 1920s: Soninke families today remain much larger than families in other regions, and the control of elders is strong, in spite of the very strong migration toward France.

190. Adam Walaszek, "Preserving or Transforming Role? Migrants and Polish Territories in the Era of Mass Migrations," Unpublished, 1992. My special thanks to Professor Walaszek, of the Jagiellonian University of Krakow, for communicating to me this text.

191. Catherine Quiminal, *Gens d'ici, gens d'ailleurs. Migrations Soninké et transformations villageoises* (Paris: Christian Bourgois, 1991), esp. Chapter 6, pp. 110–146.

192. ANM 1E-36, Nioro, 3d quarter 1923.

193. Pollet and Winter, *Société soninké*, pp. 128, 439.

194. The impression of a crisis of the traditional family is reinforced by the fact that still today the Soninke are reluctant to solve matters of divorce through official channels, unless traditional channels have proved inoperative. Pollet and Winter, *Société soninké*, pp. 437–442.

195. F. de Kersaint-Gilly, "Essai sur l'évolution de l'esclavage en Afrique occidentale française. Son dernier stade au Soudan français, " *Bulletin du Comité d'Etudes Historiques et Scientifiques de l'A.O.F.*, 1924, vol. 9, pp. 469–478.

196. Adams, *Terre et gens du fleuve*, p. 73.

197. ANS 2 G 20/22, Bakel, January 1920.

198. Adams, *Terre et gens du fleuve*, p. 72.

199. I. D. Bathily, "Notices," p. 86.

200. ANM 1E-19 Kayes, Report, July 1929.

201. Pollet and Winter, *Société soninké*, pp. 260–261.

202. Saint-Père, *Sarakollé du Guidimakha*, p. 183.

203. The criticism was made by Governor Sanmarco, himself a former liberal colonial administrator, in *Colonisateur colonisé*, pp. 60–63.

Chapter 7

1. *L'Ouest Africain Français*, 12 March 1929, quoted by Adrian Adams, *Long voyage des gens du fleuve*, p. 47. Colonial administrators in the valley had criticized the railway project even before it was completed, see ANS 4G 167, Rapport d'inspection concernant le cercle de Matam, 1922. For a forceful criticism of the railway with reference to the Upper Senegal region, see Chief Ibrahima Jaman Bacili, "Bakel sous les cendres de l'oubli," ["Bakel under the ashes of oblivion"] *L'A.O.F.*, 22 November 1946, in I. D. Bathily, "Notices," p. 95–99.

2. For example, Adams, *Long voyage des gens du fleuve*, pp. 46–48.

3. ANSOM, TP AOF, 28, 3, Rapport Mathy, 1904.

4. ANS O 62, Commandant Belle to Gov. general French West Africa, No. 29, 2 June 1903.

5. ANSOM, TP 91, 1, Rapport Rougier, 3 June 1903.

6. Apt formulation by Assane Seck, paraphrasing the Rougier report (ANSOM TP 91, 1, 3 June 1903), *Dakar, métropole ouest-africaine* (Dakar: I.F.A.N., 1970), p. 394.

7. ANSOM TP 91, 1, Rapport Rougier, 3 June 1903.

8. ANSOM, TP 91, 1, Rapport Rougier, 3 June 1903; ANSOM, TP AOF, 28, 3, Rapport Mathy, 1904.

9. Additionally, a railway could improve the transportation of European civil servants to the Soudan, resulting in substantial savings in pay (civil servants were paid during their journey to the Soudan) and lives (sick civil servants could be sent by railway to the coast for treatment), ANSOM TP 91, 1, Rapport Rougier, 3 June 1903.

10. It was proposed in 1878 to build a railway between Saint-Louis and Médine, which would connect with the projected Dakar–Saint-Louis railway and also with a projected railway to the Niger River Valley (this third section was eventually built as the Kayes-Niger railway). A study mission showed that the Saint-Louis–Médine railway would have to be built at some distance from the river in order to avoid building bridges across countless small tributaries, and that the project was unfeasible at the time because of Fuutanke hostility to it. The French Parliament rejected the project in 1880. See Paul Gaffarel, *Le Sénégal et le Soudan français* (Paris: Delagrave, 1892), pp. 185–188; Idowu, "Conseil General of Senegal," pp. 19–20; Seck, *Dakar*, p. 300.

11. Such a project was studied in the nineteenth century. See Marc Merle neveu et Robert, "Chemin de fer de Médine à Saint-Louis (Sénégal) adressé à M. le Ministre des Travaux Publics, pour être soumis à la Commission supérieure du Transsaharien," in *Haut-Sénégal, Concessions aurifères et chemin de fer de Médine au littoral par le Djoloff et le Ferlo* (Bordeaux: Gounouilhou, 1880), pp. 81–96.

12. Which had been anticipated from the 1910s; Pheffer, "Railroads and Social Change," p. 251.

13. Pheffer, "Railroads and Social Change," pp. 224–258. In my opinion, Pheffer overemphasizes the administration's wish to develop the harbor of Dakar and does not realize the importance of the 1902 transportation breakdown in demonstrating the river's unreliability. See ANSOM, T.P. 91, 1, Chemin de fer Thiès-Kayes, Mission

Rougier-Belle, 1903–1904. On the work necessary to improve the river, see ANSOM, T.P. 23, 3, Mission hydrographique du Sénégal, 1904; T.P. 28, 1, Amélioration de la navigabilité du Sénégal, 1904. Note sur la situation des études du régime du fleuve Sénégal, 1896; T.P. 28, 3, Avant-projet d'aménagement du Sénégal (Rapport Mathy, 1904).

14. Seck, *Dakar*, pp. 368; 170.

15. Ibid., p. 372.

16. Brévié, "Le déblocage du Soudan—Deux grands ports: Dakar et Abidjan," *L'Afrique française*, 1932, p. 845.

17. Ibid., p. 846.

18. Seck, *Dakar*, p. 372. It is true that an important part of river traffic was comprised of coal for the Kayes-Niger railway.

19. Seck, *Dakar*, pp. 349–489; and "Les escales du fleuve Sénégal," *Revue de géographie de l'Afrique occidentale*, Nos. 1–2, 1965, passim.

20. Saint-Père, *Sarakollé du Guidimakha*, p. 51.

21. ANS 2G 34-66, Bakel, Yearly Political Report, 1934.

22. Adams, *Terre et gens du fleuve*, pp. 27–29.

23. The reference is important because, among the Soninke, women traditionally grew peanuts. The reference shows that the custom had no absolute binding value and that men also grew peanuts when they found it profitable to do so.

24. Ibid., pp. 74–75.

25. Boyer, *Un peuple de l'ouest soudanais*, p. 110.

26. Bradley et al., *Guidimakha mauritanien*, p. 144.

27. Adams, *Terre et gens du fleuve*, p. 99. In Nioro, the only problem reported during the decade was locust infestation in 1933, which caused extensive damages, although it was not necessary for the administration to send food aid. In Kayes, only a partial drought in 1932, which caused extensive damages to the peanut crop, is reported. ANM 1E-36: 1E-19.

28. Ibid., pp. 80–81. Estimates of cereal production are usually made on the basis of one hectare of cultivation per adult male and 700 to 800 kilograms of millet per hectare. It should be noted that Adrian Adams is a privileged observer since she has been living more than a decade in Kungani.

29. Ibid., p. 62.

30. ANS 2G 34–66, Bakel, Pol. Report, 1934.

31. Jan S. Hogendorn, *Nigerian Groundnut Exports: Origins and Early Development* (Zaria; Ibadan: Ahmadu Bello University Press; Oxford University Press, 1978), passim; figures on pp. 98, 133. Soudanese figures after 1932 in David, *Navétanes*, p. 138.

32. Pheffer, "Railroads and Social Change in Senegal," p. 510.

33. Seck, "Escales," see pp. 82–84.

34. Pollet and Winter, *Société soninké*, p. 99.

35. Including Bakel: 2,463 persons; ANS 2 G 37–88, Bakel, Pol. report, 1937.

36. David, *Navétanes*, p. 132. If we look at *departures* from the Soudan (excluding migrants reported as in Senegal already at the time of the survey), out of 4,811 depar-

tures from these cercles (Nioro excepted), 3,561 (74 percent) left by railway. Ibid., p. 133. On the influence on navetanat of the completion of the railway, see ANM 1E-19, Telegramme-lettre, Delegate Kayes to Gov. Soudan, No, 922, 28 May 1924.

37. David, *Navétanes*, pp. 127–141.

38. Ibid., p. 138.

39. For Henri Labouret, the decline was due to the low returns of migration this year; Labouret, "Main-d'oeuvre dans l'ouest africain," pp. 242–243. There apparently was a temporary crisis that year, but overall peanut prices stayed stable (and on the whole quite high) during the entire period from 1920 to 1930 (price per kilogram: 1924, 1 franc; 1925, 1.11 francs; 1926, 1.52 francs; 1927, 1.52 francs; 1928, 1.43 francs; 1929, 1.36 francs—the drop began in 1930 (0.98 franc) and especially 1931 (0.67 franc). Guiraud, *L'arachide sénégalaise*, p. 37. It is interesting to note that the Gambia, which had a much older history of navetanat, began experiencing a shortage in seasonal farm labor as early as 1922; David, *Navétanes*, p. 205; also 209–215ff.

40. David, *Navétanes*, pp. 61–64.

41. Ibid., pp. 73–74.

42. David, *Navétanes*, pp. 82–83. Their visit appeared to reverse roles, with the commandant of Nioro complaining to Duranthon about alleged lack of official action to force navetanes to return to their homeland after their agricultural campaign in Senegal. ANM 1E-36, Nioro, Extract of pol. report, 3d quarter 1933; see also 1st quarter 1933. A decade before it had been Duranthon, while an administrator in Nioro, who had made this kind of complaint. (See Chapter Six.)

43. Sources: Soudan 1932, David, *Navétanes*, p. 132; Guinea 1936, ibid., p. 152; Guinea 1937, ibid., p. 153; Soudan 1937, ibid., p. 134; Soudan 1943 (forced recruitment), ibid., p. 300; Soudan 1944(forced recruitment), ibid., p. 303; Soudan 1945 (return to free recruitment), ibid., p. 305; Soudan and Guinea 1947 (1947a), ibid., p. 256; Soudan 1947, other figures (1947b), ibid., p. 307; Soudan 1948, ibid., p. 307; Soudan 1950 ("navétanes officiels" sent between 9 May and 14 June), ibid., p. 309; Soudan 1952 ("départs officiels"), ibid., p. 311; Soudan 1955 ("enregistrés à Tambacounda"), ibid., p. 387 (the figure for Nioro comprises both Nioro and Yelimane).

44. On the distinction between these two categories of migrants, see Chapter Six.

45. These figures were probably incomplete (there were no figures for Koutiala, for example), but the dominance of districts with a Soninke population appears in the figures until 1947.

46. ANM 1E-36, Nioro, Extract from the Pol. Report, 2d quarter 1933.

47. Moussa Oumar Sy, "Provinces, cantons et villages du Soudan Français des origines à l'indépendance," *Bulletin de l'I.F.A.N.*, vol. 40, ser. B, no. 3, 1978, pp. 489–512.

48. It should be noted that the cercle of Baninko (Kutiala) was merged with Bamako in 1935; thus the large increase in figures of navetanes for Bamako between 1932 and 1937 may also reflect this administrative change.

49. David, *Navétanes*, p. 113.

50. Saint-Père, *Sarakollé du Guidimakha*, pp. 52, 183.

51. ANS 2 G33-67, Bakel, Yearly Pol. Report, 1933 (see p. 9, "Mouvement des populations—émigration") refers to migration to the "cercles of the [railway] line where gains are higher," which may still mean navetanat, but ANS 2G 34-66, Bakel, Yearly Pol. Report 1934 (pp. 9–10, "Mouvement des populations. Emigration"), speaks about "young people attracted by the trading posts [*escales*] of the railway line and by Dakar."

52. See Chapter Five.

53. ANS 2G 46/77, Bakel, Rapport d'ensemble au 30 mai 1946.

54. David, *Navétanes*, pp. 120–122.

55. Adams, *Terre et gens du fleuve*, pp. 99–104.

56. ANM 1E-32, Nara, 3d quarter 1924; 1st quarter 1927.

57. ANM 1E-32, Nara, 1st quarter 1926.

58. ANM 1E-36, Nioro, 1st and 2d quarters 1925.

59. ANM 1E-36, Nioro, 4th quarter 1927.

60. ANM 1E-36, Nioro, Extract from pol. report, 2d quarter 1933.

61. ANM 1E-36, Nioro, Rapport de tournée Youri, Sandaré, Samantara, Lakamané, Sansanké, Sambadigané, Diéma, Fougoune, Tinkaré, 31 Dec. 1941.

62. ANM 1E-36, Rapport de tournée effectuée du 21 Septembre au 7 Octobre 1944 par M. Cancel Jean, Administrateur Adjoint des Colonies, Adjoint au Commandant de cercle de Nioro.

63. Pollet and Winter, *Société soninké*, pp. 126–139, and 140–142.

64. Villagers in Kungani ("Jamané") made the same assertion to Adrian Adams in 1975 to 1976; *Long voyage des gens du fleuve*, p. 75.

65. Labouret, "Main d'oeuvre dans l'Ouest africain," p. 247 (there is a printing mistake in the article, which reports "17,000" francs). The income of 1,700 francs was from an exceptional year: in normal years, navetanes brought back between 1,200 and 1,500 francs; Labouret, "Grande détresse de l'arachide," p. 732.

66. It is interesting to compare African urban wages with average industrial wages in France at the same time, which were 8,000 francs a year. Brown and Browne, *A Century of Pay*, p. 201. One would have perhaps expected a greater gap between African and French wages.

67. They made in 1922 francs between 3.50 francs (beginning wages) and 4.50 to 5 francs a day; Senegal, Conseil Colonial, session ordinaire, 4 November 1922, p. 80. The franc between 1918 and 1926 was generally worth three times less than the pre-1918 franc. After 1926, with the "franc Poincaré," it was stabilized at five times less than the pre-1918 franc.

68. Monique Lakroum, "Les salaires dans le port de Dakar," *Revue française d'histoire d'outre-mer*, vol. 63, nos. 232–233, 1976, pp. 640–653. She gives a figure for a laborer's yearly income similar to mine (about. 4,000 francs a year).

69. See Chapter Four.

70. See Pheffer, "Railroads and Social Change," pp. 322–323; Saint-Père, *Sarakollé du Guidimakha*, p. 52. Saint-Père mentions that Soninke locomotive drivers were employed in the railways in Senegal, French Soudan, Morocco, French Guinea, and the Ivory Coast; see also Chapter Five. There were also Soninke laborers especially on

the Dakar–Saint-Louis railway. Migrants probably obtained such jobs as a result of working seasonally as laborers employed in the building of these railways. Pheffer, "Railroads and Social Change," pp. 312, 345 note 58.

71. ANS 13G 201, No. 1, Bakel, December 1898, Pol. Comm. and Agr. Report: ANS 2D 4-12, Bakel, Maubert, 1904.

72. ANM 1E-36, Nioro, 1st and 2d quarter 1925.

73. Michel Samuel, *Le Prolétariat africain noir en France* (Paris: Maspéro, 1978), p. 58.

74. Robert Delavignette, *Paris-Soudan-Bourgogne* (Paris: Grasset, 1935), pp. 107–108; see also David, *Navétanes*, p. 106.

75. The growth was most spectacular in Siin-Saalum, whose urban population was multiplied tenfold over a period of ten years from 1925 to 1934. Sources of table: Pheffer, "Railways and Social Change in Senegal," pp. 521–522; I have no figure for Dakar in 1925, so I used a figure for 1926 from Seck, *Dakar*, p. 211. There are similar figures (although less detailed) for the urban population throughout the first half of this century in the *Annuaire statistique de l'A.O.F.*, 1949, vol. 1, pp. 83–88; see also for Dakar, Seck, *Dakar*, pp. 210–211.

76. See Seck, *Dakar*, pp. 334–335. A boom in construction had already begun in Dakar after 1922; ibid., pp. 113–114.

77. Apart from harbor, road, and railway building, public works construction included water conveyance for major cities in French West Africa. Brévié, "Situation générale de l'Afrique occidentale française," p. 42; on public works in general see pp. 42–45. Work on the Dakar harbor was interrupted only in 1943, due to the war; Seck, *Dakar*, p. 335.

78. Chatelain, *Migrants temporaires en France*, pp. 775–895; Raison-Jourde, *Colonie auvergnate de Paris*, pp. 86–87; Chevalier, *Formation de la population parisienne*, pp. 110–111.

79. See Labouret, "Main d'oeuvre dans l'Ouest africain," pp. 243, 247; see also for comparison to migrants to the Gold Coast, ibid., pp. 246–247.

80. ANS 9 G-86, Gov. general FWA to Gov. Mauritania, No. 376 APA, 30 June 1933. The Soninke were probably not new in the building trade. As we have seen (Chapter Three), a large number of Soninke were recruited in Dakar for the Congo Free State in the 1890s. This was the period when the building of the city and harbor of Dakar effectively began. (See Johnson, *Emergence of Black Politics*, pp. 31–37).

81. Seck, *Dakar;* Régine Van Chi-Bonnardel, *Vie de relations au Sénégal* (Dakar: I.F.A.N., 1978); Suret-Canale, *French Colonialism*, pp. 210–212.

82. Adams, *Terre et gens du fleuve*, pp. 99, 101.

83. Ibid., p. 89.

84. Ibid., p. 90; Samuel, *Prolétariat africain en France*, pp. 242–243.

85. Adams, *Terre et gens du fleuve*, pp. 67–92.

86. See Chapter Five.

87. Ibid., p. 80.

88. See Chapter Two.

89. Denise Bouche, "Dakar pendant la Seconde Guerre Mondiale: problèmes de

surpeuplement," in *Le sol, la parole et l'écrit. Mélanges en hommage à Raymond Mauny* (Paris: Société Française d'Histoire d'Outre-Mer, 1981), p. 965.

90. See graph "Heads of immigrants households according to ethnic group and date of arrival in Dakar (Polls Dagoudane Pikine 1959 and Family Budgets 1960)," *Recensement démographique de Dakar (1955)* (Paris: République du Sénégal, Ministère du Plan, du Développement et de la Coopération Technique, Service de la Statistique et de la Mécanographie, 1962), vol. 2, D 30, p. 48.

91. Ibid., vol. 1, p. 6.

92. Samuel, *Prolétariat africain noir en France*, p. 58–59.

93. *Recensement démographique de Dakar (1955)*, vol. 1, p. 70.

94. See immediately below.

95. The population of Gwey and Bakel, according to a 1937 census, was 12,198. ANS 2 G 37– 88, Bakel, yearly political report, 1937. I have no figure for Kammera, but it can be safely assumed that its population was equal to that of Gwey. There were 15,000 Soninke in the Mauritanian half of Gidimaxa and an equivalent number in the Soudanese half in the mid 1920s. Saint-Père, *Sarakollé du Gidimaxa*, p. 19. Finally, to these figures should be added the Soninke population of the Matam region (Damga), which numbered 10,000 in 1904 (I unfortunately have no later figure for Damga). ANS 1 G 292, Notice sur le cercle de Matam, 1904. Increasing this latter figure by one-third, we obtain a total of 67,000 for the Upper Senegal.

96. Samuel, *Prolétariat africain en France*, pp. 58–59.

97. See ibid., tables pp. 73–76.

98. Most Soninke chambres in the 1930s were in the downtown area; Bakel (Rue Raffenel), Kungani (Rue Raffenel), Jagili (Rue Sandiniéry prolongée), Gucube (Rue Escarfait), Muderi (Rue Valmy), Manayeli (Rue Félix-Faure), Tiyaabu (Rue Thiers); ANS 9 G-86, gov.-general FWA to gov. Mauritania, 30 June 1933; interviews Bakeli Jabira and Gay Jabira, Kungani, 17 August 1982 (location of Kungani chambre); ANS 2 D 4-21, Bakel, Affaires des Bathily, Réclamation des Bathily de Dakar Samba Diama et consorts et de Samba Kadiata chef du Goye Inférieur contre l'assesseur du tribunal Fodé Saloum de Tuabo. Correspondance. Rapports. 1917–1918 (Tuabo chambre). After the war, most appear to have moved to Niaye Thioker (e.g., Jagili) or Médine (Kungani); interviews Bakeli and Gay Jabira, and complementary information Jabe So, Kungani, 17 August 1982. On the history of Dakar, see Seck, *Dakar*, esp. Part One; and *Recensement démographique de Dakar (1955)*.

99. Samuel, *Prolétariat africain en France*, p. 243. See also p. 242.

100. Adams, *Long voyage des gens du fleuve*, pp. 75–82; *Terre et gens du fleuve*, 80–90.

101. A. Hauser, *Rapport d'enquête sur les travailleurs des Industries Manufacturières de la région de Dakar* (Dakar: Université de Dakar, I.F.A.N., 1965); see also by the same author, *Les ouvriers de Dakar. Etude psychosociologique* (Paris: O.R.S.T.O.M., 1968).

102. Hauser, *Rapport d'enquête*, pp. 19–20. Of the workers surveyed, 6.3 percent were Soninke.

103. Hauser, *Rapport*, p. 21. It is worth noting that the Petersen factory was estab-

lished before the Second World War, in 1932 according to Seck. *Dakar*, p. 83. Employment in oil pressing plants appears as a logical outgrowth of earlier employment as navetanes.

104. See above.

105. Hauser, *Rapport*, p. 21.

106. Ibid., pp. 38, 40, 64, 68, 80.

107. Ibid., p. 75.

108. Ibid., pp. 38, 80

109. Hauser, *Rapport*, p. 49.

110. Chatelain, *Migrants temporaires en France*, especially pp. 880–1005.

111. Samuel, *Prolétariat africain noir en France*, p. 58.

112. Daniel Bleneau and Gérard La Cognata, "Evolution de la population de Bamako," *Etudes maliennes*, No. 3, 1972, p. 26.

113. Ibid., p. 33.

114. Ibid., p. 28.

115. Ibid., p. 33.

116. In addition, I have no data on the proportion of males, females, and children among the Bamako "Soninke" population.

117. Colette Le Blanc, "Un village de la vallée du Sénégal: Amadi-Ounaré." *Cahiers d'outre-mer*, vol. 17, no. 66, 1964, pp. 145–147.

118. Ibid., pp. 145–146.

119. *Terre et gens du fleuve*, p. 85.

120. Ibid., p. 89.

121. *Long voyage des gens du fleuve*, p. 77.

122. *Terre et gens du fleuve*, pp. 90; 91; *Long voyage des gens du fleuve*, p. 77.

123. Adams, *Terre et gens du fleuve*, p. 85; Suuleyman Saaxo, Interview, Dakar, 17 December 1978.

124. See, e.g., for Jafunu, Pollet and Winter, *Société soninké*, p. 116.

125. See Chapter One.

126. René Caillé, for example, stayed at the home of a Soninke during his visit to Tengrela in the early nineteenth century. Paul Marty, *Etudes sur l'Islam en Côte d'Ivoire* (Paris: Leroux, 1922), p. 122.

127. Marty, *Etudes sur l'Islam en Côte d'Ivoire*, p. 174; for other examples, see pp. 121, 123.

128. ANM 1E-36, Nioro, No. 22, Annual report 1922; 1E-32, Nara, 3d quarter 1924; 1st quarter 1927; 1st quarter 1932. See also Boyer, *Un peuple de l'ouest soudanais*, p. 110.

129. On Malian (Mande) migration to the Ivory Coast, see Marguerat, "Des ethnies et des villes"; Françoise Dureau, *Migration et urbanisation. Le cas de la Côte d'Ivoire* (Paris: ORSTOM, 1987); Jean-Loup Amselle, *Les négociants de la savane. Histoire et organisation sociale des Kooroko (Mali)* (Paris: Anthropos, 1977), pp. 131–142. On Mande migration to the Ivory Coast in the precolonial period, see Person, *Samori*.

130. Saint-Père, *Sarakollé du Guidimakha* [1925], p. 52; Marty, *Etudes sur l'Islam au Sénégal*, pp. 128–129. Migrants from Soudan were employed in the building of the railway in the Ivory Coast in the 1910s, David, *Navétanes*, p. 123.

131. ANS 2G 34-66, Bakel, Yearly report 1934, Census; see also ANS 2G 34-66, Bakel, Pol. Report annuel 1934, pp. 9–10, "Movement of populations. Emigration" and ANS 2G 40-91, Bakel, Yearly political report 1940.

132. Le Blanc, "Un village de la vallée du Sénégal," pp. 145–146. On Bouaké, see *Recensement démographique de Bouaké, Juillet-Août 1958* (République de la Côte d'Ivoire: n.p., [ca. 1960]).

133. *Terre et gens du fleuve*, p. 79; see also *Long voyage des gens du fleuve*, p. 80.

134. Adams, *Terre et gens du fleuve*, pp. 79, 84, 88; *Long voyage des gens du fleuve*, p. 81; ANM 1E-36, Rapport de tournée Youri, Sandara, Samantara, Lakamané, Sansanké, Sambadigané, Diéma, Tougoune, Tinkaré, 1941; Rapport de tournée effectuée du 21 septembre au 7 octobre 1944 par M. Cancel, Jean, administrateur-adjoint des colonies, adjoint au commandant de cercle de Nioro; Boyer, *Un peuple de l'ouest africain*, p. 110.

135. Al-Haj Mamadu Jaaxo, Kungani, 12 August 1982.

136. Interviews in Dakar of Lasana Jaaxo (nephew of Kinshasa's first *cadi*) 13 December 1979; 24 January 1980; Papa Kane (Senegalese official and scholar, born in the Congo), 9 January 1980; Lasana Ndaw, 17 December 1979; and interviews in Kungani of Al-Haj Mamadu Jaaxo (last Soninke *cadi* of Kinshasa), 11, 13, 15 August 1982.

137. Lasana Jaaxo, 13 December 1979.

138. Al-Haj Maxan Darame (Soninke *cadi* of Brazzaville before Senegalese and Malians were expelled from Congo), Bamako, 1 September 1982.

139. Al-Haj Maxan Darame and Xadi Darame, with reference to migrants from the village of Tafasiriga (Kamera). Bamako, 1 September 1982.

140. Al-Haj Mamadu Jaaxo, Kungani, 13 August 1982; Papa Kane, Dakar, 9 January 1980; Lasana Jaaxo, Dakar, 13 December 1979.

141. Al-Haj Mamadu Jaaxo, Kungani, 13 August 1982.

142. See Adams, *Terre et gens du fleuve*, pp. 75–76.

143. Indeed that same informant mentioned that leftover space could be rented to tenants.

144. Sandra T. Barnes, *Patrons and Power: Creating a Political Community in Metropolitan Lagos* (Bloomington: Indiana University Press, 1986).

145. By 1935, cloth was bought in Lagos with money transferred from banks in the Congos to banks in Nigeria. Lasana Jaaxo, interview, Dakar, 13 December 1979.

146. Saydu Nay So, Dakar, 21 December 1979. Kola nuts were at first imported for the migrants' consumption, but later were adopted by the Zairians and the Congolese.

147. Lasana Ndaw, Dakar, 17 December 1979.

148. Chiefs were also elected; they served as intermediaries with the colonial administration and for this reason were chosen before the Second World War among the Wolof, many of whom spoke French and were French citizens. Papa Kane, Dakar, 9 January 1980; Al-Haj Mamadu Jaaxo, Kungani, 12 August 1982; Al-Haj Maxan Darame, Bamako, 1 September 1982; Jean Comhaire, "Note sur les musulmans de Léopoldville," *Zaïre*, 1948, II, 3, pp. 303–304; Al-Haj Maxan Darame, 1 September 1982; Lasana Ndaw, 21 December 1979.

149. When a bull was slaughtered in Kinshasa, its head was sent to the Tanjigora (Jaaxo) family (which held the office of *cadi*, see immediately below). This was a customary honor reserved to chiefs among the Soninke. Lasana Jaaxo, Dakar, 24 January 1980. Also Lasana Ndaw, Dakar, 17 December 1979; Al-Haj Mamadu Jaaxo, Kungani, 13 August 1982; ANF (Aix-en-Provence) 10 F (17), sous-dossier "Léopoldville, 1948–55"; Al-Haj Maxan Darame; Al-Haj Mamadu Jaaxo.

150. Lasana Jaaxo, Dakar, 13 December 1979; Al-Haj Mamadu Jaaxo, Kungani, 13 August 1982. "Since a *talibé* could not be the chief of his marabout," the Tanjigora became from the beginning chiefs of the Soninke in Zaire, Lasana Ndaw, Dakar, 17 December 1979. On the beginnings of Soninke migration to Zaire, see Chapter Five.

151. Interestingly, whereas the Darame were dominant in Gajaaga, the Jaaxo dominated in Kinshasa, then a booming commercial metropolis, while the Darame had to remain content with Brazzaville, the sleepy capital of French Equatorial Africa. This situation apparently provided new fuel to the traditional rivalry between the two families.

152. Samir Amin gives a figure of 4,000 to 5,000 "Senegalese" in Zaire. Of these, 1,000 were really from Senegal and were mostly Soninke. Two thousand or more (half of the "Senegalese") were Malians, "and especially, Guineans" (these were more recent migrants); this suggests that a little less than half of this figure were Malians, most certainly Soninke. A thousand or more (one-fourth of the "Senegalese") were Hausa migrants. Amin, *Monde des affaires sénégalais*, p. 163. I do not have figures for the Congo.

153. J. S. La Fontaine, *City Politics: A Study of Léopoldville, 1962–63* (Cambridge: Cambridge University Press, 1970), p. 91.

154. Al-Haj Maxan Darame, Bamako, 1 September 1982.

155. On plantations, Jabe So, Kungani, 15 August 1982.

156. Amin, *Monde des affaires sénégalais*, p. 165.

157. Ibid., pp. 163–165. To convert from CFA francs to dollars, I have used the standard 1960s rate of 5 French francs to 1 dollar; 1 CFA franc equalled 0.02 French franc.

158. Professor Xadi Darame (a Wahabi, and son of Al-Haj Maxan Darame, last Soninke cadi of Brazzaville), Bamako, September 1982.

159. ANS 21 G 57, Colonie du Sénégal, Inscription maritime to M. l'Administrateur de l'inscription maritime, Marseille, 28 January 1920.

160. ANS 21 G 115 (48), Le chef du service de l'inscription maritime du Sénégal à M. le Délégué du Gouvernement du Sénégal à Dakar, No. 145, 24 February 1923.

161. ANSOM Senegal XI, 48.

162. Such neglect also occurred in Dakar, although less frequentlyp; ANS 21 G 57, Senegal, Inscription maritime, Dakar to Administrator, Inscription maritime, Marseilles, 28 January 1920.

163. Jabe So, Kungani, 17 August 1982.

164. ANS 21 G 57, Senegal, Inscription maritime, Dakar to Administrator, Inscription maritime, Marseilles, 28 January 1920.

165. ANS 21 G 57, Senegal, Inscription maritime, Dakar to Administrator, Inscription maritime, Marseilles, 28 January 1920.

166. See ANS 21 G 115 (48), Head of Register of Sailors *(inscription maritime)* of Senegal to Delegate of government of Senegal in Dakar, No. 145, 24 February 1923; ANSOM, Slotfom III, 41 (3).

167. ANSOM III, 41 (whole file).

168. ANSOM, Slotfom III, 41, Ministry of Colonies to Under-Secretary of State to Public Works in charge of Ports, Merchant Marine and Fisheries, No. 1460, 5 June 1926.

169. See esp. ANSOM Slotfom III, 41, Gov.-gen. FWA to CAI, Paris, No. 1157 AP/I, 27 December 1930. Not all stowaways were undocumented; ship officials appear to have tolerated or even facilitated the irregular passage to France of documented sailors by employing them as unpaid casual labor.

170. ANSOM Slotfom III, 41, Head Inscription maritime of Senegal, to Delegate of CAI, Marseilles, No. 473, 24 July 1931.

171. ANSOM III, 41; e.g., Delegate CAI Marseilles to Head, Inscription maritime Dakar, No. 1428, 2 October 1933.

172. Suuleyman Saaxo, Dakar, Dec. 17, 1978. Musa Saaxo was the leader of the migrants from Jawara in Dakar. See ANS 2 D 4/21, Bakel, Affaire Moussa Sakho.

173. ANS, unclassified document, Ct. Matam to Gov. Senegal, No. 42, 17 September 1937; ANSOM Slotfom III, 41, Gov.-gen. FWA to Min. Colonies, No. 19 DS, 17 May 1932; Magatte's role was mentioned to me by several former sailors. For more on Magatte, see ANS 21 G 115 (48), Government-General, Direction de la police et de la sûreté générale, No. 119, 12 May 1923.

174. ANSOM, Slotfom III, 27, see Reports by agent "Ernest" to M. Lucien Harlée, Administrateur des Colonies, No. 1, 7 July 1926; No 3, 12 July 1926; No 4, 14 July 1926.

175. ANS 21 G 44, Delegate CAI Marseilles to Dir. Pol. Affairs, Ministry of Colonies, 21 February 1930.

176. Collective interview with former sailors who had begun employment in the 1930s, held at the chambre of the village of Muderi (Gwey), Dakar, 21 December 1979. ANS 2 G 30-67, Bakel, Rapport politique, 1930; 2 G 30-69, 1930; 2 G 33-67, 1933; 2 G 34-66, 1934; 2 G 35-81, 1935, etc.; ANS 2 G 34- 92, Matam, Rapport politique annuel, 1934; ANS 2 G-33-15, Mauritania, Rapport politique annuel, 1938; 2 G 39-1, 1939.

177. Mamadu Jimera, during general conversation on the prestige of sailors, with Abdulay Sakiné (sailor for twenty-seven years, beginning in 1929), Dakar, 13 December 1979.

178. Gay Jabira, Kungani, 17 August 1982.

179. See Chapter Six.

180. I. D. Bathily, "Notices socio-historiques," p. 98.

181. David, *Navétanes*, p. 120.

182. ANS 4 G 163, Rapport d'inspection concernant le cercle de Bakel, January 1922. Parents often wrote to the French administrator in Bakel to obtain information

about young men who had left without their consent and to try to prevent them from obtaining sailing documents in Dakar; interview, Lasana Ndaw (former sailor), Dakar, 21 December 1979.

183. [*Sic*], instead of the correct plural, *caporaux*. The name could come from Italian or Provençal.

184. Saydu Nay So, Dakar, 21 December 1979.

185. ANSOM, Slotfom III, 27, Delegate CAI to Pol. Affairs, Paris, No. 2313, 26 August 1929.

186. There is unfortunately no comprehensive information on these *bars* and hotels in Marseilles, but the Soninke had their own *bar* there; see ANS 21 G 44, Delegate CAI to Min. Colonies, Dir, Pol. Affairs, No. 229, 21 February 1930; and below on Tumaani Sangare. A 1931 document lists the cafes frequented by Blacks in Bordeaux: one *bar* was frequented by the Senegalese and Soudanese (Soninke, Futanke, Wolof, Bambaras, and also Mossi and Susu); two were frequented by Casamançais (southern Senegal); one by Cameroonians (Duala), Baule, and Fanti; and two were ethnically mixed. ANSOM VI, 8, Bordeaux, Commissariat spécial, 12 June 1931.

187. On these organizations, see J. S. Spiegler, "Aspects of Nationalist Thought among French-Speaking West Africans," D. Phil. thesis, Oxford University, Nuffield College, 1968; Philippe Dewitte, *Les mouvements nègres en France, 1919–1939* (Paris: L'Harmattan, 1985).

188. See ANSOM Slotfom III, 36; ANS 17 G 62, No. 17; and ANS 21 G 44. One important reason for Kouyaté's failure was that the LDRN was then committed to the deportation of undocumented sailors. Kouyaté was also opposed in principle to the emigration of Africans to Europe. ANSOM, Slotfom III, 36, Ligue de défense de la race nègre to Minister of Public Works [and Marine], 24 Apr. 1930.

189. ANSOM, Slotfom III, 41, Delegate CAI Marseilles to Inscription maritime, Marseilles, 15 May 1933; Delegate CAI Marseilles to Direction Political Affairs, 5 June 1936.

190. Spiegler, "Aspects of Nationalist Thought," p. 208; see also ANSOM, Slotfom VI, 8, Commissaire spécial Chauvineau to Directeur Sureté Générale (Contrôle de la police administrative), à Paris, 18 January 1932.

191. ANSOM, Slotfom III, 45, Minister of Interior, Direction de la Sureté Générale, to Minister of Colonies, No. 2178, 12 February 1935; on Diara's activity in the Ligue, see Spiegler, "Aspects of Nationalist Thought," pp. 206, 208 and passim. See also ANSOM, Slotfom II, 36, Report of Agent Paul, Ligue de Défense de la Race Nègre, General Assembly, 3 May 1930.

192. My opinion on this was confirmed by Professor G. Wesley Johnson, who is currently writing a political history of Senegal in the interwar period, in conversations, 1986.

193. Spiegler, "Aspects of Nationalist Thought," pp. 209, 211–213; Dewitte, *Mouvements nègres*, p. 333–334, 181–182.

194. ANS K 116 (26), Les soussignés délégués des camarades navigateurs dont la liste est ci-jointe à M. Galandou Diouf, Député du Sénégal, 31 October 1934.

195. Spiegler, "Aspects of Nationalist Thought," p. 213, note 1.

196. Letter William Bertrand, Minister of Merchant Marine to Galandou Diouf, No. 2547, 13 November 1935, in ANSOM, Slotfom III, 41. See also in ibid., Delegate CAI Marseilles to Min. Colonies, Dir. Pol. Affairs, No. 1619 D.G., 15 November 1935; No. 1730 D.G.C.C., 11 December 1935; Galandou Diouf, Compte-rendu de l'audience que nous avons eue ce matin avec M. le Ministre de la Marine marchande, 30 October 1935.

197. ANSOM, Slotfom III, 41, Note au sujet des embarquements de marins indigènes à bord des navires des Messageries Maritimes, [Delegate CAI] Marseilles, 6 August 1937; Auguste Guèye, President, Société amicale des originaires de l'A.O.F. to Delegate CAI Marseilles, 4 August 1937.

198. ANSOM, Slotfom III, 41, Delegate CAI Marseilles to Inscription Maritime, Chef de quartier, Marseilles, 15 May 1933.

199. ANSOM, Slotfom III, 27, Société Amicale des Originaires de l'A.O.F. to President du Conseil [Daladier], 20 May 1939; Slotfom III, 41, Auguste Guèye, President, Société Amicale des Originaires de l'A.O.F. to Delegate CAI Marseilles, 4 August 1937.

200. See ANSOM, Slotfom III, 27, Société Amicale des Originaires de l'A.O.F. to Minister of Colonies Georges Mandel, 4 January 1939. This domination was probably not absolute because the Amicale came under increasing criticism for its ethnic exclusivism, including from the French administration, and could not too blatantly favor Saint-Louisiens. One of my informants was employed by the Messageries Maritimes in 1937, that is, before the transformation of the Amicale in 1938. Saydu Nay So, Dakar, 21 December 1979.

201. ANSOM, Slotfom III, 119, Excerpt on the Comité from Le Petit Provençal (Marseilles), 9 November 1935.

202. ANSOM, Slotfom III, 41, Delegate CAI to Min. Colonies, Dir. Pol. Affairs, No. 289 D.A., 3 March 1936; ANS 21 G 44, Delegate CAI to Min. Colonies, Dir. Pol. Affairs, No. 229, 21 February 1930. Sangare was born in Birgo in the French Soudan.

203. ANSOM, Slotfom III, 41, Delegate CAI Marseilles to Min. Colonies, Dir. Pol. Affairs, No. 1619 D.G., 15 November 1935.

204. ANSOM Slotfom III, 41, Note au sujet de l'Agit.Prop dans le milieu des originaires de l'A.O.F., 1937; compare the names with the signatures on the letter informing the CAI of the ousting of Auguste Guèye. ANSOM Slotfom III, 27, [Amicale] to M. Fouque, Delegate CAI Marseilles, 14 April 1938. It is worth noting that Kouyaté had insisted on keeping a strict ethnic balance in his organization. See ANS 21 G 44, Report by Romain [n.d. but ca. 1930]. On contacts between Pierre Mbaye and Emile Faure's Ligue (in 1935), see Spiegler, "Aspects of Nationalist Thought," p. 208.

205. ANSOM Slotfom III, 119, excerpt from Le petit Provençal, 9 November 1935; Delegate CAI Marseilles to Dir. Pol. Affairs, No. 283, 2 March 1936.

206. See the list of officials in Spiegler, "Aspects of Nationalist Thought," p. 208. But, of course, the name Amadu Njaay is a most common Wolof (and even Soninke) name.

207. ANSOM Slotfom III, 27, Minutes of meeting of Amicale on 5 June 1938, en-

closed with Head of Native Immigration to Pol. Affairs, No. 585, 29 June 1938; ANSOM Slotfom III, 27. The council of renewed Amicale comprised one delegate of "Jeunesse Africaine." This would be an indication of ties with Kouyaté, whose friends in West Africa attempted to create a Fédération Française des Jeunesses Africaines in 1939. Spiegler, "Aspects of Nationalist Thought," pp. 271–274.

208. Foreign members of the C.G.T. jumped from 50,000 to 350,000 or 400,000 between 1935 and mid 1937, according to the union's claims, which were probably exaggerated. The French unions had previously been either lukewarm or hostile toward foreign laborers, except for unions having ties with the Communist party, see Gary S. Cross, *Immigrant Workers in Industrial France: The Making of a New Working Class* (Philadelphia: Temple University Press, 1983), p. 207; Léon Gani, *Syndicats et travailleurs immigrés* (Paris: Editions sociales, 1972), pp. 23–24.

209. ANS 2 G 38-1, Mauritania, Annual Political Report, 1938; 2 G 40-3, 1940; and ANS (unclassified letter), Administrator Matam to Gov. Senegal, 17 September 1937.

210. In twenty-six years of emigration, Mr. Jabe So met only two Wolof sailors. Wolof sailors continued to be present though. The Amicale was, in fact, re-formed in 1947 under the name Société Amicale de l'Afrique Noire Française. The name suggests that this was no longer an association of sailors, but a number of its officials had been members of the Amicale in the 1930s. Archives des Bouches-du-Rhône, M 15 9343.

211. Jabe So, Kungani, 14 August 1982; Diarra, "Travailleurs africains," pp. 888–889.

212. Interview of Mr. Jean-Marc Masseaut, who worked as a deck officer between 1975 and 1985 on freighters of several French companies (Chargeurs Réunis, Société navale de l'Ouest, Nouvelle Compagnie Havraise Péninsulaire), La Baule, 1 July 1992.

213. Jean-Marc Masseaut, interview, La Baule, 1 July 1992. For Mr. Masseaut, the main reason why French shipping companies continue to employ Soninke sailors (who generally have no skill or education, although they are serious and hard working) is "political," that is, the bilateral agreements mentioned above.

214. Hotels and bars also occasionally provided useful services to the sailors. For example, sailors often deposited valuables in hotel safes.

215. My source on this is a former sailor who participated heavily in smuggling at the time. For obvious reasons, I cannot quote his name here.

216. Eugène Saccomano, *Bandits à Marseilles* (Paris: Julliard, 1968).

217. Abdulay Sakine, interview, Dakar, 13 December 1979.

218. Jabe So, Kungani, 16 August 1982.

219. Jean-Marc Masseaut, La Baule, 1 July 1992; and personal observations in Marseilles, 1982.

220. ANS J 27; Denise Bouche, "Une source pour l'étude de la société sénégalaise dans la première moitié du XXe. siècle: les monographies d'écoles," *L'école primaire sénégalaise*, supplement, No. 1, January 1967, pp. 51–56; No. 2, February 1967, pp. 45–52. Many Soninke I interviewed gave me an even harsher description of the education situation of the Soninke. See also I. D. Bathily, "Notices socio-historiques," p. 68. The rejection of modern education was not uncommon in rural Senegal at the

time; see Denise Bouche, *L'enseignement dans les territoires français de l'Afrique occidentale de 1817 à 1920* (Lille: Atelier de reproduction des thèses; Paris: Champion, 1975), passim.

221. Marc Michel, *Appel à l'Afrique*, pp. 110, 116 note 89.

222. Bathily, "Notices," pp. 31–105. Page references will be given whenever needed. I have also drawn from the transcripts of I. D. Bathily's papers in the I.F.A.N. library in Dakar, "Papiers Ibrahima Jaman Bacili." See also Jean Robin, "Autour d'un suicide sénégalais, *2d International West African Conference, Bissau, 1947*, vol. 5, 1952, pp. 295–299.

223. As explained, tunkas were usually so old that their business was carried out by a younger relative.

224. Chapter Five.

225. I. D. Bathily, "Notices," p. 64.

226. Papiers Ibrahima Jaman Bacili.

227. ANS 2 G 37-88, Bakel, Yearly pol. report, 1937; see also 4 G 252, Rapport d'inspection relatif à l'administration du cercle de Bakel par Théroud, 1939.

228. ANS 2 G 44-95, Bakel, Monthly pol. report, September 1944.

229. I. D. Bathily, "Notices socio-historiques," p. 32.

230. Seck, "Escales du fleuve Sénégal," p. 84.

231. Papiers Ibrahima Jaman Bacili.

232. I. D. Bathily, "Notices," pp. 86–87.

233. Ibid., pp. 85–88.

234. Ibid., pp. 76–79 and 88.

235. I. D. Bathily, "Notices," pp. 33 and 72.

236. "Papiers Ibrahima Jaman Bacili."

237. I. D. Bathily, "Notices," p. 72.

238. It is possible that Chief Bacili, had he been more diplomatic, could have received help from at least some of the more progressive returned sailors. See Adams, *Terre et gens du fleuve*, p. 107.

239. I. D. Bathily, "Notices," pp. 80; 98.

240. ANS 2 G 30-69, Bakel, Yearly pol. report, 1930; 2 G 38-78, Bakel, Yearly pol. report, 1938; 4 G 252, Rapport d'inspection relatif à l'administration du cercle de Bakel par Théraud, 1939; ANS 2 G 38-1, Mauritania, Yearly pol. reports, 1938; 2 G 39-1, 1939; 2 G 40-3, 1940.

241. See also ANS 2 G 40-91, Bakel, Yearly pol. report, 1940; 4 G 320, Rapport d'inspection relatif à l'administration générale de la subdivision de Bakel par Théraud, 1941.

242. I. D. Bathily, "Notices," p. 68.

243. ANS 2 D 4/21 (12), Bakel, Conflit opposant la ramille des Goundiame de Galladé à la famille des Bathily de Tuabo. Affaire des terrains de culture dans le Goye inférieur [Administrative inspection report], 1932.

244. ANS 2 G 45-81, Bakel, Rapport d'ensemble, 3d quarter 1945; also 2 G 46-77, Rapport trimestriel d'ensemble, 1st quarter 1946; I. D. Bathily, "Notices," pp. 33–34.

245. "But alas, young and old have been embittered. Farewell, tranquillity. Struggle, struggle, poison, witchcraft, delation, anonymous letters, false accusations, scandalous enquiries, courts. No more chiefs—Right of vote—No more tax—No more provident granaries—*Laisser aller, vive la liberté*," "Papers Ibrahima Jaman Bacili," written on 5 June 1947, 21 days before Chief Bacili's suicide; date of suicide in Robin, "Autour d'un suicide sénégalais," p. 295.

246. For comparative material, see Bernard Lacombe et al., *Exode rural et urbanisation au Sénégal: sociologie de la migration des Serer de Niakhar vers Dakar en 1970* (Paris: O.R.S.T.O.M., 1977).

247. This ideal persisted into the 1960s and 1970s; see the interview of a young migrant in Samuel, *Prolétariat africain noir en France*, pp. 174–175; see also the interviews on pp. 172–175.

248. Chatelain, *Migrants temporaires en France*; Raison-Jourde, *Colonie auvergnate de Paris*; and "Endogamie des migrants auvergnats"; Chevalier, *Formation de la population parisienne*.

249. See especially Chatelain, *Migrants temporaires en France*.

250. The "Parisians" tend to emphasize ecology and the defense of local architectural traditions, of the natural landscape, often in a romantic fashion, while villagers emphasize the modernization of agricultural equipment; see Jean-Luc Chodkiewicz, "L'Aubrac à Paris. Ecologie d'une migration culturelle à Paris" in *L'Aubrac* (Paris: C.N.R.S., 1973), vol. 4, pp. 203–267.

251. P. C. W. Gutkind, "African Responses to Urban Wage Employment," *International Labour Review*, vol. 97, No. 2, February 1968, pp. 135–166; Van Velsen, "Some Methodological Problems of the Study of Labour Migration," pp. 32–42.

252. Moreover, many Soninke migrants *did* live with their wives and children in the towns, as we saw in the cases of Dakar and migration to the Congos. Yet even they generally returned to their villages.

253. To emphasize the point, construction workers in the French *département* of the Creuse, for example, began to migrate in the *thirteenth century*, but it was only in the 1840s that their descendents began to abandon seasonal migration for definitive migration and brought their wives to live with them in the cities; see Chatelain, *Migrants temporaires en France*, vol. 2, p. 781; and the analysis of the memoirs of Martin Nadaud by Louis Chevalier, *Formation de la population parisienne*, p. 218.

254. Fascinating historical account of Corsican emigration in Chatelain, *Migrants temporaires en France*, pp. 978–999.

255. Caroline Hutton, *Reluctant Farmers: A Study of Unemployment in Uganda and Planned Rural Development in Uganda* (Nairobi: East African Publishing House, 1973).

256. Jabe So, Kungani, 13 August 1982.

Conclusion

1. Unfortunately, such schemes, in particular in Senegal, have often been introduced by government agencies without consultation of the Soninke and without regard for their needs. For an overview of the question, see in particular Adams, *Terre et gens du fleuve*.

2. One journalistic source even mentions *November* 1958 as a beginning date. That was the month when French West African territories attained independence within the commonwealth-type French Community. The appearance of a "turning point" must have come from the fact that African migrants were now recorded in official documents as foreign nationals, thereby acquiring greater visibility. The authors of the cited article, incidentally, contradicted themselves when they quoted an executive from a large Parisian automobile plant (most certainly Renault), who dated the beginning of African migration from 1956 to 1957. J.-P. Rosier and J. Leriche, "Africains noirs présents et au travail en France," *Cahiers nord-africains*, no. 86, October–November 1961, pp. 8–30, see p. 18.

3. These are official figures that are certainly underestimated: for 1953 figure, see Diarra, "Travailleurs africains," p. 889; for 1956 figure, see M. Aubin, "Les Jeunes et les territoires d'outre-mer," *Informations sociales*, no. 4, April 1957, p. 450; Jean-Pierre N'Diaye, "Noir, pauvre et sans travail, le drame de l'émigration noire en France," *Réalités africaines*, no. 5, May–June 1963. For various conflicting 1960s figures, see Diarra, "Travailleurs africains en France," pp. 892–894.

4. In fact, according to Soninke testimonies collected in Mauritania (especially in Gidimaxa) in the early 1970s, Soninke migration to France began *in 1954*. Elizabeth Dussauze-Ingrand, "L'émigration Sarakollaise du Guidimakha vers la France," in Amin, *Modern Migrations*, p. 243.

5. Georges Tapinos, *L'immigration étrangère en France*, Institut National d'Etudes Démographiques, Cahier No. 71 (Paris: P.U.F., 1975), pp. 10–46.

6. Successive devaluations of the French franc until 1954 also made France an unattractive destination for foreign migrants as compared with other Western European countries such as Germany.

7. Ahsène Zerhaoui, *Les travailleurs algériens en France* (Paris: Maspéro, 1971), p. 23; also Tapinos, *Immigration étrangère en France*, pp. 51–53.

8. Tapinos, *Immigration étrangère en France*, pp. 34, 48, 61.

9. Diarra collected interesting figures about the African worker community in Rouen in the 1950s. These figures show a dramatic increase in the number of migrants from 100 to 300 in 1958 to more than a thousand in 1959; Diarra, "Travailleurs Africains," p. 902.

10. On Algerian migration to France, see Ahsène Zerhaoui, *Travailleurs algériens en France*; Andrée Michel, *Les travailleurs algériens en France* (Paris: C.N.R.S., 1956); Abel Chatelain, "Les Algériens dans la région parisienne," *Bulletin de la Société d'études historiques, géographiques et scientifiques* (Paris), No. 91–92, April–September 1956, pp. 23–29; Association France-Algérie, *Compte-rendu des travaux du colloque . . .*

du 13 au 15 octobre 1966 (Paris: Association France-Algérie, 1966); Pierre Demondion, "L'emploi de la main-d'oeuvre algérienne en France," *Droit social*, vol. 24 (3), 1961, pp. 153–163; see also Madeleine Trébous, *Vie et travail des Algériens en France* (Paris: Jour, 1974); Alain Gillette and Abdelmalek Sayad, *L'immigration algérienne en France* (Paris: Entente, 1976); Alain Girard and Jean Stoetzel, *Français et immigrés*, I.N.E.D., Cahier No. 19, 2 vols, (Paris: P.U.F., 1953), see vol. 2.

11. On the transformation of the Algerian labor force during this period, see Demondion, "Emploi de la main-d'oeuvre algérienne en France," esp. p. 160; Zerhaoui, *Travailleurs algériens en France*, pp. 90–91; Association France-Algérie, *Compte-rendu du colloque de 1966*, pp. 22, 64, 68. Construction, despite its seasonal pattern of unemployment, provides better-skilled and better-paid occupations than manufacturing, and attractive opportunities for social promotion in the contracting business. Theodore Caplow, *The Sociology of Work* (Minneapolis: University of Minnesota Press, 1954); Richard H. Hall, *Occupations and the Social Structure* (Englewood Cliffs, N.J.: Prentice-Hall, 1975). It was a booming trade in France during this period; Tapinos, *Immigration étrangère en France*, pp. 47–67. Algerians were not the first migrants to have taken this route of social betterment: in the nineteenth century, French migrants from Limousin dominated the building trades, followed by Germans, and finally by Italians. See Chatelain, *Migrants temporaires en France*, pp. 775–894; Martin Nadaud, *Léonard, maçon de la Creuse* (Paris: Maspéro, 1976), introduction by Jean-Pierre Rioux; see also the other edition with a preface by Maurice Agulhon; Corbin, "Paysans de Paris," pp. 169–176.

12. Tapinos, *Immigration étrangère en France*, esp. pp. 55–62.

13. See, e.g., Michel Friedman, "Il mangera son pain à la sueur de son front: enquête sur les travailleurs africains en France," *Jeune Afrique*, No. 190, 29 June 1969, p. 17.

14. Jabe So, Kungani, 13, 14 August 1982; Jean-Pierre N'Diaye, "Noir, pauvre et sans travail"; Friedman, "Il mangera son pain à la sueur de son front," pp. 16–18, see p. 17; Dr. Jean Brincourt, "Les noirs africains dans un hopital parisien," *Esprit*, vol. 34, No. 348, 1966, pp. 758–762; Diarra, "Travailleurs africains."

15. Diarra, "Travailleurs africains," p. 890.

16. Diarra, "Travailleurs africains," p. 889.

17. Marc Nacht, "Les travailleurs noirs en France ou la misère organisée." *Les Temps Modernes*, No. 218, July 1964, pp. 152–162; "Le quartier noir de Marseilles n'est pas le paradis qu'on imagine en Afrique," *Libération*, 26 March 1964. According to Mr. Jean-Marc Masseaut, who was a deck officer on French freighters servicing the West African coast between 1975 and 1985, sailors in Marseilles often mentioned to him that some African *bar* and cafe owners acted as intermediaries for employers in Marseilles, but he had no specific information to substantiate this rumor. Interview, La Baule, 1 July 1992.

18. Jabe So, Kungani, 14 August 1982.

19. Dr. Jean Brincourt ("Noirs africains dans un hôpital parisien," p. 759) talks about direct recruiting by French enterprises in Saint-Louis, Dakar and Kayes. Another author talks about a short-lived experiment made in 1960 by French automobile plants

with workers recruited directly in Dakar, who were employed in unskilled cleaning tasks; Maurienne, "La nouvelle traite des noirs," *Révolution africaine* [Algiers], No. 13, 27 April 1963. Diarra mentions that the first Africans hired by the Paris automobile plants were employed in cleaning tasks. See Diarra, "Travailleurs africains noirs en France," p. 953.

20. Urbain Dia Moukari, "L'Histoire et les faits," *Faim et soif*, No. 61, 1965, quoted in Bradley et al., *Guidimakha mauritanien*, p. 48. I was unable to obtain a copy of this article.

21. The story here recalls the excessive dramatizing of the beginnings of the migration to the Congos in the 1890s by French colonial administrators, Chapters Four and Five.

22. Nacht, "Travailleurs noirs en France," p. 161, note (Nacht misspells "Moudéri" as "Mounery").

23. In 1973, the chambres were obligatory stopovers for migrants to France, for whom they provided housing, as the migrants waited for an opportunity to depart, and contacts necessary to arrange for a journey as an illegal migrant. Guillebaud, "De la brousse aux bidonvilles," *Le Monde*, 18, 19, 20–21 May 1973.

24. Chapter Seven.

25. Diarra, "Travailleurs africains," pp. 947, 967.

26. Rosier and Leriche, "Africains noirs en France," p. 18.

27. Adams, *Long voyage des gens du fleuve*, p. 76.

28. An additional 8.2 percent of the migrants spoke French fairly fluently and could even read and write it, although with some difficulty, a remarkable observation considering the appalling state of modern education in the Soninke homeland, even after the Second World War (on this topic, see Chapter Seven); Diarra, "Travailleurs africains," pp. 929–930.

29. Ibid.

30. Thus Soninke and Fuutanke migrants (37 percent) no longer dominated Senegalese migration to France in absolute terms.

31. OECD statistics quoted in Senegal, Direction de la Statistique, *Situation économique du Sénégal*, 1983, p. 11.

32. I traveled back from Senegal in 1982 with a young Frenchman who had lived for some time in Dakar. Once in Paris, we remarked jokingly that we heard about as much Wolof on the Metro as in Dakar. These new Wolof migrants are obviously not students, and they often speak French quite well, a clear indication of urban background.

33. See official statistics of the French Ministry of Interior in 1981 (only 52,000 out of 130,000 recorded Africans in France were from Senegal, Mali, and Mauritania), quoted in Patricia Mahot, "Une épopée sans joie," *Autrement*, no. 49, April 1983, pp. 83 and 85.

34. On Hausa migrants, see immediately below. On the Mossi, see the interesting interview of a Mossi couple, who migrated to France from the Ivory Coast, Anne Per-

ret, "J'oublie Dieu pour gagner de quoi vivre," *Autrement,* no. 49, April 1983, pp. 94–107. In 1981, of 130,000 recorded Africans, 8,500 came from the Ivory Coast, with probably an important proportion of Mossi; see Patricia Mahot, "Une épopée sans joie," *Autrement,* No. 49, April 1983, pp. 83 and 85.

35. Paul Lovejoy, "Kola in the History of West Africa," *Cahiers d'Etudes Africaines,* vol. 20, no. 77–78, 1980, pp. 97–134; "The Role of the Wangarawa in Central Sudan," *Journal of African History,* vol. 19, 1978, pp. 173–193.

36. The Hausa still sing traditional songs in Soninke language; Lasana Jaaxo, Dakar, 24 January 1980; Mamadu Jimera, Dakar, 24 January 1980; see on similar influence of Soninke on the Songhay, Hale, *Griot, Scribe and Novelist* and Troisième Colloque International de l'Association SCOA, 30 novembre–6 décembre 1977, *Actes du colloque* (Paris: Association SCOA pour la recherche scientifique en Afrique Noire), p. 79.

37. Mamadu Jaaxo, Kungani, 15 August 1982. I was shown the area where these migrants live in Dakar in 1979 to 1980.

38. Dubresson, "Travailleurs soninké et toucouleur," p. 207; also Jacques Barou, *Travailleurs africains en France, rôle des cultures d'origine* (Grenoble: Presses universitaires de Grenoble; Publications orientalistes de France, 1982), p. 35.

39. See Chapter Seven. In 1982, Zairian "refugees" (most of them appear to have been voluntary migrants who entered France passing for political refugees) came into France at the rate of 150 a month; Elimane Fall, "Nabab chez les toubabs," *Jeune Afrique,* no. 1115, 19 May 1982. There is a sizeable Zairian and Congolese community in Paris, centered around the Place de la République; Guide "Paris Black," *Autrement,* no. 49, April 1983.

40. The Soninke did likewise during the dry season in West Africa.

41. John Salt and Hugh Clout, eds., *Migration in Post-War Europe: Geographical Essays* (London: Oxford University Press, 1976), pp. 126–167. Compare the early migrations of the Kabyle, selling indigenous crafts, with the winter migrations of the French mountaineers described by Chatelain, *Migrants temporaires en France,* vol. 1, pp. 377–545. For information on Kabyle migration prior to 1920, see Ageron, *Algériens musulmans et la France,* pp. 849, 885, 854–858.

42. Salt and Clout, *Migration in Post-War Europe,* pp. 126–167.

43. Dirck Hoerder, "An Introduction to Labor Migration in the Atlantic Economies, 1815–1914," Introduction to Dirck Hoerder, ed., *Labor Migration in the Atlantic Economies, The European and North American Working Classes During the Period of Industrialization* (Westport, Conn.; London: Greenwood Press, 1985), pp. 3–31, see quotation pp. 6–7. See also the other essays in this collection, esp. Jonathan D. Sarna, "The Myth of No Return: Jewish Return Migration to Eastern Europe, 1881–1914," ibid., pp. 423–434 [compare with Green, *Pletzl of Paris,* also questioning the "uprooting" thesis for Jewish migration from Eastern Europe]. Excellent and impressive international bibliographical essay on modern European migrations by country, ibid., pp. 449–465.

44. Radio France Internationale broadcast, 29 July 1992, reporting on latest French

census data: 3 million foreigners live in France today, of which *22 percent* are from Africa. Note that this figure does not include Black Africans who have obtained French citizenship.

45. See statistics in [Berg], *Accelerated Development in Sub-Saharan Africa: An Agenda for Action* (Washington, D.C.: World Bank, 1981), p. 179.

46. Franco Rizzi, "Rome devient noire," *Le Monde Dimanche*, 25 October 1981; Momar Kébé Ndiaye, "Mamadou au pays des ritals," *Jeune Afrique*, no. 1098, 20 January 1982; Robert Solé, "Immigrés chez l'immigrant," *Le Monde*, May 22, 1986.

47. A young Soninke scholar has recently devoted an excellent Ph.D. dissertation to the problems of identity and integration of Soninke permanent migrants and migrants' children born in France. Mahamet Timera, "Les immigrés *sooninke* dans la ville: situations migratoires et stratégies identitaires dans l'espace résidentiel et professionnel," Ph.D. thesis, Ecole des Hautes Etudes en Sciences Sociales, Paris, 1993.

48. Papa Kane, Dakar, 9 January 1980.

49. For example, the Jawara clan is also found among the Xaasonke of Sanga, a tie that probably played some role in the extension of navetanat in this region. See Chapter Six.

50. See Chapter Four.

51. ANS 2D 4-9 (3), Rapport de l'administrateur adjoint Gaillardon, tournée effectuée dans le Goye supérieur en février et mars 1912.

52. ANS 2 D 4-12, Etat nominatif des villages du cercle, Bakel, 16 March 1904.

53. Adams, *Terre et gens du fleuve*, pp. 68; 80–81.

54. ANS 2G 38-78, Bakel, Yearly political report, 1938.

55. Kane and Lericollais, "Emigration en pays soninké," p. 179.

56. On Breton migration: Chatelain, *Migrants temporaires en France*, pp. 715–756; On Sereer migration: Bernard Lacombe et al., *Exode rural et urbanisation au Sénégal: sociologie de la migration des Serer de Niakhar vers Dakar en 1970* (Paris: O.R.S.T.O.M., 1977).

57. On migration from Aquitaine at the turn of the nineteenth century: Chatelain, *Migrants temporaires en France*, pp. 992–993. Migrants from Aquitaine, like the Corsicans, despised farming in their homeland and left it to immigrants from Vendée, Spain, Britanny, and Italy.

58. Lubeck, "Islamic Networks"; Salem, "De la brousse au Boul' Mich."

59. See the review of David Robinson's *Holy War of Umar Tal* by Jean Schmitz, "Rhétorique et géopolitique du *jihad* d'al-Hajj Umar Taal," *Cahiers d'Etudes Africaines*, vol. 28, no. 109, 1988, pp. 123–133.

Bibliography

ARCHIVAL SOURCES

Archives Nationales du Sénégal, Dakar (ANS)

The National Archives of Senegal in Dakar comprise three distinct archival funds. Fonds Ancien and Fonds Moderne regroup the archives of the former French West African colonial federation in Dakar. *Fonds Ancien* is for the period prior to 1920 and *Fonds Moderne* for the period after 1920 (access to documents is limited to the period until 1946.) *Fonds Sénégal* is the archives of the former colonial territory of Senegal, previously located in St. Louis. Access to the documents in the Fonds Sénégal is also limited to the period until 1946.

A. Fonds Ancien (before 1920)

6 B: Correspondance de la Division Navale de l'Atlantique Sud au Commandant de Gorée

6 B 62, Correspondance du Commandant de la Division Navale de l'Atlantique Sud et des Commandants de navire, 1848–1853.

6 B 63, [Idem,] 1861–1882.

3 E: Conseil d'Administration du Sénégal

3 E 28, Conseil d'Administration du Sénégal, 1859.

Série G: Politique et administration générale (1782–1895)

1 G: Notices et monographies

1 G 37, Notes sur un voyage dans le fleuve, 1872.

1 G 41, Mission Galliéni à Bafoulabé, 1879.

1 G 43, Mission Jacquemart, 1879.

1 G 47, Mission Monteil dans le Djoloff et le Ferlo, 1879.

1 G 49, Villages du cercle de Bakel, 1880.

1 G 71, Mission Rouvier, recrutement pour le Congo [c. 1885].

1 G 135, Tournée du Capitaine Roux dans le cercle de Bakel, 1892.

1 G 292, Notice sur le cercle de Matam, 1904.

1 G 294, Monographie du cercle de Podor, 1904.

1 G 310, Monographie du cercle de Kayes, 1903–1904.

1 G 315, Monographie du cercle de Médine, 1903–1904.

1 G 344, Monographie du cerle du Guidimakha.

2 G: Rapports périodiques
The 2 G series, in fact, straddles the Fonds Ancien and Fonds Moderne since it begins roughly in 1900 and goes on to 1946 and beyond (documents after this date are not yet accessible to the public). It comprises periodical reports (political, economical) for Senegal, Dakar, and the Communes and all the regions of Senegal. The 2 G series is an important source for Senegalese local history. It would take too long to list all the files consulted. I systematically consulted all the documents for Senegal (annual reports to the Governor-General), Bakel, and Matam, and spot checked documents for Podor.

6 G: Congo-Tchad-A.E.F. (1892–1920)
Correspondence between the French West African and French Equatorial Africa federations.

6 G 12, Documents concernant le Gabon, 1862–1886

13 G: Affaires politiques et administratives et musulmanes: Sénégal (1782–1919)
The 13 G series is also an important source for Senegalese local history. It is comparable to the 2 G series for the period prior to 1900. In addition, it comprises local correspondence between the commandants de cercle and the governor of Senegal. In addition to the Bakel documents, I also briefly reviewed a number of documents for Dakar.

13 G 164 to 175, 181 to 203, Bakel, Correspondance, rapports périodiques, bulletins agricoles et commerciaux, 1823–1909 [Systematic review].

21 G: Sureté Générale A.O.F.
21 G 27, Création d'associations, 1908.

21 G 28, Création d'associations professionnelles, 1915–1919.

21 G 30, Rapatriements, 1905–1914.

21 G 35, Rapatriement des indigènes originaires de l'A.O.F.

21 G 35, Emigration et circulation des indigènes.

Série J: Enseignement (1820–1920)

J 27, Ecole de Bakel, 1900–1920.

J 35, Ecole de Kayes, 1900–1920.

Série K: Travail et main d'oeuvre

This is a very important series comprised of documents about labor, and slavery and emancipation in French West Africa.

K 13, Captivité au Sénégal (1893–1894).

K 14, Rapports sur la captivité [Nioro, Médine, Kayes, 1894].

K 18, Questionnaires sur la captivité, 1904 [Bakel, Matam].

K 19, Questionnaire sur la captivité, 1904 [Bamako].

K 25, L'esclavage en A.O.F., étude historique, critique et positive par M. Deherme, 1906 [June–Sept. 1906].

K 26, Captivité et répression de la traite en A.O.F., 1907–1915.

K 27, Captivité et répression de la traite au Sénégal, 1902, 1907.

K 30, Travail et main d'oeuvre, 1878–1894.

K 31, Recrutement au Sénégal et émigration d'ouvriers indigènes pour la construction du chemin de fer du Congo Belge; affaire Laplène, 1890–1894.

Série O: Chemin de fer

O 57, Chemin de fer du Soudan, rapports et correspondance, 1880–1888,

O 58, [idem], 1893–1898.

O 59, [idem], 1899–1900.

O 60, [idem], 1901–1904.

O 61, [idem], 1900–1903.

O 62–O 65, Chemin de fer Thiès-Kayes.

Série Q: Affaires économiques (1782–1919)

Q 51, Rapports commerciaux des cercles de la Sénégambie-Niger, 1903–1904.

B. Fonds Moderne

6 E: Conseil de Gouvernement de l'A.O.F.

6 E 49, No. 135, Conseil de Gouvernement de l'A.O.F., 1925 [pertaining to the regulation of emigration outside of French West Africa].

10 F: Correspondance avec les Consulats de France à l'étranger

10 F 16, Documentation et correspondance du Consulat de France à Léopoldville, 1920–1955.

2 G: Rapports périodiques Sénégal

This is the continuation of the 2 G Series of the Fonds Ancien; see my remarks above.

9 G: Affaires politiques, Mauritanie

All the yearly reports were consulted. The series does not comprise local reports, but the yearly reports have extensive sections reporting on local affairs in the various cercles, which are obviously summaries of local reports.

17 G: Affaires politiques, A.O.F.

17 G 68, Propagande révolutionnaire.

21 G: Sureté générale

21 G 35 (17), Rapatriement des indigènes originaires de l'A.O.F., 1927–1931.

21 G 44, Syndicats de navigateurs—Renseignements d'ensemble. Renseignements sur l'évolution des associations de travailleurs de couleur en Europe, Amicale des originaires de l'A.O.F.—Ligue de Défense nègre-Syndicat nègre de Marseilles, 1930–1932. [Comprises also documents for 1927.]

21 G 48, Grève des manoeuvres des compagnies à Dakar et à St. Louis, 1926.

21 G 57, Rapatriement des indigents. Circulaires—Instructions.

21 G 115, Syndicat des marins indigènes 1923, Union Amicale des marins de l'A.O.F., 1924.

21 G 143, Questions indigènes, 1928–1942. [Comprises "Grève des marins indigènes à St. Louis, 1928."]

Série K: Travail et main d'oeuvre

K 28 (1), Grève des dockers du Dakar-Niger, en Nigéria, 1945–1946.

K 54 (19), Main d'oeuvre: recrutement de main d'oeuvre pour l'extérieur, 1921–1925.

K 81 (26), Problèmes de la main d'oeuvre dans les entreprises privées de la fédération—Questions diverses, 1921–1930.

K 89 (26), Enquête du département sur la main d'oeuvre aux colonies, 1926–1929. Enquête sur la main d'oeuvre en A.O.F. Rapport d'ensemble, 1927.

K 166 (26), Emploi de la main d'oeuvre indigène hors de sa région d'origine, [1931.]

K 162 (26), Recrutement des travailleurs. Emigration des indigènes. Mouvements migratoires vers les colonies étrangères. Transport des ouvriers saisonniers. [1903–1935.]

K 172 (26), Etude sur le programme de la main d'oeuvre. Rapport sur le danger de dépopulation que fait courir le recrutement excessif, 1936.

K 209 (26), Accidents du travail maritime, 1937–1938.

K 217 (26), Problème de la main d'oeuvre. Rapport de tournée de M. le Gouverneur Tap Inspecteur du Travail à travers l'A.O.F., 1937–1939.

K 392 (39), Sénégal. Divers. Grève de marins indigènes, 1928.

K 397 (132), Recrutement de main d'oeuvre sénégalaise destinée au Congo belge. Correspondance et documentation diverse, 1896–1906. [These documents should normally have been with *Fonds ancien;* perhaps they were found after *Fonds ancien* was fully organized.]

K 398 (132), Questionnaire se rapportant à la main d'oeuvre africaine. Exportation. Immigration. Travail des enfants. Projet de règlementation, 1897–1916. [Same remark as immediately above.]

BIBLIOGRAPHY

1 Q Affaires Economiques

1 Q 300 (77), Sénégal—Syndicats, 1911–1939.

1 Q 326 (77), A.O.F., Travail et main d'oeuvre (législation du travail; chômage; prestations; exodes—navétanes; office du Niger—colonisation nord-africaine), 1935–1944.

1 S: Marine de guerre

2 S, 1-5 (1).

C. Fonds Sénégal

At the time I did research in the Senegal Archives, reclassification of the *Fonds Sénégal* was just beginning. Some of the series numbers I am listing here may still be current (I was told this would be the case of the 4 G series, which was due to retain its name, but undergo internal reclassification), others will have changed. The Senegal Archives keeps records of the old classification system, and conversion from the numbers given below to the new numbers should not be too difficult.

*Correspondance confidentielle au départ [Governor Senegal
to Administrators of the cercles, 1922–1938]*

[Unclassified register.]

Courrier confidentiel départ au Gouverneur Général

[Interwar period, unclassified.]

Série B: Correspondance

1 B: Correspondance, Ministre de la Marine et colonies—Gouverneur du Sénégal
[Systematically consulted for the 1880s–1890s.]

2 B: Correspondance départ du Gouverneur du Sénégal au Ministre (1816–1896)
[Idem.]

*3 B: Correspondance départ du Gouverneur du Sénégal à toutes autres
personnes que le Ministre (1788–1893)*
Contains numerous letters pertaining to African sailors (notably letters to the maritime registration administration in Gorée). I consulted this series systematically for the 1870s–1890s.

2 D: [Archives des cercles]
2 D 4: Bakel

2 D 4/7, Bakel, Correspondance, 1923–1934.
2 D 4/8, Bakel, Affaires administratives, 1886–1910.

2 D 4/9, Bakel, Rapports de tournées, 1902–1934.

2 D 4/12, Bakel, Copies mensuelles du journal de poste, 1901–1908 [contains hardly any diary, but contains the important "Etude sur la formation des populations qui constituent le cercle, monographie," by Maubert, Administrateur-adjoint, Bakel, Mar. 16, 1904].

2 D 4/20, Bakel, Etat-civil.

2 D 4/21, Bakel, Affaires diverses, 1900–1932. [Important local litigations.]

2 D 4/22, Bakel, Justice indigène, 1901–1909.

2 D 4/23, Bakel, Affaires civiles, 1901–1909.

2 D 4/24, Bakel, Affaires civiles, 1918–1919.

2 D 10: Matam—Kaédi—Saldé

2 D 10/4, Matam—Kaédi—Saldé, Correspondance, 1908–1920.

2 D 10/9, Matam—Kaédi—Saldé, Rapports de tournées, 1894–1917. [Contains an important "Notice sur le cercle de Matam par l'administrateur Palmède de Raffin, 1917."]

2 D 10/10, Notice et études sur le cercle, 1917–1920.

2 D 11: Podor

2 D 11/14, Podor, Emigration de populations, 1895–1903.

2 D 11/23, Podor, Dossiers divers, 1893–1912.

Série 3 G: [?] (unclassified)

3 G 2-9, Limitation de la population de Dakar "pour lutter contre un afflux désordonné de la population indigène, 1934–35."

Série 4 G: Inspection des affaires administratives du Sénégal

4 G 52, Rapport d'inspection du cercle du Guidimakha, 1942.

4 G 112, Rapport concernant le cercle de Matam, 1908.

4 G 117 1–4, Rapports d'inspection concernant le cercle de Bakel, 1908.

4 G 120, Rapport d'inspection relatif aux cercles du fleuve, 1909.

4 G 132, Correspondance et rapports du 13 janvier 1912 au [?] octobre 1913.

4 G 133, Correspondance et rapports, 1913–1918, 1920–1921.

4 G 145 1–2, Rapports d'inspection concernant le cercle de Matam, 1914.

4 G 160, Correspondance et rapports d'inspection, 1924.

4 G 163, Rapport d'inspection concernant le cercle de Bakel, janvier 1922.

4 G 167, Rapport d'inspection concernant le cercle de Matam, 1922.

4 G 252, Rapport d'inspection relatif à l'administration du cercle de Bakel par Théroud, 1939.

4 G 320, Rapport d'inspection relatif à l'administration générale de la subdivision de Bakel par Théroud, 1941.

Série L: Marine

Unclassified documents.

Archives de l'Institut Fondamental d'Afrique Noire (Dakar)

Papiers Ibrahima Diaman Bathily.

Archives Nationales du Mali (Bamako)

The Malian National Archives are also comprised of a *Fonds ancien* (documents before 1920) and a *Fonds récent*. Documents until 1946 may be consulted by researchers after obtaining the authorization of the Ministry of Culture of the Republic of Mali.

SH Fonds ancien

IE-38, Goumbou, Rapports politiques, 1897–1920.

IE-44, IE-45, Kayes, Rapports politiques, 1891–1920.

IE-60, Nioro, Rapports politiques, 1891–1920.

SH Fonds récent

IE-19, Kayes, Rapports politiques et tournées, 1921–1942.

IE-32, Nara, Rapports politiques et de tournées, 1921–1958.

IE-36, Nioro, Rapports politiques, 1921–1949.

IE-44, Yélimané, Rapports politiques et tournées, 1922–1955.

French Archives

Documents were consulted at three archival depots. The main French archival depot on the Rue des Archives in Paris *(Archives Nationales de France)* contains interesting nineteenth-century documents on Soninke sailors in the French Navy (mostly the Senegal River service) in Senegal. The colonial archives depot *(Archives Nationales, Section Outre-Mer)* contains documents and reports on French West Africa that often duplicate documents in the Senegalese Archives, hence I simply surveyed most of these documents, except for the important Slotfom fund (see below.) The French colonial archives are in *Aix-en-Provence*, which also holds the French Algerian archives and the French Equatorial African archives. I consulted a number of the French Equatorial African documents in Aix. I also consulted the Archives départementales of the Bouches-du-Rhône in Marseilles.

Archives Nationales de France (ANF)

Série CC: Personnel (Marine)

CC 3 1182, Recrutement de troupes indigènes, Sénégal-Gabon, 1864–1893.

CC 3 1183, Recrutement de troupes indigènes, Sénégal-Gabon, 1864–1893.

Archives Nationales, Section Outre-Mer (ANSOM)

A. Main Archival Fund

Afrique IV: Expansion
Afrique IV, 47, Congo Belge, 1886–1898, a, b, and c, Chemin de fer du Congo.

Afrique VI, Affaires diplomatiques
Afrique VI, 77, Congo indépendant, 1889, c, Recrutement d'indigènes dans les colonies françaises.

Afrique VI, 86, Congo indépendant, 1890, c, Douanes et recrutement d'indigènes.

Afrique VI, 161, Congo indépendant, 1899, b, Situation des Sénégalais licenciés par la Compagnie du chemin de fer de l'Etat indépendant.

Sénégal I: Correspondance
Correspondence of the Governor of Senegal to the Minister of Colonies for the years 1889–1899.

Sénégal II: Mémoires sur le Sénégal
Sénégal II, 4, Mémoire Carrère, 1854.

Sénégal VI: Affaires diplomatiques
Sénégal VI, 30, Congo Belge, Rapatriements d'ouvriers sénégalais, 1890–1895.

Sénégal XIII: Agriculture. Commerce. Industrie
Sénégal XIII, 10, Commerce du fleuve.

Sénégal XIII, 17, Correspondance et mémoires relatifs à l'agriculture et aux produits naturels.

Sénégal XIII, 24–33, Traite de la gomme.

Sénégal XIII, 40, Commerce du mil.

Sénégal XIV: Travail et main d'oeuvre
Sénégal XIV, Immigration africaine aux Antilles et en Guyane, 1857–1870.

Sénégal XIV, Recrutement de travailleurs indigènes, 1872–1895; Décret du 27 juin 1895, 26, Rapatriement d'un travailleur sénégalais ouvrier en France, 1872.

Sénégal XIV, 27, Emigration, 1896.

Sénégal XIV, 28, 1882–1899, Recrutement de travailleurs indigènes par l'Etat indépendant du Congo, 1886–1897. Recrutement de Sénégalais pour les milices du Congo, 1899. Recrutement d'ouvriers et de coolies chinois pour les travaux du Haut Fleuve, 1882.

Sénégal XIV, 29, Esclavage et traite, 1902, Envoi de maçons pour les travaux du chemin de fer de Madagascar.

Travaux Publics (T.P.)

T.P. 23, 3, Mission hydrographique du Sénégal, 1904.

T.P. 28, 1, Amélioration de la navigabilité du Sénégal, 1904. Note sur la situation des études du régime du fleuve Sénégal, 1896.

T.P. 28, 3, Avant-projet d'aménagement du Sénégal (Rapport Mathy, 1904.)

T.P. 91, 1, Chemin de fer Thiès-Kayes, Mission Rougier-Belle, 1903–1904.

B. *Slotfom Fund*

The Slotfom fund regroups documents from the official French services in charge of the welfare and police surveillance of French colonial subjects on the metropolitan soil. All the documents consulted were for the interwar period.

Slotfom III, 20, (. . .) Liaison entre Indochinois et Africains vivant à Marseilles.

Sltofom III, 27, Association Amicale des originaires de l'A.O.F. à Marseilles. (. . .) Société de secours mutuel des Nègres (5e. arrondissement.)

Slotfom III, 31, (. . .) C.G.T.U. (. . .) Formation de syndicats communistes indigènes.

Slotfom III, 34, (. . .) Colonie indigène du Havre (. . .) Foyer des Noirs de Dunkerque (. . .)

Slotfom III, 36, Syndicat nègre de Marseilles. Syndicat nègre de Bordeaux (. . .) Constitution d'un comité international des ouvriers nègres.

Slotfom III, 41, Arrestations à Marseilles d'indigènes de l'A.O.F. (1937.) Commerce et usage illicite des cartes de navigateurs effectué par les marins de l'A.O.F. Décret du 11 Mars 1937 sur le droit syndical des travailleurs indigènes de l'A.O.F. (. . .) Réunions secrètes de navigateurs indigènes de Dakar. Répression des embarquements clandestins. (. . .)

Slotfom III, 45, L.U.D.P.R.N. Amicale des anciens marins du Sénégal. Ligue de lutte pour la liberté du peuple du Sénégal et du Soudan. (. . .)

Slotfom III, 87, (. . .) Affaire Amadou Fall—Mannet. (. . .)

Slotfom III, 112, (. . .) Foyer colonial de Marseilles (. . .) C.G.T.U.

Slotfom III, 119, (. . .) Comité de défense des travailleurs de la mer originaires d'outre-mer. (. . .)

Slotfom III, 125, Main d'oeuvre indigène en France et dans les colonies.

Slotfom III, 136, Union des Travailleurs Nègres.

Slotfom VI, 8, Demandes de duplicata de livrets de marins (A.O.F.). Contrôle des navigateurs de l'A.O.F. Correspondances diverses provenant des marins indigènes. Navigateurs de passage à Dunkerque (. . .) Rapatriement de marins indigènes.

Slotfom IX, 9, Liaison entre le service du C.A.I. et les compagnies de navigation.

Aix-en-Provence Archival Depot

The documents consulted in Aix are correspondence and reports for the Moyen-Congo colony (today the Republic of the Congo) and correspondence and reports for the city of Brazzaville during the interwar period. The following files contain information about Soninke migrants.

4 (2) D 54.

4 (2) D 61.

5 D 85.

10 F 16 (17) Fonds moderne.

Belgian Colonial Archives

I consulted the Belgian colonial Archives in Brussels (M.O.I.) in the hope of finding information about the Soninke in Zaïre (formerly the Belgian Congo.) Results were disappointing owing to the apparent lack of local material in these archives.

INTERVIEWS

Bakeli Jabira (Bakéli Diabera), former sailor, Koungany, Senegal, Aug. 17, 1982.

Wadi Fili (Gay) Jabira (Wadi Fily (Gaye) Diabera), former sailor, Koungany, Senegal, Aug. 17, 1982.

Lasana Jaaxo (Lassana Diakho), former merchant in Zaire, nephew of the first *cadi* of Kinshasa, interviews in Dakar, Senegal, Dec. 13, 1979; Jan. 24, 1980.

Al-Haj Mamadu Jaaxo (El Hadj Mamadou Diakho), second and last Soninke *cadi* of Kinshasa, Zaire, interviews in Koungany, Senegal, Aug. 12, 13, 15, 1982.

Manca Jawara (Manthia Diawara), from Kingi Diawara, scholar and former labor migrant, interviews and conversations in Santa Barbara, Feb. 1984.

Mamadu Jimera (Mamadou Djimera), civil servant, formerly at the Commission on National Languages of Senegal, Dakar, Dec. and Jan. 1979.

Xadi Darame (Khady Dramé), Professor at the Ecole Normale Supérieure of Bamako, Personal conversations and interviews in Bamako, Aug. 31; Sept. 1982.

Al-Haj Maxan Darame (El Hadj Makhan Dramé), last Soninke cadi of Brazzaville, Congo, interview in Bamako, Mali, 1 Sept. 1982.

Papa Kane, Director, Formation permanente, Ministère de l'Enseignement supérieur, born in Zaire, family from the village of Golmy (Goye, Senegal), interview in Dakar, Senegal, 9 Jan. 1980.

Alpha Oumar Konaré, formerly Minister of Culture of the Republic of Mali, interview and conversations, Bamako, Sept. 1982.

Jean-Marc Masseaut, Mate, formerly employed between 1975 and 1985 as deck officer on freighters servicing the West African coast (companies: Chargeurs Réunis, Société navale de l'Ouest, Nouvelle Compagnie Havraise Péninsulaire), La Baule, 1 July 1992.

Chambre de Moudéri, Dakar, collective interview, 21 Dec. 1979.

Lasana Ndaw (Lassana N'Dao), former merchant in Zaire, former sailor, Dakar, 17 Dec. 1979.

Sally N'Dongo, President of the Union Générale des Travailleurs Sénégalais en France, Paris, France, 3 Jan. 1977.

Suuleyman Saaxo (Souleymane Sakho), former sailor, merchant in Dakar, Dakar, 17 Dec. 1978.

Abduulay Sakine (Abdoulaye Sakiné), former sailor, Dakar, 13 Dec. 1979.

Jabe So (Diabé Sow), former sailor and labor organizer, founder of the Foyer du Marin Sénégalais in Marseilless, farm organizer, Koungany, 14, 16, 17 Aug. 1982.

Saydu Nay So (Seydou Naye Sow), former sailor, Dakar, 21 Dec. 1979.

FRENCH GOVERNMENT PUBLICATIONS

Annales du Sénat.

Annales du Sénat. Documents parlementaires.

FRENCH WEST AFRICAN PUBLICATIONS

Annuaire statistique de l'A.O.F.

Recensement démographique de Dakar (1955), Paris: Haut Commissariat de la République en Afrique Occidentale Française, 1958.

Journal Officiel de l'A.O.F.

SENEGALESE GOVERNMENT PUBLICATIONS

Conseil Général du Sénégal. *Procès-verbaux des séances.*

Conseil Colonial du Sénégal. *Procès-verbaux des séances.*

Journal Officiel du Sénégal. [This publication was first called the *Moniteur du Sénégal.*]

Population du Sénégal par canton et groupe ethnique (population autochtone). Renseigne-ments au 1er. janvier 1956. Saint-Louis: Imprimerie du Gouvernement, 1956.

Situation économique du Sénégal.

NONGOVERNMENT PUBLICATIONS

Newspapers and Weeklies

Senegalese newpaper collections are rare and never complete. *L'Afrique occidentale* (published c. 1896–1898) was consulted at the Versailles branch of the Bibliothèque Nationale in Paris. *L'Ouest Africain Français* (published during the interwar period) was consulted at the I.F.A.N. library in Dakar. All are daily publications except for the weekly *Jeune Afrique.*

L'Afrique occidentale (Dakar) c. 1896–1898.

Jeune Afrique (Paris) 1960–1987.

Libération (Paris) 1986.

Le Monde (Paris) 1978–1987.

L'Ouest Africain Français (Dakar) c. 1920–1938.

Le Temps (Paris) 1885–1900.

Other Non-Government Publications

Académie des Sciences Coloniales, Compte-rendus des séances.

L'Afrique française (Paris) [Bulletin of the Comité de l'Afrique Française]

Revue Indigène (Paris)

Quinzaine coloniale (Paris)

BOOKS, ARTICLES, AND DISSERTATIONS

Abbott, Daniel; see Clinard, Marshall B. *Crime in Developing Countries.*

Adam, Jean. *L'Arachide, culture, produits, commerce, amélioration de la production.* Paris: Challamel, 1908.

Adams, Adrian. *Le long voyage des gens du fleuve.* Paris: Maspéro, 1977.

———. *La terre et les gens du fleuve. Jalons, balises.* Paris: L'Harmattan, 1985.

Adanson, Michel. *A Voyage to Senegal, the Isle of Gorée and the River Gambia*, Translated by an English gentleman [*sic*] London: J. Nourse, 1759.

Adedeji, Adebeyo. "The Future of Personal Income Taxation in Nigeria." In Milton C. Taylor, *Taxation for African Economic Development*, pp. 257–278.

Ageron, Charles-Robert. *Les Algériens musulmans et la France (1871–1919)*. Paris: P.U.F., 1968. 2 vols.

———. *France coloniale ou parti colonial?* Paris: P.U.F., 1978.

Agier, Michel. "Etrangers, logeurs et patrons. L'improvisation sociale chez les commerçants soudanais de Lomé." *Cahiers d'Etudes Africaines*, vol. 21, nos. 81–83, 1981, pp. 251–266.

Agulhon, Maurice. "Un problême d'ethnologie historique: les "chambrées" en Basse-Provence au XIXe siècle." In Maurice Agulhon, et al., *Ethnologie et histoire, forces productives et problêmes de transition*. Paris: Editions sociales, 1975.

———. *La République au village*. Paris: Plon, 1970.

———. *Une ville ouvrière au temps du socialisme utopique: Toulon de 1815 à 1870*. Paris; The Hague: Mouton, 1970.

Aliber, Robert Z. *Money, Banking and the Economy*; see Meyer, Thomas, ed.

Allain, Jean-Claude. *Joseph Caillaux*. Paris: Imprimerie Nationale, 1981. 2 vols.

Amin, Samir. *Le monde des affaires sénégalais*. Paris: Editions de Minuit, 1969.

———. "La politique coloniale française à l'égard de la bourgeoisie commerçante sénégalaise (1820–1960). In Claude Meillassoux, ed., *The Development of Indigenous Trade and Markets in West Africa*, pp. 361–376.

———. *Trois expériences africaines de développement: le Mali, la Guinée et le Ghana*. Paris: P.U.F., 1965.

———. "Underdevelopment and Dependence in Black Africa—Origins and Contemporary Forms." *The Journal of Modern African Studies*, vol. 10, 1972, pp. 503–524.

———, and Forde, Daryll, eds. *Modern Migrations in Western Africa*. London: Oxford University Press, 1974.

Amselle, Jean-Loup. *Logiques métisses. Anthropologie de l'identité en Afrique et ailleurs*. Paris: Payot, 1990.

———. *Les négociants de la savane. Histoire et organisation sociale des Kooroko (Mali)*. Paris: Anthropos, 1977.

———. "Parenté et commerce chez les Kooroko." In Claude Meillassoux, ed., *The Development of Indigenous Trade and Markets in West Africa*, pp. 253–265.

Andrew, Christopher, and Kanya-Forstner, A. S. *The Climax of French Imperial Expansion, 1914–1924*. Stanford: Stanford University Press, 1981.

Andromedas, John N. "The Enduring Urban Ties of a Modern Greek Folk Sub-Culture." In Perestiany, *Contributions to Mediterranean Sociology*, pp. 269–278.

Anfreville de la Salle, Docteur d'. *Notre vieux Sénégal*. Paris: Challamel, 1909.

Angoulvant, Gabriel. "L'Afrique occidentale française." *Le monde colonial illustré*, no. 5, Feb. 1924, p. 98.

———. *La Côte d'Ivoire*. Bingerville: Imprimerie du Gouvernement, 1915.

———. *Les Indes néderlandaises*. Paris: Le monde nouveau, 1926. 2 vols.

———. *La pacification de la Côte d'Ivoire, 1908–1915, méthode et résultats, lettre-préface par le Général Gallieni*. Paris: Larose, 1916.

———. "Le problème des voies de communication et des débouchés mairtimes de l'Afrique occidentale française." *Colonies et marine*, no. 26, 1920, pp. 531–563.

———. "La réorganisation administrative de l'A.O.F." *Colonies et marine*, Mar.–Apr. 1921, pp. 161–178.

"L'Année économique 1937 au Soudan français." *Bulletin mensuel de l'Agence économique de l'A.O.F.*, no. 119, 1938, pp. 157–160.

"Approches de la migration noire en France." Special issue of *Hommes et migrations* (Paris), no. 104, [1966].

Arensberg, M., ed.; see Polanyi, Karl, et al., eds., *Trade and Markets in the Early Empires*.

Ardouin, Claude Daniel. "Une formation politique précoloniale du Sahel occidental malien: le Baakhunu à l'époque des Kaagoro." *Cahiers d'Etudes Africaines*, vol. 28, nos. 111–112, 1988, pp. 463–483.

Arnaud, Robert; see Randau, Robert (pseudonym).

Aspe-Fleurimont, [Lucien-Auguste]. *La Guinée française*. Paris: Challamel, 1900.

———. *L'organisation économique de l'Afrique Occidentale française. Liberté. Règlementation. Rapport à M. le Ministre du commerce*. [Paris], 1901.

Association France-Algérie. *Compte-rendu des travaux du colloque sur la migration algérienne qui s'est tenu du 13 au 15 octobre 1966 au Centre des Conférences Internationales, 19, Avenue Kléber, Paris, XVIe*. Paris: Association France-Algérie, 1966.

Aubert, Vilhelm, ed. *The Hidden Society*. Totowa, N.J.: Bedminster Press, 1965.

———. "A Total Institution: The Ship." In Vilhelm Aubert, *The Hidden Society*, pp. 236–258.

———, and Arner, Oddvar. "On the Social Structure of the Ship." In Vilhelm Aubert, *The Hidden Society*, pp. 259–287.

Aubin, M. "Les jeunes et les territoires d'outre-mer." *Informations sociales*, no. 4, Apr. 1957, pp. 446–457.

Ba, Amadou Hampâté. *L'étrange destin de Wangrin, ou les roueries d'un interprête africain*. Paris: Union générale d'éditions, Collection "Dix-Dix-huit," 1978.

Ba, Oumar. *Le Fouta Toro au carrefour des cultures*. Paris: L'Harmattan, 1977.

Baier, S.; see Lovejoy, Paul, and Baier, S., "Desert-Side Economy."

Baillaud, Emile. *Sur les routes du Soudan*. Toulouse: Privat, 1902.

Banton, Michael. *West African City*. London: Oxford University Press, 1957.

Barbour, Kenneth, ed.; see Prothero, R. Mansell, and Barbour, Kenneth Michael, eds., *Essays on African Population*.

Barlett, Peggy F., ed. *Agricultural Decision Making: Anthropological Contributions to Rural Development*. New York; London: Academic Press, 1980.

Barnes, Sandra T. *Patrons and Power: Creating a Political Community in Metropolitan Lagos*. Bloomington; Indianapolis: Indiana University Press, 1986.

Baroja, Julio Caro. "The City and the Country: Reflexions on Some Ancient Commonplaces." In Charles Tilly, ed., *An Urban World* (Boston; Toronto: Little, Brown, 1974), pp. 473–487.

Barou, Jacques. *Travailleurs africains en France, rôle des cultures d'origine*. Grenoble: Presses universitaires de Grenoble; Publications orientalistes de France, 1982.

Barrows, Leland Conley. "The Merchants and General Faidherbe: Aspects of French Expansion in Senegal in the 1850s." *Revue française d'histoire d'outre-mer*, vol. 61, no. 223, 1974, pp. 236–283.

Barry, Boubacar. *Le royaume du Waalo: le Sénégal avant la conquête*, Preface by Samir Amin. Paris: Maspéro, 1972.

Barton, Josef J. *Peasants and Strangers: Italians, Rumanians and Slovaks in an American City, 1890–1950*. Cambridge, Mass.: Harvard University Press, 1975.

Bates, Robert H., and Lofchie, Michael F., eds. *Agricultural Development in Africa: Issues of Public Policy*. New York: Praeger, 1980.

Bathily, Abdoulaye. "La conquête française du haut-fleuve (Sénégal), 1818–1887." *Bulletin de l'I.F.A.N.*, vol. 34, série B, 1972, pp. 67–112.

———. "Imperialism and Colonial Expansion in Senegal in the Nineteenth Century; with Particular Reference to the Economic, Social and Political Development of the Kingdom of Gajaaga (Galam.)" Ph.D. dissertation, Centre of West African Studies, University of Birmingham, U.K., 1975.

———. "Mamadou Lamine Dramé et la résistance anti-impérialiste dans le Haut-Sénégal (1885–1887.)" *Notes africaines*, no. 125, Jan. 1970, pp. 20–32.

———. *Les Portes de l'or. Le royaume de Galam (Sénégal) de l'ère musulmane au temps des négriers (VIIIe-XVIIIe siècle)*. Paris: L'Harmattan, 1989.

———. "La traite atlantique des esclaves et ses effets économiques et sociaux en Afrique: le cas du Galam, royaume de l'hinterland sénégambien au dix-huitième siècle." *Journal of African History*, vol. 27, 1986, pp. 269–293.

Bathily, Ibrahima Diaman. "Notices socio-historiques sur l'ancien royaume du Gadiaga. Présentées, annotées et publiées par Abdoulaye Bathily." *Bulletin de l'I.F.A.N.*, vol. 31, série B, 1969, pp. 31–105.

Bauer, P. T. *West African Trade: A Study of Competition, Oligopoly and Monopoly in a Changing Economy*. London: Routledge and Kegan Paul, 1963; reprint of Cambridge: Cambridge University Press, 1954.

Bazin, Jean, and Terray, Emmanuel, eds. *Guerres de lignages et guerres d'Etats en Afrique*. Paris: Editions des archives contemporaines, 1982.

Ben Jalloun, Tahar. *Hospitalité française: racisme et immigration maghrébine*. Paris: Seuil, 1984.

Béranger-Féraud, L.F.-B. *Les peuplades de la Sénégambie: histoire, ethnographie, moeurs, coutumes, légendes, etc.* Paris: E. Leroux, 1879.

Béraud, Médard. *L'agriculture et la colonisation au Congo français, la main d'oeuvre. Rapport présenté au comité consultatif de l'Agriculture, du Commerce et de l'Industrie (Ministère des Colonies.)* Paris: Chaix, 1899.

Berg, Elliot J. *Accelerated Development in Sub-Saharan Africa: An Agenda for Action.* Washington, D.C.: World Bank, 1981.

———. "Backward-Sloping Labor-Supply Functions in Dual Economies: The Africa Case." *Quarterly Journal of Economics,* vol. 75, 1961, pp. 468–492.

———. "The Development of a Labor Force in Sub-Saharan Africa." *Economic Development and Cultural Change,* vol. 13, 1965, pp. 394–412.

———. "The Economics of the Migrant Labor System." In Kuper, Hilda, *Urbanization and Migration in West Africa,* pp. 160–181.

Bernard, Augustin. "La main d'oeuvre aux colonies." *Questions diplomatiques et coloniales,* vol. 10, 1900, pp. 333–350.

Bernus, E., and Savonnet, G. "Les problèmes de la sécheresse dans l'Afrique de l'Ouest." *Présence africaine,* 1973, p. 113–138.

Betts, Raymond F. *Assimilation and Association in French Colonial Policy, 1890–1914.* New York: Columbia University Press, 1961.

Biebuyck, Daniel, ed. *African Agrarian Systems.* London: International African Institute; Oxford University Press, 1963.

"Black." [Special issue.] *Autrement,* no. 49, 1983.

Blanc, E. "Contributions à l'étude des populations et de l'histoire du Sahel soudanais." *Bulletin du Comité d'Etudes Historiques et Scientifiques de l'Afrique Occidentale Française,* vol. 8, no. 2, 1924, pp. 258–314.

Bleneau, Daniel, and La Cognata, Gérard. "Evolution de la population de Bamako." *Etudes maliennes,* no. 3, 1972, p. 26.

Bohannan, Paul. "The Impact of Money on an African Subsistence Economy." *Journal of Economic History,* vol. 19, 1959, pp. 491–503.

Boilat, Abbé P.-D. *Esquisses sénégalaises.* Paris: P. Bertrand, 1853.

Bouche, Denise. "Dakar pendant la Seconde Guerre Mondiale: problèmes de surpeuplement." In *Le sol, la parole et l'écrit. Mélanges en hommage à Raymond Mauny.* Paris: Société Française d'Histoire d'Outre-Mer, 1981, pp. 960–976.

———. *L'enseignement dans les territoires français de l'Afrique Occidentale de 1817 à 1920: mission civilisatrice ou formation d'une élite?* Lille: Atelier de reproduction des thèses; Paris: Champion, 1975.

———. "Une source pour l'étude de la société sénégalaise dans la première moitié du XXe. siècle: les monographies d'écoles." *L'école primaire sénégalaise,* Supplement, no. 1, Jan. 1967, pp. 51–56; no. 2, Feb. 1967, pp. 45–52.

———. *Les villages de liberté en Afrique noire française, 1887–1910.* Paris: Mouton, 1968.

Bouët-Willaumez, E. *Commerce et traite des noirs aux côtes occidentales d'Afrique.* Paris: Imprimerie Nationale, 1848.

———. *Description nautique des côtes de l'Afrique occidentale comprises entre le Sénégal et l'Equateur.* Paris: Imprimerie Royale, 1846.

Boulègue, Marguerite. "La presse au Sénégal avant 1939, bibliographie." *Bulletin de l'IFAN,* B, vol. 27, pp. 715–733.

Boutillier, J.-L., et al. *La moyenne vallée du Sénégal (étude socio-économique.)* Paris: P.U.F.; République Française; République Islamique de Mauritanie; République du Sénégal, 1962.

Boyer, G. *Un peuple de l'ouest soudanais: les diawara.* Dakar: I.F.A.N., 1953.

Brasseur, Paule. *Bibliographie générale du Mali.* Dakar: I.F.A.N., 1964.

Brazza, Pierre Savorgnan de. *Lettre à M. Paul Bourde écrite de Brazzaville à la veille de son retour en France sur les impressions et les conclusions de l'enquête qu'il vient de terminer au Congo (24 Août 1905.)* Paris: L. de Soye, 1906.

Brévié, Jules. "Le déblocage du Soudan." *Europe nouvelle,* no. 14, June 20, 1930, pp. 844–846.

———. "La situation générale de l'Afrique occidentale française." *L'Afrique française, Renseignements coloniaux,* 1932, pp. 23–48.

Brincourt, Dr. Jean. "Les noirs africains dans un hôpital parisien." *Esprit,* vol. 34, no. 348, 1966, pp. 758–762.

Britsch, Amédée. *Pour le Congo français: la dernière mission Brazza d'après le registre de correspondance inédit de P. Savorgnan de Brazza, extrait du Correspondant du 10 janvier 1906.* Paris: L. de Soye, 1906.

Brokensha, David. *Social Change in Larteh, Ghana.* Oxford: Clarendon Press, 1966.

———; and Riley, Bernard. "Introduction of Cash Crops in a Marginal Area of Kenya." In Robert H. Bates and Michael F. Lofchie, eds., *Agricultural Development in Africa,* pp. 244–274.

Brooks, George E. *Landlords and Strangers: Ecology and Society in Western Africa, 1000–1630.* Boulder, Colo.: Westview Press, 1992.

———. "Peanuts and Colonialism: Consequences of the Commercialization of Peanuts in West Africa, 1830–70." *Journal of African History,* vol. 16, 1975, pp. 29–54.

Brossard de Corbigny, P. "Le commerce dans le haut fleuve." *Moniteur du Sénégal,* vol. 85, No. 10, 1857, pp. 1–3.

Brown, Benjamin H. *The Tariff Movement in Great Britain, 1881–1895.* New York: A.M.S. Press, 1966.

Brown, C. Harold; see Tilly, Charles, "On Uprooting, Kinship and the Auspices of Migration."

Brown, E. H. Phelps; with Browne, Margaret H. *A Century of Pay: The Course of Pay and Productivity in France, Germany, Sweden, and the United States of America, 1860–1900.* London: MacMillan; New York: St. Martin's Press, 1968.

————. *The Inequality of Pay.* Berkeley: University of California Press, 1977.

Browne, Margaret H.; see Brown, E. H. Phelps, *A Century of Pay.*

Buell, Raymond Leslie. *The Native Problem in Africa.* London: Frank Cass, 1965; reprint of Cambridge, Mass.: Bureau of International Research of Harvard University, 1928. 2 vols.

Byl, A. "History of the Labor Market in French-Speaking West Africa." *Cahiers économiques et sociaux*, vol. 5, June 1967, pp. 167–188.

Caillié, René. *Travels through Central Africa to Timbuctoo.* Translated from the French. London: F. Cass, 1968; reprint of London: Henry Colburn and Richard Bentley, 1830. 2 vols.

Caldwell, John C. *African Rural-Urban Migration: The Movement to Ghana's Towns.* New York: Columbia University Press, 1969.

————. *The Theory of Fertility Decline.* London; New York: Academic Press, 1982.

Camara, Camille. *Saint-Louis du Sénégal: évolution d'une ville en milieu africain.* Dakar: I.F.A.N., 1968.

Campbell, J.K. *Honour, Family and Patronage: A Study of Institutions and Moral Values in a Greek Mountain Community.* Oxford: Clarendon Press, 1964.

Caplow, Theodore. *The Sociology of Work.* Minneapolis: University of Minneapolis Press, 1954.

Caron, François. *An Economic History of Modern France.* New York: Columbia University Press, 1979.

Carrère, Frédéric, and Holle, Paul. *De la Sénégambie française.* Paris: F. Didot, 1855.

Castles, Stephen, and Kosack, Godula. *Immigrant Workers and Class Structure in Europe.* Oxford: Oxford University Press, 1985.

Cauwès, Paul-Louis. *Cours d'économie politique.* Paris: Larose, 1893. 3 vols.

————. "Les nouvelles compagnies de colonisation privilégiées." *Revue d'économie politique*, vol. 6, 1892, pp. 1–35.

Chaffard, Georges. "Les travailleurs d'Afrique noire en France." *Chronique de la Communauté*, no. 4, Mar. 1960, pp. 10–20.

Challaye, Félicien. *Le Congo français: la question internationale du Congo.* Paris: F. Alcan, 1909.

Chambers, J. D. "Enclosure and the Labour Supply in the Industrial Revolution." *Economic History Review*, series 2, vol. 5, 1953, pp. 319–343.

Charbonneau, Jean. *Marchés et marchands d'Afrique Noire.* Paris: Editions du Vieux Colombier, 1961.

Chastanet, Monique. "Les crises de subsistances dans les villages soninké du cercle de Bakel. Problèmes méthodologiques et perspectives de recherches." *Cahiers d'Etudes Africaines*, vol. 23, nos. 89–90, .pp. 5–36.

————. "Cultures et outils agricoles en pays soninke (Gajaaga et Gidimaxa)." *Cahiers de l'ORSTOM*, série sciences humaines, vol. 20, no. 3–4, 1984, pp. 453–459.

————. "L'état soninké du Gajaaga de 1818 à 1858 face à l'expansion commerciale au Sénégal." Mémoire de maîtrise, Université de Paris I Sorbonne (Centre de Recherches Africaines), 1975–1976.

————. "Les plantes de cueillette, alimentation d'appoint ou de substitution," in *Les ressources génétiques végétales, atouts du développement?* (Paris: ORSTOM, 1987), pp. 39–51.

————. "De la traite à la conquête coloniale dans le Haut Sénégal: l'Etat soninké du Gajaaga de 1818 à 1858." *Cahiers du C.R.A.*, no. 5, October 1987, pp. 87–108.

Chatelain, Abel. "Les Algériens dans la région parisienne." *Bulletin de la Société d'études historiques, géographiques et scientifiques* (Paris) nos. 91–92, Apr.–Sept. 1956, pp. 23–29.

————. *Les migrants temporaires en France de 1800 à 1914.* Lille: Publications de l'Université de Lille; C.N.R.S., 1976. 2 vols.

Chauveau, Jean-Pierre. "Notes sur les echanges dans le Baule precolonial." *Cahiers d'Etudes Africaines*, vol. 36, no. 68, 1977, pp. 567–601.

Chevalier, Louis. *La formation de la population parisienne au XIXe siècle.* Paris: P.U.F., 1950.

Chodkiewicz, Jean-Luc. "L'Aubrac à Paris. Ecologie d'une migration culturelle à Paris." In *L'Aubrac.* Paris: C.N.R.S., 1973, vol. 4, pp. 203–267.

Chudeau, René. "Itinéraire de Kayes à Nioro et Nara, au nord du plateau mandingue." *Bulletin du Muséum national d'histoire naturelle*, no. 2, 1919, pp. 84–94.

Clayton, Anthony, and Savage, Donald C. *Government and Labour in Kenya, 1895–1963.* London: F. Cass, 1974.

Cline, Catherine. *E. D. Morel, 1873–1924.* Belfast: Blackstaff Press, 1980.

Clout, Hugh; see Salt, John, and Clout, Hugh, eds., *Migration in Post-War Europe.*

Cohen, Abner. *Custom and Politics in Urban Africa: A Study of Hausa Migrants in Yoruba Towns.* Berkeley: University of California Press, 1969.

Cohen, Michael A. "Urban Strategy and Development Strategy." In I. William Zartman and Christopher Delgado, *Political Economy of the Ivory Coast*, pp. 57–75.

Cohen, Nicholas; see Dumont, René, and Cohen, Nicholas, *The Growth of Hunger.*

Cohen, William B. *The French Encounter with Africans: White Response to Blacks, 1530–1880.* Bloomington; London: Indiana University Press, 1980.

————. "Robert Delavignette: The Gentle Ruler (1897–1976)." In L. H. Gann and Peter Duignan, eds., *African Proconsuls*, pp. 185–205.

————. *Rulers of Empire: The French Colonial Service in Africa.* Stanford: Hoover Institution Press, 1971.

Colin-Noguès, Renée; see Dia, Oumar, and Colin-Noguès, Renée, *Yakarê: autobiographie d'Oumar.*

Colloque de Nouakchott, 17–19 Décembre 1973, *La désertification au sud du Sahara.* Dakar; Abidjan: Nouvelles Editions Africaines, 1976.

Colombani, F.-M. "Le Guidimakha, étude géographique, historique et religieuse." *Bulletin du Comité d'Etudes Historiques et Scientifiques de l'Afrique Occidentale Française*, vol. 14, 1931, pp. 365–432.

Colvin, Lucy Gallistel, et al. *The Uprooted of the Western Sahel: The Migrants' Quest for Cash in the Senegambia*. New York: Praeger, 1981.

Comhaire, Jean. "Note sur les musulmans de Léopoldville." *Zaïre*, vol. 2, no. 3, 1948, pp. 303-304.

Comité de défense des indigènes. "Lettre à Vigné d'Octon." *Le Temps*, vol. 7, 1899.

"Commerce du Soudan par le fleuve Sénégal pendant l'année 1897." *Revue coloniale*, vol. 1, 1899, pp. 38–42.

Condé, Julien. "Migration in Upper Volta." *Demographic Aspects of Migration in West Africa*, vol. 2, pp. U.V.i–U.V. 156.

Congrès d'Agriculture Coloniale, 21–25 May 1918. *Compte-rendu des travaux*. Paris: Challamel, 1920. 4 vols.

Conrad, David. "Oral Sources on Links between the Great States: Sumaguru, Servile Lineage, the Jariso, and Kaniaga." *History in Africa*, vol. 11, 1984, pp. 35–55.

Conrad, David; and Fisher, Humphrey. "The Conquest that Never Was: Ghana and the Almoravids." *History in Africa*, vol. 9, 1982, pp. 21–59; vol. 10, 1983, pp. 53–78.

Conzen, Kathleen Neils. *Immigrant Milwaukee, 1836–1860: Accommodation and Community in a Frontier City*. Cambridge, Mass.: Harvard University Press, 1976.

Cookey, S. J. S. "West African Immigrants in the Congo, 1885–1896." *Journal of the Historical Society of Nigeria*, vol. 3, no. 2, Dec. 1965, pp. 261–270.

Copin, Noël. "L'Afrique noire au coeur de Paris." *La Croix*, Dec. 12, 13, 14, 1962.

Coquery-Vidrovitch, Catherine. "Les idées économiques de Brazza et les premières tentatives de compagnies de colonisation au Congo français, 1885–1898." *Cahiers d'Etudes Africaines*, vol. 5, no. 17, 1965, pp. 57–82.

———. *Le Congo au temps des grandes compagnies concessionnaires, 1898–1930*. Paris; The Hague: Mouton, 1972.

Corbin, Alain. "Migrations temporaires et société rurale: le cas du Limousin." *Revue historique*, no. 500, Sept.–Dec. 1971, pp. 293–334.

———. *Archaïsme et modernité en Limousin au XIXe siècle, 1845–1880*. Paris: Marcel Rivière, 1975. 2 vols.

———. "Les paysans de Paris: histoire des Limousins du bâtiment au XIXe siècle." *Ethnologie française*, vol. 10, no. 2, 1980, pp. 169–176.

Cosnier, Henri. *L'Ouest africain français*. Paris: Larose, 1921.

Courtet, M. *Etude sur le Sénégal*. Paris: Challamel, 1903.

Craven, Kathryn; and Tuly, A. Hasan. "Rice Policy in Senegal." In Pearson, Scott R.; Stryker, J. Dirck; and Humphreys, Charles P., eds., *Rice in West Africa*, pp. 229–295.

Crew, David F. *Town in the Ruhr: A Social History of Bochum, 1860–1914.* New York: Columbia University Press, 1979.

Cross, Gary S. *Immigrant Workers in Industrial France: The Making of a New Working Class.* Philadelphia: Temple University Press, 1983.

Crowder, Michael. *West Africa under Colonial Rule.* London: Hutchinson, 1968.

Cruise O'Brien, Donal. *The Murids of Senegal.* London: Faber and Faber, 1971.

Cultru, P. *Histoire du Sénégal du XVe. siècle à 1870.* Paris: Larose, 1910.

Curtin, Philip D. *The Atlantic Slave Trade: A Census.* Madison: University of Wisconsin Press, 1969.

———. *Cross-Cultural Trade in World History.* Cambridge: Cambridge University Press, 1984.

———. *Economic Change in Precolonial Africa: Senegambia in the Era of the Slave Trade.* Madison: University of Wisconsin Press, 1975. 1 vol. and a supplementary vol.

———. "Jihad in West Africa: Early Phases and Inter-Relations in Mauritania and Senegal." *Journal of African History,* vol. 12, 1971, pp. 11–24.

Cuvillier-Fleury, Henri. *La mise en valeur du Congo français.* Paris: Larose, 1904.

Dahl, Gudrun, and Hjort, Anders. *Having Herds: Pastoral Herd Growth and Household Economy.* Stockholm: Department of Social Anthropology, University of Stockholm, 1976.

Dalton, George. "The Impact of Colonization on Aboriginal Economies in Stateless Societies." *Research in Economic Anthropology,* vol. 1, 1978, pp. 131–184.

Daniel, Fernand. "Etude sur les Soninkés ou Sarakolés." *Anthropos,* vol. 5, 1910, pp. 25–49.

David, Pierre. *Journal d'un voiage fait en Bambouc en 1744,* publié par André Delcourt. Paris: Société française d'histoire d'outre-mer, 1974.

David, Philippe. *Les navétanes. Histoire des migrants saisonniers de l'arachide en Sénégambie des origines à nos jours.* Dakar; Abidjan: Nouvelles Editions Africaines, 1980.

Davis, J. *People of the Mediterranean: An Essay in Comparative Anthropology.* London: Routledge, 1977.

Davis, Ronald W. *Ethnohistorical Studies on the Kru Coast.* Newark, Del.: Liberian Studies, 1976.

Dean, Warren. *Rio Claro: A Brazilian Plantation System, 1820–1920.* Stanford: Stanford University Press, 1976.

Deblé, Isabelle; and Hugon, Philippe. *Vivre et survivre dans les villes africaines.* Paris: P.U.F., 1982.

Degler, Carl N. *Neither Black Nor White: Slavery and Race Relations in Brazil and the United States.* New York: Macmillan, 1971.

Delafosse, Louise. "Comment prit fin la carrière coloniale de Maurice Delafosse." *Revue française d'histoire d'outre-mer,* vol. 61, 1974, no. 222, pp. 74–115.

―――. *Maurice Delafosse, le Berrichon conquis par l'Afrique,* preface by Léopold Sédar Senghor and postface by Felix Houphouët-Boigny. Paris: Société française d'histoire d'outre-mer, 1976.

Delafosse, Maurice. *Broussard ou les états d'âme d'un colonial.* Paris: Larose, 1922.

―――. *Enquête coloniale dans l'Afrique française sur l'organisation de la famille indigène.* Paris: Société d'études géographiques, maritimes et coloniales, 1930.

―――. *Haut-Sénégal-Niger.* Paris: Larose, 1912.

―――. "Monographie du cercle de Bamako." *L'Afrique française, Supplément,* Mar. 1910, pp. 57–67.

―――. "Les points sombres de l'horizon en Afrique occidentale." *L'Afrique française,* June 1922, pp. 271–285.

Delaunay, Daniel. *De la captivité à l'exil: histoire des migrations paysannes dans la moyenne vallée du Sénégal.* Paris: O.R.S.T.O.M., 1984.

Delavignette, Robert. "L'Afrique occidentale française au travail." *L'Afrique française,* 1932, pp. 403–407.

―――. "Le discours du gouverneur-général Brévié." *L'Afrique française,* 1932, pp. 721–729.

―――. "Le dynamisme de l'A.O.F." *L'Afrique française,* 1932, pp. 476–481, 528–533, 577–580.

―――. *Freedom and Authority in French West Africa.* Translated by M. Fortes, Daphne Trevor and M. Manoukian. London: F. Cass, 1968.

―――. *Paris Soudan Bourgogne.* Paris: Grasset, 1935.

―――. *Les Paysans noirs.* Paris: Stock, 1947.

―――. "La vie économique en Afrique occidentale française." *L'Afrique française,* 1932, pp. 163–166.

―――. *Les vrais chefs de l'empire.* Paris: Gallimard, 1939.

―――, and Julien, Charles-André. *Les constructeurs de la France d'Outre-mer.* Paris: Corréa, 1946.

Delcourt, André. *La France et les établissements français au Sénégal entre 1713 et 1763.* Dakar: I.F.A.N., 1952.

Delgado, Christopher L.; see Gbetibouo, Mathurin, and Delgado, Christopher L., "Lessons and Constraints of Export-Led Growth: Cocoa in the Ivory Coast."

Delgado, Christopher, ed.; see Zartman, I. William, and Delgado, Christopher, *The Political Economy of the Ivory Coast.*

Demondion, Pierre. "L'emploi de la main d'oeuvre algérienne en France." *Droit social,* vol. 24, no. 3, 1961, pp. 153–162.

Den Tuinder, Bastiaan A. *Ivory Coast: The Challenge of Success.* Baltimore; London: Johns Hopkins University Press for the World Bank, 1978.

Désiré-Vuillemin, G. M. *Essai sur le gommier et le commerce de la gomme dans les escales du Sénégal.* Dakar: Clairafrique, 1963.

Dessare, Eve. "Dakar-sur-Seine." *Jeune Afrique*, no. 99, Sept. 10–16, 1962.

Dessertine, A. *Un port secondaire de la côte occidentale de l'Afrique: Kaolack, étude historique, juridique et économique, des origines à 1958*. Kaolack, Senegal: Chambre de commerce, [1967?]

Dewitte, Philippe *Les mouvements nègres en France, 1919–1939*. Paris: L'Harmattan, 1985.

Dia, Oumar, and Colin-Noguès, Renée. *Yakarê: autobiographie d'Oumar*. Paris: F. Maspéro, 1982.

Diagana, Ousmane Moussa. *Chants traditionnels du pays soninké (Mauritanie, Mali, Sénégal)*. Paris: L'Harmattan, 1990.

Diarra, Souleymane. "La population du Sénégal." *Bulletin de l'I.F.A.N.*, vol. 33, série B, no. 3, 1971, pp. 642–657.

————. "Les travailleurs africains noirs en France." *Bulletin de l'I.F.A.N.*, vol. 31, série B, 1969, pp. 884–1004.

Dictionnaire de biographie française. Paris: Letouzey et Ané, 1933–[1982]. 15 vols. published.

Diderot, Denis. *Oeuvres*. Paris: Gallimard, Bibliothèque de "La Pléiade," 1951.

Dike, Kenneth Onwuka. *Trade and Politics in the Niger Delta, 1830–1885*. Oxford: Clarendon Press, 1956.

Diop, Abdoulaye Bara. *Société toucouleure et migration (enquête sur l'immigration toucouleure à Dakar)*. Dakar: I.F.A.N., 1965.

Dobb, Maurice. *Studies in the Development of Capitalism*. London: Routledge, 1947.

Doutressoule, G. *L'élevage au Soudan français*. Algiers: E. Imbert, 1952.

Dubresson, Alain. "Les travailleurs soninké et toucouleur dans l'ouest parisien." *Cahiers de l'O.R.S.T.O.M.*, Série sciences humaines, vol. 12, no. 2, 1975, pp. 189–208.

Duby, Georges; and Wallon, Armand, eds. *Histoire de la France rurale*. Paris: Seuil, 1976. 4 vols.

Duesenberry, James; see Meyer, Thomas, ed., *Money, Banking and the Economy*.

Duignan, Peter, ed.; see Gann, L. H., ed., *African Proconsuls*.

————; see Gann, L. H., ed., *The Rulers of Belgian Africa*.

————; see Gann, L. H., ed., *The Rulers of German Africa*.

Dumont, René. *False Start in Africa*. Translated by Phyllis Nauts Ott. New York: Praeger, 1966.

————, and Cohen, Nicholas. *The Growth of Hunger*. London; Boston: Marion Boyars, 1980.

————, and Mottin, Marie-France. *Stranglehold on Africa*. Translated by Vivienne Menkes. London: A. Deutsch, 1983.

Dupon, Jean-François. "Tambacounda: capitale du Sénégal oriental." *Cahiers d'outre-mer* (Bordeaux), vol. 17, no. 66, Apr.–June 1964, pp. 174–214.

Durand, Jean-Baptiste Léonard. *Voyage au Sénégal fait dans les années 1785 et 1786*. Paris: Dentu, 1807.

Dureau, Françoise. *Migration et urbanisation. Le cas de la Côte d'Ivoire*. Paris: ORSTOM, 1987.

Durkheim, Emile. *The Division of Labor*. Translated by George Simpson. New York: Free Press, 1966.

Dussauze-Ingrand, Elizabeth. "L'émigration sarakollaise vers la France." In Samir Amin, *Modern Migrations in Western Africa*, pp. 239–257.

Echenberg, Myron. *Colonial Conscripts: The Tirailleurs Sénégalais in French West Africa, 1857–1960*. Portsmouth, N.H.: Heinemann, 1991.

———. "Slaves into Soldiers: Social Origins of the Tirailleurs Sénégalais," in Paul E. Lovejoy, ed., *Africans in Bondage: Studies in Slavery and the Slave Trade* (Madison: University of Wisconsin Press, 1986), pp. 311–333.

Eicher, Carl K., and Liedholm, Carl, eds. *Growth and Development of the Nigerian Economy*. East Lansing: Michigan State University Press, 1970.

Eisenstadt, S. N., and Roniger, Louis. "Patron-Client Relations as a Model of Structuring Social Exchange." *Comparative Studies in Society and History*, vol. 22, no. 1, 1980, pp. 42–77.

Ela, Jean-Marc. *La ville en Afrique noire*. Paris: Khartala, 1983.

Elkan, Walter. *Migrants and Proletarians: Urban Labour in the Economic Development of Uganda*. London: Oxford University Press, 1960.

———. "Migrant Labor in Africa: An Economist's Approach." *American Economic Review*, May 1959, pp. 188–202.

Encyclopédie ou dictionnaire raisonné des sciences, des arts et des métiers. Berne; Lausanne: Sociétés typographiques, 1781.

Epstein, T. Scarlett. *Urban Food Marketing and Third World Rural Development: The Structure of Producer-Seller Markets*. London; Camberra: Croom Helm, 1982.

Etienne, Eugène. *Les compagnies de colonisation*. Paris: Challamel, 1897.

Etude historique sur les impôts en France jusqu'en 1789. Chalons, France: Imprimerie-Librairie T. Martin, 1867.

Evans-Pritchard, E. E. *The Nuer*. Oxford: Clarendon Press, 1940.

Fabre, Jean. "Le marquis de Mirabeau, interlocuteur et protecteur de Rousseau," in *Les Mirabeau et leur temps*, pp. 71–91.

Faidherbe, Louis. "Le Gadiaga." *Moniteur du Sénégal et dépendances*, Jan. 15, 1857, pp. 3–4.

———. *Le Sénégal: la France dans l'Afrique occidentale*. Nendeln: Klaus reprints, 1974; reprint of Paris: Hachette, 1889.

Fall, Babacar. "Une entreprise agricole privée au Soudan français: la Société anonyme des cultures de Diakandape (Kayes), 1919–1942." In Catherine Coquery-Vidrovitch, ed., *Entreprises et entrepreneurs en Afrique au XIXe et XXe siècle*, vol. 1 (Paris: L'Harmattan, 1983), pp. 335–350.

Faur, Jean-Claude. "La mise en valeur ferroviaire de l'A.O.F. (1880–1939)." Thèse de doctorat, Faculté de lettres de Paris, 1969.

Fenaltoa, Stefano. "Migration," unpublished presentation to the Banca d'Italia, November 1991.

Finnegan, Gregory A. "Employment Opportunity and Migration among the Mossi of Upper Volta." *Research in Economic Anthropology,* vol. 3, 1980, pp. 291–322.

Fisher, Humphey J. "The Early Life and Pilgrimage of Al-Hajj Muhammad Al-Amin the Soninke." *Journal of African History,* vol. 11, 1970, pp. 51–69.

————; see Conrad, David, and Fisher, Humphrey, "The Conquest that Never Was: Ghana and the Almoravids."

Flanagan, William; see Gugler, Joseph, and Flanagan, William, *Urbanization and Social Change in West Africa.*

Foltz, William J. *From French West Africa to the Mali Federation.* New Haven; London: Yale University Press, 1965.

Fondation S.C.O.A. pour la recherche scientifique en Afrique noire (projet Boucle du Niger). *Actes du Premier colloque international de Bamako, 27 janvier-1er février 1975.* Paris: Fondation S.C.O.A. pour la recherche scientifique en Afrique noire, 1975.

————. *Actes du Deuxième colloque international de Bamako, 16 février–22 février 1976.* Paris : Fondation S.C.O.A. pour la recherche scientifique en Afrique noire, 1976.

————. *Actes du Troisième colloque international de l'Association S.C.O.A., Niamey 30 novembre–6 décembre 1977.* Paris: Association S.C.O.A., 1980.

Forde, Daryll, ed.; see Amin, Samir, and Forde, Daryll, eds., *Modern Migrations in Western Africa.*

Fortes, Meyer, and Patterson, Sheila. *Studies in African Social Anthropology: Essays Presented to Professor Isaac Schapera.* London; New York: Academic Press, 1975.

Fouquet, Joseph. *La traite des arachides dans le pays de Kaolack, et ses conséquences économiques, sociales et juridiques,* Etudes sénégalaises no. 8. Saint-Louis: I.F.A.N., 1958.

Fox-Genovese, Elizabeth. *The Origins of Physiocracy: Economic Revolution and Social Order in Eighteenth-Century France.* Ithaca; London: Cornell University Press, 1976.

Fraser, Derek; and Sutcliffe, Anthony, eds. *The Pursuit of Urban History.* London: Edward Arnold, 1983.

Freeman, Gary P. *Immigrant Labor and Racial Conflict in Industrial Societies: The French and British Experience, 1945–1975.* Princeton: Princeton University Press, 1979.

Frey, Henri. *Campagne dans le Haut Sénégal et le Haut Niger (1885–1886).* Paris: Plon, 1889.

Friedman, Michel. "Il mangera son pain à la sueur de son front: enquête sur les travailleurs africains en France." *Jeune Afrique,* no. 190, 29 June 1969, pp. 16–18.

Gaffarel, Paul. *Le Sénégal et le Soudan français*. Paris: Delagrave, 1892.

Galarza, Ernesto. *Merchants of Labor: The Mexican Bracero Story*. Charlotte; Santa Barbara: MacNally and Loftin, 1964.

Gallieni, Joseph Simon. *Deux campagnes au Soudan français, 1886–1887*. Paris: Hachette, 1891.

Gani, Léon. *Syndicats et travailleurs immigrés*. Paris: Editions sociales, 1972.

Ganier, Germaine. "Lat Dior et le chemin de fer de l'arachide, 1876–1886." *Bulletin de l'I.F.A.N.*, vol. 27, série B, nos. 1–2, 1965, pp. 223–281.

————. "Maures et Toucouleurs sur les deux rives du Sénégal. La mission de Victor Ballot auprès de Sidi Ely, roi des Maures Bracknas, février–juin 1884." *Bulletin de l'I.F.A.N.*, vol. 19, série B, no. 4, 1968, pp. 182–226.

Gann, L. H. *The Birth of a Plural Society*, Preface by Max Glucksman. Manchester: Manchester University Press, 1961.

————; and Duignan, Peter. *The Rulers of Belgian Africa, 1884–1914*. Princeton: Princeton University Press, 1979.

————; and Duignan, Peter. *The Rulers of German Africa, 1884–1914*. Stanford: Stanford University Press, 1977.

————; and Duignan, Peter, eds. *African Proconsuls*. New York: Free Press; London: Collier MacMillan; Stanford: Hoover Institution Press, 1978.

Gbetibouo, Mathurin, and Delgado, Christopher L. "Lessons and Constraints of Export-Led Growth: Cocoa in the Ivory Coast." In I. William Zartman and Christopher Delgado, eds., *The Political Economy of the Ivory Coast*, pp. 115–147.

Gessain, Monique. *Les migrations des Coniagui et des Bassari*. Paris: Société des Africanistes, 1967.

Gibbs, Jack P., and Martin, Walter T. "Urbanization, Technology and the Division of Labor: International Patterns." *American Sociological Review*, vol. 27, 1962, pp. 667–677.

Gillette, Alain, and Sayad, Abdelmalek. *L'immigration algérienne en France*. Paris: Entente, 1976.

Girard, Alain, and Stoetzel, Jean. *Français et immigrés*. I.N.E.D., Cahier No. 19. Paris: P.U.F., 1953. 2 vols.

Giraud, Arthur. *The Colonial Tariff Policy of France*. Oxford: Clarendon Press, 1916.

Glucksman, Max. "Analysis of a Social Situation in Modern Zululand." *Bantu Studies*, vol. 14, 1940, pp. 1–30; 147–174.

————. "Anthropology and Apartheid: the Work of South African Anthropologists." In Fortes, Meyer; and Patterson, Sheila, *Studies in African Social Anthropology*, pp. 21–39.

————. "Malinowski's Functional Analysis of Social Change." Reprint from *Africa*, vol. 17, no. 2, April 1947, pp. 207–234. In Glucksman, Max, *An Analysis of the Sociological Theories of Bronislaw Malinowski*. Rhodes-Livingstone Paper No. 16. London: Oxford University Press, 1949.

Gray, J. M. *History of the Gambia*. London: F. Cass, 1966; first ed. 1940.

Green, Nancy L. *The Pletzl of Paris: Jewish Immigrant Workers in the Belle Epoque*. New York; London: Holmes and Meier, 1986.

Griffen, Clyde, and Griffen, Sally. *Natives and Newcomers: The Ordering of Opportunity in Mid-Nineteenth Century Poughkeepsie*. Cambridge, Mass.; London: Harvard University Press, 1978.

Grigg, David. *Population and Agrarian Change: An Historical Perspective*. Cambridge: Cambridge University Press, 1980.

Grove, A. T. "A Note on the Remarkably Low Rainfall of the Sudan Zone in 1913." *Savanna*, vol. 2, no. 2, December 1973, pp. 133–138.

Guèye, Youssouf. "Essai sur les causes et les conséquences de la micropropriété au Fouta Toro." *Bulletin de l'I.F.A.N.*, vol. 19, série B, nos. 1–2, 1957, pp. 28–42.

Gugler, Joseph, ed. *Urban Growth in Subsaharan Africa*. Kampala: Nkanga, 1970.

———, and Flanagan, William. *Urbanization and Social Change in West Africa*. Cambridge: Cambridge University Press, 1978.

Guillard, Xavier. "Un commerce introuvable: l'or dans les transactions sénégambiennes du XVIe au XVIIIe siècle." *Cahiers du C.R.A.* [Centre de Recherches Africaines, Université de Paris I Sorbonne], no. 5, 1987, pp. 31–75.

Guillebaud, André. "De la brousse aux bidonvilles." *Le Monde*, May 18; 19; 20–21, 1973.

Guiraud, Xavier. *L'arachide sénégalaise*. Paris: Librairie technique et économique, 1937.

Gulliver, P. H. "Nyakusa Labour Migration." *Rhodes-Livingstone Journal*, vol. 21, 1957, pp. 32–63.

Gutkind, P. C. W. "African Responses to Urban Wage Employment." *International Labour Review*, vol. 97, no. 2, Feb. 1968, pp. 135–166.

———. "Tradition, Migration, Urbanization, Modernity, and Employment in Africa: The Roots of Instability." *Canadian Journal of African Studies*, vol. 3, no. 2, 1969, pp. 343–365.

Guy, Camille. "L'Avenir de l'Afrique Equatoriale Française, les projets de M. Antonetti." *L'Afrique française*, Jan. 1926, pp. 7–13.

Hale, Thomas. *Scribe, Griot and Novelist: Narrative Interpreters of the Songhay Empire*. Gainesville: University of Florida Press/Center for African Studies, 1990.

Hall, Richard H. *Occupations and the Social Structure*. Englewood Cliffs, N.J.: Prentice-Hall, 1975.

Halperin, Rhoda. "Polanyi, Marx, and the Institutional Paradigm in Economic Anthropology." *Research in Economic Anthropology*, vol. 6, 1984, pp. 245–272.

Handlin, Oscar. *The Uprooted*. Boston; Toronto: Atlantic-Little, Brown, 1973.

Hanna, William J., and Hanna, Judith Lynne. *Urban Dynamics in Black Africa: An Interdisciplinary Approach*. Chicago: Aldine Atherton, 1971.

Hanson, John. "Islam, Migration, and the Political Economy of Meaning: *Fergo Nioro* from the Senegal River Valley, 1862–1890." *Journal of African History*, vol. 35, no. 1, 1994, pp. 37–60.

Hanson, John Henry. "Umarian Karta (Mali, West Africa) during the Late Nineteenth-Century: Dissent and Revolt among the Futanke after Umar Tal's Holy War." Ph.D. dissertation. Michigan State University, 1989.

Hardy, Georges. *La mise en valeur du Sénégal de 1817 à 1854*. Paris: Larose, 1921.

Harrison, Christopher. *France and Islam in West Africa, 1860–1960*. Cambridge: Cambridge University Press, 1988.

Hauser, A. *Les ouvriers de Dakar. Etude psychosociologique*. Paris: O.R.S.T.O.M., 1968.

————. *Rapport d'enquête sur les travailleurs des Industries Manufacturières de la région de Dakar*. Dakar: Université de Dakar, I.F.A.N., 1965.

Hecksher, Eli. *Mercantilism*. Translated by Mendel Shapiro, revised edition by E. F. Söderlund. London: Allen and Unwin; New York: Macmillan, 1955.

Heisler, Helmuth. *Urbanization and the Government of Migration: The Inter-Relation of Urban and Rural Life in Zambia*. London: C. Hurst, 1974.

Heisser, David C. R. "The Impact of the Great War on French Imperialism, 1914–1924." Ph.D. dissertation, University of North Carolina at Chapel Hill, 1972.

Henderson, Barbara. *Internal Migration during Modernization in Late Nineteenth-Century Russia*. Princeton: Princeton University Press, 1980.

Herrick, Bruce H. *Urban Migration and Economic Development in Chile*. Cambridge, Mass.; London: M.I.T. Press, 1965.

Hill, Polly. "Landlords and Brokers: A West African Trading System." *Cahiers d'Etudes Africaines*, vol. 6, 1966, pp. 349–366.

————. *The Occupations of Migrants in Ghana*. Ann Arbor: The University of Michigan Press, 1970.

————. *Population, Prosperity and Poverty: Rural Kano, 1900 and 1970*. Cambridge: Cambridge University Press, 1977.

————. *Rural Hausa: A Village and a Setting*. Cambridge: Cambridge University Press, 1972.

Hincker, François. *Les français devant l'impôt sous l'Ancien Régime*. Paris: Flammarion, 1971.

Hjort, Anders; see Dahl, Gudrun, *Having Herds*.

Hodge, Carleton T., ed. *Papers on the Manding*. Bloomington: Indiana University Press, 1971.

Hoerder, Dirck. "An Introduction to Labor Migration in the Atlantic Economies, 1815–1914." In Dirck Hoerder, ed., *Labor Migration in the Atlantic Economies*, pp. 3–31.

————. *Labor Migration in the Atlantic Economies: The European and North American*

Working Classes during the Period of Industrialization. Westport, Conn.; London: Greenwood Press, 1985.

Hogendorn, Jan S. *Nigerian Groundnut Exports: Origins and Early Development.* Zaria; Ibadan: Ahmadu Bello University; Oxford University Press, 1978.

Hohenberg, Paul M., Lees, Lynn Hollen. *The Making of Urban Europe, 1000–1950.* Cambridge, Mass.: Harvard University Press, 1985.

Holle, Paul; see Carrère, Frédéric, *De la Sénégambie française.*

Hommes et destins (dictionnaire biographique d'outre-mer). Paris: Académie des sciences d'outre-mer, [1981.]

Hopkins, A. G. *An Economic History of West Africa.* New York: Columbia University Press, 1973.

————. "The Lagos Strike of 1897: An Exploration in Nigerian Labour History." *Past and Present,* no. 35, Dec. 1966, pp. 133–155.

Hopkins, J. F. K., and Levtzion, N., eds. *Corpus of Early Arabic Sources for West African History.* Cambridge: Cambridge University Press, 1981.

Horii, Toshio. "La crise alimentaire de 1853 à 1856 et la Caisse de la Boulangerie de Paris." *Revue historique,* no. 552, Oct.–Dec. 1984, pp. 375–401.

Hrbek, Ivan. "The Early Period of Mahmadu Lamin's Activities." In John Ralph Willis, ed., *Studies in West African History,* pp. 211–232.

Hubert, Lucien. *L'agriculture et la République.* Préface by Joseph Ruau. Paris: Librairie d'Education Nationale, 1906.

Hughes, Everett C., and Hughes, Helen MacGill. *Where People Meet: Racial and Ethnic Barriers.* Glencoe, Ill.: Free Press, 1952.

Humphreys, Charles P., ed.; see Pearson, Scott R., et al., *Rice in West Africa.*

Hutton, Caroline. *Reluctant Farmers: A Study of Unemployment in Uganda and Planned Rural Development in Uganda.* Nairobi: East African Publishing House, 1973.

————. "Unemployment in Kampala and Jinja, Uganda." *Canadian Journal of African Studies,* vol. 3, no. 2, 1969, pp. 431–440.

Idowu, H. Olu. "Assimilation in Nineteenth Century Senegal." *Bulletin de l'I.F.A.N.,* vol. 30, série B, no. 4, 1968, pp. 1422–1447.

————. "The Conseil General of Senegal, 1879–1920." Ph.D. dissertation, University of Ibadan, 1966.

————. "The Establishment of Elective Institutions in Senegal, 1869–1880." *Journal of African History,* vol. 9, 1968, pp. 261–277.

I.L.O.; see International Labor Office.

International Bank for Reconstruction and Development [World Bank.] *The Assault on World Poverty: Problems of Rural Development, Education and Health.* Preface by Robert S. MacNamara. Baltimore; London: World Bank, 1975.

————. *Demographic Aspects of Migration in West Africa.* World Bank Staff Working Paper, no. 415. Washington, D.C.: World Bank, 1980. 2 vols.

―――. *Senegal: Tradition, Diversification and Economic Development*. Washington, D.C.: World Bank, 1974.

International Labor Office. *Conventions and Recommendations adopted by the International Labour Conference, 1916–1966.* Geneva: I.L.O., 1966.

―――. *Why Labour Leaves the Land: A Comparative Study of the Movement of Labour out of Agriculture*. Geneva: I.L.O., 1960.

Jackson, John Ander. *Profession and Professionalization*. London: Cambridge University Press, 1970.

Jaugeon, Renée. "Les sociétés d'exploitation au Congo et l'opinion française de 1890 à 1906." *Revue française d'histoire d'outre-mer*, no. 172–173, 1967, pp. 253–437.

Jarrett, Bede. *Social Theories of the Middle Ages, 1200–1500*. New York: Frederic Ungar, 1966; reprint of 1926 edition.

Jelloun, Tahar ben; see Ben Jelloun, Tahar.

John, A. H. *The Industrial Development of South Wales, 1750–1850*. Cardiff: University of Wales Press, 1950.

Johnson, D. Gale, and Schuh, Edward, eds. *The Role of Markets in the World Food Economy*. Boulder, Colo.: Westview Press, 1983.

Johnson, G. Wesley. "African Political Activity in French West Africa, 1900–1940." In *History of West Africa*, ed. J. F. A. Ajayi and Michael Crowder. Harrow, England: Longman, 1974, vol. 2, pp. 542–567.

―――. *Emergence of Black Politics in Senegal: The Struggle in the Four Communes, 1900–1920*. Stanford: Stanford University Press, 1971.

―――. "William Ponty and Republican Paternalism in French West Africa (1866–1915)." In L. H. Gann and Peter Duignan, eds., *African Proconsuls*, pp. 127–156.

―――, ed. *Double Impact: France and Africa in the Age of Imperialism*. Westport, Conn.; London: Greenwood Press, 1985.

Jollivet, Marcel, ed.; see Mendras, Henri, ed., *Les collectivités rurales françaises*.

Jolly, Jean, ed. *Dictionnaire des parlementaires français*. Paris: P.U.F., 1960–1977. 8 vols.

Jones, William O. *Marketing Staple Foods in Tropical Africa*. Ithaca; London: Cornell University Press, 1972.

Joucla, E. *Bibliographie de l'Afrique Occidentale Française*. Paris: Société d'éditions géographiques, maritimes et coloniales, 1937.

Julien, Charles-André. *Histoire de l'Algérie contemporaine*. Paris: P.U.F., 1964–1979. 2 vols.

―――; see Delavignette, Robert, *Les constructeurs de la France d'Outre-mer*.

Kaba, Lansiné. *The Wahhabiyya: Islamic Reform and Politics in French West Africa*. Evanston, Ill.: Northwestern University Press, 1974.

Kamara, Sylviane. "Analphabètes mais millionaires." *Jeune Afrique*, no. 989, Dec. 19, 1979.

————. "Personne n'en veut." *Jeune Afrique,* no. 1032, Oct. 15, 1980.

Kane, Francine; and Lericollais, André, "L'émigration en pays soninké." *Cahiers de l'O.R.S.T.O.M.,* Série sciences humaines, vol. 12, 1975, pp. 177–187.

Kanya-Forstner, A.S. *The Conquest of the Western Sudan: A Study in French Military Imperialism.* Cambridge: Cambridge University Press, 1969.

————; see Andrew, Christopher, *The Climax of French Imperial Expansion.*

Keita, Rokiatou N'Diaye. *Kayes et le Haut-Sénégal.* Bamako: Editions populaires, 1972. 3 vols. [Bound as 2 vols.]

Kersaint-Gilly, F. de. "Essai sur l'évolution de l'esclavage en Afrique occidentale française. Son dernier stade au Soudan français." *Bulletin du Comité d'Etudes Historiques et Scientifiques de l'A.O.F.,* vol. 9, 1924, pp. 469–478.

Kingsley, Mary. *West African Studies.* New York: Barnes and Noble, 1964; 1st ed. 1899.

Klein, Martin A. *Islam and Imperialism in Senegal: Sine-Saloum, 1847–1914.* Stanford: Stanford University Press, 1968.

————. "Servitude among the Wolof and Sereer of Senegambia." In Susan Miers and Igor Kopytoff, eds., *Slavery in Africa,* pp. 335–366.

————. "Slave Resistance and Slave Emancipation in Coastal Guinea." In Suzanne Miers and Richard Roberts, *The End of Slavery in Africa* (Madison: University of Wisconsin Press, 1988), pp. 203–219.

————. "Slavery and Emancipation in French West Africa." Colloquium Paper, Woodrow Wilson International Center for Scholars, June 5, 1986 (unpublished).

————; see Roberts, Richard, and Klein, Martin A., "The Banamba Slave Exodus of 1905."

Kolchin, Peter. *Unfree Labor: American Slavery and Russian Serfdom.* Cambridge, Mass; London: Belknap Press of the Harvard University Press, 1987.

Kopytoff, Igor, ed.; see Miers, Suzanne, ed., *Slavery in Africa.*

Kosack, Godula; see Castles, Stephen, and Kosack, Godula, *Immigrant Workers and Class Structure in Europe.*

Kuper, Hilda, ed. *Urbanization and Migration in West Africa.* Berkeley: University of California Press, 1965.

Labat, Père. *Nouvelle relation de l'Afrique occidentale . . . .* Paris: G. Cavelier, 1728.

Labouret, Henri. "Le coton et l'indigène (Afrique Occidentale Française)." *Africa* (London), vol. 1, 1928, pp. 320–337.

————. "La grande détresse de l'arachide." *L'Afrique française,* 1932, p. 732.

————. "Irrigations, colonisation intérieure et main d'oeuvre au Soudan français." *Annales d'histoire économique et sociale,* 1929, pp. 365–376.

————. "La main d'oeuvre dans l'ouest africain." *L'Afrique française,* 1930, pp. 240–250.

————. "Maurice Delafosse." *Africa* (London), vol. 1, no. 1, Jan. 1928, pp. 112–115.

―――――. *Paysans d'Afrique occidentale*. Paris: Gallimard, 1941.

La Cognata, Gérard; see Bleneau, Gérard, and La Cognata, Gerard, "Evolution de la population de Bamako."

Lacombe, Bernard, et al. *Exode rural et urbanisation au Sénégal: sociologie de la migration des Serer de Niakhar vers Dakar en 1970*. Paris: O.R.S.T.O.M., 1977.

La Fontaine, J. S. *City Politics: A Study of Léopoldville, 1962–63*. Cambridge: Cambridge University Press, 1970.

Landes, David S. *The Unbound Prometheus: Technological Change and Industrial Development in Western Europe from 1750 to the Present*. Cambridge: Cambridge University Press, 1969.

Lanrezac, H. C. "Le cercle de Nioro." *Bulletin de la Société de Géographie commerciale de Paris*, vol. 27, pp. 227–261.

Lapidus, Ira M. *A History of Islamic Societies*. Cambridge: Cambridge University Press, 1988.

"Des laptots du Sénégal et en général des esclaves envoyés en France." *L'Abolitionniste français*, 1848, pp. 387–398.

Lartigue, Commandant de. "Notice géographique sur la région du Sahel." *L'Afrique française, Renseignements coloniaux*, no. 5, 1898, pp. 116–126.

―――――. "Notice historique sur la région du Sahel." *L'Afrique française, Renseignements coloniaux*, 1898, pp. 69–101.

Lasnet, Dr., et al. *Une mission au Sénégal*. Paris: A. Challamel, 1900.

Laufenberger, Henry. *Histoire de l'impôt*. Paris: P.U.F., Collection "Que sais-je?," 1954.

Leach, E. R. *Political Systems of Highland Burma: A Study of Kachin Social Structure*. London: Athlone Press, 1st ed. 1954.

Le Blanc, Colette. "Un village de la vallée du Sénégal: Amadi-Ounaré." *Cahiers d'outre-mer*, vol. 17, no. 66, 1964, pp. 117–148.

Le Bris, Emile; Rey, Pierre-Philippe; Samuel, Michel. *Capitalisme négrier, la marche des paysans vers le prolétariat*. Paris: Maspéro, 1976.

Le Clair, E. E.; and Schneider, Harold K. *Readings in Economic Anthropology: Readings in Theory and Analyses*. New York: Holt, Rhinehart and Winston, 1968.

Lees, Lynn Hollen. *Exiles of Erin: Irish Migrants in Victorian London*. Ithaca, N.Y.: Cornell University Press, 1979.

―――――; see Hohenberg, Paul M., *The Making of Urban Europe, 1000–1950*.

Lefébure, Jules. *Le régime des concessions au Congo*. Paris: "L'université de Paris," 1904.

Legris, Michel. "Quarante mille esclaves volontaires: les travailleurs noirs en France." *Le Monde*, Feb. 22; 23; 24, 1963.

Leriche, J.; see Rosier, J.-P., "Africains noirs présents au travail en France."

Lericollais, André. "Peuplement et migrations dans la vallée du Sénégal." *Cahiers de l'O.R.S.T.O.M.*, Série sciences humaines, vol. 12, 1975, pp. 123–135.

———; see Kane, Francine, "L'émigration en pays soninké."

Leroy-Beaulieu, Paul. *De la colonisation chez les peuples modernes*. Paris: Alcan, 1908. 2 vols.

Lévi, G. "Mobilita della popolazione e immigrazione a Torino nella prima metta del settecento." *Quaderni Storici*, vol. 17, 1971, pp. 510–554.

Levtzion, Nehemia. *Ancient Ghana and Mali*. London: Methuen, 1973.

———. "Merchants vs. Scholars and Clerics in West Africa: Differential and Complementary roles." In Levtzion and Fisher, *Rural and Urban Islam in West Africa*, pp. 21–37.

———. *Muslims and Chiefs in West Africa: A Study of Islam in the Middle Volta Basin in the Pre-Colonial Period*. Oxford: Clarendon Press, 1968.

———, and Fisher, Humphrey J., eds. *Rural and Urban Islam in West Africa*. Boulder, Colo.: Lynne Rienner, 1987.

———; see Hopkins, J. F. P., and Levtzion, N., eds. *Corpus of Early Arabic Sources for West African History*.

Liedholm, Carl, ed.; see Eicher, Carl K., and Liedholm, Carl, eds., *Growth and Development of the Nigerian Economy*.

Lipton, Michael. *Why Poor People Stay Poor: Urban Bias in World Development*. Cambridge, Mass.: Harvard University Press, 1977.

Little, Kenneth. *Urbanization as a Social Process: An Essay on Movement and Change in Contemporary Africa*. London: Routledge and Kegan Paul, 1974.

Lizelair. "M. Brévié et la politique indigène en A.O.F." *Le monde colonial illustré*, vol. 8, 1931, p. 196.

Lodhi, A. Q., and Tilly, Charles. "Urbanization, Crime and Collective Violence in Nineteenth Century France." *American Journal of Sociology*, vol. 79, 1973, pp. 297–318.

Lofchie, Michael F., ed.; see Bates, Robert H., ed., *Agricultural Development in Africa*.

Louis, William Roger, ed.; see Morel, E. D., *E. D. Morel's History of the Congo Reform Movement*.

Lovejoy, Paul. "Kola in the History of West Africa." *Cahiers d'Etudes Africaines*, vol. 20, nos. 77–78, 1980, pp. 97–134.

———. "The Role of the Wangarawa in Central Sudan." *Journal of African History*, vol. 19, 1978, pp. 173–193.

———. *Transformations in Slavery: A History of Slavery in Africa*. Cambridge: Cambridge University Press, 1991.

———, and Baier, S. "The Desert-Side Economy of the Central Sudan." *International Journal of African Historical Studies*, vol. 7, 1975, pp. 551–581.

Lubeck, Paul M. "Islamic Networks and Urban Capitalism: An Instance of Articulation from Northern Nigeria." *Cahiers d'Etudes Africaines*, vol. 21, nos. 81–83, 1981, pp. 67–78.

MacDonald, D. F. *Scotland's Shifting Population*. Glasgow: Jackson, 1937.

MacDonald, John S., and MacDonald, Leatrice D. "Chain Migration, Ethnic Neighborhood Formation, and Social Networks," reprinted from *Milbank Memorial Fund Quarterly*, vol. 42, 1964 in Charles Tilly, ed. *An Urban World*. Boston: Little, Brown, 1974, pp. 226–236.

————. "Urbanization, Ethnic Groups, and Social Segmentation." *Social Research*, vol. 29, 1962, pp. 431–448.

MacDougall, Elizabeth Ann. "The Idjil Salt Industry: Its Role in the Pre-Colonial Economy of the Western Sudan," Ph.D. thesis, University of Birmingham, U.K., 1980.

MacNamara, Robert S.; see International Bank for Reconstruction and Development, *The Assault on World Poverty*.

Mage, Abdon M. Eugène. *Voyage dans le Soudan occidental (Sénégambie-Niger) 1863–1866*. Paris: Hachette, 1868.

Mahot, Patricia. "Une épopée sans joie." *Autrement*, no. 49, April 1983.

Manchuelle, François. "Background to Black African Emigration to France: the Labor Migrations of the Soninke, 1848–1987." Ph.D dissertation, University of California, Santa Barbara 1987.

————. "Forced Labor in French West Africa, 1881–1946: A Reappraisal." Presentation at the annual meeting of the (U.S.) African Studies Association, Denver, Colorado, 22 November 1987. (Unpublished.)

————. "Garveyism in French West Africa, 1920–1932." Presentation at the annual meeting of the Southeastern Regional Society of African Studies, Columbia, South Carolina, 2 March 1990. (Unpublished.)

————. "Métis et colons: la famille Devès et l'émergence politique des Africains au Sénégal, 1881–1897." *Cahiers d'Etudes Africaines*, vol. 24, no. 96, 1984, pp. 477–504.

————. "Origins and Impact of Soninke Migrations from Senegal and Mali to France." Presentation at the annual meeting of the (U.S.) American Historical Association, Chicago, 28 December 1986. (Unpublished.)

————. "Origines républicaines de la politique d'expansion coloniale de Jules Ferry, 1838–1865." *Revue française d'histoire d'outre-mer* (Paris) vol. 75, no. 279, 1988, pp. 185–206.

————. "The Patriarchal Ideal of Soninke Labor Migrants: From Slave Owners to Employers of Free Labor Migrants." *Canadian Journal of African Studies*, vol. 23, 1989, pp. 106–125.

————. "Slavery, Emancipation and Labor Migration in West Africa: The Case of the Soninke." *Journal of African History*, vol. 30, 1989, pp. 89–106.

Mangin, Eugène. *The Mossi: Essay on the Manners and Customs of the Mossi People in the Western Sudan*. Translated by Ariane Brunel and Elliott Skinner. H.R.A.F. microform, 1959; first published Paris: Challamel, 1921.

Manning, Patrick. *Francophone Sub-Saharan Africa, 1880–1985*. Cambridge: Cambridge University Press, 1988.

Marguerat, Yves. *Analyse numérique des migrations vers les villes du Cameroun*. Paris: O.R.S.T.O.M, 1975.

————. "Des ethnies et des villes. Analyse des migrations vers les villes de Côte d'Ivoire." *Cahiers de l'O.R.S.T.O.M.*, vol. 18, série sciences humaines, no. 3, 1981–1982, pp. 303–340.

Marion, Marcel. *Histoire financière de la France depuis 1715*. Paris: Rousseau, 1914–1931. 6 vols.

Martin, Walter T.; see Gibbs, Jack P., "Urbanization, Technology and the Division of Labor."

Marty, Paul. *Etudes sénégalaises*. Paris: Société de l'histoire des colonies françaises; Leroux, [n.d., 192–.]

————. *Etudes sur l'Islam en Côte d'Ivoire*. Paris: Leroux, 1922.

————. *Etudes sur l'Islam au Sénégal*. Paris: Leroux, 1917.

————. *Etudes sur l'Islam au Soudan*. Paris: Leroux, 1921. 4 vols.

————. "L'Islam en Mauritanie et au Sénégal." *Revue du monde musulman*, vol. 31, 1915–1916, pp. 29–479.

Mauny, Raymond. *Tableau géographique de l'ouest africain au moyen âge*. Amsterdam: Swets et Zeitlinger N.V., 1967.

Maurienne. "La nouvelle traite des noirs." *Révolution africaine* (Algiers), no. 13, 27 Apr. 1963.

Mbaye, Saliou. "La représentation du Sénégal au Parlement français sous la Seconde République (1848–1851)." *Bulletin de l'I.F.A.N.*, vol. 38, série B, no. 3, 1976, pp. 517–551.

Meillassoux, Claude. *Anthropologie économique des Gouro de Côte d'Ivoire*. Paris: Mouton, 1974.

————. "Le commerce pré-colonial et le développement de l'esclavage à Gumbu du Sahel (Mali)." In Claude Meillassoux, ed., *The Development of Indigenous Trade and Markets in West Africa*, pp. 182–195.

————. "Essai d'interprétation du phénomène économique dans les sociétés traditionnelles d'auto-subsistance." *Cahiers d'Etudes Africaines*, vol. 1, no. 4, 1960, pp. 39–67.

————. "Etat et condition des esclaves à Gumbu (Mali) au XIXe. siècle." In Claude Meillassoux, ed., *L'esclavage en Afrique précoloniale*, pp. 221–247.

————. *Femmes, greniers et capitaux*. Paris: Maspéro, 1975.

————. "Les origines de Gumbu (Mali)." *Bulletin de l'I.F.A.N.*, vol. 34, Série B, no. 2, 1972, pp. 268–298.

————. *Urbanization in African Community: Voluntary Associations in Bamako.* Seattle; London: University of Washington Press, 1968.

————, ed. *The Development of Indigenous Trade and Markets in West Africa.* London: International African Institute; Oxford University Press, 1971.

————, ed. *L'esclavage en Afrique précoloniale.* Paris: Maspéro, 1975.

————; Doucouré, Lassana; and Simagha, Diaowé. *Légende de la dispersion des Kusa (épopée soninké).* Dakar: I.F.A.N., 1967.

Mendras, Henri. *La fin des paysans; changement et innovation dans les sociétés rurales françaises.* Paris: A. Colin, 1970.

————, ed. *La sagesse et le désordre.* Paris: Gallimard, 1980.

————, and Jollivet, Marcel, eds. *Les collectivités rurales françaises.* Paris: A. Colin, 1971.

Méniaud, Jacques. *Les pionniers du Soudan.* Paris: Société des publications modernes, 1931. 2 vols.

Mercier, René. *Le travail obligatoire dans les colonies françaises.* Paris: Larose, 1933.

Merle, Marc neveu et Robert. "Chemin de fer de Médine à St. Louis et Dakar, Mémoire relatif à la mise en communication, par voie ferrée, de Médine à St. Louis (Sénégal) adréssé à M. le Ministre des Travaux Publics, pour être soumis à la Commission supérieure du Transsaharien." In Haut-Sénégal. *Concessions aurifères et chemin de fer de Médine au littoral par le Djoloff et le Ferlo* (Bordeaux: Gounouilhou, 1880), pp. 81–96.

Merlin, Pierre. *L'exode rural.* Cahier de l'I.N.E.D., no. 59. Paris: P.U.F., 1971.

Mersadier, Yves. "La crise de l'arachide sénégalaise au début des années trente." *Bulletin de l'I.F.A.N.*, vol. 28, série B, nos. 3–4, 1966, pp. 826–877.

Meuvret, Jean. "Comment les Français du XVIIe siècle voyaient l'impôt." In Jean Meuvret, *Etudes d'histoire économique*, pp. 295–308.

————. *Etudes d'histoire économique.* Paris: A. Colin, 1971.

————. "Les idées économiques en France au XVIIe siècle." In Jean Meuvret, *Etudes d'histoire économique*, pp. 281–293.

Meyer, Thomas; Duesenberry, James Stumble; and Aliber, Robert Z., eds. *Money, Banking and the Economy.* New York: Norton, 1984.

Michel, Andrée. *Les travailleurs algériens en France.* Paris: C.N.R.S., 1956.

Michel, Marc. *L'appel à l'Afrique. Contributions et réactions à l'effort de guerre en A.O.F. (1914–1919).* Publications de la Sorbonne, Série Afrique, 6. Paris: Université de Paris I-Panthéon Sorbonne, Institut d'histoire des relations internationales contemporaines, 1982.

————. *La mission Marchand, 1895–1899.* Paris: Mouton, 1972.

————. "Un programme réformiste en 1919: Maurice Delafosse et la politique indigène en A.O.F." *Cahiers d'Etudes Africaines*, vol. 5, no. 58, 1975, pp. 313–327.

Miers, Suzanne, and Kopytoff, Igor, eds. *Slavery in Africa: History and Anthropological Perspectives.* Madison: University of Wisconsin Press, 1977.

Miers, Suzanne, and Roberts, Richard, eds. *The End of Slavery in Africa*. Madison: University of Wisconsin Press, 1988.

Mille, Pierre. *Le Congo Léopoldien*. Paris: Cahiers de la Quinzaine, 1905.

Mitchell, J. Clyde. "The Causes of Labour Migration." *Bulletin of the Inter-African Labour Institute*, vol. 6, no. 1, 1959, pp. 12–47.

―――. "The Growth of Towns." In Prudence Smith, ed., *Africa in Transition*. London: Max Reinhardt, 1958, pp. 47–53.

―――. "Wage Labour and Population in Central Africa." In Prothero, R. Mansell, and Barbour, Kenneth Michael, eds., *Essays on African Population*, pp. 193–248.

Moch, Leslie Page. *Paths to the City: Regional Migration in Nineteenth-Century France*. Preface by Louise and Charles Tilly. Beverly Hills; London; New Delhi: Sage, 1983.

Monteil, Charles. *Les Bambaras du Ségou et du Kaarta*. Paris: Larose, 1924.

―――. "Fin de siècle à Médine (1898–1899)." *Bulletin de l'I.F.A.N.*, vol. 28, Série B, nos. 1–2, 1966, pp. 84–171.

―――. *Les Khassonké, monographie d'une peuplade du Soudan français*. Paris: E. Leroux, 1915.

―――. "La légende du Ouagadou et l'origine des Soninké." In Charles Monteil, *Mélanges ethnologiques*. Mémoires de l'I.F.A.N., no. 23. Dakar: I.F.A.N., 1953, pp. 359–408.

―――. *Monographie de Djenné*. Tulle: J. Mazeyrie, 1903.

Morel, E. D. *Affairs of West Africa*. London: Heinemann, 1902.

―――. *The British Case in the French Congo*. New York: Negro University Press, 1960; reprint of London: Heinemann, 1903.

―――. *E. D. Morel's History of the Congo Reform Movement*. Edited by William Roger Louis and Jean Stengers. Oxford: Clarendon Press, 1968.

Mottin, Marie-France; see Dumont, René, and Mottin, Marie-France, *Stranglehold on Africa*.

Nacht, Marc. "Les travailleurs noirs en France ou la misère organisée." *Les Temps Modernes*, no. 218, July 1964, pp. 152–162.

Nadaud, Martin. *Léonard, maçon de la Creuse*. Introduction by Jean-Pierre Rioux. Paris: Maspéro, 1976.

N'Diaye, Francine. "La colonie du Sénégal au temps de Brière de l'Isle (1876–1881)." *Bulletin de l'I.F.A.N.*, vol. 30, série B, 1968, pp. 463–510.

N'Diaye, Jean-Pierre. "Noir, pauvre et sans travail, le drame de l'émigration noire en France." *Réalités africaines*, no. 5, May–June 1963.

N'Diaye Keita, Rokiatou; see Keita, Rokiatou N'Diaye, *Kayes et le Haut-Sénégal*.

N'Diaye, Magatte Louis. "Libres opinions." *L'Ouest Africain Français* (Dakar), 25 Feb. 1928.

―――. "Tribune libre: sur la loi sur les accidents du travail." *L'Ouest Africain Français* (Dakar), 18 Feb. 1928.

N'Diaye, Momar Kébé. "Emigrés de tous les pays, divisez-vous . . ." *Jeune Afrique*, no. 1091, 2 Dec. 1981.

N'Dongo, Sally. *La coopération franco-africaine*. Paris: Maspéro, 1972.

———. *Exil, connais pas*. Paris: Editions du Cerf, 1976.

Nègre, Pierre. *Essai sur les conceptions économiques de Saint Thomas d'Aquin*. Aix-en-Provence: Imprimerie universitaire de Provence, 1927.

Newbury, C. W. "The Formation of the Government General of French West Africa." *Journal of African History*, vol. 1, 1960, pp. 111–128.

Ninine, Jules. *La main d'oeuvre indigène dans les colonies africaines*. Paris: Jouve, 1932.

Niane, Djibril Tamsir. *Sunjata: An Epic of Old Mali*. Translated by G. D. Pickett. London: Longmans, 1965.

Nordhaus, William D.; see Samuelson, Paul, *Economics*.

Nyambarza, Daniel. "Le marabout El Hadj Mamadou Lamine d'après les archives françaises." *Cahiers d'Etudes Africaines*, vol. 8, no. 33, 1969, pp. 124–145.

Olivier, Marcel. *Six ans de politique sociale à Madagascar*. Paris: Grasset, 1931.

Oloruntimehin, B. Olatunji. "Muhammad Lamine in Franco-Tukulor Relations, 1885–1887." *Journal of the Historical Society of Nigeria*, vol. 4, no. 3, December 1968, pp. 375–396.

Ortiz, Sutti, ed. *Economic Anthropology: Topics and Theories*. Longham, Md.; New York; London: University Press of America; Society for Economic Anthropology, 1983.

Ould Mohammed, Moussa. "Cinq villages au travail." *Jeune Afrique*, no. 1245, no. 14, 1984.

[Oxfam]; see Thomas, Harford, ed., *A Picture of Poverty*.

Park, Mungo. *The Travels of Mungo Park*. London: J. M. Dent and Sons; New York: E. P. Dutton, 1910 and 1915.

Parkin, David, ed. *Town and Country in Central and Eastern Africa*. London: International African Institute, 1975.

Paques, Viviana. *Les Bambara*. Paris: P.U.F., 1954.

Pasquier, Roger. "Villes du Sénégal au XIXe. siècle." *Revue française d'outre-mer*, vol. 47, 1960, pp. 387–426.

Patterson, Orlando. *Slavery and Social Death: A Comparative Study*. Cambridge, Mass.: Harvard University Press, 1982.

Patterson, Sheila, ed.; see Fortes, Meyer, and Patterson, Sheila, eds., *Studies in African Social Anthropology*.

Pearson, Harry W., ed.; see Polanyi, Karl, and Arensberg, M., eds., *Trade and Markets in the Early Empires*.

Pearson, Scott R., Stryker, J. Dirck, Humphreys, Charles P., et al., eds. *Rice in West Africa: Policy and Economics*. Stanford: Stanford University Press, 1981.

Pélissier, Paul. *Les Paysans du Sénégal: les civilisations agraires du Cayor à la Casamance.* Saint-Yriex, France: Imprimerie Fabrègue, 1966.

Perret, Anne. "J'oublie Dieu pour gagner de quoi vivre." *Autrement,* no. 49, April 1983, pp. 94–107.

Perinbam, B. Marie. "Notes on Dyula Origins and Nomenclature." *Bulletin de l'I.F.A.N.,* vol. 36, série B, 1974, pp. 676–690.

Person, Yves. *Samori, une révolution dyula.* Dakar: I.F.A.N., 1968–1975. 3 vols.

Péter, Georges. *L'effort français au Sénégal.* Paris: Brocard, 1933.

Pheffer, Paul Edward. "Railroads and Aspects of Social Change in Senegal, 1878–1933." Ph.D. dissertation, University of Pennsylvania, 1975.

————. "Political and Economic Strategies for French Colonial Railroads in Africa." *French Colonial Historical Society Proceedings,* vol. 2, 1977, pp. 60–69.

Pietri, Capitaine. *Les français au Niger: voyages et combats.* Paris: Hachette, 1885.

Pinchemel, Philippe. *Structures sociales et dépopulation rurale dans les campagnes picardes de 1836 à 1936.* Paris: A. Colin, 1957.

Pitié, Jean. *Exode rural et migrations intérieures en France: l'exemple du Poitou-Charentes.* Poitiers: Nevers, 1971.

Pitt-Rivers, J. "Honour and Social Status." In G. Perestiany, ed., *Honour and Shame. The Values of Mediterranean Society.* London: Weidenfeld and Nicolson, 1965, pp. 19–78.

Poidevin, Raymond. "Protectionnisme et relations internationales: l'exemple du tarif douanier de 1910." *Revue historique,* no. 497, 1971, pp. 47–62.

Polanyi, Karl. "The Economy as an Institutional Process." In Karl Polanyi, M. Arensberg, and Harry W. Pearson, eds., *Trade and Markets in the Early Empires,* pp. 243–269.

Polanyi, Karl, Arensberg, M., and Pearson, Harry W., eds. *Trade and Markets in the Early Empires.* Glencoe, Ill.: Free Press; Falcon's Wings Press, 1957.

La politique coloniale de la France. Paris: Alcan, 1924.

Pollet, Eric, and Winter, Grace. *La société soninké (Diahunu, Mali).* Brussels: Université Libre de Bruxelles, Editions de l'Institut de Sociologie, 1971.

Poquin, Jean-Jacques. *Les relations économiques extérieures des pays d'Afrique noire, 1925–1955.* Paris: A. Colin, 1957.

Poulet, Georges. *Les Maures de l'Afrique occidentale française.* Paris: Challamel, 1904.

Priestley, Herbert Ingram. *France Overseas: A Study of Modern Imperialism.* New York; London: Appleton-Century, 1938.

Prothero, R. Mansell; and Barbour, Kenneth Michael, eds. *Essays on African Population.* New York: Praeger, 1961.

Quiminal, Catherine. *Gens d'ici, gens d'ailleurs. Migrations Soninké et transformations villageoises.* Paris: Christian Bourgois, 1991.

Quinn, Charlotte A. *Mandingo Kingdoms of the Senegambia.* Evanston, Ill.: Northwestern University Press, 1972.

Raffenel, Anne. "Exploration du pays de Galam, du Bondou et du Bambouck et retour par la Gambie." *Revue coloniale,* vol. 4, Oct. 1844, pp. 136–218.

———. "Le haut Sénégal et la Gambie en 1843 et 1844." *Revue coloniale,* vol. 8, Mar. 1846, pp. 309–340.

———. *Nouveau voyage dans le pays des nègres.* Paris: Chaix, 1856.

———. "Second voyage d'exploration dans l'intérieur de l'Afrique, entrepris par M. A. Raffenel." *Revue coloniale,* Dec. 1849, pp. 217–276.

———. *Voyage dans l'Afrique occidentale . . . exécuté en 1843 et 1844.* Paris: A. Bertrand, 1846.

Raison-Jourde, Françoise. *La colonie auvergnate de Paris au XIXe siècle.* Paris: Ville de Paris, Commission des Travaux Historiques, 1976.

———. "Endogamie et stratégie d'implantation professionnelle des migrants auvergnats à Paris au XIXe siècle." *Ethnologie française,* vol. 10, no. 2, 1980, pp. 153–162.

Rançon, André. *Dans la Haute-Gambie, voyage d'exploration scientifique.* Paris: Société d'éditions scientifiques, 1894.

Recensement démographique de Bouaké, Juillet–Août 1958. République de la Côte d'Ivoire: n.p., [ca. 1960].

Read, Margaret. "Migrant Labour in Africa and its Effects on Tribal Life." *International Labour Review,* vol. 45, no. 6, June 1942, pp. 6055–631.

Redford, Arthur. *Labour Migration in England, 1800–1850.* Manchester: Manchester University Press, 1964; 1st ed., 1926.

Renard, Capitaine. *La colonisation au Congo français.* Paris: Kugelmann, 1901.

Renault, François. *L'abolition de l'esclavage au Sénégal: l'attitude de l'adminstration française, 1848–1905.* Paris: Société française d'histoire d'outre-mer, 1972.

Rey. "Voyage à Farabana (haute Sénégambie)." *Revue coloniale,* série 2, Jan. 1854, pp. 34–62.

Rey, Pierre-Philippe; see Le Bris, Emile, Rey, Pierre-Phillipe, and Samuel, Michel, *Capitalisme négrier.*

———. *Colonialisme, néo-colonialisme et transition au capitalisme, l'exemple de la "Comilog" au Congo-Brazzaville.* Paris: Maspéro, 1971.

Richards, Audrey I. *Hunger and Work in a Savage Tribe.* Preface by B. Malinowski. London: Routledge and Sons, 1932.

Riembau, Frédéric. *De Dakar au Niger: la question du chemin de fer et la mise en valeur des territoires de la Sénégambie et du Niger.* Paris: Challamel, 1908.

Riley, Bernard; see Brokensha, David, and Riley, Bernard, "Introduction of Cash Crops in a Marginal Area of Kenya."

Roberts, Richard. "The End of Slavery in the French Soudan, 1904–1914." In Suzanne Miers and Richard Roberts, eds., *The End of Slavery in Africa,* pp. 282–307.

———. "Long-Distance Trade and Production: Sinsani in the Nineteenth Century." *Journal of African History*, vol. 21, 1980, pp. 169–188.

———. *Warriors, Merchants and Slaves: The State and the Economy in the Middle Niger Valley, 1700–1914*. Stanford: Stanford University Press, 1987.

———. "Women's Work and Women's Property: Household Social Relations in the Marka Textile Industry of the Nineteenth Century." *Comparative Studies in Society and History*, vol. 26, 1984, pp. 229–250.

———, and Klein, Martin A. "The Banamba Slave Exodus of 1905 and the Decline of Slavery in the Western Sudan." *Journal of African History*, vol. 21, 1980, pp. 375–394.

———, and Miers, Suzanne, eds.; see Miers, *The End of Slavery in Africa*.

Roberts, Stephen H. *History of French Colonial Policy*. London: P. S. King, 1929. 2 vols.

Robin, Jean. "Autour d'un suicide sénégalais." *2d International West African Conference, Bissau, 1947*, vol. 5, 1952, pp. 295–299.

Robinson, David. *Chiefs and Clerics: Abdul Bokar Kan and Futa Toro, 1853–1891*. Oxford: Clarendon Press, 1975.

———. *The Holy War of Umar Tal: The Western Sudan in the Mid-Nineteenth Century*. Oxford: Clarendon Press, 1985.

Rocheteau, Gabriel. "Société wolof et mobilité." *Cahiers de l'O.R.S.T.O.M.*, Série sciences humaines, vol. 12, 1975, pp. 3–18.

Rondet-Saint, Maurice. *L'Afrique Equatoriale Française*. Preface by Marcel Saint-Germain. Paris: Plon, 1911.

Roniger, Louis; see Eisenstadt, S. N., and Roniger, Louis, "Patron-Client Relation as a Model of Structuring Social Exchange."

Rosier, J.-P., and Leriche, J. "Africains noirs présents au travail en France." *Cahiers nord-africains*, no. 86, Oct.–Nov. 1961, pp. 8–30.

Rouch, Jean. "Problêmes relatifs à l'étude des migrations traditionnelles et actuelles en Afrique Occidentale." *Bulletin de l'I.F.A.N.*, vol. 22, série B, nos. 3–4, 1960, pp. 369–378.

Rousseau, Jean-Jacques. *Oeuvres complètes*. Paris: Gallimard, Bibliothèque de "La Pléiade," 1959–1969. 4 vols.

Rueschmeyer, Dietrich. *Power and the Division of Labour*. Stanford: Stanford University Press, 1986.

S.C.O.A.; see Fondation S.C.O.A. pour la recherche scientifique en Afrique noire (projet Boucle du Niger).

Sabot, R. H. *Economic Development and Urban Migration in Tanzania, 1900–1971*. Oxford: Clarendon Press, 1979.

Saccomano, Eugène. *Bandits à Marseilles*. Paris: Julliard, 1968.

Saint-Martin, Yves. *L'empire toucouleur et la France: un demi-siècle de relations diplomatiques (1846–1893)*. Dakar: Université de Dakar, Publications de la Faculté des lettres et sciences humaines, 1967.

————. "Papiers Brière de l'Isle Sénégal-Soudan 1878–1891 (Fonds privé B. Dunoyer de Segonzac). Présentation et inventaire par Yves Saint-Martin." *Bulletin de l'I.F.A.N.*, vol. 38, série B, no. 3, 1976, pp. 552–591.

————. "Les relations diplomatiques entre la France et l'Empire toucouleur de 1860 à 1887." *Bulletin de l'I.F.A.N.*, vol. 27, série B, nos. 1–2, 1965, pp. 183–222.

————. *Une source de l'histoire coloniale du Sénégal: les rapports de situation politique (1874–1891).* Dakar: Université de Dakar, Publications de la Faculté de lettres et sciences humaines, 1966.

Saint-Père, Jean-Hubert. *Les Sarakollé du Guidimakha.* Paris: Larose, 1925.

Salem, Gérard. "De la brousse sénégalaise au Boul'Mich: le système commercial mouride en France." *Cahiers d'Etudes Africaines*, vol. 21, nos. 81–83, 1981, pp. 267–288.

Salt, John; and Clout, Hugh, eds. *Migration in Post-War Europe: Geographical Essays.* London: Oxford University Press, 1976.

Samuel, Michel; see Le Bris, Emile, and Rey, Pierre-Philippe, *Capitalisme négrier.*

————. *Le prolétariat africain noir en France.* Paris: Maspéro, 1978.

Samuelson, Paul; and Nordhaus, William D. *Economics.* New York: McGraw-Hill, 1985.

Sanmarco, Louis. *Le colonisateur colonisé.* Paris: Fabre, 1983.

Sanneh, Lamine O. *The Jakhanke.* London: International African Institute, 1979.

Sar, Moustapha. *Louga et sa région (Sénégal).* Dakar: I.F.A.N., 1973.

Sarna, Jonathan D. "The Myth of No Return: Jewish Return Migration to Eastern Europe, 1881–1914." In Dirck Hoerder, ed., *Labor Migration in the Atlantic Economies*, pp. 423–434.

Sarraut, Albert. *Grandeur et servitude coloniales.* Paris: Sagittaire, 1931.

————. *La mise en valeur des colonies françaises.* Paris: Payot, 1923.

Saugnier. *Relation de plusieurs voyages à la côte d'Afrique . . .* Paris: Gueffier jeune, 1791.

Saulnier, Eugène. *Une compagnie à privilège au XIXe siècle: la compagnie de Galam au Sénégal.* Paris: Larose, 1921.

Sautter, Gilles. *De l'Atlantique au fleuve Congo, une géographie du sous-peuplement. République du Congo. République gabonaise.* Paris; The Hague: Mouton, 1966. 2 vols.

————. "Migrations, société et développement en pays mossi." *Cahiers d'Etudes Africaines*, no. 79, vol. 20, 1980, pp. 215–253.

————. "Note sur la construction du chemin de fer Congo-Océan, 1921–1934." *Cahiers d'Etudes Africaines*, vol. 7, no. 26, 1967, pp. 219–299.

Sawadogo, Patrice. *Impact de la croissance démographique sur le développement économique et social en République de Côte d'Ivoire.* [Nairobi:] Commission économique des Nations Unies pour l'Afrique, [1980].

Sayad, Abdelmalek; see Gilette, Alain, and Sayad, Abdelmalek, *L'immigration algérienne en France.*

Schapera, I. *Migrant Labour and Tribal Life.* London: Oxford University Press, 1947.

Schmitz, Jean. "Anthropologie historique de quelques villages et territoires de la région de Matam (Rapport de mission effectuée auprès de l'I.D.A.)," May 1989 (unpublished).

———. "Rhétorique et géopolitique du *jihad* d'al-Hajj Umar Taal." *Cahiers d'Etudes Africaines,* vol. 28, no. 109, 1988, pp. 123–133.

———. *West African Slavery and Atlantic Commerce: The Senegal River Valley, 1700–1860.* Cambridge: Cambridge University Press, 1993.

Schneider, Harold K.; see Le Clair, E. E., *Readings in Economic Anthropology.*

Schob, David E. *Hired Hands and Plowboys: Farm Labor in the Midwest, 1815–60.* Urbana; Chicago; London: University of Illinois, 1975.

Schoelcher, Victor. *L'esclavage au Sénégal en 1880.* Paris: Librairie centrale des publications populaires, 1881.

Schuh, Edward, ed.; see Johnson, D. Gale, ed., *The Role of Markets in the World Food Economy.*

Searing, James F. "Aristocrats, Slaves, and Peasants: Power and Dependency in the Wolof States, 1700–1850." *International Journal of African Historical Studies,* vol. 21, no. 3, 1988, pp. 475–503.

Seck, Assane. *Dakar, métropole ouest-africaine.* Dakar: I.F.A.N., 1970.

———. "Les escales du fleuve Sénégal." *Revue de géographie de l'Afrique occidentale,* nos. 1–2, 1965, pp. 71–118.

Sée, Henri. *Histoire économique de la France.* Paris: A. Colin, 1942. 2 vols.

Sembène, Ousmane. *Le docker noir.* Paris: Présence africaine, 1973.

Sewell, William H. *Structure and Mobility: The Men and Women of Marseilles, 1820–1870.* Cambridge: Cambridge University Press; Paris: Maison des sciences de l'Homme, 1985.

Shelley, Louise I. *Crime and Modernization: The Impact of Industrialization and Urbanization on Crime.* Carbondale: Southern Illinois University Press, 1981.

Sibert, Edmond. "Développement de la consommation du riz en A.O.F. et extension de la riziculture dans la vallée du Niger." *Riz et riziculture,* vol. 4, 1929–1930, pp. 21–34.

Skinner, Elliott P. "Labor Migration among the Mossi of Upper Volta." In Kuper, Hilda, ed., *Urbanization and Migration in West Africa,* pp. 60–84.

———. "Labour Migration and its Relationship to Socio-Cultural Change in Mossi Society." *Africa,* vol. 30, 1960, pp. 375–401.

Soleillet, Paul. *Voyage à Ségou, 1878–1879.* Paris: Challamel, 1887.

Songre, Ambroise. "Mass Emigration from the Upper Volta: The Facts and Implications." *International Labour Review,* vol. 108, 1973, pp. 209–225.

Southall, Aidan W. *Alur Society: A Study in Processes and Types of Domination.* Cambridge: W. Heffer, 1953.

―――. "Population Movements in East Africa." In R. Mansell Prothero and Kenneth Michael Barbour, eds., *Essays on African Population*, pp. 157–192.

Spiegler, J. S. "Aspects of Nationalist Thought among French-Speaking West Africans." D. Phil. thesis, Oxford University, Nuffield College, 1968.

Steinkamp-Ferrier, Lucie. "Sept villages du Guidimakha Mauritanien face à un project de développement: l'histoire d'une recherche." Doctorat de Troisième cycle, Ecole des Hautes Etudes en Sciences Sociales, 1983.

Stengers, Jean. "King Leopold's Imperialism." In Roger Owen and Bob Sutcliffe, eds., *Studies in the Theory of Imperialism.* London: Longman, 1972.

―――, ed.; see Morel, E. D., *E. D. Morel's History of the Congo Reform Movement.*

Stewart, C. C. "Emergent Classes and the Early State: The Southern Sahara." In Donald Crummey and C. C. Stewart, eds., *Modes of Production in Africa: The Precolonial Era.* London; Beverly Hills: Sage, 1981, pp. 69–91.

―――. *Islam and Social Order in Mauritania: A Case Study in the Nineteenth Century.* Oxford: Clarendon Press, 1973.

Stoetzel, Jean; see Girard, Alain, *Français et immigrés.*

Stryker, J. Dirck, ed.; see Pearson, Scott R., et al., eds., *Rice in West Africa.*

"Sur le chemin de fer du Sénégal." *Revue économique française*, vol. 5, 1882–1883, pp. 403–404.

Suret-Canale, Jean. *Afrique noire occidentale et centrale.* Paris: Editions sociales, 1964. 3 vols.

―――. *French Colonialism in Tropical Africa, 1900–1945.* Translation by Till Gottheiner of *Afrique noire occidentale et centrale.* New York: Pica Press, 1971.

Sutcliffe, Anthony, ed.; see Fraser, Derek, ed., *The Pursuit of Urban History.*

Swindell, Ken. *The Strange Farmers of the Gambia.* Swansea: University College, Centre for Development Studies, 1981.

―――. "Serawoolies, Tillibunkas and Strange Farmers: The Development of Migrant Groundnut Farming along the Gambia River, 1848–95." *Journal of African History*, vol. 21, 1980, pp. 93–104.

Sy, Cheikh Tidiane. *La confrérie sénégalaise des Mourides.* Paris: Présence Africaine, 1969.

Tapinos, Georges. *L'économie des migrations internationales.* Paris: Presses de la fondation internationale des sciences politiques, 1974.

―――. *L'immigration étrangère en France.* Cahier de l'I.N.E.D., no. 71. Paris: P.U.F., 1975.

Tardieu, Amédée. *Sénégambie et Guinée.* Paris: F. Didot, 1847.

Tautain, L. "Etudes critiques sur l'ethnologie et l'ethnographie des peuples du bassin du Sénégal." *Revue d'Ethnographie*, vol. 4, 1885, pp. 61–80.

Tauxier, Louis. *The Black Population of the Sudan, Mossi and Gurunsi Country.* Translated by Ariane Brunel. H.R.A.F. microfiche, 1959; 1st ed., Paris: Larose, 1912.

———. *La religion bambara.* Paris: P. Geuthner, 1927.

Taylor, Milton C., ed. *Taxation for African Economic Development.* London: Hutchinson International, 1970.

Tellier, G. *Autour de Kita.* Paris: Henri-Charles Lavauzelle, [c. 1898].

Terray, Emmanuel, ed.; see Bazin, Jean, ed., *Guerres de lignages et guerres d'Etat en Afrique.*

Terray, Emmanuel. "Commerce précolonial et organisation sociale chez les Dida de Côte d'Ivoire." In Claude Meillassoux, ed., *Development of Indigenous Trade and Markets,* pp. 145–152.

———. "Long Distance Exchange and the Formation of the State: The Case of the Abron Kingdom of Gyaman." *Economy and Society,* vol. 3, no. 3, 1974, pp. 315–343.

Tessier, G. "La Mise en valeur du Congo français." *L'année coloniale,* no. 1, 1899, pp. 60–81.

Tharaud, Jérome; and Jean. *The Long Walk of Samba Diouf.* Translated by William Steel. New York: Duffield, 1924.

Thernstrom, Stephan. *Poverty and Progress: Social Mobility in a Nineteenth-Century City.* Cambridge, Mass.: Harvard University Press, 1964.

Thomas, Harford, ed. *A Picture of Poverty: The 1979 Oxfam Report.* Oxford: Oxfam, 1979.

Tilly, Charles; and Brown, C. Harold. "On Uprooting, Kinship and the Auspices of Migration." *International Journal of Comparative Sociology,* vol. 8, 1967, pp. 139–164.

———; see Lodhi, A. Q., "Urbanization, Crime and Collective Violence in Nineteenth-Century France."

Todaro, Michael. *Internal Migration in Developing Countries: A Review of Theory, Evidence, Methodology and Research Priorities.* Geneva: I.L.O., 1976.

Toupet, Charles. *La sédentarisation des nomades en Mauritanie centrale sahélienne.* Lille: Atelier de reproduction des thèses, 1977.

Trébous, Madeleine. *Vie et travail des Algériens en France.* Paris: Jour, 1974.

Tuly, A. Hasan; see Craven, Kathryn, "Rice Policy in Senegal."

U.G.T.S.F. [Union Générale des Travailleurs Sénégalais en France]. *Le livre des travailleurs africains en France.* Paris: Maspéro, 1970.

Van Chi-Bonnardel, Régine. *Vie de relations au Sénégal.* Dakar: I.F.A.N., 1978.

Van Velsen, J. "Some Methodological Problems of the Study of Labour Migration." In *Urbanization in African Social Change.* Proceedings of the Inaugural Seminar, Centre for African Studies, University of Edinburgh, [c. 1961,] pp. 12–47.

Van Vollenhoven, Joost. *Une âme de chef.* Paris: Imprimerie Henri Deval, 1920.

————. *Etude sur le fellah algérien*. Paris: Rousseau, 1903.

Villard, André. *Histoire du Sénégal*. Dakar: Ars Africae; Maurice Viale, 1943.

Villasante Cervello, Mariella. "Collectivités tribales, restructuration des stratégies sociales de reproduction et de pouvoir. Quelques aspects du système foncier dans la région de l'Assaba, République islamique de Mauritanie." Université de Genève, Institut Universitaire d'Etudes du Développement, Mémoire No. 46, 1989.

Walaszek, Adam. "Preserving or Transforming Role? Migrants and Polish Territories in the Era of Mass Migrations." Unpublished, 1992.

Wallerstein, Immanuel. "Migration in West Africa: The Political Perspective." In Hilda Kuper, ed., *Urbanization and Migration in West Africa*, pp. 148–159.

Wallon, Armand, ed.; see Duby, Georges, ed., *Histoire de la France rurale*.

Watts, Michael. *Silent Violence: Food, Famine and Peasantry in Northern Nigeria*. Berkeley: University of California Press, 1983.

Webb, Jr., James L. A. *Desert Frontier: Ecological and Economic Change along the Western Sahel, 1600–1850*. Madison: University of Wisconsin Press, 1995.

————. "Ecological and Economic Change along the Middle Reaches of the Gambia River, 1945–1985." *African Affairs*, vol. 91, no. 4, 1992, pp. 543–565.

————. "The Evolution of the Idaw al-Hajj Commercial Diaspora. *Cahiers d'Etudes Africaines*, vol. 35, nos. 138–139, 1995, pp. 455–475.

————. "The Mid-Eighteenth-Century Gum Arabic Trade and the British Conquest of Saint-Louis du Sénégal, 1758." *Journal of Imperial and Commonwealth History*, vol. 25, no. 1, 1997, pp. 37–58.

Weber, Max. *The Theory of Social and Economic Organization*. Translated by A. M. Henderson and Talcott Parsons. Glencoe, Ill.: Free Press, 1947.

Weigel, J.-Y. *Migration et production domestique des Soninké du Sénégal*. Paris: O.R.S.T.O.M., 1982.

Weinstein, Brian. *Eboué*. New York: Oxford University Press, 1972.

Weiskel, Timothy C. *French Colonial Rule and the Baule Peoples: Resistance and Collaboration, 1889–1911*. Oxford: Clarendon Press, 1980.

————. "The Precolonial Baule: A Reconstruction." *Cahiers d'Etudes Africaines*, 1978, vol. 18, no. 72, pp. 503–560.

Wesselring, H. L. "Le modèle colonial hollandais dans la théorie coloniale française, 1880–1914." *Revue française d'histoire d'outre-mer*, vol. 68, 1976, no. 231, pp. 222–255.

Wilks, Ivor. *Asante in the Nineteenth Century: The Structure and Evolution of a Political Order*. Cambridge: Cambridge University Press, 1975.

Willis, John Ralph, ed. *Studies in West African Islam, vol. 1, The Cultivators of Islam*. London: F. Cass, 1979.

Winter, Grace; see Pollet, Eric, *La société soninké*.

Works, John A. *Pilgrims in a Strange Land: Hausa Communities in Chad*. New York: Columbia University Press, 1976.

World Bank; see International Bank for Reconstruction and Development.

Young, Arthur. *Voyages en France en 1787, 1788, et 1789*. Translated and edited by Henri Sée. Paris: A. Colin, 1931. 3 vols.

Zartman, I. William; and Delgado, Christopher. *The Political Economy of the Ivory Coast*. New York: Praeger, 1984.

Zeltner, F. de. "Tissus africains à dessins réservés ou décolorés." *Bulletins et mémoires de la société d'anthropologie de Paris*, 6e. série, no. 1, 1910, pp. 224–227.

Zerhaoui, Ahsène. *Les travailleurs algériens en France*. Paris: Maspéro, 1971.

Zion, Henri. "Le poste de Bakel à l'époque du gouverneur Faidherbe, 1855–1865." Mémoire de maîtrise, Université de Dakar, Faculté de lettres et sciences humaines, 1968.

Zuccarelli, François. "L'entrepôt fictif de Gorée entre 1822 et 1852: une exception au régime de l'exclusif." *Annales Africaines*, 1959, pp. 261–282.

———. "Les maires de St. Louis et Gorée de 1816 à 1872." *Bulletin de l'I.F.A.N.*, vol. 35, série B, no. 3, 1973, pp. 551–573.

———. "Le recrutement de travailleurs sénégalais par l'Etat indépendant du Congo (1888–1896)." *Revue française d'histoire d'outre-mer*, vol. 47, 1960, nos. 168–169, pp. 475–481.

———. "Le régime des engagés à temps au Sénégal (1817–1848)." *Cahiers d'Etudes Africaines*, 1962, no. 7, pp. 420–461.

Index

Delafosse, Maurice, 133, 146, 149, 154, 155, 166, 167–169
Delavignette, Robert, 188
Demba Jango, 127
Demba Jangu Bacili, 83
Demba Kona, 127
Descemet, Governor, 123–124
desiccation, 158–159
Devès family, 106
Diagne, Blaise, 127–128, 184, 199, 204
Diarra, Souleymane, 2, 216
Diaxite, of Jawara, 111
Dida, 38
Didelot, Governor, 169
Diouf, Galandou, 199–200
Diourbel, 193
Doué River, 113
drought, 11, 212
dubangandi komo, 36
Dukure, of Jawara, 111
Dukure clan, 16, 18, 23
Dunkerque, 200
Duranthon, Commandant: administrative reports critical of colonial policy, 152–155, mentioned, 160; incomplete 1921 census by, 172–174; sets head tax in Yelimane, 174; beliefs about migration and social change, 175; appointment as recruiter of navetanes, 184

Ecole Normale (Teachers' College) of Gorée, 204
Elkan, Walter, 80–81
emancipation: condition of former slaves after, 134–140; different responses from the Marka and Soninke toward explained, 139; impact on adult migration, 140–143; impact on youth migration, 143. See also slavery, slaves
ethnicity: diversity in Soninke homeland, 11; Soninke compared with Fuutanke, who have no weaver caste, 26; in Congo migrant sample, 113–114; Marka and Soninke responses to emancipation explained, 139; composition of migrants from cercle of Nioro, 173; and periods of migrants' residency in Dakar, 192
exodes, 161–163. See also migration

Faidherbe, Governor: proposal to reform the tax system, 67–69; creation of embryonic administration in Senegal, 69
Fado, 20
Fajele Sise, 85
Falemme River Valley, 42
falo, 11. See also agricultural lands
famine: in Upper Senegal region, 70; in Bundu in 1900, 100; in 1913–1914, 147; in Bandiagara, 148. See also subsistence crisis
Fatick, 141
Faure, Emile, 199, 200
Félou cataracts, 50
Fenaltoa, Stefano, 64
Fergo Umar, 114, 227
Ferlo semidesert, 38
firdou, 160
Fode Mamadu Jaaxo, 182
Fode Saalum Saaxo, 127
Fofani clan, 111
forced labor: colonial belief in value of, 7–8; and colonial taxation, 8; in Upper Senegal in 1880s, 94; suspended in Gwey, 97; revival after First World War, 148–149; periodization of, in French West Africa, 148; for Jaxandappe plantation, 150–151; resistance to, in cercles of Kayes and Nioro, 151; impact on temporary migration evaluated, 161–163; in French Congo, 163–167; Delafosse's critique of military draft, 167–169
Fort-Lamy, 122
Foyer du Marin Sénégalais, 201–202, 211
Franco-Prussian war, 74
free labor, 103–104
freed-slave villages, 131
French Congo: forced labor in, 163–167; concessionary companies, 163–164; 1921 estimate of population in, 167
French Parliament, 97, 130, 165, 167, 184
French Soudan, 93–94, 98, 108, 130
French West Indians, 226
Frey, Commandant: description of river traffic, 75; on Soninke investments in slaves, 81, 82; on commercial expansion in Soninke homeland, 90–91; on war booty from suppression of Mamadu Lamin Darame's revolt, 96; estimate of Gidimaxa taxes paid to Umarians, 97; wages war on Gidimaxa, 103
Fuuta Tooro, 38
Fuutanke migrants: village origins of, 113–114; and Fergo Umar, 114, 227

Gabon, 123
Gajaaga: and hydrographic system of Upper Senegal River, 10; historical evolution of, 16; affected by marigotier trade, 49; partitioned under French guidance, 51; increase in cereal production as a result of gum trade, 53; labor migrants to Congo from, 109; names and villages of migrants to Congo from, 110; women in, grow peanuts and grain for sale, 181–182; clan ties in, and migration, 220
gajaba, 11–12. See also cereals
Galadio Terewele, 186

Office National de l'Immigration, 213, 214
Olivier, Marcel, 154
Ololdu, 87–88
Oudourou, 113
Ourossogui, 4

Park, Mungo, 23
patriarchy: under stress as result of migration, 175–177; under stress as result of emancipation of slaves, 177. *See also* Political Order, Social Order
peanuts: expansion of production in Upper Senegal region, 51–52; early experience in the Gambia, 54–55; expansion of trade in, and exports from Bakel, 75–77; expansion in years 1910–1912, 141; impact of railways, 141–142; golden age of, in Senegambia, 169; song about peanut boom, 170–171, 198–199
Peloponnesos, 92
Peterson peanut oil factory, 190
Pineau, Commandant de, 70–72
Pinet-Laprade, Governor, 73
Podor, 51
Polish migrants, 176
political order: segmentary states, 15; institutions of formalized clientship, 17; royal clans, 17–18; praise-songs, 18–19, 20; politics of clientage, 14–22; clientage and honor, 20
Pollet, Eric and Grace Winter, 58, 132, 134, 136, 177–178
polygyny, 16
Popular Front, 149, 201
population: African migrants in France, 2, 213, 216–217, 218; of Soninke today, 9; 1893 census of, in eastern Soninke provinces, 96; estimate of, in French Equatorial Africa, 167; urban, of Senegal in 1914–1934, 189; increase in Soninke, in Dakar, 191; Soninke, in Bamako, 193; Soninke, in Belgian Congo, 196
Pontac, Captain Jean-Baptiste, 52
Ponty, Governor-General, 126
Poulet, George, 47
Pout, 204
praise-singers, 83. *See also* praise-songs
praise-songs: of Jaabe Siise, manga of Wagadu, 18; of the Saaxo-Wakkane of Jawara, 20
Protet, Governor, 52

rainfall: in Bakel, Yelimane, Nioro, and Selibaby beween 1930s and 1960s, 10; in Bakel and Matam, 159
Raison-Jourde, Françoise, 189, 209
Rebel, Captain, 78
remittances, 171, 196
Renault, 1, 214

rent (state revenue), 23
Robinson, David, 70, 96, 227
Roger, Governor, 43
Rufisque, 58, 75

Saalum, 108
saarido, 33
Saaxo, of Jawara, 111
Sabourault, Paul, 126
Saint-Domingue, 43
Saint-Louis, 50, 71, 77, 96, 181
Saint-Père, J.-H., 135–137, 152, 177
Salde, 113
salt: trade with Beydan, 25; historical link with gum trade, 48; sea-salt, 53–54
saluma, 31
salumo, 31
Samba Hawa, 122
Samba Kajata, 127, 204
Samba Njaay, 134
Samba Njaay Bacili, 63
Samba Suumare, 201–202
Samba Suuley, 83, 125–126
Samori, 103
Samuel, Michel, 191
Sanga, 147
Sarakole. *See* Soninke
Sarraut plan, 149
Saugnier, 59
Sautter, Giles, 145
Savoie, 38
Schapera, I., 145
Schmalz, Julien, 43
Schmitz, Jean, 114, 227
School of the Sons of Chiefs (in Saint-Louis), 204
Scipio, Charles, 61
Searing, James, 32, 61
Sédhiou, region of, 57
Seexu Jomo, 120
Segala, 109
segmentary states. *See* political order
Segu, 27, 227
Selibaby, 10, 100
Sengalu, 109
Senedubu, 51
Sereer, 226
serfdom. *See* slaves, slavery
S.F.I.O. (French Socialist party), 205
sharecropping, 134–135
Shell Company, 186, 190
Sierra Leone, 3
Siima, 16
Siin, 108
Siin-Saalum, 101
Sila, 13
Simca, 214

urban migration. *See* migration

Valière, Governor, 73
Van Velsen, J., 4
Van Vollenhoven, Governor-General, 149, 154, 155
village de liberté. *See* freed-slave villages
Vivier de Streel, Edmond du, 153

waalo (land), 11. *See also* agricultural lands
Waalo (state), 43, 68
Wagadu, 13
Wahabiyya, 196
Wangara, 217
war (as source of wealth), 22–23
wealth (as source of power in Soninke society), 82–83
Webb, James, 45
Weigel, Jean-Yves, 136
Woermann, 121
Wolof, 78, 91, 195, 197
women: and agriculture, 31–32; prices of, as slaves, 35; as urban migrants, 191

woroso, 33, 139

Xaabu Kammera, 109
Xaara Xooro, 10
Xaaso, 10, 49, 53, 67, 94
Xaasonke, 173
Xoolinbinne River Valley, 10, 174, 220

Yaafera, 70, 74, 89, 90, 100. *See also* Goye Annexé
Yaagine, 109
Yarse, 27
Yatera, 20
Yelimane, 9, 150; 155; 156; 174
Yellingara, 110
Yeresna, 13, 27

Zabrama, 65
Zaire, 3, 196,
zakkat, 86–87. *See also* taxation
Zambia, 3.